The Future Middle East without Islamic Republic

REGIME CHANGE IN IRAN

The Future Middle East without Islamic Republic
REGIME CHANGE IN IRAN

ERFAN FARD

The Future Middle East without Islamic Republic
Regime Change in Iran
Author: Erfan Fard
Design & Layout: Rasa

Copyright© 2025 By Erfan Fard
All rights reserved.
First Edition: January 2025

No part of this book may be reproduced in any manner without the express written consent of the publisher, except in the case of brief excerpts in critical reviews or articles.

For information about permission to reproduce selections from this book, write to:

www.Ketab.com
12701 Van Nuys Blvd., Suite H
Pacoima, CA, 91331, USA

ISBN: 978-1-59584-848-2

With utmost sincerity, I dedicate this book to the counterterrorism analysts within the intelligence agencies of the United States and Israel, whose tireless efforts have illuminated and unraveled the web of transnational terrorism tied to the Islamic Republic of Iran.

Erfan Fard

www.ingramcontent.com/pod-product-compliance
Lightning Source LLC
Chambersburg PA
CBHW070040080526
44586CB00013B/869

Contents

Islamic Caliphate,	15
The Succession Scenario.	15
IRGC-QF is an Imminent	22
Threat for US Forces	22
U.S. Homeland Security and	29
Terrorist plots of Iran.	29
CIA Ring in Iran: "All lies!"	33
The Hamas and Islamic Terrorism.	52
Biden's Iran policy is a disaster!	59
CIA, Mossad, and regime change in Iran	63
The wordless West and	68
regime change in Iran.	68
The Mullah's regime, Saudi Arabia,	74
and Netanyahu	74
Iranian-backed "sleeper cells"	80
and US Counterintelligence	80
The likelihood of regime change in Iran	86
Reformists are plotting a coup against the Iran's Revolt	91
The Iranians will never forget or	95
forgive Qatar!	95
A mullah's flag with a hole in it is now the symbol of the revolution	99
80 days of protests in Iran and	103
still no leader	103
The young protesters have sculpted the New Iran	108

Iranian protesters feel 113
a huge sense of betrayal 113
When will the Mullahs' regime fall? 117
To the mullahs: Will you soon be the ones swinging from lampposts? . 122
First Charlie Hebdo, then the world 126
Khamenei's new police commander is a lunatic thug 132
Labeling IRGC as a terrorist 138
Antisemitism is a long-cherished value for the mullahs 142
Terrorist Mullahs: quitting nuclear non-proliferation and assaulting Israel . 145
The extravagant boasting of an Iranian thug threatens US and Israeli national security. ...150
Biological terror in Iranian schools 154
Israel, a friend of Iran's historic legacy 158
The consequences and import of.. 162
  Reza Pahlavi's visit to Israel 162
If they are laughing at Khamenei to 167
his face, change is imminent 167
The intricate labyrinth of.. 171
  the political stage in Iran 171
The Mossad Spymaster, an architecture of relations with Saudi Arabia 174
A way that the Iranian Mandela will change Iran. 178
Central Tensions of Mullah's Regime 183
THE U.S. INTELLIGENCE COMMUNITY: 187
Iran is a worldwide threat! 187
Raisi rubs salt into Kurd's wound! 191
The crown prince of Iran is frontrunner. 195
A way that the Iranian Mandela will change Iran 198
THE U.S. INTELLIGENCE COMMUNITY: 204
Iran is a worldwide threat! 204
The Holy War of Israel on PIJ Terrorists 208
Policy of "Seeking Regime Change in Tehran" 212
Read the Mullahs' book Mr. 216
Biden! 216
Haley knows the criminal mullahs practically. 219
IDF in the War Against Terrorism 223
Mullah's Regime is at Death's Door. 226
Freedom of Speech in Mullah's Regime 229
35 Years After the Death of that Villain Khomeini 233
Carter: The President Who Failed to Understand Iran 236
Chaotic Iran and Its Ruthless Dictator 240
Iranian Regime's Threat to 246

Global Democracy 246
A Fearful and Perilous Future Awaits Iran's Nation............................. 251
Behind Mullah's Iron Curtain: 257
Propaganda and Repression... 257
Countering the IRGC:... 263
A Global Call to Action 263
Donald Trump 's Challenges with the Iranian Regime 268
Early Elections in Iran: 273
Public Apathy and the Specter of 273
Continued Oppression... 273
Echoes of Dissent: The Silent Boycott Against Iran's Authoritarian Rule................. 278
Fanning the Fires: The Islamic Republic's Global Terror Campaign . 282
HRH Pahlavi at IAC: "United for Freedom, Time to Act Together"...................287
Haniyeh's Elimination A Turning Point in Middle East..................... 292
Harris, Trump: The Reluctance for Regime Change in Iran.............. 296
Israel's Next Front? Iran, Hezbollah, and the Coming War in Lebanon 301
Fanning the Fires: The Islamic Republic's Global Terror Campaign . 307
Sham Elections: Iran is under the Rule of a Junta 312
The Iranian people reject war, but the regime seeks it....................... 318
Iran's Sham Elections: 324
A Threat to U.S. and Israel Interests.. 324
Iran's Crossroads: 329
A Regime Paralyzed by Its Own Failures 329
Israel's War with the World's Terrorist Supreme Leader 334
Israel's Next Front? Iran, Hezbollah, and the Coming War in Lebanon. 340
Israel's Next Front? Iran, Hezbollah, and the Coming War in Lebanon 346
Khamenei's Call for Total War 352
Against Israel.. 352
Khamenei's Assassination Threats Against Trump 355
Khamenei: Iran's Warmonger Leading the Nation to Ruin 361
Khamenei's Dictatorship and Pezeshkian's Servitude Role............... 367
Khamenei's Paper Boat on... 370
Turbulent Waters 370
Leftists fearing the regime's 375
collapse in Iran... 375
A Ticking Time Bomb for the Middle East.. 381
Fear of Mossad: Shaking Iran's 384
Intelligence Community... 384
Netanyahu's Direct Appeal:... 390
A New Chapter in Middle East Politics.. 390
Pezeshkian, Khamenei's New Operative and the Mirage of Reform . 395

Qaani in Baghdad: Mobilizing Iran's Terror Axis Against Israel   398
Reza Pahlavi: Guiding Iran Toward Democratic Change 403
Silent Veils: Unveiling Tehran's Theocracy 408
Status Quo Remains: 412
The Persistent Stagnation of Regime 412
The Battle for Iran's Presidency Amidst Power Struggles 418
The CIA in the Biden Era: 423
Successes and Failures 423
The Circus of "Fools, Frauds, and Firebrands" in Iran 434
"Mullahs' Reign in Iran: Decades of Deception and Brutality 438
The Final Solution is Regime Change in Iran 443
The Iranian Dictator Continues to Order Assassinations 449
The MOIS: A Legacy of Shame for Mullahs 455
The Mirage of Reform in Iran's Eternal Theocracy 461
The Paper Tiger Has Collapsed 465
The Regime of Lies, Terror, and Deception 470
The Return of Trump: The Mullahs' 476
Nightmare of Death in Iran 476
An Opportunity for Regime Change: Rejecting the Illusions of Diplomacy 482
Iran's Endless Winter and a Nation in Ruins 487
Kristi Noem: A Terrorist's Worst Nightmare - A New Era of American Homeland Security 492
Shifting Sands: The Mullahs' Nightmare in the U.S. Defense Department ... 498
The First Solution is Regime Change in Iran 503
The New CIA Director and the Tehran Regime Headache 509
Trump's NSA and the Frailty of Khamenei's Chaos 515
The US Intelligence Community and Its Hidden Enemies 522
Dictator's Nightmare: Khamenei's Fear 527
of the Trump-Netanyahu Alliance 527
The Fearful Message of IRGC to Trump and Netanyahu 532

Acknowledgement 538
ABOUT THE AUTHOR 553

PROLOGUE

This book is a compilation of my articles on the clerical regime and the criminal Ayatollahs in Tehran. Over the past two years, these pieces have been published in The Jerusalem Post, Israel Hayom, and National News Israel. My primary objective has been to expose the intricate networks of Islamic terrorism tied to Iran's religious dictatorship and to provide an unfiltered analysis of its malign influence.

With years of experience analyzing the complexities of the Middle East, I have strived to offer a realistic understanding of the Islamic Republic—an entity I view as a cancerous force undermining regional and global stability. The regime's propaganda apparatus frequently disseminates misleading portrayals in Western media, crafting an illusion dangerously detached from reality. These distortions obscure the true nature of a system built on repression, corruption, and violence.

In writing these articles, I sought to counter such false narratives and present an unflinching view of Iran's sociopolitical reality. My hope is that readers will gain a clearer understanding of the dangers posed by this regime and its network of proxies. If this collection helps readers see through the fog of propaganda and grasp the true dynamics of modern Iran, then my mission will be accomplished.

After the repeated failures of Biden and Obama in their diplomatic engagements with the mullahs, and the West's futile attempts to normalize relations with the Islamic Republic, I have consistently argued that the modern, civilized world of the 21st century cannot coexist with this malignant and deadly regime. The only viable path is to support regime change in Tehran. In my discussions with U.S. political, intelligence, and military entities, I have persistently underscored this point. This conviction inspired the title of this book: Regime Change.

The Shiite mullahs understand only the language of force. Their rise to power in 1979 —enabled by Marxist and Islamic terrorist groups—established a religious dictatorship that has since thrived on terrorism, repression, and propaganda. This vicious cycle must be dismantled to pave the way for peace and stability in the Middle East. Breaking this chain of terror and oppression is not merely an option; it is an imperative for achieving a region free from the shadow of extremism and conflict.

The Islamic Republic's Legacy of Terror and Repression

The essays in this book take you on a journey to uncover

the criminal face of the Islamic Republic, which, in the 46 years since the 1979 revolution, has brought disaster upon Iran and the broader Middle East. Political Islam and Khomeinism have proven to be deeply flawed and destructive—both a regional blight and a global menace.

Beyond the regime's propaganda in international media, I explore how Iran, an ancient and proud civilization, has lost its identity, credibility, and honor under the mullahs' rule. Clinging desperately to power, the regime has committed countless crimes and betrayals, while the Iranian people have borne the humiliation of living under this theocratic dictatorship.

The Islamic Republic's sponsorship of terrorism—through organizations like Hezbollah and the Islamic Revolutionary Guard Corps (IRGC)—has made it one of the most destabilizing forces in global politics. Its relentless pursuit of nuclear capabilities threatens to spark a regional arms race, further jeopardizing international security. Domestically, the regime's suppression of fundamental freedoms and flagrant human rights violations highlight its tyrannical nature.

Iran's involvement in conflicts across the Middle East—fueling wars in Syria, Iraq, and Yemen—exacerbates instability and suffering. Meanwhile, the regime's history of deceptive diplomacy has exposed the failure of past international negotiations in curbing its destructive ambitions.

Given these realities, the necessity of regime change in Iran is not just a matter of national liberation—it is a global security imperative. A free and democratic Iran would not only liberate its people but also help restore peace and stability to the region.

1
ISLAMIC CALIPHATE, THE SUCCESSION SCENARIO.

"The rule or reign of a caliph or chief Muslim ruler" is the popular meaning of Caliphate. Historically, after the death of Mohammad (June 8, 632 CE), an Arab political leader and the religious founder of regional Islam in Hijaz; the successors shaped the 1st Islamic Caliphate. Even though, With Muhammad's death, disagreement broke out over who his successor would be, but for preserving the spoils of war and confiscated wealth, Women and power, they solved the problem by sword accordingly.

Because, after the unexpected death of Mohammad, it was a serious crisis and bloody power struggle all over the occupied places and among the Arab rebellious tribes. Astonishingly, most of the tribes, in Bahrain, Yemen, and Oman, converted to this new faith [The History of al-Tabari & Stories of the Prophets] considerably, most of the nonbelievers were killed and beheaded by Islamic atrocious commanders. [Arnold Toynbee, A Study of History]

This is a famous point that the Companions and followers of Mohammad, before his burial and funeral, had started plotting and intriguing against each other. intrinsically they seized the opportunity to get wealth and power, there were many challengers for succession. [Ibn Hisham; The Life of the Prophet] With the announcement of the emergency situation, the first Caliph tried to oppress any crisis and resistance of opponents through all Arabian Peninsula, viciously. He labeled the opponents as Infidels!

Astonishingly, similar to Mohammad, there were some pretenders to the throne of Islam who claimed to be the prophet of God [The Collection of histories and Tales].
Hurriedly, the council of Mohammad's friends solved the problem, and they created a new government under the name of the Caliphate; they wanted to monopolize the Islamic Power. So, they brand the rivals as liars! [The Arabs in History, Bernard Lewis.]

There was no vision about the future of the Islamic Caliphate after appointing the 1st Caliph. There was no election by the vote of the Islamic Caliph. Fundamentally, there was no divine legitimacy. Undeniably, he found legitimacy with this ruthless policy and suppression of rebellion. [History of Arabx, P.K.Hitti.]

Then, The Rashidun Caliphate was the first mechanism of the four major caliphates instituted following the death of Muhammad. It was ruled by the first of 5 successive caliphs (successors).

The Rashidun Caliphate is portrayed as a 25-year era of rapid military expansion, subsequently a five-year period of internal strife. Four of these Islamic caliphs were assassinated by the hands of Muslim opponents (Omar, Uthman, Ali, Hassan).

Intentionally and erroneously, they announced that their faith is for all the world! But in reality, it was a local religion based on Arab Peninsula's culture [Quran; Nahl 36 & Sojdeh 23 & Haj 34]. Furthermore, Islam was an Arabic faith and religion was created specifically for Arabs in Arab Peninsula.

Remarkably, For the purpose of development in their caliphate, they started to use military forces to declare wars on other lands and to attack them brutally. their main goal was seizing power and wealth. [Sir William Muir; The Life of Muhammad & 23 Years, Ali Dashti & Hubert Grimme, Muhammad.]

More to the point, The Rashidun Caliphate had started Islamic Jihad (a struggle or fight against the enemies of Islam, nowadays is labeled as Islamic Terrorism) under the name of Islam and Holy Wars. [T.W.Arnold; The Preaching of Islam] in the possible scenario, the main purpose was an economical and political motivation. likewise, most of the verses regarding jihad were added to Quran during the 2nd and third Caliph which leads to political developments in the Islamic Caliphate.In 637, a Muslim army under the 2nd Caliph Umar ibn al-Khattāb defeated a larger Persian force. The Arabs captured Ctesiphon shortly afterward. Thus, the Muslims were able to seize a powerful financial resource, leaving the Sassanid government strapped for funds. [R. Dollinger, Muhammad's Religion.]

The abrupt fall of the Sassanid Empire was completed in a period of just five years, and most of its territory was absorbed into the Islamic caliphate; however, many Iranian cities resisted and fought against the invaders several times. in reality, Islamic caliphates, with the flag of Islamic States in their hands, repeatedly suppressed revolts in cities [The Caliphs and Their Non-Muslim Subjects. A. S. Tritton ; Zarinkoob, Abdolhossein, Ruzgaran] during the victories of Islamic rebels, they had thousands of war prisoners. they started slavery, trades with slaves and looting. admittedly, in

Iran the Iranians never accept this new religion peacefully. The Arabs raided 83 cities harshly and destroyed everything which was in 200 dark years [Zarinkoob, Abdolhossein, 200 years silence; The History of Tabari]. Another example was Baghdad, where the new comers slaughtered thousands of opponents [Nafisi, Saeed , Iranian Social History ; R.Frye, The Abbasid Revolt].

Later, 14 centuries after death of Mohammad, Islamic Caliphate had three directors who developed their mutual project. after four Caliphs of Rashidun Caliphate (632–661) it was 14 Caliphs of The Umayyad Caliphate (661–750 CE], 37 Caliphs of Abbasside in Baghdad (566–653 CE ; 750-1258), 22 Caliphs of Abbasid, Caliphate of Cairo (1261-1517), 16 Caliphs of Umayyad governors in al Andalus [711 – 1492] ; 17 Caliphs of The Fatimid Caliphate, in North of Africa [909–1171] ; 34 Caliphs of The Ottoman Caliphate [1517-1923]. totally Islamic history had 144 *Amir al-Mu'minin* or "Commander of the Faithful" or "Leader of the Faithful".

In Iran, the Shias (Shi'ite, schism), one of the branches of Islam, had power in the society of Iran by religious institutions and network of Mosques. Shia consider Ali to have been divinely appointed as the successor to Muhammad, and as the first Imam.

In The Safavid dynasty (from 1501 to 1736) conversion of Iran to Shia Islam was a process that took place roughly over the 16th through 18th centuries and turned Iran (Persia), which previously had a Sunni majority, into the spiritual bastion of Shia Islam. It was a process that involved forced conversion [Arshin Adib-Moghaddam, Psycho-nationalism; The Lure of the Other; Islam: Art and Architecture, Könemann; Melissa L. Rossi , What Every American Should Know about the Middle East]. During 235 years, Shia' Mullahs influenced in all parts of Iranian Society. They were the supporter of tyrant kings of Safavid. The Kings of Safavids called themselves as the legitimate representative of Imam Zaman/al-Mahdi (born 870 CE).

Based on Shia belief, he is the final Imam of the Twelve Imams who will emerge with Isa (Jesus) in order to fulfill their mission of bringing peace and justice to the world. even though, most Sunni Muslims reject that he was Mahdi and believe that Mahdi has not yet been born. [An Introduction to Shi'i Islam]

A couple of years later, it was another religious system with same ideology. The Qajar Dynasty which was an Iranian royal dynasty of Turkic origin, specifically from the Qajar tribe, ruling over Iran from 1789 to 1925. [Abbas Amanat, The Pivot of the Universe; William Bayne Fisher. Cambridge History of Iran; Choueiri, Youssef M., A companion to the history of the Middle East]

The religious atmosphere of Iran got transition in its religious traditions with the rise of Safavids who used the religious card throughout their tenure and emerged as the champions of Shi'ism in Iran. Qajars being their successors also fallowed almost the same religious policy as matter-of-fact up to their times Shi'ism had become dominant faith in Iran. Shia traditions were always used by Qajar rulers for legitimization of their power. The Qajars shrouded themselves in a religious aura. They declared themselves Protectors of Shi'ism, Keepers of the Koran, Commanders of the Faithful, and Girders of Imam Ali's Sword.

During these two paradigms – Safavids and Qajar – the religious network of Mullahs in Iran had developed dramatically. but on the contrary, after emergence of Reza Shah Pahlavi (15 December 1925 - 16 September 1941), Mullahs had no power anymore. Shia Mullahs During these

years, from 1501 until 1925, claimed that the king in the Shia Land of Iran is a trustee to preserve the power, because power is related to Imam Zaman/al-Mahdi. historically and logically, it is a insignificant. but after 1941, Shia Mullahs tries to reestablish their power in Iranian Society.

For that reason, they used Islamic Terrorism in some Islamic and Marxist Militia Groups against the Shah. After 1979, a Shia Mullah came to power and the religious circle around Khomeini seized the power in Iran. The Shia Mullahs shaped the Shia Islamic Caliphate, or an autocratic regime in Tehran. when Khomeini died in 1989, Khamenei succeeded him. Khamenei is now 83 years old. although he calls himself the leader of all Muslims in the entire world, he is only the leader of a Shia country like Iran and during 31 years, he has shaped a Shia Crescent in the Middle East.

Currently, one of the potential scenarios for Khamenei's

succession is his son. Mojtaba is behind the scenes and controls all the issues related to Khamenei. This scenario is a reminder of Abbasside Caliphate that the power was hereditary, and in another scenario we have Ebrahim Raisi, the current candidate for the circus of presidential election in June 2021.

2
IRGC-QF IS AN IMMINENT THREAT FOR US FORCES.

The Middle East is highly unstable. The serious threat for US forces in this turbulent region is the hostility of Iranian regime. this regime is a bad and malign actor is this volatile region of the globe. Iran policy has a multiplicity of factors and it operates with a multi-faceted strategy. The main policy of Mullahs is Iran's Global Terrorism Network.

Regionally, the US allies –Israel, Saudi Arabia, some of the GCC States, Jordan, Egypt– are confused with understanding the destroying role of Mullah's autocratic regime which is similar to a cancer tumor. they see threats, in large part, much better than Americans do. US regional partners want to counter Iran's destabilizing influence.

On the ground, the US has not yet responded beyond the rhetoric in actions. But, in the middle of this turmoil,

President Biden has had strong rhetoric and attacked some of the IRGC-QF's network in Iraq and Syria which is not enough and effective.

Since 1979, Iranian regime has worked to develop a wide-reaching global network of terrorist organizations, criminal networks, and terrorist proxies stretching from Afghanistan to West Africa and Latin America in the western hemisphere. This transnational network has engaged in terrorism, supported militias, and fomented instability.

During recent three decades, IRGC-Quds Force is the main threat for USA and its allies. the IRGC is a multilayered political, ideological, and security institution and its Quds Force is the largest terrorist network in the world today.

Gratuitously, the threats of IRGC-QF cause tremendous harm to the Middle East and US forces. The threats posed by a wide range of terrorist networks, supported by Iranian regime. The Iranians regime is uncertain about US-ISRAEL-Saudi Arabia's ultimate intentions. The head of the IRGC, Hussein Salami, has referred Israel, Saudi Arabia and US as —the triangle of Iranian adversaries.

The criminal mullahs in Iran face four main threats, which destabilize and strike at the foundations of the regime. First, the succession of Khamenei and a challenge of naming the new supreme leader.

Second is the growing dissatisfaction among Iranians such as strikes. To predict the plausibility of additional protests in the future, regime faces the loss of legitimacy and inefficiency. Third, the clerical leadership is under increasing pressure over its rumored pursuit of nuclear weapons, its suppression of human rights at home, and its support of terrorism abroad. After re-imposition of US sanctions, Iran feels itself under increasing pressure. this is the Achilles heel of regime. Last of all is the international isolation. The regime believes to be facing an imminent threat of regime change from the US– a situation comparable to what Saddam faced in 2003.

Shockingly, after 42 years of vicious life in making crisis, it is too late, but the US faces an imminent threat and US is under attack of IRGC-QF!

Literally, IRGC-QF and its Shia terrorist militias is the largest terrorist network in the world today. The IRGC-QF operates a large network of non-combatant associates in Latin America, Europe, Asia, and Africa. however, IRGC-QF provides material, weapons, logistical assistance, training, funding, and guidance to militants and terrorist operatives throughout the world. The main purpose of IRGC-QF's terrorism and regional aggression is targeting Americans. this point is not negligible for White House and the US intelligence community.

As time goes on, the US's lack of action increase the threat to the US, US forces across the Middle East, and US regional allies. Doubtlessly, it is too late. the militant Shias have formed a united bloc, a sectarian-political organizations across the region, led by IRGC-QF. Potently, President Trump understood the threat and he had an accurate intelligence information from CIA and DIA.

From 2003, The IRGC-QF network, with worldwide operators, controls dozens of well-organized groups, battle-tested militia, and media from Middle East to Latin America and inside the US. This countless anti-American motivated militia is an imminent danger and significant threat for US and its allies.

Since 2011, IRGC-QF have deployed Shia militia to the conflicts, civil wars, and insurgencies that erupted in the region. The collapse of state structures in Iraq, Syria, Libya, and Yemen has facilitated the growth in power and influence of a wide range of regional non-state terrorist networks. Iran creates sectarianism and radicalism and then progressively put the label on this coalition which is the Axis of Resistance. But it means Axis of Anti-America or Axis of Islamic Terrorism!

The immediate and imminent threats of regional interstate conflict come from Iranian use of terrorist proxies in the Middle East and growing of state and non-state use of weapons of mass destruction. Then, The IRGC commands a growing missile capability. Tehran already has the largest inventory of ballistic missiles in the Middle East. Tehran's desire to deter the US might drive it to field an ICBM.

The IRGC-QF involves in all current conflicts in the region. Operationally, America's ability to confront Iran's support for terrorism is unproductive. This lack of a clear regional strategy has allowed Iran and its partners to continue to destabilize the Middle East and undercut U.S. interests and allies. USA is not going to be able to stop ―Iran's Global Terrorism Network‖ stabilizing the region— USA is ignoring too much. Truth be told, the elimination of Baghdadi and Soleimani were great steps forward.

The U.S. has identified the IRGC-QF as the Iranian regime's primary mechanism for supporting terrorists abroad, "but all of these organizations have worked to expand Iran's power and influence in the region". Scandalously, Iran's support for the Popular Mobilization Committee (PMC) and Shia militants remains the primary threat to US personnel in Iraq. IRGC-QF militias in Iraq have killed Americans in the past and pledge to do so again. U.S. forces since the 2000's have been the target of the IRGC-QF and will continue to face danger.

During the 2003–2011 Iraq War, the IRGC-QF led and supported Iraqi militia group in a deadly campaign against the U.S. forces in the country. Today, the IRGC-QF bolster and shares close links with an estimated 40 of the 67 largest militias in the PMF Forces, dominated Iraq and undermine nearly 15 years of American stabilization and humanitarian efforts in the country.

In Afghanistan: Iran and its expansive terrorist network have increased instability to force US forces to leave the region. Iran's anti-US instincts led the IRGC-QF into a tactical coalition with the Taliban. The IRGF-QF strategy became raising the cost of U.S. IRGC-QF has benefited financially from the illicit drug trade flowing out of Afghanistan, the world's largest producer of opium.

In Syria, Iran is working to consolidate its influence while trying to prevent US forces from gaining a foothold. Or In Qatar the IRGC-QF in Qatar with HAMAS are monitoring the US Forces and US Embassy daily.

Notably, IRQC-GF creates Iran's land-bridge, connecting Iran through Iraq to Syria, Lebanon, and the Israeli northern fronts. this land corridor will allow the IRGC-QF to transfer arms and personnel through Iraq into Syria and Lebanon, all the way to the Israeli front and the Mediterranean.

Additionally, Iran is increasing Hezbollah's capability to target Israel with more advanced and precision-guided rockets and missiles. Iran poses many threats to the interests and security of the US, especially through funding and support for terrorist groups like Hezbollah and Hamas—groups that routinely attack and antagonize our allies in Israel.

The presence of IRGC-QF-led forces near the Israeli border is part of the Iranian strategy to exert maximum pressure on Israel. IRGC-QF continues to develop and improve a range of new military capabilities to target US and allied military assets in the region.

As well, IRGC-QF supports Hezbollah which is active in the Middle East, Latin America, and here in the USA. Iran enjoys Hezbollah's international network. Iran constantly is a threat to US interests abroad, US international allies, and policies of US National Security in the homeland.

Hezbollah designated as a trans-national criminal organization, operating budget and finance through drug proceeds and working with criminal syndicates. More to the point, Iran's terror proxy networks in Latin America, the back yard of US, are run by sophisticated operatives. Operatives dispatched to Latin America to run drug smuggling, gun running, and money-laundering activities. Iran has viewed Latin America as a prolific ground for the export of its ideology and Anti-Americanism.

In actuality, IRGC-QF wants the Western Hemisphere to become a hotbed of anti-Americanism and a forward operating base for Iran. Hezbollah's networks in Latin American have cooperated with violent drug cartels and criminal syndicates, often with the assistance of local corrupt political elites. This toxic crime-terror nexus is fueling both the rising danger of global Jihadism [Global Terrorism] and the collapse of law and order across Latin America that is assisting drive drugs and people northward into the US soil.

Furthermore, Iran and Hezbollah operatives and their global network, running illicit drug trafficking and money laundering operations on a global scale, are threat to the integrity of the U.S. financial system. Along with smuggling drugs to the US and plotting attacks on US targets inside the US and overseas, Hezbollah's illicit finance networks often use US-based front companies, launder money through U.S. banks, and invest in the U.S. real estate sector to support their terror finance schemes. They therefore constitute a threat to US homeland security.

Iranian MOIS and IRGC back conspiracies to target the US inside the soil. Iran continuously seeks to strike again inside the US. Finally, Iranian MOIS and IRGC-QF continue to view the US as a primary threat.

3
U.S. HOMELAND SECURITY AND TERRORIST PLOTS OF IRAN.

The rogue state in Iran continues the work towards acquiring nuclear weapons, building long-range missiles, and supporting terrorism. it is a threat to the international community, building weapons of mass destruction. It is a threat to the Middle East, dominating the region through intimidation and support of terrorist organizations. The US Intelligence community should prevent "Iranian Terror Operations on American Soil." Now, the Iranian government is a threat to US Homeland Security by attempting to assassinate its opponents on US soil using drug cartels operating at the US's door.

The fact that Iran plotted attacks in the United States is surprising, and not only because Iranian agents have traditionally carried out such attacks in Europe, South America, or the Middle East. But the fact that Iranian agents engage in assassination plots abroad is not itself news.

From 7 March 2017 to 28 July 2020, several times in different meetings, I informed the US Department of Homeland security that "Iranian intelligence operatives have also engaged in activity in support of potential terrorist operations in the United States" but, regrettably, DHS had no clear vision about traditional *modus operandi* of Iran's Ministry of Intelligence and Security MOIS and the IRGC-Quds Force! It was an unbelievable experience in my academic life and 12 years field research in international security studies!

The U.S. State Department considers Iran the world's most active state sponsor of terrorism. Since its inception in 1979, the Islamic state has used terrorism as an integral part of its foreign and military policies. For U.S. DHS, Iran's terror operations on American soil is an important issue. Iran's actions are wrong. There's no doubt in that, following the sham elections, the Iranian regime has had its legitimacy wounded. Their own paranoia has increased. Indecently, they have called on Islamic extremists in the region to increase their violent posture.

Iran's known and speculated alliances with terrorist organizations pose an actual threat to the United States homeland. some Iranian-Americans working on behalf of and members of Iran's Quds Force, have a lobby and media mafia!

Frankly, the United States and Iran have a long history. Even before restarting J.C.P.O.A. deals, the United States had designated Iran as a terrorist country. The CIA reported that Iran is vigorously pursuing nuclear weapons and has strong ties to Al-Qaeda are additional reasons why the United States should pay close attention to Iranian clandestine activities inside the soil of US. However, Iran is a nation that has already isolated itself from the world community. It has long lost even more credibility following its latest round of illegitimate sham elections which leads to emergence of a criminal such as Ebrahim Raisi and Mohseni Ejei.

Let me conclude with this: There will be a new wave of Terrorism in the tenor of Raisi as a Mullah president. It will be merely a new example of hostile behavior by Iran.

Moreover, we must ask ourselves: Has US policy with respect to Iran been working? We appear to have a policy of rhetorical condemnation when the Iranians engage in behavior adverse to the United States interests. We also engage in negotiations which are on-again, off-again, while the Iranians continue to pursue nuclear weapons.

All that said, it is time to review our strategy for Iran against the harsh reality that despite our rhetoric, attempts to negotiate, isolate, and sanction, the fact is the Iranians continue to use their proxies against US interests and continue to pursue nuclear weapons.

Therefore, one must conclude the obvious: That our policy has failed, and failed miserably. What can we do? First and foremost, begin to treat Iran as the strategic enemy they truly are. As such, develop a strategic competitive framework that counters every major interest the Iranian regime engages in.

The question now facing the United States and its intelligence community is how best to respond.

But let me tell you President Biden, American Diplomacy is not effective! To be sure, the Mullah regime's use of terrorism as a tool of foreign policy! It is very clear, with no ambiguity inside! As you know well, in recent years, Iran has continually worked against the interests of the United States, Israel and the international community.

The Iranian regime will continue to kill us, will continue to sponsor terrorism and use their proxies against our interests, and will continue to pursue nuclear weapons. The next nightmare the world is awaiting is around the corner, and it is an unchecked Iran with nuclear weapons!

4
CIA RING IN IRAN: "ALL LIES!"

During the cold war, the Iranian intelligence SAVAK (Intelligence and Security Organization of the Country) and the Central Intelligence Agency (CIA), formed on September 18th, 1947, were allies. SAVAK was the foreign and domestic security and intelligence service of Iran during the reign of the late Shah of Iran, and was established by Mohammad Reza Shah Pahlavi with the assistance of the CIA, MI6 and Mossad.

SAVAK operated between 1957 and 1979, and was a combination of both the FBI and CIA. In the wake of the 1979 rebellion of Iranian Shia Mullahs lead by Khomeini, the organization was ruined. "The Shah of Iran had been a great friend of the United States and the CIA, and his intelligence service, the SAVAK, had been the agency's main pipeline in Iran".

SAVAK was trained and equipped by the CIA. The CIA wanted SAVAK to serve as its eyes and ears against the Soviets. The Shah wanted an intelligence organization to protect his country because of a dreaded network of Islamic and Marxist-Leninist terrorists operating in Iran.

In the Islamic world of the Middle East, the late Shah became the centerpiece of American foreign policy. For years to come, it would be the CIA station chief, not the American ambassador, who spoke to the Shah for the US. The CIA wove itself into Iran's political culture, locked in "a passionate embrace with the Shah," said Andrew Killgore, a State Department political officer.

Fascinatingly, Richard Helms who served as Director of Central Intelligence (DCI) from 1966 to 1973, after leaving the leadership of the CIA, began his service as US ambassador to Iran as designated by President Nixon. From April 1973 Helms had his residency in Tehran, where he served as the American representative until resigning effectively in January,
1977. "One can only guess at the wry smile that must have come to the Shah's face when he first heard that Nixon was proposing to send the CIA's top man to be the American envoy". Helms was certain to be warmly received by the late Shah.

Richard Helms was all ears and all eyes of the President, one of the enduring symbols, controversies and legends of the CIA, had been US ambassador to Iran from 1973 to 1976. When Richard Helms was the director of CIA, he advised the White House that "it is in our own interest to support this concept of a special relationship with Iran". Helms had a strong relationship with SAVAK, because of the USSR.

SAVAK and CIA had a mutual project against the activities of the KGB in Iran as the CIA dealt for two Soviet-missile-monitoring stations in north of Iran.

Helms had good knowledge regarding the dangerous game of the KGB in the region and the communist militia as well. Iran had an increasingly important role in the Middle East. "I just wish there were a few more leaders around the world with his foresight", President Nixon reflected in 1971. "Helms himself had negotiated with the late Shah for permission to place intelligence installations on Iran borders in 1957" and "During those years, Helms carried out sensitive negotiations with the Shah that often bypassed the State Department and kept many Washington officials in the dark."

Parviz Sabti - the head of the internal section of SAVAK, counter-terrorism division, the director of the SAVAK's third division—had a meeting with Helms in the house of Amir Asadollah Alam, then the Minister of the Royal Court, in Tehran.

In that moment, Birch Bayh came to Iran. Bayh was a US Senator from Indiana - from 1963 to 1981 - and also Chair of the Senate Intelligence Committee (January 3, 1979 – January 3, 1981). "Bayh had a meeting with Shah and his main mission was visiting those two Soviet-missile-monitoring stations in north of Iran. he asked Shah to be briefed. for that reason, Shah sent him to visit Sabeti."

During the party in house of Alam, Helms had a short private talk with Sabeti. "It's not a right place now, but I will send someone to talk to you!". Oddly enough, some of the prisoner's families sent letters to US Senate regarding SAVAK and they wanted that US put Iran under pressure to prepare a reasonable answer to them. "this was against diplomatic norms!"

At the Same day, the agent of CIA in Iran - with the nickname JIM- went to SAVAK to visit Sabeti. with sophistication, Sabeti offered: "These prisoners are a bunch of miscreants and thugs. it is more reasonable that the senators answer the families shortly, its related to internal matters of Iran!" Then, the Shah was fumed and furiously sent a message for Sabeti regarding the lack of cooperation. "In reality, It was not related to the CIA. those families wanted to act politically. why CIA should be involved in an unrelated matter like that? Sabeti solved the issue professionally!"

On January 30th, 1976, President Ford brought George Herbert Walker Bush back to Washington to become the 11th DCI, placing him in charge of the CIA. During Bush's years in charge of the CIA until January 20, 1977, SAVAK was busy with operations against Islamic terrorists and Marxist-Leninist terrorist guerrillas. Bush's tenure at the CIA ended after Carter narrowly defeated Ford in the 1976 presidential election. Then Bush was the special guest of SAVAK in Iran. In so much as, he went there and visited some historical places of Iran, such as Isfahan. Bush had a friendly relationship with SAVAK directors, and he met Shah twice.

Shah respected the CIA. Impenetrably, CIA was implicated in an impertinence and impiety with Mike Wallace. "This interview was part of an ongoing smear campaign in the western media against the Shah of Iran that would eventually culminate in his abdication in 1979, and his untimely and unnecessary death in 1980."

In October 1976, Wallace, in the introduction said "The Shah of Iran is one of the most powerful men in the world". Mike Wallace revealed to the Shah of Iran that "the CIA considered him a dangerous megalomaniac and an uncertain ally." During this 1976 interview on 60 Minutes, Wallace challenged the Shah of Iran about CIA. It was enormously grotesque!

"*Wallace: Are you aware of a CIA about sir?*
Shah: No. What is it?
Wallace: This secret study portrays the Shah as a brilliant but dangerous megalomaniac who is likely to pursue his own aims in disregard of US interests.
Shah: So how could I be your man, your agent?
Wallace: How do you mean?
Shah: Say guarding your interests?
Wallace: Well, it says that the Shah is an uncertain ally.
Shah: Oh, ahh. I know. So you would like me to be stooge?
Wallace: Do you want me to go on or shall I forget about this, Your Majesty?
Shah: Well, if some funny points why not?"

It was a laudatory answer! A smashing one! And Wallace was in a lather. Abnormally, on October 22nd, 1976, the New York Times published the interview with censorship and censorious comments. It was the exact opposite of American Media toward Khomeini. exaggeratedly, they supported Khomeini and labeled that brutal radical Mullah with meaningless adjectives, such as «Ayatollah» [sign of God!]

One year before the crisis of 1979, CIA invited a famous figure of SAVAK to Langley, who was Parviz Sabeti. "the rumors say that you will be the next director of SAVAK" one friend in Shah's Palace in Niavaran told Sabeti. Alas, it was a wrong and a weak person who was appointed instead of that patriotic well-educated figure.

The new director became General Nasser Moghaddam "it was a tragedy, most of the well-informed CIA's experts were out of Langley because of Carter's new policy. Some of those CIA's experts had no knowledge regarding Khomeini or Islamic terrorism or the role of KGB in Iran! On top of that, Moghaddam was related to those terrorist revolutionaries and followers of Khomeini. he wanted to preserve his situation."

In June 1977, when Adm. Stansfield Turner was DCI, the Director of Near Eastern Division or chief of the Near East and South Asia division and European division in CIA - More likely, he was Mr. Alan Douglas Wolfe - had a meeting with Parviz Sabeti, in his political directorate.

Mr. Sabeti was philosophically against Marxism and radical Islamism, and he irreverently explained to the officials of CIA that the terrorist of MEK confessed in the prison that KGB is in the picture. Apparently, Wolf was not convinced and replied "normally, you label all opponents as the agents of Russia!"

However, the Agent of CIA in Iran had interrogated Vahid Afrakheh (from MEK) in the cell. Also, Sabeti insinuated: "CIA brought Jan Šejna (Honza Šejna) to Iran, the former head of military intelligence who was seeking asylum in the US. In the time of communist Czechoslovakia, Šejna was a Major General of the Czechoslovak Army. In 1977 Šejna shared all his experience and intelligence with SAVAK regarding the contacts among KGB and Iranian Marxist-Leninist or Islamic Marxist terrorist groups in Europe.

Implausibly, Šejna announced in the conference in Tehran,

that Russia "endorsed the revolution in Iran"...

In Langley, Sabeti reminded the story of Šejna and asked graciously "if you believe that Russia is not involved , why CIA brought Šejna to Iran?" Indigently, Wolfe denied the credibility of those points. However, CIA knew pretty well that these Marxist underground groups had been active in Iran since 1970, and about 200 of its members had been killed in battles or executed.

Though, nowadays, there are plenty of documents regarding the relations between MEK (The People's Mujahedin Organization of Iran, or the Mujahedin-e-Khalq, PMOI, or MKO), and also OIPFG (The Organization of Iranian People's Fedai Guerrillas ; simply known as Fadaiyan-e-Khalq) and KGB as well, on the subject of secret relations between ROTPI (The Revolutionary Organization of the Tudeh Party of Iran) with China, there are also plenty evidences.

Similarly, most of the terrorist Islamic groups - such as the FMI (The Freedom Movement of Iran or Liberation Movement of Iran; L MI) - spent their trainings in the camps of Palestinians or Qaddafi in Libya or Egypt.

When MEK assassinated Americans in Iran [on Col. Paul R. Shaffer, Lt. Col. Jack J. Turner were killed in Tehran on May 21st, 1975. then on 1976/08/28, six members of this Islamic Marxist group killed another three Americans in Iran -Robert Krongard, William Cotrell and Donald Smith- with machine guns and pistols and left their car and ran from the crime scene.] The killers went to Paris and presented the briefcase of Shaffer and Turner to the USSR's Embassy. In all of these recently published in Persian, insidiously, they narrated these malevolence events with exaggeration.

On the other hand, in South Yemen where was center of communist activities, the USSR and KGB established a radio station for MEK. Additionally, OIPFG sent some secret letters to their followers in Tehran, that U.S.S.R. asked them to gather intelligence information regarding Imperial Iranian Army. Painstakingly, the SAVAK gathered those confiscated documents and wrote a report to the CIA. But the CIA, with indifference, hesitated to hear the voice of SAVAK. Wistfully, CIA did not like to see the chaos. After 1979, most of the leaders and members of OIPFG went to Russia. They themselves have narrated their memoires publicly.

In December 1978, "about six weeks before the revolution drove the Shah out of Iran, Eugene Tighe had visited Tehran, he recalled. The CIA station chief there was pleading for more Farsi speaking agents. He didn't get them; almost no one was able to find out what was going on. To get a firsthand view, Tighe had walked around for three hours. One million demonstrators poured into the streets, whipped into an anti-American frenzy. It was a stunning display, showing true emotion or precision organization, or both. It was clear that dramatic forces were at work, that a hurricane was about to hit."

Soon after, at the American Embassy, the head of SAVAK, "Nasser Moghadam, had taken Tighe to a private room for three hours and pleaded for crowd-and riot-control equipment. What were the lines of communications from the Iranian government to the US government? Apparently, the lines were screwed up and there was paralysis in both countries. Iran was a ghastly intelligence failure. It deserved more searching analysis, even now."

As a matter of fact, CIA knew nothing to suggest that

the Shah was in trouble. "it said the Shah might survive for another 10 years!" on January 16, 1979, the late Shah of Iran left Tehran. In his book, he blamed the CIA as a deaf and blind agency toward Khomeinism. The Shah was right! "we did not understand who Khomeini was!" then after Shah's ouster, Carter bluntly said "Fuck the Shah. I am not going to welcome him here when he has other places to go where he'll be safe".

In the chaos of 1979, a CIA agent was captured a few days after the Shah's fall by an armed group of supporters of Khomeini, and escaped execution by appealing to a Mullah, who agreed that the Koran did not sanction such punishment." Howard Phillips Hart was a career Near East Division officer, Hart's overseas postings included two years as a Chief of Station (COS) in the Persian Gulf; a three-year posting in Iran, before, during and after 1979 (where he was Chief of Station after the Shah fell and the American Embassy was overrun by Khomeini elements). In 1978 Hart began working the streets of Tehran. His reports that, contrary to over 15 years of CIA estimates, the Shah's rule was far from stable or secure were suppressed by more senior personnel within the CIA.

In the summer of 1979, the CIA station was a four-man operation, and all four were newly arrived in Iran. Howard Hart had returned to headquarters. In July, leaving behind a new station chief, Tom Ahern, who had spent the past 13 years in Japan; an experienced case officer, Malcolm Kalp; a communications technician, Phil Ward; and a thirty-two-yearold marine veteran, William J. Daugherty, who had joined the CIA nine. Tehran was Daugherty's first CIA tour. "I knew little about Iran," he recalled.

Since Carter and Turner had hit an iceberg in Iran, "Casey read everything he could find in the CIA on the subject. Like many he was still wondering, What had the CIA been doing? Could American intelligence have failed as badly as DIA chief Tighe said? How had the CIA missed the precariousness of the Shah's position, his physical condition, his utter weakness?"

In fact, when the Shah raised the price of Oil, Henry Kissinger and Gerald Ford advised Shah to reduce the price. Hereupon, Shah overlooked and answered the letter of Ford impudently but he did not like to make the answer public. Strategically, the Shah did not like to make an obstacle in his relations with the West or the US during the Cold War.

In the US, at the end of December 1974, When Jimmy Carter began his presidential Campaign in the US, he lambasted the Shah harshly. Heedlessly, Carter poured scorn on Shah and he was slapdash to the consequences of his debates. Carter and Ford faced off in three televised debates. He had a scurvy show off and he enamored to bluster and blew his own trumpet. Lastly, on November 2nd, 1976, Carter was elected as president of US. Leaving a rambling jeremiad, Shah sent a letter to congratulate him, but Carter answered back three weeks later!

Before the presidency of Carter, the prestigious figure of SAVAK, Sabeti, sent a private letter to the Shah and advised him "the political opponents like the period of Kennedy, would repeat a similar scenario. We should stand firmly. Otherwise, these opponents will take advantage of the situation." But the Shah decided to be patient. Next, Shah followed the advice of American authorities and made some changes gradually. Then, bit by bit, Shah started to withdraw from the battlefield and finally he lost the ground."

Inconsequentially, it was a string of events. In one side, The Shah had no strong will nor desire to stay in the country. He knew the meaning of Islamic Terrorism pretty well. from another side, the CIA was confused. Correctly, Sabeti thought: "CIA and DIA were not against Shah until the last months of 1978, the analysis of CIA were about the stability of Shah's power". After that, incorrigibly, CIA accepted the reality because Shah decided to go!

At Langley, "Casey was determined that there be no estimate on his watch that said something like "The Shah of Iran will have five years in power" and then he's out in months». In reality, the CIA had missed the Iranian revolution. "The senior Iran analyst at the CIA, Ernest Oney, said he got four or five kind notes from people up the line who liked the reports, but he was never really questioned; there was no effort to sit down and puzzle it out; there was no indication that there was even a problem to puzzle out. Intelligence had been reduced to unintelligence—getting a lot of facts and throwing them at people; if intelligence was going to answer the "tomorrow" question, it would be necessary to make assumptions, but assumptions were speculation, and that was bad."

The CIA station in Tehran was split over what was going on in Iran, but the disagreements among the members did not show up in the cables and reports. The formal priorities for the CIA station in Tehran listed the Soviets first, and Iran's efforts to obtain nuclear weapons second. "no one considered the Shia religious octopus or the terrorist groups." Near the bottom was the internal political situation. "Several months before the upheaval in Iran, the CIA station started to change the priorities, but there was only a tentative sense that a political struggle was under way".

A CIA paper of August 1978 said, "Iran is not in a revolutionary or even a prerevolutionary situation." And a November 22nd, 1978, the paper concluded specifically that the Shah was "not paralyzed with indecision" and was generally "in accurate touch with reality." A National Intelligence Estimate that year was never completed as the situation in Iran fell apart, but on an early draft Turner's only comment was: "What would happen if Russia invaded Iran?"

After a while, The Shah was bewildered. He did not trust Carter's policy at all. "National-security adviser Brzezinski had wanted the Shah to use force to quell the street rebellions;

Secretary of State Vance opposed force. The President couldn't decide. And the crux was that the Shah would not act unless he was told by the President of the U.S. what to do. Carter's hesitation, the Shah's hesitation, was all the revolutionaries had needed to flourish and eventually win".

The Shah left Iran for exile on 17th January, 1979. Soon thereafter, the Iranian monarchy was formally abolished, and Iran was declared an Islamic Republic led by Khomeini and radical Mullahs; the emergence an outlaw regime in the Middle East.

Ironically, in public, Montazeri appreciated Carter's help to Khomeini and his Islamic revolution. After some time, one of the top analysts of the CIA was travelling to Tehran under his own name on a diplomatic passport. Robert Ames had a meeting with some opportunist revolutionaries in the new Iranian regime. It was an infertile effort and CIA could not make a base or establish the normal relations once more. "The CIA had tried to rebuild a network of agents in Iran but failed. The CIA was in ruins. It was broken in Iran."

The CIA decided to replace those lost assets in Iran. after a while Ames was killed in Lebanon bombing or 1983 United States embassy bombing in Beirut. Certainly there was an Iranian hand in the embassy bombing and payment was made from the Iranian Embassy in Damascus.

The exiled Shah was sick dramatically. Thanks to eagerness of Kissinger, on October 22nd, 1979, "the Shah arrived in New York and checked into a hospital to treat his cancer". It lead to Iran's hostage crisis. On November 4th, 1979, fifty-two US diplomats were held hostage after a pro-Khomeini and pro-Russia radical group, took over the US Embassy in Tehran and seized hostages.

Extraordinarily, when the Shah of Iran came to the U.S. for medical treatment in October 1979, two weeks before the American hostages were taken in Tehran, "the White House had wanted the CIA to bug the deposed Iranian ruler's hospital room to discover what the mercurial, cancer-stricken man intended to do. Turner had argued that the Shah had the same rights as a US citizen and that, by law, the CIA couldn't gather intelligence in the US. But he was given a written order.

He swallowed hard and authorized the electronic surveillance of the Shah's three private rooms on the seventeenth floor of a New York City hospital, though he still thought it improper. Carter and Brzezinski regarded intelligence as a tool, like the plumbing."

After the Iran hostage crisis - apparently it was a plan of KGB or pro-Russia mullahs - the US terminated diplomatic relations with the Iranian government. No ambassadors have since been appointed.

Former ambassador Richard Helms had a friendly relation with Shah. After being exiled, Shah was in hospital. "During his stay at a New York hospital in 1979, Helms and his wife Cynthia paid their last visit to the defrocked Shah of Iran. With bitterness, the monarch kept asking them why the US had abandoned him, asking, 'Why did you want to destroy what we had?'"

He seemed certain that the Carter administration had played no minor role in his overthrow. He hinted on repeated occasions that the revolution had been the disastrous result of Carter's desire to replace the Pahlavi monarchy with a democratic government that would be more palatable to Washington. He wondered why Carter repeatedly reassured him of America's support if he didn't mean it. Confined to his hospital bed, depressed, and gravely ill, the Shah kept confronting them with the question, "Why did you do it?" The Helms' silence prompted him to respond with something that smacked of his sense of betrayal: "The real difficulty was caused by too precipitate liberalization," he mused.

Continuously, inside the inner circle of Khomeini, CIA liked to have some deep plants and useless players such as Ebrahim Yazdi or Mohammad Hosseini Beheshti, but it was the emergence of the Iran-Iraq war (Sep 22, 1980 – Aug 20, 1988). During eight years, sadistically, Iran executed military officers as a spy of CIA.

Casey knew that Iran could not be trusted, and he wanted

to shape a stage for Khomeini's political opposition. While the CIA was supporting the Iranian opposition in exile, and the backers of the Shah's son, who wanted to overthrow Khomeini. "in CIA, We decided to run the story". Since 1982, the CIA had been supporting the main anti-Khomeini Iranian-exile movement, the Paris-based Front for the Liberation of Iran (FLI) at $100,000 a month. Casey had no realistic expectation that the group could ever mount a coup, but their contacts did provide some sketchy intelligence.

The New York Times reported on March 14th, 1982 "The agency reportedly is secretly financing two paramilitary groups in eastern Turkey near the Iranian border - 6,000 to 8,000 men under Adm. Ahmad Madani, a commander in the Shah's navy, and an unsuccessful presidential candidate, and 2,000 followers of Gen. Bahram Arynana, the Shah's army chief of staff. In addition, Washington is spending several million dollars a year on propaganda beamed into Iran in competition with long-active Soviet broadcasts. The agency is also aiding Iranian exiles in France and Egypt, including leftists (but not former President Abolhassan Banisadr) and rightists. Reports that the CIA is also working with monarchists were denied. Washington wants to unite the exiles, most of whom would apparently rather continue old feuds."

Financially, the CIA supported Ali Amini, Manouchehr Ganji ($250,000) and Shapour Bakhtiar ($150000),General Gholam-Ali Oveissi as well, CIA endorsed Khosrow Qashqai a Qashqai tribal leader, $100000. "However, another $20,000 to $30,000 a month went to support Radio Liberation, which broadcast anti-Khomeini programs from Egypt to Iran for four hours a day».

Then, on September, the CIA had supplied a miniaturized television transmitter for an eleven-minute clandestine broadcast to Iran by Reza Pahlavi, the son of the late Shah. "The son of the Shah, had declared, "I will return." Khomeini and his circle in Tehran were traumatized! then, Rafsanjani wanted to open the door for CIA through the back channels." "Casey was impressed that new secret channels into Iran had been developed".

CIA went into overdrive. "What a mistake, Turner had come to realize. He and his CIA had studiously misread Khomeini as a benign, senile cleric, and now he held the US hostage. No one, Turner concluded, could surprise like a friend. It was almost easier with unfriendly nations; the CIA knew what to expect".

The CIA already had provided intelligence for Iraq to use against Iran. In one stage, one of the directors of CIA planned to give out intelligence to assist the Iranians in their war with Iraq. brutally, the Iranian commanders of IRGC used "human waves" of teenagers and irregular soldiers, and almost a million had been killed, wounded or captured on both sides.

Two pillars of Reagan's foreign policy—no deals with terrorists, no arms for Iran—tumbled down in secret. In contrary, "President Reagan signed the finding the next day, authorizing the arms sales to Iran through the CIA". in this period, "The CIA had made two trivial mistakes on the Iran arms sales, they shipped the Iranians all sorts of advanced missiles and military equipment". In general, US policy denying arms to Iran and preparing to respond to Iranian-sponsored terrorism.

The agency's leadership and many of the officers "directly involved in the Iran arms shipments". actually, CIA had a deal with a notorious salesman. Ghorbanifar, and the CIA had no other channel into Iran. Manucher Ghorbanifar, a wealthy Iranian arms salesman who had been a secret CIA source and "he was a deep plant of Ranfsanjani to misguide CIA!" Casey set Ledeen and North up with the chief of the CIA's Iran desk.

During that Period, Iran shaped Hezbollah. Even though the CIA had reports that its Beirut station chief Buckley, a hostage now for nearly eighteen months, had been killed, Casey clung to the hope that he might turn up if there were some renewed relations with the Iranians.

After 1988, sporadically, this saga continued and the mullah's regime, killed some figures as an agent of CIA. As a matter of fact, MOIS had no power to monitor the CIA's activities inside Iran. between 1979 to 1999, the CIA was in dire straits. "the agency actually knew less about those nuclear programs, terrorist activities, missiles program and Shia Crescent in Middle East than it had known 30 years before." after 2000, through the channel of Intelligence Services of Persian Gulf monarchies or Israel, CIA knew much better.

Currently, the CIA analyst Norm Roule who spent 34 years at the CIA, where he was the intelligence community's Iran mission manager. -analyzes past administration failures dealing with Iran, the consequences of inaction and he believes that lesson should be learn from "Past U.S. failures in dealing with Iran" is important issue.

For the last time, it was July 22nd, 2019, that Iranian media reported "MOIS in Iran had broken up a CIA spy ring and captured 17 spies working for the U.S. CIA and some have been sentenced to death". or Iranian state television published images it said showed the CIA officers who were in touch with the suspected spies and a CIA officer recruiting an Iranian man in the United Arab Emirates. "The identified spies were employed in sensitive and vital private sector centers in the economic, nuclear, infrastructure, military and cyber areas... where they collected classified information," At a press conference, read the ministry statement. In an unusual move, the official did not identify himself at the press gathering. then he added "in April that it had uncovered nearly 300 CIA spies working in Iran over the past few years".

Pompeo and Haspel's tenure at the CIA, were full of these propaganda of MOIS. Predictably, the U.S. officials did not respond to those groundless allegations. The Iranian government made similar claims and it was not immediately possible to determine whether they were legitimate. The U.S. government never acknowledges CIA recruitment abroad. Mockingly, a Diplomat in Jordan said "Alavi was a brilliant idiot! the dreaded MOIS could tell a barefaced lie with a straight face".

Affirmatively, it was a comic story. Another joke is "an accusation of CIA guilt for overthrowing the Mosaddeq regime in 1950's Iran". A dictator Prime Minister who wanted to be King of Iran. However, Mosaddeq was not an elected PM by Iranians, instead he was appointed by the Shah according to the constitution of Iran. But he was a nagger, who closed the parliament and all independent newspapers in Iran. The media in the west over and over again, repeated this illusion. Similarly, "the Iranian regime, in their illusion are stronger than CIA, with the same mentality in fabricating a groundless story".

President Donald Trump categorically denied the reports of Iran capturing spies from the CIA. He tweeted the claims are "totally false" and that the Middle Eastern state "is a total mess! Iran is a mess and it is fabricating stories."

Meanwhile, then Secretary of State Mike Pompeo poured more scorn on the claims, saying "the Iranian regime has a long history of lying." He declined to comment specifically on the arrests, but added: "I would take with a significant grain of salt any Iranian assertion about actions that they've taken."

When I told Michael Morell, the former deputy director of the CIA from 2010 to 2013 and twice as its acting director, in 2011 and then 2012, that "this is only a propaganda of regime and groundless claim of that bad guys in MOIS", he wrote to me "I agree with you. All lies!"

"I take it that all of this propaganda is for internal enthusiastic pro-regime followers. all of them are a preposterous tale only. Continuously in these 42 years, the MOIS or IRGC's intelligence organization act like an overgrown schoolboy." Sabeti said.

5
THE HAMAS AND ISLAMIC TERRORISM.

The young man killed in a cowardly terror attack in Jerusalem's Old City on Sunday, November 21st, 2021. His name was Eli Kay (Eliyahu David Kay), 26 years old, from the central Israeli city of Modiin. The shooting attack took place in the morning hours and the terrorist attack carried out by a terrorist Hamas gunman.

Jen Schiff Kay was an immigrant from South Africa. "He worked as a tour guide for the Western Wall Heritage Foundation. He was to be wed to his fiancée in six months". The Rabbi eulogized Kay, calling him "an incredible boy, full of smiles and from a good family that wanted to add the study of the Torah to his life." Kay served in the Israel Defense Forces as a lone soldier (one of the soldiers from foreign countries who move to Israel without family) in the Paratroopers Brigade, until August 2019. Kay's girlfriend said that "Eli loved this country. He fought for it."

Kay had been walking to work when the terrorist, an East Jerusalem resident whom Hamas identified as one of its members, opened fire. "It was heartbreaking Eli was murdered for one reason and one reason only today... He was a Jew!".

Blissfully, thanks to IDF, the assailant or the Palestinian terrorist, 42-year-old Fadi Abu Shkhaydam from the Shuafat refugee camp in Jerusalem, was shot and killed by security forces. Hamas gunman Fadi Abu Shkhaydam was a senior member of the Hamas terrorist group's political wing and a teacher in an East Jerusalem school. The Hamas heinous cold-blooded murderer, kills one or two, wounds four in terror shooting. The terrorist Palestinian man dressed up as an Orthodox Jew and opened up fire indiscriminately. This was Palestinian terrorism, not a "confrontation."

Surely, there is no difference between the people who blow up mosques in Iraq and Afghanistan, or ISIS that killed whoever disagrees with them. Hamas has the same mentality. Prime Minister Naftali Bennett ordered to shore up police presence in the capital for fear of copycat attacks. However, the attack came four days after a 16-year-old Palestinian from East Jerusalem stabbed and wounded two Border Patrol troops near the Nablus Gate in the Old City.

It was a horrific scene. blood on the streets of Jerusalem was a terrible sight. The blood of the innocents washed away in the streets of the Holy City of Jerusalem. This was the result of Palestinian terrorism in Israel! In actuality, the main perpetrator of this bloodshed is sitting in Tehran and supporting these crimes with the wealth of the Iranian people.

The best option to end terrorism in the region is to focus on overthrowing the autocratic regime in Iran. in other words, Swift and decisive action is needed.

Audaciously, Hamas took responsibility and issued a statement in which it praised the attacker, saying that "the Holy City continues to fight against the foreign occupier and will not surrender to the occupation."Unavoidably, the international community should blacklist the Islamist group's political wing as a terrorist organization. It was an act of terrorism, which reminds us that anti-Semitism is a present and future threat.

Surely, it's not freedom fighting or an Islamic Resistance Movement. without hesitation, its "Islamic Terrorism" and a clear sign of radical Islam. The fact of the matter if, "it is Not a freedom fighter, he was a terrorist."

Horrible enough, "CNN Couldn't even distinguish between the victims and the shooter and New York Times couldn't label a Palestinian as a terrorist... Shamelessly, CNN seeks to equate the Palestinian Hamas terrorist and the innocent Israeli man he murdered, on same level! Why is it that difficult to just call Hamas TERRORISTS? Hamas has already taken responsibility. What exactly is CNN waiting for?", Credit to the Washington Post for getting this right; at least Washington Post got the headline right!

These days, UK did a great job because Britain outlaws Palestinian militant group Hamas. "Since 2001 the UK has solely recognized Hamas's military wing as a terrorist organization. Now the entire apparatus will be designated as such." In addition, the UK made the right choice to seek to ban Hamas and label it a terrorist group. "This is clear that Why does Israel need security walls? Because Jewish blood is not cheap and Israelis have the right to self-defense." Israel surrounded by transnational terrorist network and the Iranian outlaw regime is behind the scene.

The situation is more complicated with respect to the emergence of transnational terrorist network. "Hamas is one of 78 terrorist groups proscribed in the UK...Hamas has significant terrorist capability, including access to extensive and sophisticated weaponry, as well as terrorist training facilities. And it has long been involved in significant terrorist violence...We must stand united against terrorism...This is an important step, especially for the Jewish community. if we tolerate extremism, it will erode the rock of security,". British Home Secretary Priti Patel announced.

Notably, the organization would be banned under the Terrorism Act and anyone expressing support for Hamas, flying its flag or arranging meetings for the organization would be in breach of the law, the interior ministry confirmed.

The world is in the midst of a crisis. Hamas has already been designated an outlawed terrorist organization by the US, Canada and the EU, meaning that its assets can be seized and its members jailed. On 10/8/1997, The US Secretary of State designated Hamas as Foreign Terrorist Organizations (FTOs) or foreign organizations. "The terrorist Hamas is fundamentally and rabidly anti-Semitic, and Anti-Semitism is an enduring evil which I will never tolerate. Jewish people routinely feel unsafe –at school, in the streets, when they worship, in their homes, and online".

Hamas has strong relations with the Islamic regime in Tehran "A spin-off of the Palestinian branch of the Muslim

Brotherhood in the late 1980s, the Islamist militant group Hamas took over the Gaza Strip after defeating its rival political party, Fatah, in elections in 2006". As well, Iranian regime provides it with material and financial support, and Turkey reportedly harbors some of its top leaders. however, Ismail Haniyeh currently serves as political chief, having replaced longtime leader Khaled Meshaal in 2017. Haniyeh has operated from Doha, Qatar, since 2020. both of them, has strong ties with IRGC-QF.

Therefore, Iran is one of Hamas's biggest benefactors, contributing funds, weapons, and training. Iran is providing hundred million dollars annually to Hamas, PIJ, and other Palestinian groups designated as terrorist organizations by the United States. also, Turkey or President Erdogan's is the fan of Hamas. "Iranian security officials have said that Tehran provided some of these weapons, but that Hamas gained the ability to build its own missiles after training with Iran's IRGC and other terrorist proxies…"

Historically, "Islamic Terrorism" is a phenomenon among the Islamic organizations in the Middle East. during all Islamic caliphates in the Islamic History. Continuously, killing their opponents, because of political or economic purposes, is a normal policy among them. In a glance at the theatres where such movements flourished shows that the political motivation of the leaders of an Islamist jihadist is stronger. It means, because of more power, they kill each other as well. But, groundlessly, the radical Islamic organizations label those irrational terrorist activities as a glorious fighting. Psychologically, this phenomenon is rooted from superstitious ideology and the underlying element in the radical Islamist worldview is power and wealth.

Alas, in 1979 the modern world and West were observers of the modern International Islamist terrorism in Iran, when a radical Mullah - Khomeini - came to the stage . They watched the events as Khomeini reshaped the Islamic Caliphate in the region. Unbelievably, the intelligence services of the Globe had no clue regarding the view of the Islamic fundamentalist groups. In point of fact Khomeini, many years before Bin Laden, triggered the stream of Islamic Terrorism and fundamentalist movements in the world. Similarly, Muslim Brotherhood has the same background in evil Islamic radicalism.

Ostensibly, Khamenei, with such a analogous philosophy, has the same pattern. Viciously, along with the renewal of the so called Islamic jihad, he attempted to mobilize Shia Muslims in the region and all over the world for a Islamic jihad which means Terrorism!

It is crucially important to know that the politics of Islamist radicalism, with a critical factors in, has two main bases: anti-Americanism and anti-Semitism. Therefore, killing the American or Israeli forces have interpreted as Islamic Jihad or Islamic resistance in their propaganda. Though, this interpretation is wrong and has no legitimacy!

Oddly enough, the West learned the meaning and usage of one Islamic word which is a genuine instrument of religious deliberation. However, fatwa or to call for violent action became branded in as a result of Khomeini's fatwa or Osama bin Laden's fatwas against the United States and Israel. in this matter, the Al-Qaida and the Islamic Republic of Iran are seen as two sides of the same coin.

Similar to preposterous propaganda of Nazism, Khomeini

or Khamenei or Bin Laden called themselves as the leaders of the Muslim society! So, they can promulgate such order to support terrorism! However, it is also true that insofar as religious establishments, it's a dilemma of the Muslim societies in the region. most of them like to participate in war against radical Islamic ideology, even though some of those states have no respect to the freedoms of religion and speech.

Paradoxically, these days in Iran, thousands of Iranians in any huge protest against tyranny of Shia Islamic Caliphate, boo Khamenei and disavow Hamas. "He is not a holly man! he is a real iniquitous mullah!" it means that Ali Khamenei has no legitimacy or credibility for Iranians. only in CNN or the New York Times he is famous with an irrelevant adjective; Ayatollah! Contrarily, in social media, footages show protesters chanting slogans against the tyranny regime and terrorist loving mullahs ruling Iran. It may not be obvious, but Hamas - a den of iniquity - has the same situation in the Muslim communities, they knew the religious nature of that threat much better than The West.

Mischievously, Khamenei and Hamas are framing the fight as an ideological struggle and the Modern world is at war with a radical component of Islam, and a political ideology based on a religion. Optimistically , the modern world blow a raspberry at these fake leaders, because their own people do not care a hoot.

6
BIDEN'S IRAN POLICY IS A DISASTER!

What is occurring are not sporadic protests or only a feminist revolution. This is a true Revolution of the Iranian people against the theocracy of the mullahs.

In Iran, we have a dictatorial regime of the worst kind and the courageous young generation is struggling to accomplish a regime change. This was not an easy decision nor is overthrowing a tyrannical regime an easy task. It is a very risky endeavor; but there is really no alternative, given the destructive ideology of Khomeinism , which has brought Iran to the brink of collapse.

It is critical to understand the actual situation on the ground in Iran, to appreciate that what is occurring are not sporadic protests or only a feminist revolution. This is a true Revolution of the Iranian people against the theocracy of the mullahs. It is indisputable that unless there is a regime change, flagrant human rights violations will continue and there will be no freedom for the Iranian people. The tyrannical regime is on the verge of self-destructing. The time is short and during this vulnerable period, the regime can do great harm in a misbegotten effort to preserve itself. The Biden administration can cut off funding and funding sources for the evil regime and curtail the damage by hastening its demise.

If the Biden Administration does not do so in support if the Iranian people, then like the collapse of so many other malevolent dictatorships in history, the process of self-destruction will be prolonged, with likely catastrophic consequences for the Iranian people - and others.

Needless to say, I and so many of my fellow Iranians are very exasperated with the Biden Administration's Iran policy. Relieving the strict crippling sanctions and allowing many billions of dollars to flow into the Iranian regime serves to enable and even embolden it to continue to harm its own people and, directly or through its proxies, commit malign acts against the US and its allies in the free world, including Israel. This threatens US national security.

The mullah's mafia-like regime is an integral part of the axis of evil with Russia and China. Ironically, while the US is supporting Ukraine in its defensive war with Russia, it is effectively undermining its own efforts by continuing to appease Iran, which is supplying Russia with weapons used to attack Ukraine. Astonishingly, it continues the improbable indirect nuclear negotiations with the malevolent Iranian regime, through Russia and China, as intermediaries.

It is increasingly clear that any negotiation with the criminal mullahs is a fruitless effort. President Biden must shut the doors to the regime's apologists, defenders, and lobbyists! The notorious pro-regime lobbies in EU and USA are grave threats to the Iranian freedom fighters. They're, effectively, partners in crime!

The tyrannical Iranian regime is not interested in genuine diplomacy and compromise, nor does it have any interest in democracy. Its stock in trade is terror and thuggery to enforce its will.

However, President Biden can speak with at least one bona-fide champion and representative of the Iranian people, in the Iranian diaspora, the crown prince Reza Pahlavi. Of course, meeting with freedom loving Iranian journalists, poets, and celebrities, at the White House is a good-will-gesture. However, meeting publicly with a prominent figure like the crown prince would send a clear message that the US stands with the good people of Iran yearning to be free and not with murderous tyranny and immoral human rights violators.

The Biden Administration should immediately terminate - and walk away from - all negotiation with the evil Iranian regime of the mullahs. It must restore the strict sanctions regime previously in place and reinforce them with crippling secondary sanctions. all economic channels to the brutal terrorist regime of the mullahs must be blocked so that they will not have any access to money to fund terrorism and their other malign activities.

The long-standing US policy of not negotiating with terrorists must be maintained. There is just no rational excuse for negotiating with the present terrorist regime in place in Iran.

President Biden should also voice strong support for the good people of Iran in their quest for freedom and to unseat the dictators. The phenomenal resilience of the protest movement in Iran is inspirational. Don't let these young people down. Support their courageous quest for freedom and human rights.

Join in their demand for regime change and installing a truly democratic government. We cannot morally accept, condone or excuse supporting the tyrannical, terrorist regime of the mullahs, which has enslaved its people with the deeply misogynistic political and legal system it imposed since 1979. We must not allow a nuclear Iranian regime or a continuation of its malign activities.

Iran can and should play a positive and peaceful role and partner with the US and its allies, including Israel, in the economic development of the region. The people of Iran share in this vision and desire to be a part of achieving these noble goals.

In the interests of the people of Iran and in the national security interests of the US. We have the opportunity to empower the wonderful young generation of Iran yearning for the freedoms we take for granted here. This is unachievable in Iran without a regime change. It's time unabashedly to support regime change in Iran. Allow the good people of Iran to join in the Circle of Peace with US allies, including Israel, and share in the benefits of peace, security, freedom, and prosperity.

7
CIA, MOSSAD, AND REGIME CHANGE IN IRAN

Mullahs have absolutely no place in the future of a free Iran, just like Nazis in today's Germany. The world must support the revolt. In a loathsome speech on Saturday October 29, 2022, the notorious Commander-in-Chief of the IRGC, Hussein Salami, warned young Iranians for continuing to protest and denounced them as villains.

Today is the last day of the riots. Do not come to the streets " again. What do you want from this nation?" Salami said amed the Central pompously. The core of the regime has interpreted the protests as a "threat to domestic stability which can lead to destabilizing the political system."

Repeatedly, Iranian officials have blame CIA for playing a key role in the current protests in Iran by meeting and cooperating with the leaders of Iran's Kurdistan region. Certainly, this is a false story! Usually, the Iranian regime prefer to sweep their problems and issues under the rug. This time, however, the Iranian public opinion has overwhelmingly rejected that CIA has any role. There is no rational behind this falsification, nor the falsification that the CIA orchestrated the coup in 1953 in Iran. I would like to quote a former CIA agent as well as a friend, "All Lies!."

In defiance of the final warning of Hussein Salami, thousands of Iranians came to the streets chanting antiregime slogans. The day after, vicious clashes took over Iranian universities as protests endured across Iran. Hundreds of videos on social media ostensibly revealed security forces firing tear gas, live bullets of AK-47s (Kalashnikov) and armed plainclothes forces firing at young students.

It is increasingly clear that the nationwide protests and wave of public anger in Iran go beyond class, geography, ideology, and ethnicity, and show no sign of diminishing. There are various anti-regime graffiti on the walls of the cities. Day after day seems to bring another embarrassment to the mullah's regime which is absolutely melting.

Needless to say, Iran's brutal regime looks progressively more perplexed by the events. In this war between the Islamic regime and the Iranian society, the brave and sharp young students are becoming more ready to endanger their lives for the cause. Be sure, it's a sign of Iran's nationalism.

A new course in the protests has been triggered. The young students are chanting "From Zahedan to Sanandaj, I sacrifice my life for ." This development may be crucial to the durability of the protests.

Most of the memorial ceremonies and university campuses

have appeared as significant centers of resistance, serving a crucial part in the rally. There is no sign of congregation at religious centers because the mullahs and religion have no credibility nor legitimacy any longer. Undeniably, Iran's protesters challenge the regime's authenticity. From a realistic point of view, "the regime can't quell the protesters with massacre, and it won't mollify them with hoary slogans and tales of martyrs for the revolutionary cause". In fact, this is the main motive behind the protests!

Another important aspect to consider is that the regime's repressive measures have not had any damping effect on nationwide street demonstrations, which means the will and inspiration of change has challenged the regime's tyrannical apparatus.

Factually, Iran was the first country to embrace fundamental Islam and will be the first to reject it after this 2022 revolution. It is also important to note that the Middle East and the world will be a safer place without the Islamic Republic of mullahs in Iran.

Iran's ongoing protesters need more support. Disappointingly, most states in the international community have no clear message for Iran's resilient demonstrators, even though they can help the Iranians who are struggling for freedom. In some regional countries, there are no solidarity rallies for Iranian opponents. Crucially, most states will profit from regime change in Iran, because power dynamics will change dramatically. Cancer cells cannot coexist with healthy body cells. As an opposition leader said, "We all need to work together to destroy the roots of Islamic fundamentalism in the region."

One of the main states in the Middle East with an influential role, is Israel. Indeed, a free Iran can cooperate and use Israel's technological experience in areas of agriculture and beyond in the future with great potential.

Israel should not help the opposition leader explained, " MEK (Mujahedin Khalgh) by any means. This terrorist group is more dangerous and more radical than mullahs. When the mullahs are gone, Syria will behave very differently, and like Hezbollah, will be less hostile to Israel, which is more good news. Consequently, Israel will be a clear and net winner in many aspects when the Islamic Republic is toppled. Hamas and Hezbollah both will become poorer and less dangerous. A free Iran will not want nuclear bombs and will not export its missiles to Israel's enemies."

Western officials clearly haven't considered what happens next. Although the consequences of regime change and collapsing of criminal mullahs in Iran are very significant on their own, even more things will change in accord. Mullahs have absolutely no place in the future of a free Iran, just like Nazis in today's Germany. Unquestionably, the new Iran will ban their uniform, books, ideology, and so on, which is good news for the region and the world.

For the first time after 1979, the regime is evidently afraid that the average people are confronting their very nature. Perhaps the biggest reason is "a barrier of fear has been broken". Thus far, the Iranian regime is deeply divided in many ways, and there is a probability for the emergence of internal dispute among the pillars of the regime's core.

This is well within the realm of possibility, where the national uprising will open the path to terminate the life of the corrupted Allah's regime in the globe. In other words, the main demand of this uprising is for an end to the Islamic republic, or regime change.

More than 50 underage children were killed in less than two months by the Islamic regime in Iran, which is led by a sick old mullah. These are part of their violent repression against protesters in the streets. The world needs to get informed and act against this terrorist regime and vicious mullahs.

Most importantly, the sole survivor of this repression will be Iran. The CIA and Mossad have no parts to play here, and these savage acts reveal the Iranian government as Islamic tyrannists. The Iranian government is at war with its own people and has raided all the schools- not the CIA or Mossad.

Eventually, the Iranian young generation will cause the brutal regime of mullahs to retire into the dustbin of history where it belongs. For this reason, Iranian school girls and boys knock turbans off disreputable mullahs as part of anti-regime protests and mass protests continue throughout Iran.

May the freedom of Iranians prevail over the tyranny of their government.

8
THE WORDLESS WEST AND REGIME CHANGE IN IRAN.

The lack of partnership among the opposition alarmed the silent West so it did not to support the Iran revolution. During the mullah's rule, thousands of Iranians were imprisoned, tortured, massacred, or disappeared. Today's revolution is against a dictatorship of mullahs and a corrupt personalist regime. . It is critically important to note that democracy cannot emerge in a religious dictatorship, as it will be collapsed dramatically. Reforming the present regime is not the answer.

There is not a shred of doubt that, since 1979, the mullah's regime showed itself in its true colours. Tthere is no choice that attempts to restore democracy because the nature of religious tyranny is against any democratic reforms or the shift from theocracy to a democratic form of government. Currently, the tumultuous and transformative events in

Iran can be a shocking upheaval in the 21st century. Surely, overthrowing this political order in Iran will change the region vastly. However, there is no possibility to change the theocratic system in Iran through peaceable reform. Under the jackboot of mullahs, their propaganda and empty words have driven the Iranians to distraction. The pro-regime reformists want to settle for a promise of jam on their daily bread. Incrementally, this violent Islamic regime is unwilling and incapable of reform and improvement.

The lobbies' propaganda, though, has poisoned the mind of the West. Yet, the ruthless repression of mullahs in Iran managed to shock many western observers. The western media have broadcasted a persuasive shared narrative of resistance in Iran.

Therefore, the causes of the Iran revolution in 2022 at this particular moment may be relatively unimportant for the West. They do not like to support the regime change nor inviting the legitimate leaders of oppositions. Apparently, the odds are not very much in their favour. Seemingly, the EU are not willing to lend a helping hand to support democracy in Iran. Nonetheless, the frayed Iranian society without the help of the West is fighting for collapse of a longstanding dictatorship in Iran and to shift toward democracy.

Alas, the West have not educated themselves in learning the ideology of mullah institutions or the aspects of mullah history and the "uncivic" culture. Since the Safavid dynasty (1501 to 1736) up to these days, they had enough time to learn it, it was a long-term historical process, but because of their political interests they were unwilling to do so.

The European mentality has this challenge to face: to

identify those trajectories which erected obstacles in Iran, for the existence of this so-called religious reason that meant Iranians could not lead to democracy and are so far away from it.

There are plenty of causes and political factors to believe in the possibility of regime change in Iran. there is a historical trend toward democracy. At a very broad level, Iran has experienced numerous "waves" of democratization in the 20th century during Pahlavi dynasty. During the almost 54 years between 1925 and 1979, the late kings struggled to adopt democracy.

With a lump in my throat, I must recount that all of them were followed by "reverse waves" after which Iran collapsed into dictatorship. This time, a fundamental regime change in Iran cannot be a smooth transition. Indeed, the institution of the mullahs is the main obstacle in this path to democracy. Traditionally, the religious background conditions and historical trajectories make some political outcomes more improbable or even impossible in Iran.

Academically, the main purpose and cause of any revolutions is clear. But, in Iran, the impact and existence of a vicious ideology of Khominisim is the most important factor. To assess this argument, it should be considered that the mullah's institution is against any civilian political institutions in the society that pursue their own private business and their predisposed affairs. These supposed Holly men believe that they should have more rights than others, and they are by their nature above the law. Plausibly, this tyrannical ideology shaped in dark mosques makes any democratization or civic culture in Iran less likely.

In contrast, the civic community of Iranians view the mullah's institution as illegitimate to rule the state. With a similar goal, the young generation of Iranians have the willingness to form a democratic transition and the emergence of democracy. In response, the political institution of mullahs uses force apparatus to suppress any peaceful demonstration.

The criminal mullahs have no respect for other views, they have no feeling of trust and shared responsibility for the expectation that others can change the mullah's inefficient and mafia system tranquilly. By the lack of economical development, the mullah's circle cannot change people's values and the growth of more support of democracy. The economic transformation from rich to poor flames this likely political transformation from dictatorship to democracy in Iran as well. The processes driving economic modernization transformed and even demolished existed economic structures across Iran since 1979. the demise of agricultural and industrial systems and commercial investment had a tremendous impact on these nationwide protests in Iran.

So, the spark of this revolution did not occur abruptly or out of the blue. It's triggered by multiple causes. For 44 years, the Iranians suffered and had showed their grievances in more than 18 protests which are the political consequences of the 1979 revolt. The logic of this argument with regard to regime change depends on the strength of newly established revolutionaries' groups. In turn, the mullahs are fighting to retain their privileged positions and access to power.

Truly, the action of Iranians positioned in the diaspora is insufficient, sluggish, sporadic and shows they have no desire for regime change. Conspicuously, the only legitimate figure is the crown prince Reza Pahlavi. Behind this belief, of course, the discourse of regime change among the opposition is full of fallacies, ambiguity, intolerance, and conspiratorial competition.

Simultaneously, there is no tendency to make a coalition among these egotistical competitors who have negative publicity. Conversely, with the lack of articulating a common strategy the most Saudi-backed narcists clique instead of assisting a figure like Reza Pahlavi, they are busy in an erosive way planning various conspiracies against him.

Without leadership and an ideological plan, it will be hard to accomplish the regime change. This points up the fact that the only influential figure with a charisma who guide his followers' energy and passion is Reza Pahlavi. He could virally communicate and spread his message to be resonated across the country. The protesters lack leadership and concrete plans for action. He could attract mass support among young generation through media.

In global perspective, the lack of partnership among the opposition alarmed the silent West so as not to support the Iran revolution. Consistently, the world is always watching with different appraisals. Soon, the West will intervene effectively if the context of revolution permit it.

More broadly, a lot of factors can influence the development of the revolutionary movement in 2022. people' aggregate contributing to a movement at various levels, they are participating in protests at varying frequencies. considerably, the only motivation for the resilient young generation is an Iranian nationalism which conceptualizes the process of inspiring regime change in Iran. Nationalism is a powerful unifying motivation which shows itself behind the goal of revolution in Iran.

This they do via a mechanism to reframing the supposed structure to maximize the likelihood of regime change and the depth of the revolutionary coalition inside Iran. Every now and then, the formal literature on citizen participation in anti-regime protests implicitly signals a successful revolution. The Iranian citizens' believe in the likelihood of success, for this reason, they are actively protesting on the streets courageously. They learned from previous protest movements' successes and failures, from their tactics and methods.

In essence, the anarchistic rebellions and revolt of 1979 in Iran based on terrorists was a tragedy - or a nightmare. Optimistically, this real revolution in 2022 might be a brilliant triumph. Emphatically, a large proportion of the Iranian society become extremely frustrated and rebellious against the mullah's regime. The truth is that, with such quality, this phenomenon of political revolution will come to fruition. Eventually, the continuance of this revolutionary movement will paralyze state administrative and coercive powers.

9
THE MULLAH'S REGIME, SAUDI ARABIA, AND NETANYAHU

Israel and Saudi Arabia's intelligence centers, GIP or Mossad, know well that IRGC head Salami is a psychopath and his words a bluff. There is no decline in Iran's malevolent and destructive activities across the Middle East. After the signing of the aggression "Abraham Accord in 2020", Iran's became "more obvious than ever". Indisputably, Iran has increaseded its engagement in regional conflicts to the effect of, intensifying, prolonging, and deepening them. The very continuation of this regime is based on tensions and creating crisis.

Since the winter of 1979 with no spring in sight, the mullah's thuggish regime in Iran increasingly expanded its radical Islamic doctrine around the globe using terrorism, infiltration, interference, invasion, involvement in conflicts, and bribery, as well as the smuggling of arms, ballistic missiles, and drugs.

Shortly after coming into power, the regime turned Iran into the world's largest and most powerful state sponsor of terrorism, and it has maintained this kind of aggressive behavior for 43 years.

Consistently and endlessly, Iran's regime has carried out attacks on international shipping, regional infrastructure, and U.S allies in the region. Today, "Iran challenges regional security, stability, and peace as aggressively as at any time in recent history," because Iran is not a rationally acting member in the international community.

The perception that "the Iranian regime would somehow become moderate enough to the point of no longer supporting such malignant activity," has proven to be wrong. Bluntly put, this view was the false propaganda of pro-regime lobbies in Washington DC.

From the very beginning, terrorism was an inseparable part of this Islamic regime. Iran doubled down on their support for terrorist groups and continued racing ahead in developing ballistic missiles and its nuclear weapons program. The regime's lethal and financial support to terrorist groups and proxies includes aid to Shia militants, such as Houthis, Hezbollah, Hamas, even an organic relation with ISIS.

Currently, the world is watching the melting down of this theocracy in Iran and the brutal suppression of antiregime protesters. The demand of the protesters is clear; in polite terms, the young generation wants regime change in Iran. One such ongoing conflict is particularly relevant to relations between Iran and Saudi Arabia.

The Saudi-Iran cold war or proxy conflict is a major ongoing struggle in the Middle East. The battle between these two bitter rivals has swamped several different countries, including both regional and international actors. Crystally clear, Iran is a primary source of conflicts and chaos in the Middle East.

However, in the near future, a free Iran can cooperate with regional states with great potential. When the mullahs are gone, Syria will behave very differently, and terrorist organization like Hezbollah will be less hostile to Israel, which is added benefit for peace.

Consequently, Saudi Arabia and Israel will be clear and net winners in many aspects when the Islamic Republic is toppled. "Hamas and Hezbollah both will be wrecked. After regime change, a free Iran will not want nuclear bombs and will not export its missiles to Israel's enemies." Certainly, it is good news for the Iranian Revolution of 2022 that Israel and Saudi Arabia wholeheartedly support democracy in Iran.

Nowadays, the threat of terrorism around the globe is vastly different compared to what it was before 9/11. The U.S. counterterrorism community has appropriately and dramatically ramped up its intelligence capabilities. On 29 October 2022, Hussein Salami, the commander of IRGC, said: "Conspiracy in Iran is the result of US-UK-IsraelSaudi policies". It is because of this mentality that democracy will only be accessible after the regime change in Iran.

In addition to his statement, Salami accused Saudi Arabia of funding hostile media which inflame the feelings of the

Iranian youth. He suggested, those behind unrest in Iran cannot tolerate the Islamic Republic's political and spiritual influence across the region, and have therefore resorted to inciting violence in the country. Salami warned "You cannot create anxiety for the Iranian nation, and yourself live in calm." Similarly, the internal media of Iran reported, "The London-based Iran International TV, which has been playing a major role in provoking unrest in Iran, is funded by Saudi Arabia. The disinformation campaign by the network is also led by Israel."

A week later, after Saudi Arabia was blamed for this socalled media war, the US and Saudi Arabia worried that Iran might be planning an attack on energy infrastructure in Middle East. Tentatively, Saudi Arabia revealed to the US intelligence information on a potential attack without mentioning any specifics. In turn, the National Security Council stated the U.S. is prepared to respond. The Saudis accurately commented regarding this matter, wants to distract from local protests".

Even though, the IRGC warns Saudi Arabia over Iran protest coverage, the reality of the situation is evident in the plethora of protester's videos which display the viciousness of the pugnacious mullah's regime in Tehran. Without a doubt, Saudi Arabia has revealed numerous fallacies in coverage by Persian-language news outlets, which pertain to tendencies such as censorship, the dirty game of reformist's factionalism of the regime, and the existence of a guest's blacklist and so on and so forth. These media only prove the real face of criminal mullahs.

There are no credible alternatives and the censorship in

those media is stubbornly ongoing. For the mullah terror entity in Iran, there will be no shortage of seemingly plausible reasons to be worried. Riyadh and Jerusalem are anticipators of the regime change in Iran. Now that Netanyahu has been elected. it is highly likely that he will get his wish and be able to form a right-wing coalition. Notably, Biden congratulated Netanyahu on the election win on 7 November 2022.

The US president told Israel's presumed next president that "we're brothers" and "we'll make history together' Who can say what will happen until the next message? It might be that a regime change in Iran will take place and they will ink additional historic peace deals in the tumultuous region.

Unquestionably, anyone with his wits about him will be more careful here. Tehran cannot change the security balance in the Persian Gulf and Iran has no capacity to solve its internal turmoil. As such, the mullahs have no military power to confront the improving ties between Israel and Arab governments in the Persian Gulf.

Most conspicuously, the internal affairs of Iran under the rule of corrupted mullahs have led to Iran's turmoil and this famous revolution in 2022. Surely, the intelligence centers of Israel and Saudi Arabia -GIP or Mossad - know well that Salami is a psychopath, and his words were only a flippant bluff. when he exclaimed: "Whatever move you make against the Iranian nation, you will receive blows several times harder,". The ongoing nationwide demonstrations serves as a great proof of mullah's failure and mismanagement.

The brave young protesters did not comply when Salami yelled "Put aside the wickedness. Today is the last day of the riots. Do not come to the streets anymore. What more do you want from the lives of these people? ". Regardless of the warning, students hit back at him and continued to protest in large numbers at several of Iran's major universities on Sunday. Sooner or later, the will of change will triumph over the will of suppression. This young generation will succeed on the long road to democracy in Iran.

10
IRANIAN-BACKED "SLEEPER CELLS" AND US COUNTERINTELLIGENCE

In case the mullah's regime is endangeredl, it could activate ‹sleeper cells' all over the US. The U.S. Intelligence Community says Iran threats to exofficials Mike Pompeo, Brian Hook persist and remain credible. From my personal view, those in 's circle are in danger because the and IRGC have a plan against Trump, , John Bolton and Gina Haspel. More specifically, this rogue regime is playing the long game. They have a high degree of patience. We may not be out of the woods yet, and we should know that they have terrorist sleeper cells all over the world.

The Director of National Intelligence (DNI) in the Biden administration, specifically the National Counterterrorism Center (NCTC) is conscious that Iran's deep cover illegal agents on U.S. soil could be extremely hazardous. The potential Terrorist Sleeper Cell operations within the U.S. represent a credible threat and would be tantamount to a new 9/11.

It is crystal clear that Iran cannot win a head-to-head conventional war against the U.S., Therefore, it will use asymmetric warfare on its allies that can give the cloud of deniability and yet deliver the message of war.

A primary concern is Iranian backed "sleeper cells" that are in the U.S. and await the code word to strike. In other words, they are positioned to attack the U.S. homeland. More recently, the American intelligence community has obtained concrete evidence about a resurgence of the Iranian sophisticated network of sleeper cells in the U.S.

In a meeting with the U.S. FBI and DHS, in 2020 and 2021, I echoed my rhetoric " the Iranian regime-backed terror cells could be implemented to launch deadly attacks in the U.S. How probable are and both of their respected agents acknowledged that point. Then, one of them asked me: terrorist attacks from Iranian-backed sleeper cell agents right here in the United States?

To put more emphasis on this point: "Preparations to terrorism broadly should clearly take into consideration the nuanced and growing Iran threat to U.S. national security. If not, no wall can thwart it. Iranian agents have already clandestinely entered the U.S. fight against Islamist some of them are apologist lobbyists!" I responded.

Since July 2013, I have been working on mapping the Iranian regime's transnational terrorist network and in my tours to Middle East for doing field research, I have been ringing alarm bells to governments warning of an exceptional built-up network of Iranian regime's "logistics hub and hideouts" in the U.S.

One decade has passed, and I have not changed that dea: "The Iranian regime may give the green light to its covert proxy rebels and its gangs if the internal crisis deepens and regime change's supporters seem to be winning in Iran.". The Iranian government is a threat to the international community and a serious threat to the homeland security of the U.S. there is no argument about that.

The U.S. Department of State considers Iran the world's most active state sponsor of terrorism. Since its establishment in 1979, the Islamic state has used terrorism as an integral part of its foreign and military policies. «The notorious coalition of IRGC-Hezbollah-Al Qaeda is almost certainly the most experienced and professional terrorist alliance in the world,» even more so than ISIS. Iran's influence in Latin America is growing for more than the past decade. That means there is a significant presence of Iranian agents in and near the United States, threatening U.S. national security.

There is mounting evidence that Iranian-sponsored terrorists are operating across the U.S. mainly unrestricted, raising concerns in the U.S. Intelligence community and counterterrorism centers that these «sleeper cell» agents are poised to launch a large-scale attack on the American homeland. " Iran Terrorists are "infiltrating" South America and setting up intelligence networks to carry out terrorist attacks in the region" was a viral sentence in the media.

Indisputably, the U.S. faces a threat, because "the Iranian

regime's networks are present in the United States." While Iran is presently more likely to use its proxies for attacks against the U.S., «those sleeper cells» positioned in the U.S. could be employed to orchestrate an attack.

In any part of the U.S. intelligence community, if you work to counter Iranian influence in the region, you agree that «it's better to go and target them, instead of looking on the sidelines at the stream of events,». Potentially, "Iran's proxy terror networks in Latin America are managed by Tehran's entirely owned Lebanese franchise Hezbollah," Among the most tenacious threats to the U.S. homeland is Iranian proxies' profound infiltration throughout Latin America, where Iran finances its terror activities.

In truth, the Shiite terror group has been developing its existence in South America since the late 1980s. During the Obama presidency, this Shiite terrorist group made inroads on the North American continent. and now they have broader penetration in the Western Hemisphere.

The matter is further complicated because "Their existence in Latin America should be regarded as a forward operating base against America's regional and internal interest". The moral of the story is, Iran has sought "to infiltrate the countries of Latin America and install secret intelligence stations with the goal of committing, fomenting and fostering acts of international terrorism in concert with its goals of exporting the revolution."

Even though plotting a sneak attack inside the U.S. is not so easy for IRGC or MOIS, the White House needs to wake up! The criminal Ayatollahs are funding the global terrorist activities in a transnational terrorist network. "The pro-regime stooges and agents stayed for years in the U.S. and established a base." Hence, it indicates that the terror of sleeper cells remains, especially in the U.S. Factually, this is the natural world of Islamic caliphates. If mullahs feel imperiled, they can call upon the network of terrorist sleeper cells to carry out atrocities.

It is important to know that this is the nature of the outlaw religious octopus. Iran's sleeper cell tactics date back to Khomeini's rise to power in Iran in 1979. Since that winter with no spring in sight, Iran has been Infiltrating the U.S. with Terrorist Sleeper Cells and vicious. terror organizations". Since it was established, the IRGC has played a pivotal role in the protection, consolidation and spread of the Islamic Revolution around the world. IRGC and MOIS aren't just in Tehran. They are in New York and Washington, too.

To highlight Iran's radical ideology, the terror cells are run by the Caliph himself. The so-called ayatollah – sign of God- has control of a network of individuals linked to terrorists, to carry out a terrorist attack in the event of a conflict.

Make no mistake, the existence of Iranian sleeper cells has long been an indicator of Iranian purpose and the precursor to Iranian terror attacks. They serve no other intention. As of today, November 2022, the Biden administration is unsuccessful in taking ample action to demolish mullah's terror networks across the Middle East, along with those in Latin American and the U.S., with a thorough approach.

Markedly, these terrorist organization are ready to rumble if the Shia Islamic caliphate wants a fight prior to the regime's collapsing. In actuality, Bush and Obama disregarded the threat. Taken together, British intelligence agencies «believe Iran has organized and funded sleeper terror cells across Europe including the U.K. and could greenlight attacks in response to a conflict in the Persian Gulf.» And in recent years, Iran has shown it is willing to strike within U.S. borders.

By using every possible means to achieve its illegitimate and illegal goals in Africa, Iran has not been reluctant to support outlawed groups and militias in countries suffering from political and social instability. It has done this either with the aim of taking revenge on its opponents, by striking their domestic interests or threatening their national security.

"We remain concerned that violent extremist organizations tied to the regime, including their various partner organizations, may continue to pose a general threat against American citizens and interests both overseas and in the homeland," the DHS bulletin said. They are in a state of preparedness but must be extra alert to be victorious in combat with the Khomeinist thugs..

In sum, history is our best testimony. This unthinkable revolution in Iran will terminate all these sleepers' cells. Victory of those fighting for regime change and the end of vindictive mullahs in Iran will lead to peace and stability in the world.

11
THE LIKELIHOOD OF REGIME CHANGE IN IRAN

Discernibly, challenges lie head, but some countries are reluctant to support it or have a role to play in helping Iran's protesters. The question is «how many lives must be lost to get the world's awareness?»

Globally, there are various demonstrations for regime change in Iran. Iranian expatriat men and women have relentlessly marched to call for "regime change" and show solidarity and support for protesters inside Iran. At the same time, the uninterrupted nationwide protests in Iran are calling for regime change. Internally, the brave young generation continue to confront the tyrannical regime and target the iron-fisted rule of the mullahs.

The viral videos show that many young protesters symbolically knock the turbans off the dishonorable mullahs in Iran. In addition, seminary schools are one of the main targets of protesters as a symbol of clerical rule in Iran. Ingeniously, the Iranians sent a clear message - which was burning down Khomeini's childhood home.

As the Iranian people are calling for regime change, Democrats in the white house and European Union are out with another request for the deceitful mullahs to revitalize the dead JCPOA. We all know the problems. So, there's no need to state the obvious. Ingratiatingly, many pro-regime stooges and lobbies are spreading fake propaganda calling for reforms. Infuriatingly, the US is wavering too much to reinforce clear demands of regime change publicly. In other words, it seems that the current administration in the US does not want regime change in Iran.

How can you succeed in reforming this demonic totalitarian mullah regime? Contrary to this claim, freedom and democracy can not happen without regime change in Iran. . Explicitly or implicitly, Iran is on the verge of regime change as tension on the streets spreads dramatically Discernibly, challenges lie head, but some countries are reluctant to support it or have a role to play in helping Iran's protesters. The question raised is «how many lives must be lost to get the world's awareness?».

Roughly 20000 are arrested and more than 500 slaughtered by the thugs of the mullah terror entity. This time, it is a highly visible reminder that this leaderless movement in 2022 is the largest and most critical antimullah demonstration the regime has seen since it came into power in 1979. Despite earlier violent suppression, the Islamic regime has faced 18 anti-protests in the past; 14 protests were against the totalitarianism of Khamenei, who is the second Caliph in the religious octopus in Iran.

Today is Iran's third month, the movement shows no indications of waning, regardless of the savage violence Iran's current governnment has implemented against the unarmed demonstrators.

It is important to note that regime change would ultimately become an appropriate idea. Now advocates of a new revolution have appeared, the main features being democracy, moderation, widespread secularization, human rights and civil liberties, friendship with Israel and the US, and peace with Arab states in the region. It will be a unique phenomenon, certainly a dramatic change in the world order. In terms of its regional affect, the likely triumph of Iranian revolution will terminate the mullah's long history of terror and aggression. In actuality, the generation is fighting against radical Islamism, Iran's aggressive contribution to theMiddle East and the Khomeinist ideology of the mullahs.

One could argue that the World is only watching the ongoing protests, but they are paralyzed in the conflict with mullahs. What is undeniable, though, is that even today, some of the intelligence organizations in Israel, the US and Europe are striving to understand the real face of Iran's revolution in 2022. The overwhelming majority of Arab states in the region, ironically, not necessarily most of them, are too confused to realize the aspects, framework and foundation of this spawned resilience and courageousness by Iran's young generation.

In fact, these intelligence analysts stick to the same question and attempt to respond to the same basic question: how to get rid of terrorist loving mullahs in Iran who want to seize and hold power after collapsing the current mullah's regime?

It should be noted that the so-called pro-regime ‹reformists' have ties with Saudi Arabia. This notorious political mafia has a verity of economic, security, propaganda system, media, lobbies, and cleric's network.

At the same time, most of the dangerous intelligence figures are related to this Islamic gang. Predictably, they would like to make a deal with Khamenei to remove Raisi from the presidency and seize the state power and agree to compromise. In a sense, it could also be said that there is no possibility their dream will come true.

True, and very surprisingly, Israel is concentrating on an aggressive approach to the mullah's terrorist loving regime. Simply put, the possibility of regime change can be after the events, of which one will be the bombardment of nuclear sites. Because Israel is capable of striking Iran's nuclear facilities to stop its nuclear program. Another scenario which can be considered is restoring Snapback. it will be restored by Security Council resolutions on Iran with all the long-term restrictions and should remain in place indefinitely. Controversially, If the US and Europe trigger and activate mechanism of 'snapback', it will lead to regime change more efficiently.

What is especially important to note, however, is that in the 21st century, there is no state more dangerous on the globe than that of the mullahs. The world should give full backing to the Iranian protesters. Immediately afterwards, Iranian activists can have a serial meeting with the US intelligence community and senators and congressmen to educate them regarding Iran.

If you ask one of the CIA's directors to have a public

meeting, certainly, the answer of this respectable veteran might be: "Unfortunately, the leaders of the Intelligence Community can't meet with Iranian activists, as it would give the regime ammunition to use in the argument that the US Government, namely the CIA, is behind the protests."

An active effort to achieve regime change is not US policy toward Iran and this has not changed at all. However, there is a taboo or paranoia in the mind of Democrats to talk about regime change in Iran. On the othe rhand, the US and Israel can facilitate regime change in Iran, even by introducing the concept. There is no question that it can be a workable and successful way to help the peace and stability in the region.

Everybody knows that "the Iranian people should complete the process of regime change independently and replace a democratic regime", however, there is one way to achieve regime change more easily. Standing on the right side of history cannot be a mistake. The US and Israel intelligence can help Iran's intelligence figures topple the mullah regime. They would like to see regime change in Iran and open the embassy out there once more.

12
REFORMISTS ARE PLOTTING A COUP AGAINST THE IRAN'S REVOLT

So-called reformists, separatist and terror groups as well as pro-regime forces are working to nip the revolt in the bud. The world is watching Iran's horrific situation and the atrocities that are taking place. But Iranian fearless and industrious protesters continue to dig in their heels, their demand is clear: Regime Change. The young generation has decided to eliminate the Shia religious octopus, which is a turning point that will transform Iran into a democracy.

Gradually, the nationwide anti-regime protests got global attention. This is a nightmare for the mullah's regime, and they are escalating the attack on unarmed mass protests. The repressive regime's structure is vulnerable. However, their response has been ferocious.

Notoriously, throughout these momentous events, all the intelligence services of the mullah's regime are working hard to describe this movement as a violent and unforgiving revolt. It is a scandal that, although ineffectively so far, MOIS and IRGS's intelligence organizations are struggling to divert the revolution from its course.

What is at issue is that Iranian protests have grown into the biggest challenge to the regime's theocracy since the 1971 revolt of Khomeini and Marxist Islamic terrorist groups. This movement is gaining power and actively increasing across Iran. Among the US intelligence community, the probability of Regime Change in Iran, has gone unheeded. There are various reasons to support this way of looking at the situation.

One of them is the existence of a corrupt, insolvent, freeloader, mafia opposition in the diaspora. The same old story is before us as these powerless figures cheer loudly and dementedly in front of cameras. On one side, they exhibit a lack of strategy and démarche, and from another side the delusion of grandeur is all they have. Another is that regionally, the competition between Saudi Arabia and Iran is often described as the "Cold War of the Middle East". The tension between the two regional powers, which can be traced since 1979, has increased. In this seemingly unending cold war, there are plenty of suspicions, hostility and aggression between the two Islamic states in the region. The Saudi Iranian rivalry has become a fight over influence, and the whole region is a battlefield.

Nowadays, Saudis are nor more Catholic than the Pope. Inexcusably, they have relations with the pro-regime reformists. They established a connection with reformists since the presidency of Rafsanjani (1989 - 1997) and Khatami

(1997 - 2005) in Iran. it's not a well-kept secret; the seditious truth is that both figures were related to Islamic leftists or so-called reformists. What is certain is that the Saudis are intimate with «reformists» who want to improve and not change the present regime, and apparently, Saudis prefer reformists over radical "regime change" in Iran.

The reformist wing is insisting on making a deal with Khamenei. For this to be possible, they have invited all their friends and lobbies to spread the folktale about olden times. It follows from what pro-regime reformists say that "referendum" or "political reform" is the solution. Remarkably, It's evidence of imbecility and a guff in the political theatre of Iran. The reformists are trying to gull radicals out of power in Iran. while climbing on the bandwagon. In actuality, Iran's revolution sounds a death knell for reformists and hardliners alike.

The tangle in the skein is the organic relationship of separatist ethnic groups with the reformist mafia. The satanic alliance among these disloyal criminals is ludicrous. There is the rub, pro regime reformists are working in parallel with separatists. Moreover, In Khomeini's last will and testament, he names those separatist groups. Indisputably, a couple of years ago a MOIS minister in the Islamic parliament named a couple of separatist groups which have diplomatic ties with the regime..

For the p'resent, the Saudis are supporting most of the Kurdish separatist groups which were allies of Saddam Hussein in Iraq. They are in the firing line. Praise the Lord! The US will never support a fight among separatist ethnic groups. The White House is reluctant to take them seriously.

The presentation of ethnic groups in the London-based Iran international TV to bandy a story about Kurdistan, have kept Iranian protesters guessing. It's anybody's guess to divine the main motivation of the Saudis. As a matter of course, the separatist literature is the bane of the ongoing revolution's existence in Iran. Furtively, the separatist groups with terrorist backgrounds will slaughter, literally, the Iranian will for change.

We can say that during the revolution in Iran, the coup de grâce is an alliance between reformists and radicals and the propaganda of separatist groups. The Iranian revolution will be engulfed in troubles if reformists and pro-regime lobbyists have a finger in the pie. Heterogeneously, they continue to present flattery to faint-hearted leaders and know how to make a fuss by fair means or foul. Some of these fast-growing numbers of grovelers, who build themselves up, have ties with the notorious NIAC. Some of them are wolves lying in wait!

Israel and the US are observing. With a fine-toothed comb, the intelligence analysts are watching the Iranian revolution. Realistically, there are still a lot of ifs and buts. I wish to goodness that the Saudis would be serious and support the regime change, and then go back to the drawing-board. There is no need to hammer a point home, they live in a dreadful neighborhood, which is controlled by a gormless lunatic Shia leader who is the pretender to the throne of Islam's history. The destructive ideology of Khomeinism is like a cancer in the Middle East which triggered all terrorist groups and shaped radical Shia militia. The terrorist loving mullahs are now embarked on a path of strife. The Saudis know all this. Will the West see through it all?

13
THE IRANIANS WILL NEVER FORGET OR FORGIVE QATAR!

The young generation in Iran will never forget or forgive Qatari flagrant support for silencing their public statements at the games.

Currently, Qatar is hosting the 2022 FIFA World Cup soccer tournament in Doha. Lamentably, the intelligence organization of this terror sponsor state helped MOIS in Iran to ban all anti-mullah's slogans in Doha. In actuality, Qatar is hosting FIFA under the banner of terrorism and charlatanism. Disgracefully, some of Qatar's police had a puerile approach to some Iranian viewers in Doha.

From one point of view, the world cannot keep turning a blind eye to Qatar's funding of terrorism, and from another point of view, the young generation in Iran will never forget and forgive the Qatari flagrant and obvious support for silencing any public statements in Qatar. It is also important to remember that while there are no clear data on numbers, most Iranians boycotted the World Cup in Qatar.

Certainly, after regime change in Iran, there will be no room for Qatar to pull the wool over everyone's eyes. Somebody should get that into the Emir's thick skull because he is a skivvy of the Shia octopus. And Al Jazeera never ever broadcast any video from the protesters. Qatar never, through its state-run news channel Al Jazeera, has spread the words of protesters.

Tangibly, Qatar's state-owned Al Jazeera has been spreading Antisemitism, Anti-Zionism and Islamic terrorism to achieve its goal of pan-Islamism among the Persian Gulf states. Al Jazeera News Station, however, has given voice to pro-regime stooges and regurgitated all the pro-regime's platitudinous propaganda or current speeches of Khamenei. Here's the rub, with servility, the Emir of Qatar has pandered to terrorist mullahs in Iran and made obeisance to IRGC. The young generation in Iran has therefore had a rude awakening and these realities are troubling.

Despite that, the nationwide protests against theocracy in Iran, are in the glare of public attention and shaking the mullah terror entity. Irrefutably, Qatar has built ties to terrorist groups, international extremism, and terrorism sponsors such as Hamas, Taliban, Al-Qaeda, IRGC , ISIS , Brotherhood, Nusra Front and other global terrorist groups. In addition, Qatar is supplying sanctuary and "safe haven" to the top Hamas leaders, hosting members of IRGC and MOIS and other religious extremists expelled from other countries such as Yemeni rebel militias.

At the same time and in certain instances, some of the Iranian intelligence organizations, under the cover of businessmen are monitoring the Israelis and American officials. To this day, most of the regional states accuse Qatar of links to terrorism and supporting ISIS insurgents. There is an organic relation between IRGC and ISIS and this hidden agenda. Most members of the Qatari royal family have provided safe haven for Al Qaeda members, ISIS, Hamas leaders. Since then, IRGC and MOIS have been sponsoring and shielding Hamas leaders and other transnational terrorist groups on the soil of Qatar.

Reportedly, the increasing presence of MOIS officials in Qatar since approximately the early 2000's, has highlighted the hide-and-seek game of Iran. It is now an explicit fact that Qatar has formed an alliance with IRGC terrorists, which has led to cooperation with Iran's MOIS. Sometimes, Qatar provided financial support in the form of ransoms for IRGC in the region. Against this reality, it is not hard to see that the doors of Qatar are open to the Iranian mullahs.

As regional tension remains high amid Iran's rapid progress toward making nuclear bomb, it will lead to undermining regional and international security. It is important to note that Qatar is a steadfast and important partner to the terrorist loving mullahs in Iran and these relations will challenge the Persian Gulf norms and stability in the region.

This reality is exclusively expressed that Doha under the supervision of the Islamic outlaw regime in Iran, and plays a pivotal role in waging the global terrorism against the US, Israel, and the free world. Qatar and the Mullah's regime in Iran have embraced their role as sponsors of terrorism.

Furthermore, Tehran has shared a massive offshore natural gas field with Doha. In fact, this alliance is a permissive environment for terror financing. The truth of the matter is that some of the Persian Gulf states know that large sums of money from this alliance between Tehran and Doha go to terror financing, funding terrorism for making never-ending tensions and destabilization.

Some of the Arab states in the Middle East and North Africa are watching the process of anti-regime protests inside Iran. They know that the likelihood of success in regime change will be a significant moment for the stability and peace of the region. The continued existence of mullahs in power will prolong a deeply problematic and longstanding tension over the region for an unforeseen future. Therefore, moving forward, this devastating coalition between Emir of Qatar with the Supreme leader of the Mullah regime is not good for the region. "this ongoing revolution in Iran will be followed by an international law, a bill of rights, human rights after disintegrating this dangerous regime. Certainly, after this horrible reign of terror, regime change will bring peace to the region once more!". Words to live by!

Imagine for a second, "life in Iran without Mullahs" All these dreams will come true and the Persian Gulf will turn over a new leaf.

14
A MULLAH'S FLAG WITH A HOLE IN IT IS NOW THE SYMBOL OF THE REVOLUTION

The revolutionaries in Iran know the historic symbolism of a flag with a hole - and their own historic symbolism of a Lion and Sun. In 1905, George Santayana said "Those who cannot remember the past are condemned to repeat it". This is true for dictators of our age. "Those who do not know history are destined to repeat it," a quote from Edmund Burke.

Khamenei, lunatic mullah in Iran, knows the history of Ceaușescu's dictatorial regime, but he is doomed to repeat it. Everybody knows that a Romanian flag with a hole in the middle symbolized the 1989 revolution. The flag of the Romanian Socialist Republic with the communist logo was perceived as a symbol of Nicolae Ceaușescu's regime. In the Revolution of 1989, protesters made a hole in it the and the ripped flag became one of the symbols of Revolution. In the course of time, the revolution engulfed a desperate Romania at the middle of December 1989. A flag with a hole in the middle, which was flown by the revolutionaries of 1989, was an object loaded with memories and emotions.

For the first time, on the 19th of June 2022, I published my article in Persian with the title: The final solution, transition from Mullahs! because I got a signal from members of the young generation inside Iran saying that they have the courage of their convictions.

As a matter of a course, one of my friends in Canada, sent me that picture. Exactly, like I said in , it was replicating the Romanians in 1989. Then, I put it on Twitter As you may or may not know, after 1979, the mullahs changed the national flag of Iran to a strange flag which is not related to the history and culture of Iran. Without doubt, the notorious institution of the mullahs crossed swords with the history of Iran.

After that winter with no spring in sight, Khomeini dragged all Iranians into doing something strange, deleting the flag with the Lion and Sun. Historically, that national flag is related to an ancient tradition of Iranians in the 12th century. These days the youths of Iran are deeply involved in the national flag of Iran with the Lion and Sun

A Shia mullah in Iran, who had no feeling for Iranian history, and was an enemy of any nationalistic interpretation, changed the flag after the 1979 revolt. Sacrilegiously, Khomeini showed a great amount of ill will and malevolence against the national flag of Iran. Disturbingly, in any demonstration against the theocratic regime of the mullahs in Iran, most of the Marxist or Islamic terrorist or separatist groups in the diaspora are against the flag with the Sun and Lion. All the partners in the 1979 revolt, paved the path to ruin Iran and set that beautiful country ablaze. After setting the stage for the mullahs, they never turned swords into ploughshares against the Iranians themselves.

The abovementioned photo had been shared hundreds of times on social media. By inference, some of the fanatical pro-regime activists regarded that as a deliberate insult to Iran, a groundless and false claim. In actuality, the mullahs' regime and thugs of the regime have no ties with the national identity or interests of Iran. Undeniably, they act like occupiers.

Now and then, I used that flag in my notes in , one of which was Cyrus the Great Day. One of my followers in , sent me a shocking video. When I saw that, I wrote" The mullah's mafia regime in will go to the «ash heap of history» where it belongs. The world community can help and facilitate. Throughout history, "A national Flag represents and symbolizes a particular nation. It is flown by the government of the nation, but typically can also be flown by its citizens. A national flag is normally designed with certain values for its colors and symbols, which may also be employed independently from the flag of the nation."

What happened for the young generation making a hole in the middle of the mullahs' flag? All is fair in war! The regime attempted to use the world cup to evoke nationalist pride, but it crashed. It is a sad fact that in the US-Iran match, when the mullahs lost the hearts and minds battle, the people came out to celebrate Iran's defeat in Qatar. Historically, in 1998, Iranians celebrated their world cup victory against the US team and waved flags. After 24 years, the

situation has deteriorated dramatically. The young generation were happy about the US victory, they went out in the streets to celebrate the regime's loss to the US loudly and joyfully, and they chanted for freedom! These videos are so embarrassing for Iran's regime.

It is not a sign of behavioral solecism, because these people have done nothing wrong. It's a sign of the wrath and anger of the people inside Iran. As might have been expected, the mullah's thugs, police and security forces could not prevail. It defies description. Reportedly, the frustrated and furious bullies of the regime attacked many people during this national celebration. It's a safe bet that the terrorist loving regime in Iran will collapse and crumble, sooner or later, it's only a matter of time. This people in Iran are in a fury. Nowadays in Iran nobody shows any respect to the flag of the mullahs or the national anthem of the Islamic Republic of mullahs in Iran. This degenerated regime is not related to Iran. Comparisons are odious!

Likely enough, if someone had doubts regarding Iran's revolution in 2022 and the likelihood of regime change, they can be convinced now. I need hardly say that the mullah's regime is weakening every day, The young generation in Iran will exorcise these criminal mullahs by fair means or foul. Wish them luck!

15
80 DAYS OF PROTESTS IN IRAN AND STILL NO LEADER

There is no way diplomacy or dialogue works with Shia' mullahs, so the rebels need a charismatic leader, but none has appeared. If everyone in Iran made it his or her goal find a way to take down one mullah or ayatollah during these months of revolution, for example, the problem would be solved, wouldn't it? All of them would be gone. Imagine for a second, life in Iran without the Mullahs. Everybody talks about it, protests against it, but does nothing about it.

There is absolutely no way diplomacy or dialogue works with Shia' mullahs. If your house is infested with cockroaches, the only way to solve the problem is to get rid of all of them. Granted, the mullahs are far worse than any cockroach and they cannot be dealt with in the way we deal with cockroaches.

You may think I am promoting "terrorism" or something resembling terrorism when in fact I am not. If all the terrorist-loving mullahs were eliminated tomorrow, and there are ways to do that without necessarily taking their lives, tens of millions of lives worldwide would be saved. That's for sure.

Let's explore this a bit further. During the regimes Muammar Gaddafi and Saddam Hussein, both of them respected Islam, but both men had absolutely no use for the mullahs in their current form as they are in Iran. They both supported Khomeini, in the rebellion of 1979, because he opposed the late king of Iran, Mohammad Reza Pahlavi, and they hated the King The late Shah- because "Pahlavi was on good terms with the USA and Israel".

But neither one ever supported the mullahs and neither one would give the mullahs any semblance of the power they currently yield in Iran. In other words, to sum it up, the mullahs are worthless. They live in the Middle Ages, they murder, rape, terrorize, torture, and eliminate anyone who stands in their way. In the 1988 executions of Iranian political prisoners, between 5000 and 6000 were murdered. in the 2019- 2020 Iranian protests also known as the Bloody November, Reuters reported the slaughtering of about 1,500 protesters. these are 2 samples of extreme barbarity of a regime that has a management model based on pure Mohammadi Islam.

The only way you can move forward is to get rid of all of these brutal and corrupted mullahs. Any true Muslim (remember now, I'm talking about true Muslims) knows I am right.

What Iran lacks right now is leadership. Granted to go against the totalitarian regime means almost certain death. But if enough Iranians - and I am talking in tens of millions here.- If enough Iranians go against the ayatollahs and the mullahs, wonders will happen. The historical examples were Ukraine [the velvet or Orange Revolution, 2004-2005] and Egypt, Tunisia. [Arab Spring, 2010-2012].

Diplomacy and dialogue, once more, I should emphasize, will never work. In fact, the only thing that has any chance of ever working is for a powerful leader to emerge, similar to one of the modern east European leaders, or somrone similar to the modern Iranian kings, Reza Shah Pahlavi (15 December 1925 - 16 September 1941), or Nader Shah Afshar [8 March 1736 - 20 June 1747].

Because regardless of what you may think, during his leadership the nation prospered, lived in peace and the majority lived well and without fear. The middle eastern people cannot have democracy identical to what they have in the west. It simply doesn't work. They need strong, tough, but fair-minded leaders - then watch them excel.

The leader I am talking about would of course recognize the importance of governing the country and worshiping his God and they are two completely different tasks. If you try to run a country based on ideology, you will have nothing but problems. From 1979, the civilized world understood the meaning of Khomeinism, an ideologyworse than Genghis Khan and the first Mongol Empire [1206-1227].

All faith has to be respected and Islam is respected faith but only to the true Muslims. Once you cross over into radical Islam or clerical fascism, you have already lost. Look at Khamenei, the current dictator of Iran — how is that working? He is the second caliphate of Shia' religious octopus in Iran since 1989.

People around the globe want the same thing. They want peace, freedom and democracy, a future for their children and the country they can be proud of. As you read this, we're waiting for this great leader to rise up. Where is he? Who is he? Unfortunately, among the opposition leaders of Iranians in the diaspora, it's very hard to find a charismatic figure. Furthermore, the life and profit of some Iranians is dependent on the survival of Mullah's regime.

The rogue regime in Tehran is the primary source of turmoil and instability in the region. The regime thirsts for ever more dominance across the region and beyond and employs a terrorist network to achieve that goal, even as it continues to move aggressively in its pursuit of nuclear weapons and weapons of mass destruction. Khamenei loves instability and chaos in the Middle East, his life depends on war, savageness, viciousness and conflicts.

Deplorably, the EU and the President of the USA are hesitating to face this reality. The Mullah regime, in their mind, is going to be around for the foreseeable future. There is a lack of will for regime change among the fake opposition which is in favor of mullah's regime. Furthermore, MOIS and the IRGC intelligence organization are supporting some related phony opposition to thwart the path of revolution.

Some of the intelligence agencies around the globe are monitoring Iran's young generation but the main issue is to find a strong and reliable figure for the transition's period after collapsing the regime. Otherwise, Iran will face an internal crisis which will be a potential threat for the region.

In sum, the main reason for the lack of leadership in Iran is the clash and conflict of interests. In an undeveloped country, the rivalry and competition among the thirsty wolves leads to this unsolved complex. In reality, some of the so-called opposition figures have a too naïve mentality to resolve the problem.

16
THE YOUNG PROTESTERS HAVE SCULPTED THE NEW IRAN

The only chance Iran has is to get rid of these toxic, worthless mullahs and ayatollahs. The harshest ever winter in Iran began on January 19,1979. It has lasted 43 years and counting. It was on that fateful day that the late Shah, Mohammed Reza Pahlavi, faltered.

The Shah, the late king of Iran, had instructed Iran's army and SAVAK to stand down. In doing so, the protesters got their wish. All their dreams came true (be careful what you wish for) and as the Shah taxied down the runway heading to Egypt, Khomeini rubbed his hands and licked his lips in glee. The nightmare the installation of the worst theocracy in the 20th century, had begun.

The turbulent Middle East would be an entirely different place today if the Shah had acted just a little bit differently.

Here is how it all went down. Khomeini had done his homework and defined his mission. He had the backing of Jimmy Carter, who was about to make a gigantic blunder (with his support for the new regime behind the scenes). The Shah blinked, saying to himself that Khomeini has the backing of the USA and CIA, so I had better get out while the getting is good. In fact, Shah was a peace loving and zealous Iran-lover! He was the best and honest friend of Israel and the USA.

In truth, had the Shah stood his ground and put down the uprising, America would have backed down and gone away. The USA didn't love Iran that much. Robert Armao, in an interview with me, is of the opinion that "history will be kind to the Shah" . It could be, but when examined closely, standing down spared the protestors for a short time only. Khomeini killed them anyway plus many, many, many more over the next 10 years. He was a murderous Shia mullah who wanted to imitate the rule of the Islamic caliphate.

Moreover, the massacres, which started in 1979, still go on today with the Mullahs in charge. They supported and extended the "transnational terrorist network (TTN)" in the world. Nowadays, that network is a cancerous tumor in the 21st century.

Had the Shah had the mindset of Gaddafi or Saddam this would never have happened. They would not have blinked and casually handed over the reins of power to Carter and Khomeini. The Shah was a respectable gentleman - in Middle Eastern terms - not a con artist or Islamic terrorist leader.

Ronald Reagan himself, just 2 years later, said "it was a disastrous move on the part of Carter" and how right he was!

Jimmy Carter, coming from the deep south of the United States was of opinion that Khomeini was a Holy man when in fact Khomeini himself was worse than the Devil himself. "Radical Islam" and "Clerical Fascism" have borne out how ridiculous the USA role in all of this was.

A year later, in 1980, the CIA toyed with the idea of putting Reza Pahlavi, the son of the Shah, back in power. How weird is that? If truth be told, the CIA had enough time to support Iranian protests for democracy in Iran. Now 43 years later, a new generation of protestors are talking about bringing Reza Pahlavi out of exile and overthrowing Khamenei, the current tyrant of Iran, who I don't need to remind you is a total disaster! Except crown prince Reza Pahlavi has neither zeal nor desire.

When you look at the twists and turns that have taken place in Iran over the last 43 years, you arrive back to middle of 1970's, when a time of harmony and stability prevailed, just where the current protesters of Iran want to go. This was a time when Jimmy Carter, George H.W. Bush, Ronald Reagan, Richard Nixon visited Iran and Iran was close ally of USA in the region, even if Iran was not an American style democracy..

The young generation realizes that the mullah's vicious network existing today is nothing more than a recipe for disaster. They are not willing to buy into the ideology of the "Islamic Terrorist", which is all the mullahs and ayatollahs have to offer. Take that away and guess what results?, "No more mullahs. mullahs gone". Now, we can say: God is great!

Two years ago, as you walked the streets of Tehran with the protesters, you could hear "peace be with you Reza Shah!" along with some slogans in favor of "prince Reza Pahlavi". They wanted Reza Pahlavi, the first Shah's grandson, to lead the Iran of the future.

Going forward, the only chance Iran has is to get rid of these toxic, worthless mullahs and ayatollahs. These protesters need to set up their game and somehow come together in unity, with one goal in mind. Their mindset must be laser-focused on the elimination, at all costs of this dead weight (criminal mullahs and ayatollahs), an albatross around the neck of Iran and the choice of a new leader.

The famous Iranian journalist, Amir Taheri, would be in total agreement with me, he has written countless articles along the same vein. His beliefs, mine along with many others, are gaining traction minute by minute. If everything goes according to plan the future of Iran will be bright.

Through the thousand years long history of Iran different brutal leaders came to power, ruled, and disappeared. It's a long story... Accordingly, just 3 years ago Farah Pahlavi, the widow of the late Shah, after being insulted by the cowardly Khamenei said:" all dictators collapsed, you will be no different!". Words to live by! The Iranians and the World will celebrate the ruin of the religious octopus in Iran and the Islamic caliphate of the Shia Mullah's autocratic regime.

Note - The MOIS has installed many fake oppositions in diaspora. Also, numerous figures among the Iranian opposition are in relation with NIAC, a notorious proregime lobby in the US, or reformists in Iran's regime. In addition, some of this nouveau riche opposition is in the hands of

Saudi Arabia, and they are playing with some spoiled cards. Surely, these political dwarfs have no desire to support regime change in Iran, and surely, these incapable figures can not have a political role in future of Iran. As an example, one of them is a puppet in hands of reformists, another one is a clown, posing in front of cameras with an insatiable appetite, making a name for herself. The leopard cannot changes its spots.

How can an opportunist journalist or a populist figure be recognized as a leader, and an organizer of demonstrations insist upon being in a fake leadership's circle? The answer is that MOIS and IRGC are making efforts to set a trap for Reza Pahlavi. It's not a laughing matter, the regime wants to keep the pot boiling and this is how it is doing so. These days in Iran, the young generation still exhibits a strong will to eliminate the mullah's terrorist regime. The mullah's notorious institution is on the edge of the precipice. The young must choose their leader wisely.

17
IRANIAN PROTESTERS FEEL A HUGE SENSE OF BETRAYAL

The Democrats seem to like to support diplomacy with the mullahs and that means no new Iran, no end to supporting terror, no freedom. Iran is endowed with impending troubles. After a hopedfor regime change in Iran, the political theatre of Middle East will be changed dramatically. For instance, one of the main results will be institutionalizing democracy, peace, and stability in the area. Unquestionably, a clear region free of Hezbollah, Hamas, Taliban, ISIS and mullahs has the capacity for entering a modern era. Just imagine life in the region without IRGC, MOIS or the Quds Force! It would be one of the wonders of the world in the 21st century.

History and geography can not be changed effortlessly. Geopolitically, Iran is a powerful neighbor of the Arab states in the Persian Gulf. However, there are numerous mutual points between Iranian and Arab culture. Furthermore, after regime change in Iran, there will be no arms race any longer among the players. Instead of squandering billions of dollars in an arms race, these states will concentrate on economic improvement, industrial technology or their educational systems.

With brutal honesty, since 1979, there is no pride, honor, and identity for Iranians. Certainly, Raisi, Ahmadinejad, Khatami or Banisadr brought dishonor on Iranian society. Once cannot unring the bell; but after the chaos of 1979 in Iran was plunged in barbarism and darkness. The mullah's regime humiliated Iran. You wouldn't wish that on your worst enemy.

While not democratically elected, the Pahlavi dynasty was not tyrannical and at least spared Iranians shame. They created modern Iran. Pahlavi's kings have records in the contemporary history of Iran. Therefore, Iranians trusted them and nowadays the young generation are reading history to learn how at decisive moments, these late great men helped Iranians.

Meanwhile, as the world is watching, the mullahs have sold Iran for a song. There is no room for doubt that the criminal mullahs, with their destructive ideology of Khominism, demolished the region by means of terrorist groups.

It will be more effective for the Arab States in the region to halt any support to the former terrorists, separatist puppets of Saddam Hussein or pro-regime reformists. Supporting 2% of Iranian society does not meet presentday needs.. How can pro-Khomeini or pro-Saddam puppets, with radical ideologies and inferiority complexes, be trustworthy? This is a crystal-clear reason to understand the argument of Shah when he labeled these criminal and malevolent marionettes as Islamic Marxist terrorists. May he rest in peace.

What can we do about it? The first best way to seek a remedy, instead of barking up the wrong tree, will be supporting the real Iranian oppositions, such as The Crown Prince Reza Pahlavi or a patriotic circle. Iran can be the best ally of Arab States and Israel in the region once more. This reality is on record before 1979.

Alas, Saudi Arabia supports MEK and some Kurdish separatist groups, all of them Islamic Marxists. They have ties with Islamic leftists (moderates and reformists), which have caused Iranians to worry. If you remind them that Iran International TV is a center of above-mentioned groups, it just goes in one ear and out the other. But this TV has blacklists of guests to force opponents off the stage. In other words, a TV related to reformists or separatist's destructive ideology cannot spread democracy in Iran.

The Saudis fell into the trap of MOIS, which is under control of reformists and has ties with terrorists and ethnic separatists. That's about par for the course. Is it not entirely implausible that a former director of the ministry of culture and Islamic guidance in Iran who is the director of Iran international, can be faithful? But that's the way it is.

The rational thing to do is to make it public. This antiregime protests in Iran cannot be reduced. Action speaks louder than words. The courageous young generation are confronting the worst terrorist power in the globe. Regime change in a theocratic regime is extremely complicated, though the mullah's regime is on the brink of an abyss.

The world will be a better place after regime change in Iran. Crown Prince Reza Pahlavi is the front runner in the show, unaware of the fact that all the other fake opposition in the diaspora is not good for Iranian society. Improbably, some of these boisterous dolls wallowed in corruption. Inexplicably and inexcusably, John Bolton and Mike Pompeo are full of praise for MEK and holding court to some old-fashioned and worthless forces. The bird has flown, it stands to reason that there is no chance for an Islamic terrorist group to rule in Iran.

The late Shah, without guile, was a very loyal ally of Israel and the USA. In 1979, Khomeini was the standard-bearer of barbarism and Jimmy Carter was up to no good. For quite some time, It will be a false dawn if we find that the current Democrat president in the White House has no desire to recognize this reality, to recognize the revolution in Iran.

Nowadays, Iran is aware of another possible source of disappointment and betrayal. To cut a long story short, if the European Union and Biden prevent resuscitating the dead JCPOA, the world will watch the melting of mullah's regime in less than 1 to 1.5 years. Any mullah's heart is in his mouth, because they know where they stand.

The Biden administration's Iran policy is shrouded in mystery.. The only problem is that nine times out of ten, the Democrats like to support diplomacy with the mullahs. And a deal with the terrorist loving mullahs, will paint a grim picture of life in the region once more.

18
WHEN WILL THE MULLAHS' REGIME FALL?

The mullahs' regime breathing its dying breath and threatened with extinction, cannot be stable due to the shrinking economy, internal crisis, devastating environmental disaster and a succession crisis. Unexpectedly, the IRGC's intelligence organization published a statement to overemphasize that 7 UKIranian dual nationals were detained over anti-regime nationwide protests in Iran. Possibly the despicable mullahs believe that lightening never strikes twice in the same place.

Apparently, this bogus report is an exaggeration and cannot be real. There are numerous reasons that the UK cannot be against the Islamic regime in Iran. such as:

-The most corrupted pro terrorism figure, a fanatic proKhamenei individual whose name is Ata'ollah Mohajerani, lives in London. Several times, he has supported Hezbollah, Qasem Soleimani, Khamenei from London.

-There is London-Based TV which is a center for propaganda of pro-regime lobbies, such as Reformists, ethnic separatists, and National-Religious figures of Islamic revolutionary Movahedin. Remarkably, the former director of censorship in Ministry of Islamic guidance is the director of this flawed TV channel.

Most of the Pro-Theocracy's mullahs in Iran, have religious centers in London, such as Naser Makarem Shirazi, a notorious Shia Marja or religious leader. Historically, the BBC Persian program had a destructive role in 1979 by propagating the words of Khomeini and his terrorist followers. Currently, most of the reporters of BBC have sympathy for the regime's reformists inside Iran. and most of them are learning journalism inside reformist circles such as Sham'sol'vaezin, Hajarian etc.

Intriguingly, some of the regime's authorities have British citizenship and their families are living in the UK. Factually, London was a sponsor of 1979's revolt in Iran. Mehdi Bazargan, a long-time pro-terrorism activist and spiritual founder of MEK, went to London many days before the return of Khomeini to Iran. And at the same time, the UK's agents inside Iran – Hossein Fardoust and Nasser Moghadam in SAVAK- deceived their country by aiding Khomeini.

Some of the ethnic separatist individuals who were the puppets of Saddam Hussein are living in the UK with British citizenship and some of these corrupt figures from London are trying to misguide the path of protests in Iran. Most of my colleagues in the Counter-terrorism Center in the UK know how the destructive ideologies of Khomeinism, Taliban, ISIS, Hezbollah and others are expanding in the.UK. They realize that potentially these toxic ideologies can give rise to massive Islamic Terrorism inside Europe.

Unpredictably, Kazemi, the IRGC's highest official, currently the head of IRGC's intelligence organization declared a fake statement regarding arresting a UKLinked network in Kerman. This planned phony news cannot bring down the decision of young generation who calls for the ruin of the mullah's ruling theocracy. They have posed one of the greatest challenges for the Shi'ite Islamic Republic since the 1979 revolt.

On one side, the regime's suppressor apparatus blames the demonstrator and brands them as subservient to foreign powers; from another side the protesters are revealing the subordination of Khamenei's regime to China-Russia's orbit.

However, Kerman can not be a target city for the UK, for numerous reasons.. Even though Kerman, Yazd and Semnans faced some unrest, these cities were not related to the hot spots during the 100 days since September 2022. However, some of the Soleimani Statues erected in this part of Iran were torched and burned.

Furthermore, most of the regime's terrorist figures were raised in this part of Iran, such as Rafsanjani, Solaimani. Bahonar, Hojati Kermani, Mar'ashi, Movahedi Kermani and others. With such influence, this news cannot be so believable.

The achievable regime change in Iran will lead to the collapse of Islamic Shia terrorism in the region. These days, the Iranian people have no pride, honor, and identity with the criminal mullahs in power. The only era of the Iran's history which furnished Iranians pride, honor, and identity was the dynasty of Pahlavi in Iran (1925-1979).

As a replacement for the civilization of Iran, currently, most of Raisi's government are worldwide terrorists such as Ali Shamkhani, Ismail Khatib, Mohsen Rezaee, Ahmad Vahidi. This mullah's terrorist regime and its criminal network (The Islamic Coalition, Party of Islamic Nations,

The Freedom Movement /MEK, Fada'iyan-e Islam) came to power in 1979 because of terrorism, Radical Islamic and fundamentalism.

Realistically, the UK cannot sacrifice its future relations with Iranian people after regime change. So, the UK can support the real Iranian opposition figures and the front runner of the show, The Crown Price Reza Pahlavi. If UK convince the US and the west to hesitate the signing of 2nd JCPOA, the possibility of regime change in Iran can be predicted for less than 1 to 1.5 years from now. The US and the West should educate themselves that diplomacy with criminal thugs of the mullah's regime is a futile endeavor. Where there's a will there's a way.

In sum, the UK foreign office and MI6 will seek further information, but they will find out the truth and must refuse all false and distorted allegations. Literally and categorically, this comedy classic is written as envisioned by Mohammad Kazemi (IRGC) and Esmail Khatib (MOIS). Even though, imaginatively, the websites of MOIS in Iran (Bultannews and Tabnak) interpreted the speech of James Cleverly, the British foreign Secretary regarding the IRGC as the UK sanctioning it in its entirely.

These days, from time to time, the regime pours oil on the flames with legendary champions (such as Ali Daei) or artists. This is a vicious approach of MOIS and IRGC, who threaten the famous figures in Iran, arousing Iranian anger on a large scale and will provoke another storm of protests in Iran.

Throughout history, Iran has been repeatedly invaded, but the invasion by the criminal mullahs shattered Iran. A warning bell started to ring when the illegitimacy of the mullahs has floated around, because their Nazi-Style propaganda struck a holy pose!

The mullahs' regime breathing its dying breath and threatened with extinction, cannot be stable due to the shrinking economy, internal crisis, devastating environmental disaster, and a succession crisis.

Some of the Israeli MOSAD and American CIA are in conversation with the patriotic and real figures of opposition to set the wheels in motion. Surely, practice makes perfect, but let's clear the decks and get the show on the road.

19
TO THE MULLAHS: WILL YOU SOON BE THE ONES SWINGING FROM LAMPPOSTS?

The mullahs undoubtedly believe they will be safe after regime change, but there is no guarantee after their present brutality. Starting several days ago, there are tsunami of reports and circulated rumors that "the notorious judge of the kangaroo Islamic court in Iran's regime was killed with 5 bullets". Is it a sign of the emergence of Iranian partisans or the armed ex-forces who are acting in sympathy with those fearless rebels? Nobody knows for sure.

Is the butcher in charge of executing protesters dead? The mullah's propaganda officials have not yet made any announcement regarding Salavati's death. Ambiguously, there is a probability that the regime's propaganda circle outside Iran is continuing this gossip. Even though the regime denies it, in Iranian public opinion it can be accepted as a confirmation. According to unconfirmed reports coming from Iran, Abolghasem Salavati, an infamous judge and prosecutor who sentenced countless political prisoners to death in many controversial cases, has been shot to death. Surely, Salavati's neutralization will be like the celebration of Soleimani's elimination from the field.

Sarcastically, some of the Iranians wrote in social media that "Salavati is already being memed as the Iranian meatball dish – Kotlet or Kofteh". Since Friday, it is claimed that the dirtiest thug had been assassinated in his 2nd wife's house on 5th Jan 2023. If this unconfirmed report is true and Salavati was eliminated, it will be a great day for the protesters and opponents of the regime. It will be a sign of approval for revolutionaries inside Iran that they are doing amazing work.

As usual, unbelievably, the mullah's brutal regime says this murderous psychopath is breathing and in good health. He was depriving prisoners of access to lawyers, and threatening defenders. He was the head of the 15th branch of the Islamic revolutionary court in Tehran. He presided over mass show trials following 2009 and imprisoned hundreds of the Iranian freedom fighters and political activists.

This so-called judge "had offered female attorneys to sleep with him in return for calling the case in their favor". Salavti was solely responsible for handing out 300 sentences, totaling 2000 years! Probably it is seen as a sign of kindness in mullah's the savage regime.

He was sanctioned by the US in December 2019 and EU in April 2011. They knew that he was a puppet of MOIS. However, he was under the influence of Iran's intelligence because of personal corruption. It means that Iran's hanging judge did not know the meaning of justice or care about those who committed human rights abuses after any protests in Iran.

Nowadays, the regime's problem is exacerbated by the out-of-control security situation. Revenge killing is occurring almost daily as the regime's violence worsened considerably throughout Sept 2022 to Jan 2023. The people will be out in the streets to show the theocratic regime that this is a right opportunity to finish the show, which is regime change in Iran. Since Sept 2022, there is a significant change in Iranian public opinion. The country is perpetually in economic difficulty and the economy iin terrible shape. The government's security apparatus is struggling to suppress all protests inside Iran.

The young generation will open a path to change. The mullahs undoubtedly believe that they will be safe and secure after regime change, but there is no guarantee. "The Iranian people crave freedom."

There is no development, transformation, or a democratic opening inside a theocratic mullah's regime. For how long can IRGC and MOIS protect the interests of the notorious mullahs in Iran? Indeed, a good mullah is a dead one, and unquestionably "pretty soon you will be swinging from lampposts". In actuality, Jihadi Shiite ideology and Global Leftists – which are in a relationship with Islamic leftist groups - never know anything called retreat, mercy and humanity. The supreme leader of terrorists, Ali Khamenei, is not a man of integrity and tolerance, he would never have punished some corrupt officials these days to win the hearts of the nation and silence the protests peacefully. Instead, he ordered more suppression and censorship because he sees himself as "a representative of God on Earth!"

Undeniably, this mafia regime is controlled by foreign stooges, and any retreat or liberation is prohibited. For the mullahs, the nation is the enemy. From another point, the mullahs and so-called judges are issuing these rulings to appease the intelligence organizations and Khamenei. It is remarkable that a security institution, with only a phone call and a gesture, orders courts to issue a verdict of execution.

This past Saturday morning, mournfully, the murderous mullah's regime executed Mohammad Mehdi Karami who had been on a hunger strike, and Mohammad Hossein simply for participating in anti-regime protests. They were executed without letting their family meet them for the last time.

The world is watching the execution of innocent human beings in the hands of mullahs, an ongoing genocide. Anyone who shakes hands with these criminal mullahs has blood on its hands. The situation in Iran cannot be normalized. It must be completely uprooted.

20
FIRST CHARLIE HEBDO, THEN THE WORLD

IRGC threats against Charlie Hebdo are the tip of the iceberg. Iran is out to control the world and a new government is crucial. The terrorist IRGC has now threatened Charlie Hebdo's staff with the fate of Salman Rushdie. Hussein Salami, the stooge of Khamenei, made an incriminating statement to that effect.

In fact, terrorism is an inseparable part of Khomienism. Since the 1960's the terror machine of criminal Shia mullahs has terrorized and eliminated all opponents of their destructive ideology.

Analytically, in studying Iranian contemporary history, knowing that khomeinism is a mixture of more than 64 different schools is essential for political evaluation.

Critically, "Khomienism" is a mixture and a bizarre amalgam of diverse schools such as *Absolutism; Activism; Alarmism; Anarchism; Antagonism; anti-Semitism; authoritarianism; autism; barbarism; blackguardism; Bolshevism; Charlatanism; Communism; Cosmopolitanism; Demagogism; despotism; Dogmatism; Egotism; Expansionism; Externalism; Extremism; Fascism; Fanatism; Fetishism; Fundamentalism; Gangesterism; Idiotism; Interventionism; Jacobinism; Imperialism; Leftism; Machiavelism; Stalinism; Medievelism; Militarism; Misoneism; Nepotism; obscurntism; Obstructionism; opportunism; Parasitism; pharisaism; Primitivism; Propagandism; Proselytism; Radicalism; reactionism; religionism; Revivalism; Rowdyism; Ruffianism; Sacerdotalism; Sanculotism; Shamanism; sensationalism; sophism; Terrorism; Threnodism; totalitarianism; Ultraism; Vandalism; Vulgarism.*

Note that this vicious ideology is running the entire regime of criminal mullahs. Nowadays, from one side, they are up the creek without a paddle. From other side, the propaganda machine of the regime spends money hand over fist to spread the prejudicial policies of the outlaw regime.

For this reason, Salami and IRGC terrorists are an integral part of this vicious regime. Salami, as expected, is a follower of the Khominist regime and looks for trouble. The knives of the mullahs are out, The leopard cannot change its spots.

Khamenei still believes that he is the center of the world, but In reality, he is a psychopath and a serial killer, worse than Qaddafi and Saddam Hussein. This is a criminal mullah who wears the mask of holiness, but there is no sanctity among criminal and corrupted mullahs.

On February 4, 1979, Mehdi Bazargan the spiritual and moral creator of the terrorist group MEK, told the New York Times "what was wanted was a government of the type seen during the 10 years of the rule of prophet of Muhammad and the 5 years under his son-in-law, Ali, the 1st Shiite Imam.» That was 1400 years ago!

How could this irrelevant example could be applied to a country half-modernized, half-traditional in 1979? It is impossible to know why a prestigious American newspaper published such meaningless superstitious and irrational propaganda of Shiism.

In fact, Bazargan, a bizarre liar, told the New York Times in February 1980: "The numbers of executed prisoners in revolutionary courts are 60 and it is less than the 100000 people that Shah killed!" Alas, the New York Times did not bother to do fact-checking or investigate such groundless gossip. This radical Shia activist and fan of Mosaddeq did not believe in democracy and played a far more crucial role in the revolt of 1979 which led to the ruin of Iran.

Historically, based on all credible sources, the period of Ali was full of suppression, violations, terrorism, and wars against opponents. So, they are proud of a fake story. All of the Islamic terrorist groups who participated in 1979 to assist Khomeini were fundamentalist and terrorist groups, such as the Islamic Nations Party or Party of Islamic Nations; The Islamic Coalition

Party; Fada'iyan-e Islam ; the followers of Mosaddeq in The National Front or The Freedom Movement of Iran or Liberation Movement of Iran, the People's Mojahedin Organization of Iran, also known as Mojahedin-e-Khalq (MEK) ; Mansoorun , and others. Beyond doubt, they were not pro-democracy or human rights. Some of these terrorist groups , after 1979, morphed into other groups such as Mojahedin of the Islamic Revolution Organization or Reformists.

Currently, it is enough to recognize that these terrorists are running the state in Iran. Incessantly and cunningly, they talk about such superstitions to suppress their opponents among young generation in Iran. The IRGC terrorist is ready to massacre all protesters only to prolong the life of the mullah's regime and delay the regime change. The mindset of a Khomeinist individual knows only an unacceptable and unreasonable demand.

The world is watching how Iran IRGC terrorist chief vows revenge against Charlie Hebdo, the French satirical newspaper, for publishing Khamenei cartoons and caricatures. Obviously, this is threatening the entire free world. Why does the West want to turn blind eyes to this matter? What's the relationship between the real Muslim believers and the Supreme leader of world's terrorism? Is a thug and dictator like Khamenei, a religious symbol for believers? He is an icon of theocracy and a symbol of Islamic Terrorism. The legacy of Khamenei is a tumultuous Middle East after 34 years of illegitimate leadership with a long and colorful history of crimes.

For most of the regional states, the Iranian regime is the archetype of a hostile rogue regime- the most notorious state sponsor of militant Islamic terrorism. For Europe and the modern world, the only realistic option is supporting regime change in Iran.. All men in the Islamic organizations call each other "Brother" and in that sense, the inner circle of these brothers in an ineffectual religious dictatorship of terrorists against the modern world, advocating universal rule.

In international relations, the Iranian awakening and the delight of young protesters will be a triumph of liberal democracy in Iran. Indisputably, the miraculous fulfillment of divine promises has no value in behavior and lifestyle of the young generation in modern Iran. Furthermore, thy will bring an end to a global religious revolution for Shia criminal officials in Iran who wanted to export their Khomeinism globally. Soon, the Ummah (the transnational community of believers) will see the failure of Khomeinism, and elimination of IRGC terrorists.

This point should be emphasized; however, the future belongs to young generation, with this essence of the faith that democracy and human rights is much better that satanic verses of the mullahs who live as leeches and spongers inside society. These days in Iran, the final goal cannot be anything less than creating a democracy.

In principle, the first performance of radical Islam and Islamic terrorism and implementation of Khomeinism as a doctrine of state power appeared in 1979. It can be argued that this destructive and amalgamated ideology ruined a long and celebrated national past and a long-recognized reverence for its pre-Islamic history. All of Iran and the Middle East is turned upside down because of Khominism, comparable to a tumor.

Since April 1, 1979, "the first day of God's government," Khominism wanted to take the first step to overthrow of all the governments in the Muslim World and set up their alternative, an "Islamic terrorist government." In a similar spirit, the IRGC terrorists challenged the World Order. Even while still hailed in the West, this regime brought darkness to Iran, and the Middle East, the world's most volatile region.

This situation cannot be inevitably permanent. Iran will have a new government and accept the western democracies and be open to fostering cooperative relations with the modern world. Speaking with cautious optimism, Iran's revolution has moved swiftly and apparently successfully to challenge the rule of mullahs.

IRGC terrorists cannot understand the hopes of fostering a peaceful atmosphere. Their life depends on chaos. Once again, the doctrine of violent intimidation challenges the hopes for world order. After thwarting IRGC terrorists, just imagine a region without mullahs, MOIS, Quds Force. This dream can be reached after regime change in Iran.

21
KHAMENEI'S NEW POLICE COMMANDER IS A LUNATIC THUG

The kangaroo Islamic court of mullahs is ruling to execute young protesters amid crack down on the anti-regime's nationwide protests.

Since 1979 in Iran the darkness is absolute, the silence oppressive. After the revolt of the terrorist Islamic-Marxist terrorists of Khomeini, darkness falls, and after 18 protests for 43 years, the young generation are calling for the dawn, for democracy. As criminal mullahs came to power, all Iran faded into darkness, ruthlessness, corruption, grief and total destruction.

Historically, Iran has some horrible periods such as the Muslim conquest of Persia (Arab invasion of Iran) from 633 to 654 AD that led to the fall of the Sasanian Empire and the decrease of the Zoroastrian religion. For 200 years, Iran fell into a time of extreme hate, savagery, and massacring. Another horrendous period was the Mongol conquest of Persia between 1219 and 1256 that led to the termination of the Khawarazmian dynasty and the Abbasid Caliphate of Baghdad. However, the criminal Shia mullahs came to power on 1979, with a horrible instrument - Islamic Terrorism.

Starting 521 years ago, the Shia mullahs were allies of Safavid's barbarous Sultans (1501 to 1722) and Qajar corrupted kings (1789 to 1925) . Particularly, the decision of Safavid's Kings to slaughter Iranians was never protested by the mullahs. The corruption of Qajar Kings was never objected to by the Shia or Sunni mullahs.

Since the modernization of Iran, the Shia mullahs in Iran are concentrated on one destructive propaganda objective, which is the guardianship of Islamic Jurist (Velayat-e Faqih). The Muslim world knows that Khomeini was a liar, con man and a bloodthirsty mullah but amazingly most of the Muslim states who were against the late Shah of Iran,advocated for Khomeini to dethrone the king of the Pahlavi Dynasty.

Muammar Ghaddafi, Muslim, Saddam Hussein, Yasser Arafat , Fidel Castro, and other international terrorists supported Khomeini in 1979 to form the 1st Islamic republic. The consequence of this assistance was facilitating an evil to unsettle the world and the founding of Islamic Radicalism.

On Tuesday, 3rd of January 2023, one of the internal news agencies (, related to the Raisi's government) said "most likely, Ahmadreza Radan will be chosen as the new police chief in Iran.»

The only concept and doctrine of Radan is following the Khomeinism playbook. Presently, Radan is the head of the Center for strategic studies of the Iranian Law Enforcement Force. He started his career as a member of Basij and IRGC. Both had been designated as Foreign Terrorist Organizations (.) He was in Kurdistan, Sistan and Baluchistan as a police commander for a while.

Personally, he has a criminal mentality and a vicious background and history of felonies. He is related to the gang of Isfahan, which is an active gang in Islamic terrorism. Ideologically, he is the follower of Montazeri and Jannati, who were two radical pro-Khomeini mullahs with a terrorist circle. Based on this ferocious ideology, Radan has a special ability to mobilize the thugs to suppress the protesters.

Is it time to reopen the file on Radan who killed hundreds of students in July 1999? He was a deputy chief from 2008 to 2014, and played a key role in the crackdown on the 2009 protests. For instance, the Kahrizak detention center, or Iran's Guantanamo, was under the supervision of Radan. He assassinated and brutalized the young people to defend the regime.

In 2011, Radan visited Syria to share his expertise in forcibly subduing protests during the Arab Spring. When Radan was a deputy Police Chief, in 2011, he gave an ultimatum to protesters to leave. On 2011 Europe announced that Radan was responsible for beatings, murder, and arbitrary arrest and detentions against protesters that were committed by the police forces.

Radan has been designated by the US as a criminal who is "responsible for or complicit in , or responsible for ordering, controlling, or otherwise directing, the commission of serious human rights abuses against citizens of the Iran and their family members". On June 2011, the to the US Congress mentioned his name publicly.

This time, the brutal and savage mullah's government is facing an internal crisis. For this reason, the only language that these so-called Holly Men know to communicate in is terrorism from Isfahan's circle. Nowadays, the notorious mullahs are a main obstacle in the long road to democracy in Iran.

As it happens, the return of Radan paints a grim picture of life in Iran. since September 2022, the mullah's regime has slaughtered more than 600 innocent protesters who were chanting for freedom and the ruin of theocracy. Ali Khamenei is not satisfied with this massacre, and he redoubles his efforts for more persecution. But this is a long road to democracy and will go on until the regime change in Iran. It's early days yet. With this decision, Khamenei made an exhibition of himself.

Historically, most of the terrorists of Isfahan's circle were trained in Palestinian Arab terrorist camps. These days, most of this circle are working in Iran's intelligence and military organizations. Under the aegis of Khamenei, some of these terrorists are playing the role of ‹reformism› inside Iran. sanctions

The US Iran morality police for violence against protesters, but the notorious Law Enforcement Forces of Iran have an independent intelligence center from May 2022. A serial killer will now be in the driving seat and will use this agency to prosecute the opponents. This issue has had a high profile in recent months. Regime change in Iran is no picnic! But the Iranians will wreak a terrible vengeance on the mullahs.

These days, quixotically, MOIS and IRGC are pointing fingers at the US and Israel as those mainly responsible for the protests. The Iranian regime has reinvented the wheel with the same policy of intimidation, bullying and brutality and threatening. For the criminal mullahs, a warning bell sounds because of the deteriorating internal security situation in Iran and the immediate effects of the nationwide antiregime protests. it is also important that, they get out of there before the balloon goes up!

These days, the kangaroo Islamic court of mullahs are ruling to execute the young protesters amid a crack down on the anti-regime's nationwide protests. including two young men hanged over killing a terrorist Basiji who was an oppressor. There is no difference between hardliners and ‹moderates' (Islamic reformists) , both of them are the two sides of the same coin. The nature of this savage regime is execution and terrorism, which are parts of Khomeinist ideology.

Surely, the mullahs will execute more people in connection with protests that have been ongoing in the country for months. The regime's lawlessness combined with Khomeinism should prompt an urgent rethink by the modern west and the USA. Regrettably, the modern world sends contradictory messages to the Iranian protesters. The protests against the mullah's regime in Iran began after the September 16 death in custody of Mahsa Amini. Local protests speak out against the theocracy of the Islamic republic of Iran.

Now, Khamenei has chosen a notorious figure as police chief. This act means that the regime wants to start massacring, to attack the unarmed protesters in Iran. Will the world remain silent? Why do the regional powers in Middle East hesitate to lend the protesters a hand?

22
LABELING IRGC AS A TERRORIST

group - it is the EU and UK's turn now The European Parliament has done so, Biden realized that he cannot whitewash them and the rest of the world must follow suit.

The US allies in the Middle East have evidenced unanimous opposition to delisting the IRGC as an FTO (Foreign Terrorist Organization) and deep concern over the Biden's administration's approach to Iran. The IRGC has conducted various strikes against the U.S and regularly attempts to attack Israel and the states in the Persian Gulf. This terrorist group is scheming active assassination efforts against former U.S. officers and has been implicated in plots to assassinate Americans even on U.S. soil.

Undeniably, the terrorist IRGC is the established chief of Iranian efforts to increase terrorism across the region. The European Parliament has realized this at last. IRGC aggressively endorses terror proxies in Syria, Lebanon, Iraq, Bahrain, and Yemen and other places around the globe.

Foolhardy offers of a compromise to the Iran regime led to this response: "Delisting the terrorists of IRGC could whitewash the group's continuing terrorism, ignore the IRGC's terror victims, and perilously politicize terror designations moving ahead". Biden decided to accept and heed the warnings of his US partners and stop the process of removing the IRGC from the FTO list. The increase of the tension in Middle East proved that American diplomacy with criminal mullahs is ineffective.

Biden conveyed his decision unambiguously, the world welcomed it, and remembered the "maximum pressure" campaign of Trump. Trump in April 2019 designated the IRGC as a FTO, but also removed the notorious mullah serving terrorist – Qasem Soleimani – from the field. Those moves were seen as intelligent.

The US has a duty to seek to activate the "snapback mechanism" and sanctions on Iran, helping the removal of the criminal mullahs from the political theatre. In retrospect, since 1979, the terrorist loving mullahs have hegemonic goals, and IRGC with its pernicious actions presents a clear and present threat to the entire world.

The IRGC supports so-called resistance groups (terrorist Islamic groups engaged in worldwide terror such as Hezbollah, Hamas, Islamic Jihad, or Houthis). Among its major local goals. Iran amplifies its threats to attack Israel and the US. substantially, while he propaganda machine of IRGC among the fake opposition and pro-regime lobbies in the EU and the US is insidious. Certainly, the IRGC-linked propaganda machine wants to downplay the capability of IRGC in supporting terrorist groups with drones, missiles, nuclear weapons etc. The mullah regime's dedication to Islamic terrorism as a tool of statecraft is overwhelming.

Most of the intelligence agencies around the globe know that the agents of IRGC control Iran's entire system and are the globe's leading architect of international terrorism. IRGC runs many commercial companies in Iran which are major parts of the Iranian economy. Moreover, the IRGC is a part of this Khomeinist mafia regime, which is an instrument for repression and massacre of the Iranian opponents internally.

The US is the first country to have recorded the IRGC as a FTO under its criminal code. The European Parliament has just called to blacklist it. In recent months, purportedly, the US is encouraging the consideration of the European Union and UK to designate the IRGC as a FTO, additionally isolating the mafia regime of criminal mullahs.

Geopolitically, such a crucial step would be interpreted as an unambiguous message to the criminal mullahs against their international terrorism. This is why the European Parliament overwhelmingly supports terror blacklisting for Iran's IRGC.

Accordingly, including the IRGC on the EU's list of terrorist organization will be a considerable step in increasing international security. Since the fall of JCPOA, the mullahs' situation has deteriorated dramatically, and it goes without saying that, inside Iran there is no legitimacy for mullahs who are continuing vicious suppression on protesters with executions of young challengers. The Iranians will rise like a phoenix from the ashes, but they have a long way to go

The EU and UK must join the branding of IRGC terrorists - the largest savage terrorist organization in the world - which is responsible for slaughtering hundreds of Americans, Israelis, and for triggering hundreds of terrorist cells in Europe, Africa, and Latin America and to the four corners of the earth. The entire world has to wake up and smell the coffee - and get the message.

23
ANTISEMITISM IS A LONG-CHERISHED VALUE FOR THE MULLAHS

Ilhan Omar spreads the mullah's lies and antisemitic tropes, equating the US and Israel with terrorist groups. One of the main policies of the savage mullah's regime in Iran is Antisemitism. In other words, Antisemitism Is Inseparable from Khomeinism "Khomienism" is a mixture and bizarre amalgam of diverse schools, one of which is Antisemitism

One of the disreputable sympathizers and an appeaser of the mullah's regime in Tehran, Ilhan Omar, after years of unapologetic antisemitism, has been removed from the committee she served on in Congress. .Notably, Ilhan Omar never endorsed the Iranian grassroots revolution and opponents of the mullahs or IRGC thugs.

The removal of Ilhan Omar from the foreign affairs

committee has nothing to do with gender, color or faith. Hating the policies and principles of the US, she spreads lies, the mullah's propaganda and used antisemitic tropes. Unquestionably, she was unsuitable for the House Foreign Affairs Committee. Diabolically, she equated the US and Israel with the IRGC-affiliated terrorist groups such as Hamas, Jihad and Taliban.

Most disturbingly and nefariously, Omar never condemned the evil activities of the savage mullahs, although doing so is well within the law. An Islamist radical Democrat, she pandered to Islamist radicals and terrorists globally and never posted a video regarding the terrorist strikes of Islamic Transnational Terrorist Network (TTN). She didn't question the reasons behind the attacks on Israel.

Ilhan Omar, an India hater and friend of Pakistan, was outraged at Qasem Soleimani's removal from the stage. She never mentioned that the dead wolf of Khamenei was a terrorist directly responsible for the murder of 500-600 US servicemen and women. This "Squad member" gave Senator Ted Cruz a roasting over the strike.

Ilhan Omar redoubled her efforts to support a dead JCPOA. Irresponsibly, she never read a line regarding the deteriorating security situation in the Middle East and its severe challenges. Ilhan Omer never criticized the IRGC thugs of Khamenei's brutal regime that massively increased the malign activities in the region. Instead, she presented them as supporting peace and cooperation and confronting islamophobia.

Today, the English-language news channel of Iran's

regime is defending her because of the Palestinian Arab ties with Iran. The Iranian propaganda channel cites Ilhan Omar, because she supported anti-Israeli terrorist groups. They never mention that she peddled in Jew hatred, bigotry, and antisemitism, the reasons she was booted. She is on the mullah's lips today. Blood is thicker than water.

24
TERRORIST MULLAHS: QUITTING NUCLEAR NON-PROLIFERATION AND ASSAULTING ISRAEL

There was a period of calm, and then a woman who removed her headscarf at a conference will lead to an uproar of nationwide protests. Regardless of savage suppression and executions, Iran protesters are still confronting the mullah's regime and have returned to the streets.

Meanwhile, the mullah's regime seeks to quell the unleashed anger of protesters with methods that bring to mind that between 1219 and 1258, the Mongols conquered Persia. There was a short period of calm, and then a woman who removed her headscarf at a conference will lead to an uproar of nationwide protests that will challenge the entire terrorist system of the regime.

Theoretically and simultaneously, the dramatic economic

situation in Iran will trigger another phase of the revolution. So, the nationwide uprising is alive, it is the peace before chaos and mayhem ensue. Also, the ruthless regime slaughtered more than 600 people and more than 100 people are facing barbaric execution in protest-related cases.

The West is trying to isolate the mullahs, not because of the bloodshed and full arsenal of repression, but because of nuclear weapons amid the power struggle in Iran. Unquestionably, re-imposing the "maximum pressure" and "Snapback Sanction" will be a promising aid for the current Iran revolution or Iran's internal pro-democracy movement.

With the existence of internal crisis and a shrinking economy, the criminal clerics cannot really develop nuclear weapons, unless aided by another regime. Rial, Iranian troubled currency, fell to a record low in the midst of escalating isolation and imposing sanctions. This horrendous situation is very comparable to the downfall of USSR in 1989.

The end of the theocratic regime in Tehran will terminate the Islamic Fundamentalism, Islamic Terrorism, Shia Crescent, Transnational terrorist Network, destabilizing activities of IRGC and Quds Force in the region, and Arms Race in the Middle East. This is why, some of the regional powers know this logic, that a real domino effect of regime change in Iran is good for reginal stability.

The European Parliament put the tyrannical military forces of the Iranian regime on the EU's terrorist list. After blacklisting the IRGC as a FTO (foreign terrorist organization), there is little reason to believe that the world grasped the reality that the mullah regime is a stooge of Russia even when they recognized the IRGC support for

Russia's invasion of Ukraine. But the political fallout is a separate matter, the pattern of the EU regarding Iran is based on economy. Paradoxically, with ample evidencs, the EU has no desire to help the pro-democracy protests or Iranian civil societies in Iran.

Truth be told, Russia has no trustworthiness in Iranian public opinion. For example, in the 19th and 20th centuries, Russia was behind the treaties of Gulistan (1813) and Turkmenchay (1813) ; separating Georgia, Azerbaijan, Armenia from Iran into the Russia Empire.

Russia laid the foundation of the Communist Party in Iran (Tudeh Party, 1941) ; Russia upported separatist ethnic groups in Tabriz (Pishevari 1945) and Mahabad (Qazee Muhammad 1945); supporting Islamic-terrorist groups who were pro-Khomeini in 1979. It is supporting mullah theocracy in recent decades for nuclear facilities. So, Tehran's policy in supporting the Kremlin, has also helped galvanize global opinion against the mullahs, specifically around the issue of nuclear weapons.

After recent increased political pressure in the international community, the pro-Russian paranoid mullahs in Iran will intensify repression of the Iranian people and will endanger the security of the EU and region.The first and best policy to combat the dangers from mullahs, is supporting regime change in Iran, what it so desperately needs.

Now, in retaliation, the terrorist loving mullahs threaten the word by going to quit NPT (non-proliferation treaty). Since 2002, the US officials asserted that Iran's regime had launched a nuclear weapons program, based on the satellite photographs of the gigantic uranium enrichment plants installed by Russia. Unquestionably, the criminal mullah plan is to build atomic weapon only against Israel. This matter of National Security in Israel leads to the ring of bells in the White house. Washington cannot disregard malign activities of the mullah's mafia in Iran against the Jews.

Potentially military confrontation will be another option unless Israel under Netanyahu presents another approach. The clearest sign that Mossad, more than CIA, knows the domestic issues and regime's insecurity at home and Iran's mounting nuclear advances is its agent's field research inside Iran.

Concurrently Iran's regime – the primary source of Middle East instability - is egregiously violating the international laws which cause potentially disastrous outcomes. It is important to note that the CIA under the Biden Administration had failed to learn a fundamental axiom of US policy: war on terrorism and the nuclear crisis is not over!

Systematic failure to act and strategic neglect in America will have terrible consequences for the entire world and impact the dynamics of regional and international politics.
The mullah's entire terrorist mafia had a nightmare, when their ammunition factory in Isfahan was destroyed, caused by drone attacks.

Intensified military aircraft activity over Tehran amid reports of blasts in different parts of the country, proved the incapability of defense system of regime. Simultaneously, Israel and the US wrapped up largest ever joint drill in message to Iran. As well, The CIA director (William Burns) held a meeting with Mossad director (David Barnea. In retrospect, Iran did not want to get the clear message of that staged massive military exercise in the Mediterranean).

Some days after this reprisal, the terrorist IRGC provoked all terrorist groups to attack Israel, one of them was the heinous murderous terrorist Jerusalem Synagogue attack which killed 7 innocent jews. It was another proof of the malign activities of a regime in which the terrorist cadre of Quds Force seeks to spread fundamentalism and violence regionally.

25

THE EXTRAVAGANT BOASTING OF AN IRANIAN THUG THREATENS US AND ISRAELI NATIONAL SECURITY.

Idle threats? This man dreams of starting a war with the US and obliterating Israel. In a broadcasted interview on Iran's TV, an IRGC commander outraged viewers who responded with negative feedback. Hajizadeh was bluffing with abundant irrational embellishments.

Amir Ali Hajizadeh has been the commander of the Aerospace force of the IRGC thugs since 2009. Many of the IRGC thugs are radicals, see " Qaani is a radical conservative hardliner" However, he endeavors to draw a redline around IRGC's missile program.

In February 2023, he asserted Iran's regime had developed a cruise missile with a range of 1650 km (1025 miles) and threatened to assassinate former US President Donald Trump and former US Secretary of State Mike Pompeo. 'We hope we can kill Trump, Pompeo, McKenzie (former CENTCOM chief) and the military commanders who gave the order to kill Soleimani'. Tehran has repeatedly vowed to take revenge for the slaying of Soleimani in January 2020.

The IRGC thug is on the radar for sending this message. On 24 June 2019, the US Treasury sanctioned him, freezing all his assets. Then, on 29 September 2022, Canada added his name to the Canadian sanctions list.

Hajizadeh is not on his own in this matter. Heretofore, Iran's intelligence Minister sent a clear signal to the Biden Administration. Most of the time, radical officials reveal their ideology. After all, analytically, the destructive ideology of Khomeinism is based on several devastating and aggressive approaches.

Factually, Hajizadeh played a part in the crime of shooting down the Boeing 737-800 which led to killing all 176 passengers and crew. Deliberately and without taking any responsibility, IRGC crushed the plane with 2 surface-toair missiles. Without doubt, as a war criminal who never tells the truth, Hajizadeh shoud be punished for this crime and put on trial.

The shades of grey in the analysis of facts on the ground in IRGC, suggest that the interests of the US and Israel will be in removing this vicious wolf from the theatre. It is time to let this extremist criminal fade into the dustbin of history.

A couple of months ago, he threatened that Israel's existence is domed for termination and that Iran will expedite its demise.

Hajizadeh is one of the radical warmongers of the mullah's regime who seeks instability in the region. He has ramped up his rhetoric against Israel and US, if regional war breaks out. The Intelligence agencies of the US know that Hajizadeh would like to strike US bases in the Middle East and start a full-fledged war with the US. Indisputably, He is responsible for firing dozens of missiles at US bases in Iran.

Hajizadeh, research shows, is responsible for supplying and weaponizing Yemen's Houthis rebels to launch drone attacks on the oil facilities in Saudi Arabia. Alarmingly, Hajizadeh's doctrine is equipping the Shia Transnational Terrorist Network in the Middle East with an effective rocket warhead and missile arsenal. Today, IRGC enjoys a huge armory of drones, of numerous sizes and capabilities. most of the Iran-backed proxies are using these operative military supplies.

The CIA and Mossad charged him of a variety of lethal attacks across the Middle East. He has a special capability for creating tensions and wants to take up Soleimani's mantle with his vicious personality. growing in stature internally and internationally. Most of the mullah regime officials are foe to all, friend to none.

Hajizadeh, the godfather of IRGC;s missile Program, is behind dozens of terrorist attacks in the region employing UAVs and missiles. For that reason, the name of this former sniper of Special Unit in IRGC, has been on the lips of Israeli intelligence officials. When he was in Syria, the American intelligence agents started his role in IRGC's missile program, as a major Khomeinist figure who plays a critical role in IRGC air force. Specifically, he says "Israel must be wiped off the face of the earth".

Hajizadeh, with no charisma, is a conservative figure with financial scandals. He has no desire to make any deal with the West or practice diplomacy. Mentally and ideologically, this hardline Anti-Israel , Anti-West and AntiUS commander of IRGC has zero tolerance for diplomatic deals. He loves to fire missiles beneath or beside urban areas. From Hajizadeh's point of view, all missiles should be ready to fire! He has close ties with SVR – Russian Intelligence- and he was behind the alliance with Putin in the war with Ukraine.

Most of the US intelligence community is studying his manner and how he works. Specifically, Mossad and the CIA are concentrating on Raisi and new malign activities of the Quds Force, but Hajizadeh is a threat for US national security, not only Israe's .Hajizadeh dreams of starting a war with the US. Remember: In 2019, he ordered to shoot down a US RQ-4A Global Hawk over the strait of Hormuz by using a surface-to-air missile.

26
BIOLOGICAL TERROR IN IRANIAN SCHOOLS

Nobody in Iran trusts officials and religious fundamentalist figures who are opposed to girls' education to find the perpetrators. In Iran, alarmingly, the second Auschwitz is at work, done by the hands of regime thugs and the criminal mullahs. All the world is still reeling from hearing the news.

It goes without saying that the crime sent shock waves through the country itself. A week after the initial dismissal by Iran's theocracy, Iran rattled over the poisoning, which had noxious fumes wafting into girls' classrooms. Sluggishly, officials began taking the claims and multiple stories seriously.

Mullah terror entity stormtroopers brutally attacked the Iranian mothers of poisoned schoolgirls. The Iranian schools gassing is a form of biological attack on girls and the world is watching. These serial biochemical attacks in the homeland are carried out by religious extremists and followers of Khomeinism.

The facts: Since November, hundreds of mostly female students, across the country, were seriously poisoned in different cities, leading to the death of numerous innocent students. As well, hundreds of unconscious students were hospitalized horrifically. They are fighting for life and experiencing significant health issues.

Since the emergence of the terrorist mullah's regime in Iran on 1979, the thugs of IRGC and MOIS have threatened all opponents to have their brains blown out. These days, under the license of Shi'ite mullahs, a different crime against humanity is in progress. Some radical thugs are deliberately attempting to target and shut down girls' schools. The number of such horrendous incidents has picked up precipitously.

The fact of the matter is that there is growing alarm in Iran. This tragedy and abhorrent act are worse than similar ones among terrorist groups such as Al Qaeda, Boko haram, ISIS, Al-Shabaab and so on. Now, in the terrorist regime, hundreds of schoolgirls fall sick in Iran with respiratory, cardiac issues, dizziness and fatigue, and neurological symptoms.

Terrifyingly, the wave of 'deliberate' new gas poisoning of schoolgirls is another side of vitrolage [an acid attack, vitriol attack] in Iran. The Khomeinist mullahs know the attackers of these incidents well, but they are refusing to admit it. None of the cowardly groups has claimed responsibility for these terrorist attacks so far.

It is significant that this chaotic and psychological chain poisoning attack has malicious intent behind it because of specific goals. The poison attacks at more than 30 schools across the country are an 'act of revenge' for protesting for women's rights. The regime has no desire to investigate these attacks and find child killers.

Amid growing uncertainty, social panic, and anger about what is happening, nobody in Iran trusts the officials and religious fundamentalist figures who are opposed to girls' education and proscribe the hijab. It stands to reason that authorities of mullah's regime have portrayed the protests as "riots" and responded with lethal force savagely. Hundreds of unarmed protesters have been killed, among them 60 were children. The public anger at the intentional poisoning prompted fresh wave of unrest.

When Reza Shah Great started modern education in Iran, most of the Shi'ite mullahs, with a history of fundamentalism, targeted the women because of freedom of dress freedom of education, voting rights for women. The criminal mullahs continue to, rub salt into the wounds of Iranian society. Since 1979, the name of Iran, with a long-civilized history, has been dragged through the mire. The ayatollahs are the black sheep of the Iranian society, and they bring discredit on Iran.

The mullahs use terrorism as an instrument to protect their fundamentalist and radical ideology. The followers of Khomeini and destructive ideology of Khomeinism were against any freedom since 1960's. There are no two ways about it. A couple of years ago, suffice to say that, they did serial acid attacks, vitriol attacks, in Iran. It's the same old story and the truth will out.

Most of the domestic extremists are allies of the Islamic Caliphate of the criminal Shi'ite mullahs. There is no question that this crime will provoke a storm of protests against the regime and may tip the balance in Iranian favor. Will Iran rise like a phoenix from the ashes? Only time will tell.

27
ISRAEL, A FRIEND OF IRAN'S HISTORIC LEGACY

A Jewish Iranian expresses the hopes of the anti-mullah Iranian diaspora and the people of Iran from Reza Phalavi's visit to Israel. For several months now, the Iranian mafia regime of mullahs has been confronting internal mayhem, the ongoing anti-regime protests in Iran. Nonetheless, the two sides of the regime, reformists, and hardliners, are battling to preserve the structure of the regime, to suppress all opponents and to keep the succession chain of mullahs intact.

Incontestably, there is astalemate and deadlock in the opposition political movement in the Iranian diaspora. The prominent political figure of the Iranian opposition is the Crown Prince Reza Pahlavi, but he was encircled by a group consisting of royalists from the 1979 regime change, pro-regime reformists, separatists, and leftist personages who had no political commonality.

Even so, Pahlavi kept working hard to connect the exiled anti-regime figures in order to bring democracy to his homeland, but he was stuck in a destructive status quo, a puppet show of political lackeys directed by a corrupted circle. This so-called opposition has no desire to facilitate the regime change in Iran.

This time, the crown prince has played the correct game, disturbing the propaganda' of the mullah's regime in Tehran and pro mullah regime lobbies in the US and EU. The Crown Prince will take part in Israel's Holocaust Memorial Day commemoration. It means that 'Cyrus Accords' are coming soon. Gila Gamliel wrote in her Twitter response: "Starting to build bridges between our nations." Israel's government announced that the Crown Prince is the "most senior Iranian personality" to ever pay a public visit to Israel. In other words, Israel and the key figure of the Iranian opposition have a mutual enemy in the criminal ayatollah regime in Tehran. There is no question that the end of the mullah regime would be a win-win scenario for the Iranian people as well as for Israel and entire of the region.

The Biden administration has not even received Netanyahu, so they may not be part of this turn of events. Meanwhile, the mullah's lobbies outside of Iran cannot hide their wrath at this historical event, at the fact that an outspoken |Iranian opposition is about to mark Israel's Holocaust Remembrance Day.

From every aspect, this trip will be a great sign that the Iranian people themselves have no problem with Israel and the Jewish community. Iranian public opinion supports this visit, because the crown prince in the monarchial history of

Iran has an historical responsibility for forging peace and stability.

This time, the Israeli government can shift the button and instead of bankrolling MEK and repeating the same disastrous mistake as the West once did, they can back the significant figure of the Iranian opposition, Reza Pahlavi. After all, writes the Council on Foreign Relations, the People's Mujahedeen of Iran, more commonly known as the Mujahedeen-e-Khalq or MEK, is a leftist Iranian resistance group founded in 1965, which then opposed the monarchy of Shah Mohammad Reza Pahlavi, Crown Prince Reza Pahlavi's father, and its supporters in the West, including the United States, It was.once listed as a Foreign Terrorist Organization (FTO) by the United States for its alleged killing of U.S. personnel in Iran during the 1970s, and for its ties to former Iraqi leader Saddam Hussein.

Notably, some of the prestigious pro-Israel lobbies in the US are supporters of this political shift and political opening. Furthermore, the Israel lobbies can help pave the way inside US diplomacy to be on the side of Pahlavi and not support the pro current regime reformists.

After the 1979,overthrow of the Shah, some select individuals went to Israel as representatives of the Crown Prince Reza Pahlavi. Some of the political figures in the Israeli administration and in Mossad approved those secret meetings. See Iranian Dissidents to Visit Israel. The policy of Iran's Jewish neighbor will be vital for the future of Iran as well as the region. The heir to the Persian throne all be a special guest of the Ministry of Intelligence in Israel. Netanyahu, Isaac Herzog and David Barnea know well that the valuable role of the Crown Prince Reza Pahlavi after regime change will be to guarantee the peace and the stability of the region.

Principally, the Persian royal's visit "is coming to honor the victims od the Holocaust and condemn the antisemitism and holocaust denial of the outlaw regime of mullahs in Iran. During this visit, Reza Pahlavi will also visit the Western Wall and host a meeting with Iranian Jews in Israel.

Meanwhile, the terrorist loving mullahs were busy with this past Friday's Al-Quds day, an annual event created by the Islamic terrorists to encourage Iranians and Shia around the globe to display anti-Israel and Anti-American hostility. Enmity towards Israel and antisemitism are longcherished values for the mullahs. Most of the prominent figures of the IRGC were promising to annihilate the existence of Israel.

In contrast, a leading voice and front runner of the opposition to Iran's despots will make a trip to Israel to symbolize hope for a secular and democratic regime in Iran after regime change and the toppling of the criminal mullahs. There will be no more heard from Hamas, Hezbollah, Islamic Jihad and other terrorist thugs in the region, now puppets of Iran. The game will be over.

The Crown Prince constantly and openly has asked the West to embrace a pluralist and parliamentary democracy government in Iran.Reza Pahlavi respects the heritage of Iranian History, the legacy of friendship from the Iranian people to the land of the Jewish People. The cruel ecclesiastical rules running Iran now can be replaced with a parliamentary monarchy that enshriness human rights, peace, and stability. Israel can galvanize support for this historical return.

28
THE CONSEQUENCES AND IMPORT OF REZA PAHLAVI'S VISIT TO ISRAEL

The Crown Prince of Iran changed the political theatre in Iran and in its diaspora. Do not let it go to waste. Op-ed. It was July 8, 1951 when in support of the Palestinian Arabs Mohammed Mosaddeq doggedly shut down the consulate of Iran in Israel. He was a spreader of an irrelevant animosity toward Israel. It was against the late Shah's views. Most of the 1979 partners of Khomeini and fans of Mosaddeq paved the way to exacerbating ideological hostility between Israel and Iran.

In fact when Ali Akbar Hashemi Rafsanjani published his book regarding the Palestinian Arab issue, Mosaddeq endorsed a check to support the book. Mohammad Reza Pahlavi was a royal friend of Jews and an honest ally of Israel. He supported the years of cooperative relations between these two states, before the revolt of the-Islamic terrorists and Marxists. The multi-dimensional cooperation with Israel during the Shah's time was based on common geopolitical interests in the Middle East facing the dangers of Nasserite PanArabism and Soviet communism. The late Shah tried all his best to be a peace maker in the Arab Israeli war. Iran was a strategic ally and a non-Arab state for the Jewish land to maintain friendly relations with, and Israel embraced relations with Iran more openly after 1956.

The Shah on no occasion formally acknowledged Israel. Iran de facto recognized the State of Israel in March 1950. Iran was the second Muslim-majority country (after Turkey) to give Israel de facto recognition which led to 18 years terrorist operations of Marxist-Islamic groups in Iran who helped Khomeini in 1979.

In actuality, the followers of Mosaddeq and Khomeini created a socio-political movement against Israel in Iran. Bizarrely, the members of the Freedom Movement of Iran (FMI) of Liberation Movement of Iran had trained in Egypt during the rule of Gamal Abdel Nasser for terrorist operations. Khomeini was like an agent of Gamal Abdel Naser and was helped by the Muslim Brotherhood in weakening the Shah. the Shah admittedly was not a dictator, and there were justified complaints against his rule, but instead of critics working to effect change, they replaced him with a cruel theocratic government of Muslim extremists.

Some of the terrorist groups in Iran, such as MEK had a relation with the terrorist camps of Palestinian Arabs in Lebanon and Al Fatah. Likewise, one of the terrorist groups inside Iran was Palestinian Arabs who were eliminated by SAVAK. Additionally, Pooyan , one of the leaders of The

Organization of Iranian People's Fedai Guerrillas (OIPFG) published his notes regarding the necessity of a military operation with an Introduction by George Habash from PFLP.

Before 1979, Iran was the "jewel in the crown of the alliance of the periphery" until the revolt of 1979 and the emergence of mullah's theocracy in Iran. One of the main points in the relation between Iran and Israel was a formal intelligence alliance between the Mossad and SAVAK in 1958. During those years of the Cold War, both of these intelligence organizations continued to expand their relations with the CIA. The Shah continued to deepen relations with the Jewish state and consolidated Iran's position as a major regional power as well.

Alas, in that crucial moment, the CIA had no clue regarding the emergence of Islamic fundamentalism in Iran, but Mossad understood the role of the USSR in supporting the Marxist-Islamic groups. After 1979, the Persian Gulf's Arab regimes, grasped the picture of the Khomeinist regime, but it was too late. The malicious mullahs painted Israel as a threat to the Arab world and ramped up rhetoric against the Jewish State in public, but secretly they purchased arms and weapons for war.

During this period, the destructive ideology of Khomeinism was based on antisemitism and enmity with Israel. Increasingly, MOIS and IRGC and Quds Force supported the terrorist groups and proxies against Israel. The current Iranian regime is a threat and central security challenge for Israel. Also, the Israeli- Palestinian conflict was an essence the ideology of the 1979's groups who participated in shaping the Iranian revolt. Nowadays, with the tensions in the region, the isolated regime of the cowardly mullahs routinely threatens Israel.

The Crown Prince of Iran changed the political theatre in Iran and in its diaspora. Pictures show the prayers of Reza Pahlavi for peace at the Western Wall. This goodwill gesture harmed the anti-Israel campaign for public opinion in Iran.

From the first hours of this visit the mullah's propaganda machine and its lobbies outside Iran tried to devalue the role of Pahlavi. If truth be told, this voyage exposed the real face of the so-called political figures in the Persian theatre. The Crown Prince calls for 'renewing historical bonds and rebuilding ties between two nations, but the political dwarfs in Iran idiotically orchestrated propaganda for Palestinian Arabs. In reality, the public of Iran loves Israel and Shahzadeh delivered a message of friendship from the Iranian people who wish to pay respect to the victims of the Holocaust.

The future of Iran will be friendship with Israel and other states on the globe. Just imagine for a second that there are no terrosrist loving mullahs in Iran and no Islamic terrorism in the region because there is be no enemy nation which threatens to annihilate Israel.

Israel and Iran can have a prosperous future, «from the children of Great Cyrus to the children of Israel, we will build this future together in friendship' said Reza Pahlavi momentously. In contrast to the photo above and to the intelligent approach of Reza Pahlavi, some of the self-titled «opposition» who were introduced by pro-regime reformist lobbies hesitated to have an interview with an Israeli Journalist. One of the vengeful separatist figures who was a puppet of Saddam Hussein angrily criticized the journey.

This figure visited the «occupied» territories, so why he should meet a radical figure like Netanyahu". This outrageous interview was broadcasted by the Iranian regime media after a couple of minutes.

Now, what forgiveness with such policiies? The current rulers love the Israeli internal riots and wish for aggressive approaches, not peace and stability. The mullah's mafia regime has numerous puppets of that ile who fuel antisemitism and anti- Israel propaganda.

The Islamic Republic has brought Iranians 44 years of war, conflict, violence and misery. Reza Pahlavi is showing Iranians there is another way. Peaceful coexistence with the world.

29
IF THEY ARE LAUGHING AT KHAMENEI TO HIS FACE, CHANGE IS IMMINENT

Khamenei, with the same ambiitions as Cyrus the Great, is now an object of laughter despite his violent dictatorship based on fear. Khameneii, who has the same ambiitions as Cyrus the Great – Cyrus ii of Persia - has becomef an object of unafraid laughter despiter his pretensions and violent dictatorship based on fear. Cyrus the Great, on the other hand, was a benevolent conqueror and a brilliant military strategist who founded the Achaemenian Empire. Cyrusm the Persian King (590-529 BCE), a mainly tolerant and merciful ruler, integrated all the Iranians and established one of the largest empires in world history.

Cyrus the Great is remembered for his impact in the sphere of religion, human rights, philosophy, and literature. The greatest conqueror of the ancient world turned ancient

Persia into a superpower in less than 15 years.

The body of the great politician and genius leader of Persia rests in Pasargadae, an immense stone tomb oriented toward the rising sun. literally, Cyrus means sun, the symbol on the Iranian flag before the mullahs' takeover. Cyrus died but the Persian empire lives on. This is the core of Persian culture and the Iranian ancient civilization. The name of Iran remained positivie after a thousand years in the globe, from the founding of the Iranian Monarchy to its fall in 1979.

Cyrus was not the only great leader, Other great kings ruled Iran in the past, and among them, despite criticisms of some of their deeds are Darius the Great (522 BCE-486 BCE), Nader the Great (1736-1747 C.E.) and Reza Shah Pahlavi (1925-1941 C.E.). This matter leads to the question of why Cyrus is relevant today.

The return of the young generation in Iran to its historical identity, ancient history, patriotism and national pride is a kind of intellectual maturity. One of the main political figures that persuaded the public and Iranian youth to study the ancient history of Iran is the act of Reza Pahlavi.

The Crown Prince is the remembrance of a Persian Kingdom. The passion of youth, its pride and national identity are far from the destructive ideology of Khameinism and fundamentalism. In his historic visit to Israel, Reza Pahlavi appeared as eventual heir of Persian throne, spreading a peaceful message to the Israeli community.

Two days later, a video of Iranian youth Mashhas, a religious city, shows the chanting of "Long Live Israel…Down with Palestine". Iranian people in Sirjan chanted: Death to

Palestine on May 1st, 2022. And now we have the video of Basij forces laughing in Khamenei's face.

These instances show that the Iranian people support peace and have no problem with Israel. They also show the absurd ideology of the theocratic regime and terrorist Shia mullahs in Tehran which supports terrori against Israel.

In any possible regime change in Iran, the only way to preserve the territorial integrity of Iran is dependent on the rise of a trustworthy person to control the volatile situation in Iran and that is why the monarchical system is alive in the mentality of Iranians, and is a permanent point in an unpredictable circumstance. Regardless of critical perspective in politics, the Late Shah is memorialized in every positive way by Persians across the world because of modern Iran that he initiated with his father. Anyone who has studied the history of Iran should have known that the collapse of the Kingdom in Iran meant turmoil for the region as well.

Today, only the outlaw regime of Iran and the fans of terrorist groups in 1979 are against the rise of Reza Pahlavi. The warm respect of Israel towards Reza Pahlavi disturbed the followers of Islamic revolutionary activists, so far, some of the political dwarfs in the so called opposition are against the return of Iran to monarchy. Perhaps no issue better illustrates Iran's ability to raise up its former pride and identity. Iran is constantly struggling for more equitable historical orde. Beyond that, it would be naïve to think that any system less than democratic monarchy will not be devastating in the future of Iran.

The nationwide protest inside Iran is a point with no return. According to most observers, what is happening in Iran is a struggle to renovate the magnificence in Iran. Monarchy is a solution for Iran; this is true no matter which metric once uses.

Now, after visiting Israel, crown prince Reza Pahlavi is in Italy. He visited significant spiritual sites and places of worship in Jerusalem, Haifa and Vatican City, with the purpose of interacting with the public and religious and political leaders, telling them that, thousands of years ago, the ancient nation of Iran was a cradle of diversity and freedom for innumerable religions and belief systems.

Historically, since the era of The Cyrus Great, the admirers of special beliefs in Iran worshipped and resided in peace and acceptance alongside each other. In truth, it was the Persian civilization. But from the moment that the Shia criminal mullah grabbed power in Iran, during a winter with no spring in sight in 1979, it embattled the lives of Iran's Jewish, Baha'i, Christian, Zoroastrian, and other communities oppressively.

In a future secular and democratic Iran, after regime change and the end of the ruling theocracy, the rule of law will be established. Therefore, Iran can revert its way to its historical roots as a nation in history. Surely, there is no room for reactionary reformists, terrorists of MEK, pro-regime puppets of Rafsanjani, Moussavi, Montazeri or Khatami in the future of Iran. The game is over!

Freedom loving Iranians will have the last laugh.

30
THE INTRICATE LABYRINTH OF THE POLITICAL STAGE IN IRAN

The political theatre in Iran is unpredictable, as numerous power-hungry figures twist facts and present a skewed picture of events. The political theatre in Iran is like a puppet show's performance stage. Most of these puppets, with their destructive ideology, are against development. Alarmingly, their passion is to sacrifice the Iranians in another version of the failed 1979 republic. Let's shed light on this matter.

The republican opposition, which was under the mask of Khomeinism, craved participating in power with a mullah, who then monopolized it viciously. In actuality, the participants in the revolt of 1979, were pretenders to power who did not know or which to know how to wield it for the benefit of Iranians and were soon cowed.

Strangely, all the Marxist-Leninist groups, Islamic terrorists, ethnic separatists, followers of Mosaddeq, Shariati, Khomeini and future Islamic leftists (reformists and moderates) in the political sphere of Iran are against a renewed Persian Kingdom, and point to the late King of Iran. The knives are out.

Historically and literally, a true and royal Persian King or crown prince today would be a defender of "territorial integrity" under any circumstances and could also promote democratic rule. In recent years, evensome of the feminist activists came from the campaign of Faezeh Hashemi Rafsanjani (the daughter of Ali Akbar, the former President of Iran who died in a Russian style biological attack). In addition, some of the leftist feminist activists were trained under the supervision of Shahindokht Molaverdi (who worked in the cabinet of Hassan Rouhani on women affairs).

The political theatre in Iran is unpredictable, as numerous power-hungry figures twist the facts and try to present a skewed picture of the events in Iran. For instance, an ethnic terrorist leader in the PJAK party, in a TV interview with BBC, alleged that "talking about territorial integrity is a sign of fascism" - an absurd idea. One of the former pro-Ba'ath separatist terrorists avowed that "federalism is the best way for Iran." The echo chamber of the pro-1979 coup terrorist groups are alleging that "defending Reza Pahlavi is a signal for farright extremism". In actuality, this propaganda is being spread by the mullah's regime and its allies outside Iran. We can wait for the dust to settle but the battle lines are drawn.

All the ashes of Khomeinist and terrorist groups are attacking crown prince Reza Pahlavi venomously. It is well known that they are afraid that the development of a Persian

Kingdom or Persian nationalism will lead to the downfall of 1979's vicious mullah ideology and the failure of Khominism. Their bark is worse than their bite. The rise of nationalism shakes the foundations of 1979's waning ideology, as the years of religion-inspired despotism proved its faults and Khominism is threatened with extinction.

It's no wonder that this disaster is the reality of the intricate labyrinth political stage in Iran. MOIS and IRGC are ready to spring into action and they are poised to die to protect the regime of terrorist loving mullahs. At this juncture, you can see which way the wind is blowing, and you can see the writing on the wall. This is the twilight world of the history of Iran.

Words fail me, but these political dwarfs cannot be allowed to seal Iranian's fate, althoough they stike a heroic pose. The opponents of a Persian Kingdom put the cart before the horse, but the young generatio do not care about them. There's not a shred of doubt that the crown prince is a man of the world, even though politically, he is on a razor edge.

In all probability, some of the terrorist groups and kindled ashes of 1979 will ruin the country and will slaughter thousands, if there is no a reliable trustworthy figure at the helm of the transitional period before elections. In particular, there are fears that the leftists and the remains of 1979 will resort to violence and will use every trick in the book. The pro-1979 groups will never respect peace and stability or respect elections.

Long live freedom, Iran still has a long way to go!

31
THE MOSSAD SPYMASTER, AN ARCHITECTURE OF RELATIONS WITH SAUDI ARABIA

The strengthening peace in the Middle East is the mullah's funeral. Since the 1979 revolt against the Shah, Iran's regime of criminal mullahs has built a network of terrorist proxies across the Middle East. In actuality, Iran's web of terrorist partners in the region could pose a significant threat to the United States, Israel and its allies in the Middle East. The violent Quds Force is at the heart of this transnational terrorist network and known for its acts of terrorism.

King Abdullah of Saudi Arabia knew where he was standing. He repeatedly encouraged the United States to "cut off the head of the snake" by launching military strikes to destroy Iran's nuclear program, according to leaked U.S. diplomatic cables. {See a copy of the cable dated April 20, 2008, published on the New York Times website.}

It is accurate to say that after 1979, a sword has fallen into the hands of a brigand. The evil-natured mullahs became leaders in Iran and their plans make for a world conflagration.

Alas, there is ambiguity in the U.S. policy and strategy to counter Iran's growing hostile presence in the region and the world. Almost certainly, there's no clear vision among the U.S. allies and partners to deter the threats to U.S. interests posed by malicious activities of Iran, IRGC, Quds Force, and Hezbollah. The thugs and agents of Iran may already be present at the U.S. borders with Mexico, Canada and at other international borders within the Western Hemisphere. .

Iran's entry into the cold war with Saudi Arabi after 1979 means that mullah's regime is seeking hegemony. The full scope of its ambitions in this part of the world isn't clear.so monitoring these activities in the region is thus extremely important for Israel.

On the credit side, there is no room for doubt that the region is no place for Iranian mullah's meddling and using their access and emerging regional nonstate actors and affinity organizations anymore. Regional order can push back Iran and close in on its borders.

The Abraham Accord was a victory for peace and stability in the region. The only opponent of the accord was that of the mullahs in Tehran who stuck by their Transnational Terrorist Network throughout. The terrorist proxies revealed their true colors and ranged against Israel and new allies in the region in the mullah's book

"Antisemitism Is Inseparable from Khomeinism." Since then, the Persian Gulf states are normalizing their relations with Israel and their relationship has taken a turn for the better. The strengthening peace in the Middle East is the mullahs' funeral. And the internal situation in Iran shows that the regime is on the edge of an abyss.

Incontestably, mutual understanding, cooperation and coexistence and respect for human dignity and freedom are the important principles of this Accord. Pursuing a vision of peace, security and prosperity leads to Israel-Saudi forthcoming relations. The modern world is persuaded by the constant attempts to strengthen and increase such friendly relations based on shared interests and a shared commitment to an effective future.

Nowadays, admirably, the director of Mossad encourages efforts to promote interfaith and intercultural dialogue to advance a culture of peace between the region of the Jews and the lands of Islam. David Barnea knows well that the potential future historic relations between Saudi Arabia and Israel will be the great picture of the modern Middle East, and that the only treacherous actor on the stage is the isolated regime in Tehran.

"Israel, a friend of Iran's historic legacy"can have a larger role in pushing for regime change in Iran. Even though "Biden's Iran policy is a disaster!", without doubt "CIA, Mossad, and regime change in Iran" will be a significant issue after declaring normalized Saudi-Israel relations. From the point of Israeli national security, the aim of Mossad is to reduce the risk from Iran's terrorism to the soil of Israel, its citizens and interests overseas, as well as responsibility for Jewish freedom and security. A byproduct of improving relations with the Persian Gulf's states is that the Jewish people can live freely and with confidence.

For obvious reasons, the priorities of Mossad are to resolutely protect Jews from terrorism and other homeland security threats. But these days, Barnea has played a key role in Israeli diplomacy. A Spymaster is more concerned in negotiating and making deal which makes his other challenges easier to meet.

32
A WAY THAT THE IRANIAN MANDELA WILL CHANGE IRAN.

Constructively and constantly, politicians and experts are at the Munich Security Conference (MSC) to exchange views on the most important current and future issues of international security policy. On 1963, back then that this conference was inaugurated, no one in the MSC could assume that the rise of Khomeini will be a threat for the future of the modern world. Since 1979, most of the policy makers and experts and politicians had faced the destructive ideology of Khominism.

Nowadays, as a result, after decades of the conference, this Friday 10 February 2023, MSC invited the Crown Prince Reza Pahlavi to participate in that conference. After the end of Cold War, and collapse of communism, the only remaining threat for the world is the Islamic fundamentalism and radicalism. irrefutably, the head of the snake is in

Tehran and terrorist loving mullahs are fueling this chaos. Over the years, rightly so, a variety of important players in international security have been concerned about this critical point. Controversially, the circle of Transnational Terrorist Network (TTN) has expanded and grew wider.

Throughout 4 decades, since 1979, the world become well-informed that the outlaw regime of savage mullahs in Tehran are exacerbating the security situation in the Middle East. Though, the existence of the Khomeinist regime depends on anarchy and turmoil. Today, the security situation of the turbulent region of Middle East has become messier and more volatile.

In this unique global platform for the international elite and political players, there is a chance to exchange information and ideas regarding Iran's regime change in corridors and rooms. Surely, the Ukraine conflict and the relationship between the west and Russia will be in the core of discussion. Additionally, the future of transatlantic relations will be under debate.

What is issue is, one of the bad players in the stage is Islamic Republic of savage mullahs in Tehran who are supporting terrorist network in Latin America, building terrorist cells in EU and aiding Russia in war with Ukraine. Add to the point, the destructive ideology of mullahs is elimination of Israel by Shia terrorist militias. How the security situation in the region can be secured when the autocratic regime of mullahs is threatening the Persian Gulf with malign activities of IRGC thugs.

In most years, the Munich Security Conference has focused in crisis far away, like Apartheid, USSR, Iraq, Afghanistan.

But for this year's gathering, one of the viral topics will be Russia and Iran. the Europe are watching the catastrophic military incursion into Ukraine by the dictator of Kremlin, Putin. Furthermore, the world knows the humanity in Iran is in danger. The criminal mullahs massacred 600 innocent people in the streets. Surely, the gathering's chairman in MSC knows well that "Khamenei is a stooge of Kremlin" and threats are multiplying, and the security of the modern world and regional norm is progressively under attack. In that way, the need for regime change in Iran has never been greater.

Most crucially, the MSC has welcomed Iranian opposition as a replacement for the authorities of the Mullah's government. For the MSC and forty heads of government who are coming to the conference in Munich, more than ever before, discussing a diplomatic way forward with mullahs is worthless. Instead, activating the "snapback mechanism" and more sanctions on Iran, helping the removal of the criminal mullahs from the political theatre. One of the most important topics can be the emergence of political potential for the Reza Pahlavi who can play a crucial role in the future of the Iran's transitional period. This conference will lead to lively discussion and offers the opportunity to make more contacts with the only respectable political figure of Iranians in diaspora. if Reza Pahlavi reaches out to European figures to rebuild a confidence, can emphasizing today that "Brand of Pahlavi is back". The importance of this reality cannot be overemphasized.

With any luck, expectedly, Benjamin Netanyahu will signify the ins and out of the matter shrewdly. Without missing this opportunity, just for the record, Bibi has lot to say that Iran's current regime needs to be collapsed which is more important than ever. Gradually, this regime is not only a threat for Israel, but also a big challenge of the West now. Essentially, No one among the EU leaders can pile on the agony regarding this issue. They can go with the flow, but Their National Security is at stake. These days Iran faces internal crisis. In the middle of crisis, the criminal mullahs are crying over split milk. Soon, the regime's authorities will take to their heels. Certainly, tomorrow is another day. These days, the young generation believe in knights in shining armor. It's a matter of courtesy to mention this point, that the crown prince Reza Pahlavi is a front runner in the ongoing Iran Revolution. However, Reza Pahlavi has the initiative, and his character speaks for itself. Honestly, he believes referendum and liberal democracy for future of Iran. His name is the talk of the town.

These days, actually, thousands of Iranians youth are active in social media and wrote " for the transition period after the Islamic Republic, Prince Reza Pahlavi is our leading representative". Last week, Reza Pahlavi in an interview outlined his vision for the Iran's revolution and declared the likelihood of playing his historical role as a legendary figure.

Even though, some of the active Islamic or Marxist terrorists of 1979 or Pro- Khomeini's yahoos, are in the position to turn up their nose at the legitimacy of the crown prince in the public opinion of Iranians. The terrorists of MEK focuses its firepower against Reza Pahlavi. From one side, MEK have a bizarre tango with the mullah's regime. From another side the spiritual father of MEK – or the Freedom Movement of Iran or Liberation Movement of Iran which is an Iranian pro-Islamic terrorism and a Khomeinist organization founded in 1961- expressed regret for Iranian opponents in the diaspora and wrote a letter to Regime's Supreme National security council with a heavy heart.

Notably, regime change in Iran will have side effects in the region's order. The transition period needs a strong figure to lead the crisis. Some of the phony oppositions are fumbling for words and blowing their own trumpet. In reality, the situation in Iran, may tip the balance in the crown prince's favor. In all but name, Reza Pahlavi plays a leading part in the nationwide protests in Iran, but the remaining of pro-regime so-called opposition of 1979 , always piles on the agony and have evil plot up their sleeves. These days the forces of 1979 are between the devil and the deep blue sea.

In the throes of crisis, the Middle East is in the grip of radical Islam and Islamic terrorism, on such a scale, which has triggered from Shia mullahs. This period will go down in history as the start of a new era in this history. A controversial debate sparked a free-for-all among The lobbies of MEK, ethnic separatists and regime's reformists, but it's no exaggeration to say that, the wind will veer to the west over again.

I like to call the Crown Prince as the Iranian Nelson Mandela , that instead of Apartheid , he is going to eliminate the destructive ideology of Khomeinism in Iran. he is a catalyst for change in future of Iran. he is a symbol of the unity that wants to help Iranians in the long journey to freedom. The Crown Prince will give up on his homeland. The Brand of Pahlavi cannot be separated from Iran's history. Pahlavi's struggle is his people's. the message of Crown Prince is clear : Justice , peace and Freedom, which is a legendary anthem worldwide.

33
CENTRAL TENSIONS OF MULLAH'S REGIME

Conceivably, more conflicts about suppression of the nationwide protests come into play. Other internal conflicts are often conveniently, but also misleadingly, termed power struggles. The regime-change demand of the young generation raised the tension among the military and intelligence apparatus in the mafia regime of Tehran. The protesters made no secret of their hatred for mullah's theocratic savage regime. Nonetheless, on the credit side, this is 130 days that brave opponents keep the pot boiling by making the ultimate sacrifice.

For the first time, a couple of days ago, one of the hardliner's media (Saberin News and an IRGC affiliated Telegram channel) signaled that "Ali Shamkhani, the secretary of the Supreme National Security Council (SNSC), is at the end of the line. After a while, NOOR website which is affiliated to Amiri, the deputy of Shamkhani, refused the issue of replacement grievously.

The rumors said that he may go soon and be replaced by one of IRGC's terrorist commanders". Most likely, Khamenei will wring his neck. He cannot see the wood for the trees. Almost certainly, Shamkhani gets caught in the crossfire. When regime's media says British "SPY" facing execution was a top former defense official and ally of Shamkhani. In Iran, Spying, is a capital offense. It is, if you like, rare for Shamkhani to miss a day at SNSC. Shamkhani has influence in some so-called anti-regime's media outside Iran. It should be remembered that he who laughs last laughs longest.

To coin a phrase, Shamkhani is one of IRGC's prominent strategists. His credentials distance the spectrum of regime's various power centers, including the IRGC terrorists, Army, MODALF etc. Specifically, Shamkhani has become more effective in recent times, predominantly his involvement and authority in the various organs within regime's military and intelligence.

If the lights down on Shamkhani, he is nothing to write home about. He is one of the regime cunning figures with terrorist background. In the mid-1970's he was in Los Angeles. Before 1979, he and Mohsen Rezaei were active in Mansorun underground group which was an Islamic terrorist group related to Khomeini in Ahwaz. In some SAVAK's oral history, Shamkhani slaughtered a police officer in Khuzestan. Lo and behold, he is proud to be numbered among those terrorists who have served Khomeini in 1979.

Sneakily and unscrupulously, Shamkhani was in the wing of Rafsanjani- Qalibaf. He knew which side his bread was buttered on. In 1997, Shamkhani played a role in the administration of Khatami and made a approachable channel with Saudi Arabia. Almost certainly since Khatami's era, Shamkhani and Mohajerani (a pro terrorism figure in Khatami's Administration) were in payroll of Saudis. As an Arab ethnic, Shamkhani is fluent in Arabic language with a gift of the gab he has. And these days, some of the opposition believes that one of the London-Based so-called opposition TV is under the influence of these abovementioned notorious and corrupted figures for the purpose of Controlling the public-opinion.

As a defense minister, Shamkhani was under the shadow of Qasem Soleimani but with a similar mindset in ruthlessness and dogma. He doesn't know the meaning of humanity and always raised his ugly head. Shamkhani is in the pro-regime's realm of moderates and reformists. For this reason, from 2009 he was in Shadow as a military officer of IRGC. What matters, in Terrorism and repression, there is no difference between reformists or hardliners.

It is not to be sneezed at, Shamkhani galloped toward power. When Rouhani triumphed in the presidential election in 2013, Shamkhani appeared on the political scene once more. Concurrently, during this course, he and his corrupted family were active in business. he himself is the holder of many companies from Tehran to India and Philippines. For Shamkhani's family, the sanctions were a great opportunity for accumulating wealth and have been lining their pockets with money. Significantly, Shamkhani is a well-known face for the intelligence community of the US and Israel. For a while in Afghanistan, he had a negotiation with American intelligence community, probably CIA. Although Mohsen Rezaei did the same and wanted to visit the US and have a presentation in a thinktank, but CIA rejected. On 20 February 2020, the US Treasury Department extended its sanctions again under Executive Order 13876 to Shamkhani amongst other individuals, following "the disqualification of several thousand electoral candidates by Iran's Guardian Council."

On 2018, quixotically, Shamkhani claimed that protests throughout Iran led by Saudi, KSA, Israel and were plot of westerners. Shamkhani was a responsible regime's officials who commanded for deadly repression of Khuzestan protests in 2021. Furthermore, Ali Shamkhani, Iran's national security chief and one of the giant corrupted and disreputable thugs of Khuzestan, went off the rail and he was behind many terrorist operations during his tenure, since 2013. Shamkhani, was seeking to end the cycle of protests and repression. He said : "We shoot all protesters, without exemption"

Not long ago, IRGC and MOIS sentenced his colleague, Alireza Akbari because of allegedly spying for MI6. It goes without saying that these internal conflicts show a crisis in the regime's corpus. In all probability, ninety-nine times out of hundred times, one of the commanders of IRGC terrorists will consolidate all positions after being at the helm, such as Ahmad Vahidi, Mostafa Najaar, Gholam Ali Rashid. People get what they deserve. It remains to be seen.

In nothing else, the departure of any terrorist figure in the mullah terror entity from stage is an important news for the intelligence structure of Iran. a warning bell rings in regime. Just so!

34
THE U.S. INTELLIGENCE COMMUNITY: IRAN IS A WORLDWIDE THREAT!

On March 8th, 2023, US The US director of National intelligence Avril Haines mentioned this point in the US Senate Intelligence Committee officially. Sagely said, Iran will persist to threaten U.S. interests as it tries to grind down U.S. influence in the Middle East, establish its influence and project power in neighboring states, and decrease threats to the mullah's regime.

The US intelligence community and the dilemma of Iran remains and it considers that Tehran will struggle to leverage diplomacy, its expanding nuclear program, its conventional, proxy, and terrorist allies, and its military sales and acquisitions to advance its vicious goals. The mullah's regime sees itself as locked in an pragmatic battle with the United States and its regional allies, while it pursues its longstanding aspirations for regional control. The criminal Shia mullahs are struggling to be a dominant power in the region based on China-Russia orbit.

Factually, JCPOA is dead. So, unquestionably, renewing any deal with the terrorist loving mullahs will be a preposterous policy. An unexplained nuclear activity in several Iranian sites, means making nuclear Bomb. Conspicuously, it will be a grave threat for all. Ferociously, the Iranian regime suppressed the most widespread and prolonged protests since the 1979 revolt. The economic or political situation in Iran is worse than failed states. Objectively, the corrupted mafia regime of Shia mullahs has no credibility and legitimacy among a wide swath of society.

The protracted protests and prolonged unrest frightened the existence of mullah's religious octopus. Even through brutal behavior and bullying, MOIS and IRGC silenced the compounding crises but more likely it will confront the regime's staying power. It will reignite unrest and result in larger volatility.

The CIA director, as a veteran in State Department, mentioned no critical point regarding Iran. Oddly enough, Biden's CIA director and Iran are two inseparable parts in intelligence community. But Biden's policy toward Iran leads to not only brazen the criminal ayatollahs in jumping forward to acquire the bomb, but also doing espionage inside the US!

Iran will persist to endanger U.S. persons directly and via terrorist proxy attacks, predominantly in the Middle East. Iran also remains committed to developing proxy networks inside the United States, an objective it has pursued for more than a decade. Undeniably, as a perennial problem, The FBI and Iranian espionage is another threat!

Regionally, Iranian-backed terrorist network of proxies will pursue to launch attacks against U.S. servicemen. Iran has intimidated to focus on U.S. officials because of Qasem Soleimani's killing. Furthermore, Iran's outlaw regime maintains threatening Israel, as a US partner, through its transnational terrorist network. In a predictable future, Iran will remain a source of chaos, terrorist attacks and instability across the region with it's provide backing of Iraqi Shia militias and proxies, which cause the most important threat to U.S. personnel in Middle East and Persian Gulf. As well, U.S. interests in the region is in danger because of Iran's aggressive approach.

Even more important, the growing Iran influence across Middle East, North Africa and Latin America should be a priority for the US intelligence community. Iran's threat is the cornerstone of CIA consideration as it should have been for Israel. However, Iran's ballistic missile programs will cause a danger to countries across the Middle East. One contentious issue is Iran has put emphasis on improving its missiles and ICBM. Steadily and tenaciously, the mullahs have enhanced the extension and implementation of its nuclear program, producing and enriching uranium and will test nuclear device almost instantaneously. There is no way to permanently alter mullah's hostile behavior.

In an analytical framework, Iran continues to message that needs to produce nuclear weapons and the reason is crystal clear. It will be threatening both Israel and the US. The recent US intelligence report indicated that. Moreover, in an unscrupulous approach, the destructive Iranian cyber-attacks and its malign influence operations for critical infrastructure is another substantial issue. This outburst of inadvertent truth, the US intelligence community did not talk about any solution to solve the issue, for instance a crucial question is why Biden – the 3rd Jimmy Carter – has no desire to support Regime Change in Iran. there is a legitimate concern that Iran is not on the top of Biden agenda. It is no small matter.

As of now, the US various policy priorities with Iran (Nuclear Bomb, Terrorism, military aggression) can not be delinked. Unfortunately, with this paralyzed policy in democrat White House, Iran mullah's regime can act with virtual impunity in the region with more bark than bite. Albeit for different reasons, IRGC, Quds Force and MOIS can make another disaster.

It's not ignorable that a lot remained to be done to having Iran's terrorist regime to its knees. It's needed to get the sanctions back in place and make the reimposed sanctions effective immediately. Furthermore, the US must impose "maximum pressure" and trigger snapback. Convincingly, It's a great start. The reason is clear, because mullah's regime is one of the top threats identified in the US national security strategy.

35
RAISI RUBS SALT INTO KURD'S WOUND!

It will all come out in the wash. Anti-Regime's protests reveal that mullah's regime is really weak. More likely, the Iran revolution will ring the knell of mullah's regime. And regime's repression intensifying. Iranian security forces continue to slay the youth amid its suppression on countrywide revolutions.

Today, unashamedly, Raisi went to Kurdistan to pile on the agony and, but mud sticks. Stop pissing about. It was 76 days ago, when Mahsa Amini was slaughtered savagely. The pride of Kurds was roused. Kurdistan rose like a phoenix from the ashes. It's not a skeleton in the cupboard, the Kurds are at the end of their rope. In all honesty, there is no successful industry, job market, economy, or any improvement. Words fail me.

The regime's repression under Raisi, has escalated. These days, Iran is on the edge of an abyss. Following Mahsa Amini's death, Iran is boiling because of nationwide uprising. More than 500 people, including 55 children, have been assassinated ruthlessly by the hands of mullah's Mullahs are still labouring under the delusion that they can prolong the regime's life. Many Iranian teenagers could face death penalty over killing of Basij thugs. there is no justice and human rights in Iran under the mullahs. What matters is, the regime wants to settle some old scores through these scandalous Islamic kangaroo courts. The regime doles out justice for pro-regime members, but no justice of the peace for the hundreds of Iranians slaughtered.

Even though, the West has been slow to recognize full magnitude and gravity of what's happening in Iran, but the situation in Baluchistan and Kurdistan should be a wake up call to the world. It's a lamentable that they have diplomatic relations with mullahs. Some people have all the luck.

Strictly speaking, only the world's people, not politicians, supported the protests in Iran, remembered the victims and they helped Iranians for regime change. Some of the world's prominent figures are hushed about the human rights crisis unfolding across the country. Secretary Blinken said "we support what young generation in Iran are asking for, demanding in the streets which is to be heard". In reality, the protesters are speaking for themselves, and they are asking for "regime change" which is a taboo in the mind of White House, and they are reluctant to have any reaction. They could stand with Iranian people practically and seriously.

The mullah's hostility against Iranians should not be lost in the mists of time. The theocracy in Iran showed a disgusting and horrific barbarism. Raisi is in Kurdistan now, for what purpose? This notorious mullah will not stop and pay respect to Mahsa Amini. He has no knowledge of the history of Kurdistan. Probably you do not know whether to laugh or cry, but this is real. After 1979, Shia mullahs boosted the number of non-existed "Imamzadeh" or type of a fake hoy person to more than 11000 shrine-tomb of these names. There's no law against it, if I tell you Imamzadehs are not traditionally women!

People get what they deserve. You ought to know better than them than mullahs that Shia Islam had 11 imams totally. Which kind of an incubator device can produce such numbers in cemeteries? Strange to say that the supercilious mullahs are happy with the business of pilgrimages. I wouldn't wish these superstitions on my worst enemy. Raisi is an icon of slaying opponents in the ear of Khomeini. After killing Mahsa, the Kurds and all Iran made no secret of their hatred for the mullah's regime. In Sanandaj, they cannot fawn over a notorious mullah who is a symbol of barbarism.

Raisi goes to Kurdistan to show a gesture of goodwill or a policy of appeasement! In actuality, he put mullah's vulgarism and charlatanism on display. Ridiculously, he will make an exhibition of himself. In all honesty, all his speech is all stuff and nonsense. The Islamic republic of criminal mullahs has been overwhelmed by a wave of anti- government protests triggered by the killing of Mahsa Amini. Protests have erupted in all Kurdistan and Kurds in the streets are chanting " my life is for Iran". surely, the mullahs can not tolerate this patriotism. They like to labeled Kurds as separatists , which is a groundless allegations. All Iranians love Iran patriotically.

Now, Raisi can not fool the angry people with old excuses or tricks of so-called reformists. It's really not worth it. The young Kurds comprehend the significance of this moment much better. Remarkably, the word unprecedented has been employed a lot to explain events in Iran. The fight continue in the streets of Iran and mullah's propaganda machine doesn't reduce speed. These courageous Kurds and all Iran are revolting against the mafia regime and its destructive ideology. They are shaking down the foundation of Khominism .

Raisi is in Kurdistan, but there is a long line of military vehicles, military equipment and forces deployed by the regime to crack down on protesters in all Kurdish cities. This is preposterous comedy show of mullahs. Raisi's face breaks into a wide grin and wants to show off in Kurdistan but this journey is twisting the knife in the wound of Kurds!

36
THE CROWN PRINCE OF IRAN IS FRONTRUNNER.

on September 16, 2022, anti-mullah's regime protests have taken place in Iran. Mahsa, a young Kurdish woman visiting Tehran, was detained, crushed, and slaughtered savagely. Iran erupted in nationwide demonstration against the criminal mullahs and the system's savagery.

Since the early days of the protests increased by Mahsa's death, some of the disreputable ethnic separatists' groups appeared in the political theatre and media's mafia of Iran. The protests were a second wind for their opportunist and populist policies. Ostensibly, one of main futures of the protests among young generation was focusing on Iranian Nationalism. In actuality, this moral support was the only approach against the Khomeinist Ideology of the regime.

Naughtily, one of the London-based TV, Iran International, showed the morose figures of the ethnic separatists. Nebulously, such guests were talking about the Ethnic Rights, Federalism and other nauseous subjects which were far from the dominant ideology of public opinion and ongoing protests in Iran. However, the mafia of Reformists uses the card of ethnic separatists to threat the patriotic opponents. Once upon a time, indisputably, these sullen figures were related to Ba'th Party and Saddam Hussein in Iraq with terrorist background. For this reason, the viewers, squeamishly, were squinting into the so-called Saudi-TV of Iranians in London.

Tersely, this treacherous policy of Iran International has sullied the main message of protests and terrorized the activists inside Iran. none of the serious political figures in diaspora had a spirit to treat with these separatists' characters. Perhaps, these worthless tales and destructive ideas has persuaded some of the activists inside Iran to change their opinion to continue the antitheocracy protests.

One of the main individuals and respected figures among the opponents is the Crown Prince Reza Pahlavi. As soon as he invited all the oppositions of Iranian activists, they have started to slap him down. It was another slapstick of so-called fake opposition in diaspora who slash a highly regarded figure in the Iranian self-explanatory political theatre.

The Crown Price Reza Pahlavi did not want to skate around the integrity of Iran and Persian Nationalism. Selfrighteously, some of these shallow activists decided to put Pahlavi to shame of an alliance, but he was too smart to accept that trick. Reverentially, they were no great shakes. Self-evidently, some of these fake opposition had no desire to help regime change in Iran, or they had no strong will to help the collapse of mullah's regime, because of self-interests.

Brazenly, one of the activists – a virago- supported a villainous separatist. A couple of years ago in London, 2 of the Kurdish separatists groups had a 4 hours meeting with the Crown Prince Reza Pahlavi. They took a picture and invited him to Kurdish region in Iran. thanks to CIA that did not believe the plan and dissuaded the Crown Prince to travel to Iraq!

It wasn't long before one of them revealed his true colors. He, with label of Democrat, wanted to abuse his relationship with Pahlavi economically and dadding him from behind. There is not a shred of doubt that Reza Pahlavi did not move an inch in the negotiations with ethnic seperatists.

Vindictively, this ethnic separatist vindicates himself and has started naïve propaganda against the eminent crown prince. Cunningly and unceremoniously, this vandal and vampire wants to portray the Late Shah of Iran as the villain of the piece before 1979. In fact, he, and his political organization with the label of Kurd believes Vandalism and treachery. Valiantly, the valorous crown prince has indicated his man unbending goal and he is a front runner. Unavailingly, any deal or alliance with the ethnic separatist groups cannot be appropriate for the Iranians young generation through the transition period. Tacitly, it is ridiculous that some of these ethnic separatist groups are in favor of pro-regime' jejune lobbies.

If the be known, Reza Pahlavi strikes out on his own and made strides to be accepted as a legitimate alternative after regime change in Iran. This issue has had a high profile in recent months. Only time will tell.

37
A WAY THAT THE IRANIAN MANDELA WILL CHANGE IRAN

Constructively and constantly, politicians and experts are at the Munich Security Conference (MSC) to exchange views on the most important current and future issues of international security policy. On 1963, back then that this conference was inaugurated, no one in the MSC could assume that the rise of Khomeini will be a threat for the future of the modern world. Since 1979, most of the policy makers and experts and politicians had faced the destructive ideology of Khominism.

Nowadays, as a result, after decades of the conference, this Friday 10 February 2023, MSC invited the Crown Prince Reza Pahlavi to participate in that conference. After the end of Cold War, and collapse of communism, the only remaining threat for the world is the Islamic fundamentalism and radicalism. irrefutably, the head of the snake is in Tehran and terrorist loving mullahs are fueling this chaos. Over the years, rightly so, a variety of important players in international security have been concerned about this critical point. Controversially, the circle of Transnational Terrorist Network (TTN) has expanded and grew wider.

Throughout 4 decades, since 1979, the world become well-informed that the outlaw regime of savage mullahs in Tehran are exacerbating the security situation in the Middle East. Though, the existence of the Khomeinist regime depends on anarchy and turmoil. Today, the security situation of the turbulent region of Middle East has become messier and more volatile.

In this unique global platform for the international elite and political players, there is a chance to exchange information and ideas regarding Iran's regime change in corridors and rooms. Surely, the Ukraine conflict and the relationship between the west and Russia will be in the core of discussion. Additionally, the future of transatlantic relations will be under debate.

What is issue is, one of the bad players in the stage is Islamic Republic of savage mullahs in Tehran who are supporting terrorist network in Latin America, building terrorist cells in EU and aiding Russia in war with Ukraine. Add to the point, the destructive ideology of mullahs is elimination of Israel by Shia terrorist militias.

How the security situation in the region can be secured when the autocratic regime of mullahs is threatening the Persian Gulf with malign activities of IRGC thugs. In most years, the Munich Security Conference has focused in crisis far away, like Apartheid, USSR, Iraq, Afghanistan. But for this year's gathering, one of the viral topics will be Russia and Iran. the Europe are watching the catastrophic military incursion into Ukraine by the dictator of Kremlin, Putin. Furthermore, the world knows the humanity in Iran is in danger.

The criminal mullahs massacred 600 innocent people in the streets. Surely, the gathering's chairman in MSC knows well that "Khamenei is a stooge of Kremlin" and threats are multiplying, and the security of the modern world and regional norm is progressively under attack. In that way, the need for regime change in Iran has never been greater.

Most crucially, the MSC has welcomed Iranian opposition as a replacement for the authorities of the Mullah's government. For the MSC and forty heads of government who are coming to the conference in Munich, more than ever before, discussing a diplomatic way forward with mullahs is worthless. Instead, activating the "snapback mechanism" and more sanctions on Iran, helping the removal of the criminal mullahs from the political theatre. One of the most important topics can be the emergence of political potential for the Reza Pahlavi who can play a crucial role in the future of the Iran's transitional period.

This conference will lead to lively discussion and offers the opportunity to make more contacts with the only respectable political figure of Iranians in diaspora. if Reza Pahlavi reaches out to European figures to rebuild a confidence, can emphasizing today that "Brand of Pahlavi is back". The importance of this reality cannot be overemphasized.

With any luck, expectedly, Benjamin Netanyahu will signify the ins and out of the matter shrewdly. Without missing this opportunity, just for the record, Bibi has lot to say that Iran's current regime needs to be collapsed which is more important than ever. Gradually, this regime is not only a threat for Israel, but also a big challenge of the West now. Essentially, No one among the EU leaders can pile on the agony regarding this issue.

They can go with the flow, but Their National Security is at stake. These days Iran faces internal crisis. In the middle of crisis, the criminal mullahs are crying over split milk. Soon, the regime's authorities will take to their heels. Certainly, tomorrow is another day. These days, the young generation believe in knights in shining armor. It's a matter of courtesy to mention this point, that the crown prince Reza Pahlavi is a front runner in the ongoing Iran Revolution. However, Reza Pahlavi has the initiative, and his character speaks for itself. Honestly, he believes referendum and liberal democracy for future of Iran. His name is the talk of the town.

These days, actually, thousands of Iranians youth are active in social media and wrote " for the transition period after the Islamic Republic, Prince Reza Pahlavi is our leading representative". Last week, Reza Pahlavi in an interview outlined his vision for the Iran's revolution and declared the likelihood of playing his historical role as a legendary figure.

Even though, some of the active Islamic or Marxist terrorists of 1979 or Pro- Khomeini's yahoos, are in the position to turn up their nose at the legitimacy of the crown prince in the public opinion of Iranians. The terrorists of MEK focuses its firepower against Reza Pahlavi. From one side, MEK have a bizarre tango with the mullah's regime.

From another side the spiritual father of MEK – or the Freedom Movement of Iran or Liberation Movement of Iran which is an Iranian pro-Islamic terrorism and a Khomeinist organization founded in 1961- expressed regret for Iranian opponents in the diaspora and wrote a letter to Regime's Supreme National security council with a heavy heart.

Notably, regime change in Iran will have side effects in the region's order. The transition period needs a strong figure to lead the crisis. Some of the phony oppositions are fumbling for words and blowing their own trumpet. In reality, the situation in Iran, may tip the balance in the crown prince's favor. In all but name, Reza Pahlavi plays a leading part in the nationwide protests in Iran, but the remaining of pro-regime so-called opposition of 1979 , always piles on the agony and have evil plot up their sleeves. These days the forces of 1979 are between the devil and the deep blue sea.

In the throes of crisis, the Middle East is in the grip of radical Islam and Islamic terrorism, on such a scale, which has triggered from Shia mullahs. This period will go down in history as the start of a new era in this history. A controversial debate sparked a free-for-all among The lobbies of MEK, ethnic separatists and regime's reformists, but it's no exaggeration to say that, the wind will veer to the west over again.

I like to call the Crown Prince as the Iranian Nelson Mandela , that instead of Apartheid , he is going to eliminate the destructive ideology of Khomeinism in Iran. he is a catalyst for change in future of Iran. he is a symbol of the unity that wants to help Iranians in the long journey to freedom. The Crown Prince will give up on his homeland. The Brand of Pahlavi cannot be separated from Iran's history. Pahlavi's struggle is his people's. the message of Crown Prince is clear : Justice , peace and Freedom, which is a legendary anthem worldwide.

38
THE U.S. INTELLIGENCE COMMUNITY: IRAN IS A WORLDWIDE THREAT!

On March 8th, 2023, US The US director of National intelligence Avril Haines mentioned this point in the US Senate Intelligence Committee officially. Sagely said, Iran will persist to threaten U.S. interests as it tries to grind down U.S. influence in the Middle East, establish its influence and project power in neighboring states, and decrease threats to the mullah's regime.

The US intelligence community and the dilemma of Iran remains and it considers that Tehran will struggle to leverage diplomacy, its expanding nuclear program, its conventional, proxy, and terrorist allies, and its military sales and acquisitions to advance its vicious goals.

The mullah's regime sees itself as locked in an pragmatic battle with the United States and its regional allies, while it pursues its longstanding aspirations for regional control. The criminal Shia mullahs are struggling to be a dominant power in the region based on China-Russia orbit.

Factually, JCPOA is dead. So, unquestionably, renewing any deal with the terrorist loving mullahs will be a preposterous policy. An unexplained nuclear activity in several Iranian sites, means making nuclear Bomb. Conspicuously, it will be a grave threat for all. Ferociously, the Iranian regime suppressed the most widespread and prolonged protests since the 1979 revolt. The economic or political situation in Iran is worse than failed states. Objectively, the corrupted mafia regime of Shia mullahs has no credibility and legitimacy among a wide swath of society.

The protracted protests and prolonged unrest frightened the existence of mullah's religious octopus. Even through brutal behavior and bullying, MOIS and IRGC silenced the compounding crises but more likely it will confront the regime's staying power. It will reignite unrest and result in larger volatility. The CIA director, as a veteran in State Department, mentioned no critical point regarding Iran. Oddly enough, Biden's CIA director and Iran are two inseparable parts in intelligence community. But Biden's policy toward Iran leads to not only brazen the criminal ayatollahs in jumping forward to acquire the bomb, but also doing espionage inside the US!

Iran will persist to endanger U.S. persons directly and via terrorist proxy attacks, predominantly in the Middle East. Iran also remains committed to developing proxy networks inside the United States, an objective it has pursued for more than a decade. Undeniably, as a perennial problem, The FBI and Iranian espionage is another threat!

Regionally, Iranian-backed terrorist network of proxies will pursue to launch attacks against U.S. servicemen. Iran has intimidated to focus on U.S. officials because of Qasem Soleimani's killing. Furthermore, Iran's outlaw regime maintains threatening Israel, as a US partner, through its transnational terrorist network. In a predictable future, Iran will remain a source of chaos, terrorist attacks and instability across the region with it's provide backing of Iraqi Shia militias and proxies, which cause the most important threat to U.S. personnel in Middle East and Persian Gulf. As well, U.S. interests in the region is in danger because of Iran's aggressive approach.

Even more important, the growing Iran influence across Middle East, North Africa and Latin America should be a priority for the US intelligence community. Iran's threat is the cornerstone of CIA consideration as it should have been for Israel. However, Iran's ballistic missile programs will cause a danger to countries across the Middle East. One contentious issue is Iran has put emphasis on improving its missiles and ICBM. Steadily and tenaciously, the mullahs have enhanced the extension and implementation of its nuclear program, producing and enriching uranium and will test nuclear device almost instantaneously. There is no way to permanently alter mullah's hostile behavior.

In an analytical framework, Iran continues to message that needs to produce nuclear weapons and the reason is crystal clear. It will be threatening both Israel and the US. The recent US intelligence report indicated that. Moreover, in an unscrupulous approach, the destructive Iranian cyber-attacks and its malign influence operations for critical infrastructure is another substantial issue. This outburst of inadvertent truth, the US intelligence community did not talk about any solution to solve the issue, for instance a crucial question is why Biden – the 3rd Jimmy Carter – has no desire to support Regime Change in Iran. there is a legitimate concern that Iran is not on the top of Biden agenda. It is no small matter.

As of now, the US various policy priorities with Iran (Nuclear Bomb, Terrorism, military aggression) can not be delinked. Unfortunately, with this paralyzed policy in democrat White House, Iran mullah's regime can act with virtual impunity in the region with more bark than bite. Albeit for different reasons, IRGC, Quds Force and MOIS can make another disaster.

It's not ignorable that a lot remained to be done to having Iran's terrorist regime to its knees. It's needed to get the sanctions back in place and make the reimposed sanctions effective immediately. Furthermore, the US must impose "maximum pressure" and trigger snapback. Convincingly, It's a great start. The reason is clear, because mullah's regime is one of the top threats identified in the US national security strategy.

39
THE HOLY WAR OF ISRAEL ON PIJ TERRORISTS

In a globe threatened by Islamic terrorism, the Palestinian Islamic Jihad, PIJ, is one of the most complicated and treacherous Arab terrorist organizations in the Middle East which endangered and threatened the region. With sharing a fundamentalist Islamic ideology, Iranian regime espoused terrorists of PIJ. The outlaw regime of mullahs in Tehran is sponsoring, aiding and organizing terrorist attacks with such notorious terrorist organizations.

Drastically, PIJ is under the ideological-religious influence of the Khomeinist criminal mullahs in Iran. accordingly, by means of religious indoctrination of mullahs, the approach of PIJ is violent confrontation, suicide operations and an aggressive approach.

Unescapably, the terrorist attempts of PIJ has denounced in international modern community. Surely, the dead operatives of this notorious groups chose to go to Hell in our time. It is a misinterpretation concerning the terrorist activities of the Islamic Jihad. Certainly, for God's sake, there is no consecration and the Lord never appreciate the terrorist Islamic Jihadists around the world. Iranian regime, as cradle of the international terrorism, generated the outgrowth of PIJ, as the anti-Israeli terrorist group. Which state their fake imagination is to be replaced in Israel? Undoubtedly, it would be a rule of radical Islamic in Palestinian Gaza Strip. In this regard, they are followers a criminal Shiite mullah, which was Khomeini. "Israel must perish from the face of the earth" was the absurd word of abovementioned outrageous ayatollah.

Purportedly, the relationship between PIJ, as a patron, and Iranian regime in far from weaponizing or financing or carrying out devastating suicide bombings. In this concept, this is the Khomieni- oriented view toward the world, because the central core of the PIJ'e terrorist activities is terrorism.

Essentially, the growth of Shiite terrorist octopus is the consequence of the 1979's revolt in Iran. The destructive ideology of Khomeinism leads to many ideological and political movements in the region. Even though, the Shiite radical ideology, the terrorist path of the Muslim Brotherhood and the Sunni extremist movements have a continuous connection with the mullah's regime in Iran.

In any stages, since 1980, The founder of this terrorist Islamic movement was a puppet in hands of the Muslim Brotherhood and mullah's regime. Both of them advocate Palestine Islamic Jihad against the west and Israel. Despite the fact that both have strong leanings toward the terrorists of PIJ, but Iran announced relationship frankly, but Muslim brotherhood never declared their sympathy. Furthermore, with regard to the impact of Shiite Islamic fundamentalism in Iran, the figures of radicalism and Islamic terrorism (Jihad) , such as Sayyid Qutb, Al-Banna, Khomeini and etc , are the spiritual leaders and an ideological frame of this notorious movement.

Apparently, the terrorist revolt of 1979 in Iran, which emerged from Muslim Brotherhood and terrorists of Palestine, came to offer a so-called Islamic version that could be followed. For that reason, the PIJ members and followers go through hard ideological indoctrination which is Khomeinism and Islamic Terrorism and training by MOIS, IRGC Quds Force and Hezbollah throughout the Middle East.

These days, after historical visit of the Crown Prince Reza Pahlavi, IRGC and MOIS have triggered PIJ to attack Israel savagely. The reason is crystal clear; the outlaw regime of Tehran is against peace and stability in the region. Therefore, PIJ played a devastating role in the clashes between Israel and Gaza. Along the way, opportunistically, the circles close to Khamenei fueled the fire wildly with a desire to destroy Israel. Albeit, the real motivation of Iran behind sponsoring this terrorist operations and its proxies' regional attacks is expanding the influence of Shiism. Relatively, it will be a failed policy, that's for sure.

Today, the reaction of Israel is more than Holy War against fundamentalism and underground violent activities of a terrorist group. In this context, most of the prominent PIJ terrorist leaders are the targets of Israeli intelligence community. Idiotically, alongside this, when IRGC praises any terrorist attacks against Israel and advocating violence,

PIK seeks to challenge the Jewish State from within, by assistance of IRGC terrorists in advancing PIJ's military arm and its terrorist infrastructure.

Alas, the challenge of the Israel which face this terrorist threats and violence, has some casualties. This fact highlights the Holy war of Israel on terrorism and has the right to eliminate this destructive ideology and an extremist group – or US designated terrorist organization – which has no link to the Israeli-Palestinian conflict. In this sense, Iranian regime is the primary source of funding these terrorist organizations towards the fundamental issues surrounding Jihad.

Markedly, in line with PIJ's ideological adherence to Iranian regime, Jihad in lexicon of Khomeinism means Islamic terrorism. Quixotically, the vision of liberating all of Palestine or Palestinian resistance is an absurd propaganda of the alliance between PIJ and Iranian regime. It is not particularly surprising that the Iranian regime uses charitable funds, religious foundations, and cultural events to raise money in Gaza.

40
POLICY OF "SEEKING REGIME CHANGE IN TEHRAN"

Above all, For all of the candidates of presidency in the U.S., this question is important "Why Washington Should Seek Regime Change in Tehran?" Most likely, some of the American political figures talk about the ruin of mullah's outlaw regime in Iran straightforwardly.

Even though, "Regime Change" is a poisonous word in Washington. Routinely, some of the politicians, like to prolong the life of the mullah's regime, others are unwilling to backing "regime change" in Tehran. The movement of Khomeinism was an alarm to ruin the region and supports of Muslim Brotherhood was behind this chaos. Factually, Islamic regime in Iran came to power by assisting a transnational terrorist network.

These days, the path across this quagmire is very narrow, because there is no way to change the aggressive behavior of a theocratic regime of criminal ayatollahs. The remaining of this regime will lead to more volatility and dramatic situation in the region as well. Surprisingly, some of the figures in political corridors in Washington almost always attempt to disregard this reality, because they have no illusion about the malicious nature of the Islamic regime.

Regime Change in Tehran will be a unique phenomenon in contemporary history, but the outlook of the international community is not so prepared for such different transformation. The terrorist proxies will resume fueling aggression, terrorism, and instability for a while. More likely, without skepticism, the collapse of mullah's regime will be more significant than the downfall of Apartheid or communism in 20th century.

Remarkably, the imposing and implementation of Maximum pressure or invoking vigorous "Snapback mechanism" will be a promising aid for regime change in Iran. Now, the modern world identified the full continuum of Iran's evil acts. Brazenly, this terrorist regime, with no borders, is a threat for the free world.

Confidently, the Iranian society will enjoy the freedom or dignity they so deeply deserve. With anticipation, the U.S. play a key role in shaping a modern Iran! A dynamic nationwide protest disturbed the Terrorist Islamic regime of mullahs in Iran. Essentially, the threatening regime of mullahs confronted a direct ideological assault on the legitimacy and credibility.

The subsequent protest movements could resurge soon, specially after the death of Khamenei and challenges after leadership succession. Khamenei, or the Supreme leader of the world's terrorists, is one of the world's longest-reigning dictators. Thus, the message of Iran's protests was so clear, they want regime change and termination of the Islamic Terrorist regime of mullahs. Academically, the subject of regime change is one of the more bolting subjects in the analysis of politics and international relations. Many factors may impact the view of White House toward Iran, regime stability and the dynamics within Iran. Therefore, to put matters in a nutshell, there is no straightforward or sharp solution to the existing quandary.

The effective regime change in Iran depends on many leverages. Crystally clear, by lack of strong will. overthrowing a terrorist regime of mullahs and the liberation of the Iranians from the tyranny cannot be so easy for the U.S. Biden and democrats, behind the scenes, want a deal with the savage mullahs in Iran. Continuously, there is no question that, democrats in white house like to underestimate and neglect the possibility of regime change.

My eyes are out on stalks. I like to wake up and smell the coffee. I don't hold out much hope…but the media said "The U.S. seeks to silence #Israeli opposition to a revived Iran nuclear deal by offering to broker a Saudi-Israeli normalization deal in exchange." Alas, from one side, the savage regime of mullahs in Iran with atrocious acts wants to oppress and censor courageous Iranians peacefully protesting for Regime Change. From another side, the political theater & competition of numerous fake opposition is a hilarious comedy!

predictably, the mullah's regime in Iran couldn't stay in power for years to come! These flames will remain! But it seems extraordinary that anyone in Washington still offers the options of war and regime change. The U.S. intelligence community know that Iran is on the verge of Internal crisis and structural transformation.

Strategically, regime change is not a bankrupt idea for the U.S. and it can be a serious policy option. If Americans want to have a saner and more peaceful foreign policy, one of the first things that needs to happen is to expand regime change from the policy for all. certainly, the regime will not be able to reunite with the Iranians. So, the regime change in an isolated regime could redesign the entire Middle East, the main allies of the U.S.

More likely, the Regime Change will ring the knell of mullah's regime. Iran will rise from her ashes; Iran will rise like a phoenix from the ashes. It's not clear that how far will the mullah's regime go. But the mullah's mafia regime in Iran will go to ash heap of history where it belongs.

41
READ THE MULLAHS' BOOK MR. BIDEN!

In November 2010, King Abdullah advised and repeatedly exhorted the US to attack Iran to demolish its nuclear weapons program, portraying Iran as a snake whose head should be cut off without any postponement. He said, "cut off the snake!", but the Saudi problem and the head of the snake remains.

If you ask, "why Washington should seek regime change in Tehran?", the answer will be: Regime Change is a poisonous word in lobbies and political corridors of Washington. In other words, the EU and White House will never consider regime change in their lexicon.

On the contrary, the European and American politicians are seeking to have a deal with criminal mullahs behind the closed doors and love to miscalculating credulously. Alas, for quite some time, the current white house attempts to sweep the scandal under the rug. to What matters is that any deal with the Shiite mullahs, the more problematic it becomes. Simply put, Its selfdeception and the aggressive approach of mullahs will blowing up in your face.

Face up to the fact that they will try to cause turmoil in the region. A tiger cannot change its stripes. To coin a phrase, nobody can change the DNA of the criminal mullahs. Apparently for the current democrat president of the US, they do not suppose it is of any consequence now. From all accounts, the main goal of Biden is investing on coming presidential election. He will shout JCPOA from the rooftops and will be thrilled to pieces. As a politician, he took a leaf from Jimmy Carter's book.

Joe Biden is old enough to recall Chamberlain and Hitler deal on 1938. The British Prime Minister didn't know Hitler at all, and he said it was "peace for our time". Almost, Hitler had got what he wanted without firing a shot. 6 months later, in March 1939, Hitler sent his soldiers into other parts of the Europe.

Similarly, Biden doesn't have a clue regarding the savage mullah's book. Naively, he is pleased with JCPOA, only for near election. Let me tell you, in all probability, the mullah's regime will make the nuclear bomb! With the recitation of a few verses of the Koran, the terrorist-loving mullahs in Iran will assemble the nuke bomb. Then like first Jimmy Carter in 1979, this democrat president of the US, in the foreseeable future, is going to ask himself " what happened?"

The democrats are always too naive. Because of the interests of the USA, The white house should learn how to read the mullahs' book! And highly predictable, Biden is under the illusion on a large scale. Historically, under no circumstances, General Patton did not believe the German general Erwin Rommel than he could beat him. As General George S. Patton surveys the positive results of the battle in progress between Allied forces and the Nazi army in northern Africa, he proclaims, "Rommel, you magnificent bastard, I read your book!" The mullahs have their own tricks, quackery and Taqiya or Taqiyya (pious denial).

It goes without saying that in their religious schools they are studying how to deceive, not how to learn physics, mathematics, or chemistry. The skeleton in the cupboard is the lack of knowledge and information regarding the Khomeinist mullahs is a recurrent theme. It is clear that the mullahs do not give a hoot about international community or peace and stability. That's why the west and the US cannot beat them or wipe them off the face of the earth.

The best solution for the international community is listening to the advice of Israel, because the snake of the region will create another major crisis in the region after a while. One day Joe Biden will wake up at 11:00 AM and will ask himself what happened? , Surely CNN will announce that these hazardous creatures obtained nuclear bomb! Like it or lump it, that day will be a tragedy for the world. "never blaspheme!," my mother said.

42
HALEY KNOWS THE CRIMINAL MULLAHS PRACTICALLY.

Former US ambassador at the UN Nikki Haley, who is a challenging criticizer of the Iranian mullah's regime will launch her candidacy for the 2024 Republican presidential nomination. More than a dozen candidates are seeking the nomination, including several long shots who announced their bids in recent weeks, in what is the party's most diverse presidential field ever.

Yet Nikki Haley, a former U.N. ambassador and South Carolina governor, is the only woman in the bunch. Only five Republican women, including Haley, have undertaken prominent campaigns this century, compared with 12 among Democrats, including six in 2020.

Announcing her intention to run at an event in the historic coastal city of Charleston, Haley said she would "stand by our friends Israel and Ukraine against Iran and Russia." We recall that how Haley backed Trump's judgment to pull out of the Iran worthless nuclear deal, the Joint Comprehensive Plan of Action or JCPOA, a signature part of former President Barack Obama's foreign policy. She named the deal "horrible" and declared it only made Iran's evil behavior worse.

However, former ambassador to the U.N., Haley hasn't shrank from her anti-JCPOA position since leaving the Trump administration. During the anti-Mullah's protests in Iran, Haley said that Washington should step up its encouragement of the raising protest movement in Iran, saying that the nationwide demonstrations that have unfolded over the past September on 2022 were exceptional. "These protests are very different than anything we've seen before," she said. "They're much more aggressive. They're much more upset about what the regime is doing, and they're fighting back." She added.

Haley said that instead of letting Iran's president deliver a speech at the U.N., the U.S. should be publicizing the stories of the anti-regime protesters. "The protests we're seeing from the Iranian people are heroic. We need to get their stories out. They don't want a regime that treats them like this."

Nikki Haley urges removal of 'fanatical' Iran from UN women's commission amid bloody crackdown on protesters. "Having the fanatical Iranian dictatorship sit on a commission focused on women's rights has always been a joke," Haley said in a statement.

Straightforwardly, Haley said that the Biden administration should undertake efforts to restore internet access, or "anything that will allow the Iranian voices to be heard." Haley criticized US President Joe Biden's administration for its efforts to negotiate with Iran and come to a compromise with the regime on its pursuit of nuclear weapons.

Furthermore, "Due to America's weakness, Iran is in the strongest position it's ever been. Everyone knows what Iran wants. It wants nuclear weapons, it wants ballistic missiles to carry those nuclear weapons, and it wants to use those missiles and nukes to destroy both Israel and America," said Haley. "The president is desperate to get back into the Iran nuclear deal. He's made that clear, and he's said he'll do almost anything to get the ayatollahs to sign on the dotted line."

She added that "we need to make sure that we start sanctioning people that are responsible for anything that led to the brutality of what happened," and that "we shouldn't consider getting into a deal with anyone that treats their people this way." Factually, Haley is a harsh critic of the Biden administration's continued efforts on this front, but she allowed for one situation in which she would support U.S. reentry into the deal: "The only way we should consider an Iran deal again is if Israel and the Arab countries are at the table because they face the threat every day. It doesn't make sense if you're doing this just with America and Europeans."

After a while, Nikki Haley says the US should only consider another nuclear agreement with Iran if it is negotiated with Israel and neighboring Arab states as well. "We've got to make confident that Israel has a voice and the Arab countries who have dealt with the terrorism that Iran has spewed for too long. They need to have a voice only then will we hold Iran accountable," she says. Republican presidential candidate, Nikki Haley, also lambasts Biden for signing off on a visa to allow Iranian President Ebrahim Raisi to address the UN General Assembly on September 2022.

Then, In July 2022, Haley indicated that she plans to run for president in 2024, telling a Christians United For Israel gala that if Biden reenters the JCPOA, "I'll make you a promise… the next President will shred it – on her first day in office." Haley was one of the key officials in the Trump administration who urged then-President Donald Trump to exit the JCPOA. Trump abandoned the deal in May 2018.

In a similar vein, she said that Biden was too reluctant in committing to the idea that the US would use military force to prevent Iran from obtaining nuclear weapons if diplomacy failed. She said it sounded like a bluff and was embarrassing. 'Treat Iran like pariah:' Haley hits Biden team for relentless pursuit of nuclear deal. Haley sharply criticized the Biden administration for its failure to confront the Iranian regime.

43
IDF IN THE WAR AGAINST TERRORISM

These days IDF personnel, specifically the agents of counterterrorism, are involved in a military operation to eliminate the terrorists o Jenin. Simply put, there is no solution in dealing with terrorists except triumph over terrorism which provoked by the outlaw regime of criminal mullahs in Iran.

To be clear, Jenin is the capital of terrorism and a center of rebellion and only the devoted officers of Israel have the responsibility to save the life of innocent citizens. The images from Jenin, shows this truth that thugs of Khamenei and IRGC's Quds Force are behind this revolt. There's not a shred of doubt that, most of the Palestinian Arab leadership are hand puppets of mullahs in Iran. Grotesquely, all the modern world sees which way the wind is blowing and gets the message. Realistically, Iranian regime , as a state sponsor of terrorism, supports various Shia militia and terrorist groups.

Ridiculously and madly, Esmail Qaani, the terrorist commander of Quds Force, played the fool. It is only to be expected, he claimed that in Jenin the young generation gave the hell to Israel. This Islamic terrorist and stooge of Khamenei reveals his true colors. He, as stubborn as a mule, believes that the revolt of 1979 which orchestrated by the Marxist-Islamic groups and followers of Khomeini is a pattern for Palestinians.

You would not wish 1979 on your worst enemy. The truth will out, the Iranian regime since 1979 impede the progress of Peace between Israel and Palestinians. Briefly, the words of Khamenei and Qaani, anybody can sketch out the hidden line. With threatening incitements, Iranian regime provoked the terrorists of Jenin only for making a chaotic situation in the vicinity of Israel borders. The thing is that the mullahs live and breathe the ruin of Israel. Only time will tell, but this is the beginning of the catastrophe.

Morgan Ortagus announced rationally that "Terror groups in Jenin have grown too big for the Palestinian government to control, thanks to Iranian supplies, training, and financing. Israel has a right to defend themselves from anti-Semitic violence on their borders. ". In reality, the mullah's regime make Palestinian's life a misery.

It is not for nothing that the disaster will be the participation of other monstrous Iran-backed proxies of the Transnational Terrorist Network, and other potential future partners. For this reason, the Israeli IDF should target the operations and clear out the terror nests of the Islamic terrorists in Jenin properly.

As Netanyahu got to the point and said:" Jenin is no longer

a safe haven!"! Then Israel will achieve victory if they destroy all the expanded terror groups and confiscate sophisticated weapons would have been used to carry out future terrorist attacks on Israeli civilians. Nobody cry for decimating the terrorists, even though the Jenin terrorists are literally being buried in the flags of their affiliated terror groups.

Currently, the unvarnished and entirely false propaganda machine of mullah's regime is focusing in elaborating the lie against reality about Jenin, sensationalizing and fan the flames. So, with a precision effort to halt terror operations, Israeli forces must continue to fight against radical Islamist Palestinian terrorists.

Confidently, under these circumstances, the Jenin operation is a stunning success and an achievement for Israel. For that reason, the people gave IDF vehicles a hero's welcome and chanted "long live Israel!".

May the lord keep you. Israel finally manages to break free from the terrorist attackers. making stability and peace still has a long way to go. Then, on the credit side, lightning never strikes twice in the same place.

44
MULLAH'S REGIME IS AT DEATH'S DOOR.

There are couple of weeks ahead for the one-year commemoration of the nationwide protests triggered by the death of Mahsa Amini. Currently, "Iranian authorities are considering a draconian new bill on hijab-wearing that experts say would enshrine unprecedentedly harsh punitive measures into law."[CNN] In reality, Mahsa Amini, a 22-year-old Kurdish-Iranian woman, passed away last September after being captured by the mullah's notorious morality police. However, purportedly, she was taken to a "re-education center," because of refusing the country's arbitrary conservative dress code.

After a while, stubbornly, the faded morality police had pulled back from pursuing protests. Though, earlier this month, the morality police decided to restart warning and then capturing women who are caught without the Islamic headscarf in public. Their promises were all stuff and nonsense.

Until hell freezes over, the mullahs will have they are following ruthlessness. Even though, the criminal mullahs are on the edge of a precipice and their outlaw regime faces extinction. For that reason, beshrewing mullahs is on everyone's lips.

Since last year, Finally, Iranians come to a decision. As expected, Regime Change becomes a reality. The die is cast. The criminal mullahs 've ruled Iran with an iron fist for 44 years. They can't think of a rose once more. They're the bane of Iranian's life. Never the twain shall meet.

It goes without saying that Mullah's institution is a cancerous tumor that has no intention of letting Modern Iranians off the hook. There's the rub that the world hold no truck with realities and facts. Times flies. After night comes the dawns. Hopefully, after Regime Change in Iran, the notorious mullah's book be burned. All things must pass. These thugs annihilated the academic institutions by spreading Superstitions and the destructive ideology of Khomeinism. Certainly, the phoenix will rise from the ashes in Iran.

Predictably, in the anniversary of Mahsa, Iran's regime will pull out all the stops to make a chaotic situation in the region. It's the same old story. Anything goes! The rascal mullahs look for trouble and will sign their death warrant.

However, this outlaw regime is on the edge of an abyss. Only time will tell. After o lot of huffing and puffing, all the mullah's lobbies in diaspora wanted to protect the regime. For example, NIAC is on the hiding to nothing. If you like, the mullah's regime in Iran doesn't have two pennies to rub together. For this obvious reason, the word "humanity" isn't in

NIAC 's vocabulary. The regime likes to surround themselves with the thugs just to prolong the life of the regime. They believe that lightning never strikes twice in the same place. In reality, internal crisis. For these reasons the young generation treat mullahs like dirt. Strangely enough, this lack of legitimacy shakes the foundation of criminal ayatollahs. In addition, the battle lines are already drawn for the next wave of protests. it is significant that nobody see which way the wind is blowing. Only time will tell, but quest of democracy in Iran throw the book at the criminal ayatollahs. Simply put, Iranians still have a long way to go.

45
FREEDOM OF SPEECH IN MULLAH'S REGIME

The Iranian Constitution declares very typical rules regarding freedom of expression. Article 24 states: "Publications and the press have freedom of expression aside from when it is detrimental to the fundamental principles of Islam or the rights of the public."

However, media freedom is strictly restricted both online and offline. The state broadcasting company, IRIB, is firmly under control of hard-liners and prompted by the mullah's security apparatus. Actually, News and analysis are profoundly censored, while critics and opposition members are once in a blue moon, if ever, given a platform on state-controlled television, which remains a main source of information for many Iranians. In addition, state television has a record of broadcasting declaration of guilt isolated from political prisoners under duress, and it characteristically carries reports pointed at humiliating dissidents and opposition activists.

On an unprecedented scale, the regime's authorities censored media, jammed satellite television channels and, added Instagram and WhatsApp to the list of blocked and filtered mobile apps and social media platforms, which included Facebook, Signal, Telegram, Twitter and YouTube. This is the kindness of the criminal mullahs on the Earth. In other words, the authorities continually shut off or interrupted internet and mobile phone networks during nationwide anti-regime protests to control mobilization and hide the magnitude of violations and interruptions by regime's security forces.

Notably, the Internet user protection bill, which has eroded online freedoms and access to the international internet, continued impending. In actuality, the regime of mullahs limiting access to online content. The fact is that the regime banned all self-determining political parties, civil society organizations and independent trade unions, and subjected dramatic workers to reprisals. Iran has severe rules when it comes to internet censorship. The Iranian regime and IRGC determinedly block social media, (Facebook, Twitter and Instagram)and many other websites (Blogger, HBO, YouTube, and Netflix. In spite of the state-wide prohibition, several Iranian politicians use social networks to communicate with their followers (Twitter, Facebook and Instagram).

As well, constantly, Iranian authorities placed considerable pressure on journalists and writers and researchers. It should be noted that journalists receive numerous summonses or threats from prosecutors and intelligence agencies sporadically. Several intellectuals were imprisoned or imprisoned or received sentences of lashes over false-news accusations during 2021 and 2022. There is no possibility for an appeals court. Also, some intelligence officers have influence in the kangaroo courts and can put anyone in court on propaganda charges or for "spreading propaganda against the system." There is no legal control at all.

Since 1979, Iran's ambiguously has explained restrictions on speech, harsh criminal penalties, and state monitoring of online communications are among several factors that discourage citizens from participating in open and free private discussion.

Regardless of the risks, threats and limitations, many do express opposition on social media, in some cases bypassing official blocks on several platforms. If truth be told, the regime's biggest victims are the Iranian people. Regime elites waste the people's resources and opportunities, while controlling freedom and prime human rights in Iran. This is the reward of the criminal ayatollah's regime.

In particular, the Iranian regime has discontinued and declined to reissuing foreign journalists' credentials or renewing correspondents permits. Furthermore, they closed a newspaper friendly to its cause, part of a deteriorating restriction in a country with an abysmal repute for press freedoms. "Journalism and publishing books in Iran near annihilation,"

"This is a typical approach devoted by absolute regimes like Iran's, to threaten and promote self-censorship mid external reporters," that's hostility to freedom of speech, for sure. The outlaw regime of mullahs in Tehran systematically targets journalists and restricts the freedom of expression.

Inordinately, hundreds of writers, intellectuals, translators and journalists and Internet activists stayed in prison to express their views online. Regarding freedom, Iran is the worst in the globe. Dramatically, If anyone writes about anti-government protests or posting comments critical of the government on social media, will face viciousness and savageness of mullahs.

Lastly, I have a personal memoire regarding this matter, that how I faced a dramatic situation when I returned to Iran. you would not wish that on your worst enemy. On 2012, after publishing my book in the US I faced jail in Iran, Ward 350 Evin prison. In my book "Nightmare of Evin" I explained the horrible situation in that notorious jail. One time they thrashed me withing an inch of my life. The agents beat the hall out of me before going to the interrogation room. Until this moment in 2023, I feel pain in my shoulders. No sooner had I sat down than the phone rang, and the agent shouted, "Agent of CIA!". "Never blaspheme," my mother said, but I was out of control that moment and I was profaning and out of breath. It goes without saying that I had a brush with death for no apparent reason! They had been fighting a rearguard action to label me as a CIA agent!

Then in the interrogation room, they were polite, but they pushed me to the breaking point mentally. MOIS used every trick in their book. The interrogator determined to win, by fair means or foul. After returning to the US, in front of Judge when he asked me did they beat you? I answered quietly, I gulped back my tears, " it was not in the interrogation room!" I dropped a real clanger. He understood but he did not say "dream on!... pigs might fly!". The judge did not like to bring to mind those violent scenes. His honor did not say a word , just looked at my book silently. It means "let bygones be bygones".

46
35 YEARS AFTER THE DEATH OF THAT VILLAIN KHOMEINI

The news of Khomeini's death was broadcast on Radio Islamic Republic of Iran 35 years ago today. He had held power for ten years, calling himself a man of God and Islam. No one had elected him; he was not chosen by the people. He seized power in Iran with the help of Islamic terrorist groups and support from countries like Syria, Libya, Afghanistan, and organizations like the Muslim Brotherhood and Yasser Arafat.

He clung to power until his death, and his bloody history symbolizes Iran's downfall, resulting in a disgraceful outcome. The true signing of Iran's fall was when the Shah left Iran, and the most unpleasant consequence of the ill-fated 1979 revolution was the brutal repression that followed. Khomeini sought to expand his Islamic caliphate across 48 Islamic countries, including 16 with Shia communities, calling it the export of revolution. Of the 1 billion Muslims, 100 million are Shia, but Khomeini aimed to rule them all. His revolution's export meant spreading Islamic terrorism, and wherever Khomeini's forces went, they brought destruction and misery. Although the mullah system dreams of hoisting the flag of their Islam over the White House, the Kremlin, the Élysée Palace, and Buckingham Palace, if humanity does not find a solution in the 21st century, this infectious Khomeinist virus will spread worldwide.

Khomeini's dark era institutionalized religious despotism in Iran. To secure power, they waged an eight-year war with Saddam without cause and executed political opponents in prisons. Even during the tenure of the Ministry of Civil Defense and Chamran, 8,000 military personnel were executed, imprisoned, or expelled. Khomeini and his associates sought to destroy Iran's national spirit and nationalism, despising knowledge and understanding. Mullahs filled Iran, and all key positions were systematically handed over to them. Instead of providing free water, electricity, oil, and bus tickets, Khomeini's government offered free death to Iranians.

Mullahs, who understand nothing but Shia superstitions and religious dogma, see Iranian women and girls as servants. Faithful followers, with self-abasement and humiliating submission, praise their savagery. Thirty-five years ago, on this day, Khamenei came to power, creating an era filled with suffocation, censorship, and repression for the Iranian people. Both under Khomeini and Khamenei, the Shia Islamic caliphate sent thousands to the graveyards. The mullahs' government even prevented hundreds from being buried in Muslim cemeteries!

Tomorrow marks 35 years since the death of the bloodthirsty villain Khomeini. In reality, Khamenei has outdone him, spreading Islamic terrorism and shedding more blood. On June 3, 2024, Khamenei plans to speak at Khomeini's grave, lamenting his death while encouraging people to participate in the mockery of elections. His entourage constantly reassures him, saying, "Rest assured, everything is under control."

However, a patriot like Reza Shah angrily dismissed a group of high-ranking officials for repeatedly telling him, "Rest assured, everything is fine." He cared deeply for his country, unlike the mullahs, who are its enemies. Young Iranians are eager to see the country's political train return to the monarchy's track. But until the mullahs' institution is dismantled, democracy cannot take root in Iran. Out of 193 UN member countries, 24 have full democracies, 50 have flawed democracies, and 34 have hybrid systems. The path to democracy in Iran is long and arduous. Of the 24 countries with full democracies, 12 are monarchies, including the UK, Japan, Spain, Sweden, Norway, Denmark, the Netherlands, Belgium, Australia, and New Zealand.

It should not be forgotten that Khomeini waged war against 28 centuries of monarchy in Iran. Today, 35 years after his death, how will Iran move forward in the 21st century? It is impossible to predict Iran's future, but surely the memory of Khomeini, Khamenei, and the corrupt Ayatollahs will only be remembered for their crimes in history

47
CARTER: THE PRESIDENT WHO FAILED TO UNDERSTAND IRAN

The role of the United States in the chaos of 1979 is an undeniable reality. President Reagan repeatedly stated that America's misguided policies in Iran caused the fall of the Shah, calling it a historical stain on the United States [Televised Debate, November 1984]. Despite the Shah's 37-year alliance with the U.S. in the Middle East, Carter effectively undermined him [George Bush, January 26, 1979], notably by dispatching General Haig to Iran to incapacitate the military [Richard Nixon, Politique Internationale, Spring 1981].

Carter himself admitted to following the duplicitous advice of U.S. Ambassador Sullivan, a sympathizer of pro-Mossadeq forces [Carter's Memoirs, 1982, p. 443]. American officials later condemned Carter's policies as deceitful and Sullivan's views as dangerously misguided [Schumer, 1980, p. 148].

Years later, Brzezinski acknowledged that the political uprising against the Shah had U.S. backing [Power and Principles, 1983, p. 356], which ultimately led to his removal from power [Kissinger, The Economist, February 10, 1979]. This policy miscalculation not only caused the Shah's downfall but also plunged Iran into chaos, leaving it a victim of history [Alexander Haig interview].

Carter observed the 1979 crisis in Iran from a distance, while his State Department displayed overt hostility toward the Shah [Brzezinski, ibid, p. 355]. The Shah soon realized that neither Carter nor the U.S. had any intention of supporting him, and he described America's policy as delusional [Sullivan's Memoirs, 1981, p. 336]. The Carter administration repeatedly instructed its ambassador to warn the Shah about human rights issues [Encounter Report, November 1984]. History has since recorded Carter's administration as confused, hypocritical, and paralyzed in the face of Iran's escalating crisis [Michael Ledeen, Failure in Iran, 1980, p. 231]. At the height of the turmoil, the Shah was abandoned [Nixon, Leaders, 1984, p. 360].

Carter lacked a true understanding of the crisis or its catastrophic consequences. He failed to make sound decisions [Nixon, ibid, p. 312] and did not grasp the irreversible damage his policies caused [Brzezinski, ibid, p. 380]. Sullivan even advised Carter to demand the Shah leave Iran immediately and to align with Khomeini [Carter, ibid, p. 443]. Meanwhile, U.S. intelligence agencies were disorganized, ignoring one another's warnings [French Interior Minister, November 6, 1980]. Most notably, the CIA failed to predict the 1979 upheaval or the disastrous rise of the mullahs in Iran, cementing Carter's role as a key figure in the fiasco.

Carter's moralizing, cloaked in populism, often bordered on naivety [Time, May 10, 1976]. He claimed to act in the name of God [Herald Tribune, April 1976] but appeared out of touch with reality [Ledeen, ibid]. The late Shah harshly criticized Carter, admitting that his gravest mistake was following U.S. advice, which led to the release of murderous terrorists who later orchestrated more violence [Washington Post, June 22, 1980]. The Shah astutely questioned Sullivan, asking, "Why is the CIA so intensely active against me?" [Sullivan, ibid, 1981, p. 156].

The Shah foresaw the devastating catastrophe that was unfolding. Carter, wielding his political and intelligence apparatus, deliberately supported opposition forces to pressure the Shah. Later, the CIA Director confirmed the Shah's concerns, stating, "Had we shown more vigilance, America's policy during Iran's turmoil could have been different" [Turner, Newsweek, March 5, 1979].

Carter's policies were unrealistic, clumsy, short-sighted, indecisive, and full of contradictions, causing global repercussions [Shafa, Crime and Punishment, p. 611]. His treatment of the Shah during his illness was inhumane. It was Carter who, among world leaders, quickly deemed Khomeini a "sacred" figure, describing him as a religious and moderate leader. The ties between Khomeini and Carter before 1979 became clear to all [BBC Report, May 21, 2016].

The Iranian Tose'eh newspaper later published an interview with Giscard d'Estaing, who said, "The U.S. rang the death knell for the Shah's rule because Carter had no hope for the regime's survival" [Tose'eh, September 23, 1998]. When Khomeini orchestrated the hostage crisis, Carter first wrote a pleading letter and then resorted to prayers [Jody Powell's Memoirs, 1984, p. 44]. Though he later sent a rescue mission, it ended in failure.

Carter's presidency was marked by indecision and weakness. His administration was a series of contradictions, errors, and incompetence, leading to global distrust in both his government and U.S. foreign policy [Shafa, ibid, p. 624].

American authors have frequently criticized Carter's populist and controversial behavior [Ronald Kessler, Presidential Secret Service, Chapter on Carter, 2003]. While Carter is now gone, his policies live on in what can be described as "Carter 2" (Obama) and "Carter 3" (Biden) regarding the Islamic Republic. Perhaps his death will mark the end of these misguided policies and their dark legacy. Yet, the world first faced the rise of Islamic radicalism during Carter's era, and the battle against terrorism continues to this day.

48
CHAOTIC IRAN AND ITS RUTHLESS DICTATOR

Iran teeters on the edge of total collapse, hurtling toward an inevitable abyss. The nation's future in today's world grows increasingly uncertain. Under the unrelenting grip of the mullahs' mafia-like religious regime, the legacy of Iran's millennia-old history, culture, and civilization hangs precariously in the balance. Time has run out, and with each passing moment, the spiral of devastation intensifies. The governance is neither legitimate nor lawful, and the nation's path forward is enveloped in darkness.

In a nation where governance lacks legitimacy and effectiveness, where the rule of law is absent, and where true government structures are nonexistent, power operates unchecked and dictatorial. This regime stands isolated, devoid of credibility on the global stage, propped up by a junta-like leadership supported by hollow, identity-less military institutions. Armed agents and security forces pervade every aspect of life, their sole mission being the preservation of the regime. The very essence of life for Iranians has been systematically extinguished.

Since the " 'springless winter" of 1979, Iranians have risen 18 or 19 times against their two dictators—Khomeini and Khamenei—expressing their rejection of a repressive, corrupt, authoritarian, and lawless regime that stifles life, joy, and peace. Each uprising has been met with brutal consequences: death, imprisonment, loss of livelihoods, blindness, and torture.Reminiscent of the tortures of the Stalin and Hitler eras, or the brutalities of various Islamic caliphs throughout the last 1400 years of history.

Over the decades, every social movement in Iran has aimed at overthrowing the regime. Though these efforts have not yet brought about regime change, they have provided invaluable lessons. Gradually, it has become evident, particularly to the younger generation, that the nation's trajectory under this decaying regime leads only to ruin. The Islamic Republic is now gasping for its final breath.

The Iranian society of 1979 bears part of the blame for its current predicament. Enthralled by fervor and excitement, the public was blind to the lessons of history and the looming threat of a religious web of superstition. They chanted slogans such as "We are all your soldiers, Khomeini" and "Dear Khomeini, tell us to shed blood," oblivious to the dire consequences. Over time, the emptiness of these slogans and the regime's hollow promises became glaringly obvious. It now appears the clerics ascended to power with a singular mission: the complete dismantling and destruction of Iran.

Today, the people's anger smolders like embers beneath

the ashes, ready to ignite. The nation is paralyzed, resources are dwindling, and the situation teeters on the brink of explosion. Iranians have lost all hope in their government. Each passing day, the regime becomes more despised and criminal, while public disillusionment and outrage grow. This is a regime that epitomizes absolutism—greedy for power, exploitative, unjust, lawless, merciless, and utterly devoid of conscience.

In Iran, the Organization of Endowments and Charity Affairsstates that there are 8,167 registered shrines attributed to descendants of Imams. However, in the entirety of Shi'a history, there have only been 11 Imams, and their 220-year era has long since ended.Even amid widespread electricity shortages, the regime prioritizes illuminating these dubious shrines, highlighting its misplaced priorities. It has become evident that, in 1979, an opportunistic regime led by deceitful leaders seized control of Iran, stripping the people of their rights while systematically plundering the nation's wealth.

The mullah's regime is likely aware that its escalating oppression, censorship, and brutal suppression will eventually spark a national uprising. Despite knowing they lack legitimacy or support among Iranians, the ruling elite prioritizes maintaining power over the well-being of the people. Fear and insecurity permeate society, with only those connected to the regime enjoying a semblance of safety.

The mayhem of 1979 echoed the deceptive rise of ideologies like Nazism and Marxism, infiltrating Iranian society through manipulation and false promises. Cloaked in claims of divine legitimacy, the new regime silenced questioning and dissent. For decades, the fundamental issue in Iran has been the persistence of the illegitimate, bankrupt, and oppressive narrative born from the 1979 revolution—a narrative centered on an imaginary Shi'a regime led by a mythical "Imam of the Age." This regime, devoid of identity and authenticity, has entrenched itself in power. Clearly, the first step toward addressing Iran's challenges is to move beyond this destructive system.

From Khomeini's rise in the early 1960s, his Islamist and Shi'a-centric ideology systematically weakened Iran, fracturing its culture and plunging the nation into turmoil. Those who embraced this religious despotism sought power and wealth at the expense of the country's well-being. Since 1979, the regime has drained Iran's resources on foreign terrorism, domestic repression, and an unrelenting propaganda machine, leaving the nation impoverished and fragmented.

Khamenei, the obtuse dictator, epitomizes ignorance, irrationality, and a lack of comprehension. He is delusional and tyrannical, embodying barbarity, terrorism, misery, religious despotism, corruption, and opposition to progress and development. His claims of divine authority insult the intelligence of Iranians and humanity at large. Why would the Lord choose an irrational, terror-driven cleric as His representative? The clerical culture of dominance and false piety belongs to the dustbin of history. The fall of the Shi'a Islamic caliphate will mark Iran's liberation, cleansing the nation of this plundering, barbaric regime. Shi'a rule is outdated and rapidly declining.

The current mafia regime in Iran is directionless and on the brink of collapse. Bereft of rationality and a modern perspective, it stands in direct opposition to Iranian civilization and culture, perpetuating only destruction and suffering.

If this deceitful regime truly represents divine will, why have thousands of Muslims been killed over the past 46 years? Why have its leaders waged war against their own people, orchestrated coups, looted the nation's wealth, incited unrest, and carried out brutal repression? What kind of divine power commands terror, swords, and missiles? There is no link between Islamic terrorism and God. Faith does not demand violence or coercion—it demands compassion and justice.

However, Iran will not transform into a democracy overnight after the fall of the clerics. The journey ahead is long and fraught with challenges. Fortunately, the younger generation has awakened to the regime's widespread deceit. They understand that the mullahs have long exploited disunity to plunder the nation's resources, actions that bear no connection to a benevolent creator.

This new generation refuses to be misled by fabricated sanctities. They recognize the irrelevance of divine pretexts and instead focus on advancing human lives and building a better future. Their vision is pragmatic and forward-thinking, prioritizing the nation's welfare over utopian illusions. The true path forward lies in breaking free from the catastrophe of 1979.

The youth reject the idea that they must sacrifice their lives for an apocalyptic regime. They choose joy, life, and a meaningful worldly existence over the falsehoods of a fabricated "Imam of the Age." Why should an entire people wager their intellect and lives on such myths? Previous generations lost everything in this gamble. The youth now aim to forge a future free from such destructive delusions.

Iran stands on the cusp of yet another attempt to overthrow its oppressive regime. Today's generation is deeply nationalist, freedom-loving, and committed to justice and human rights. They recognize that religion is a personal matter, with no rightful place in the governance of a nation. Rejecting apocalyptic clerical rhetoric as fraudulent, they see through the facade of sanctity and divinity, understanding that nothing in the cosmos inherently possesses such attributes.

This youth, guided by a strong sense of national conscience and ethical awareness, refuses to be confined by religious dogma. They reject the deceit and ineffectiveness of a disgraceful and widely despised religious government. Fully aware of the damage inflicted by Shi'a political ideology, the new generation is resolute in their refusal to tolerate the clerics' relentless pursuit of power and control over their lives. They are determined to forge a future free from the chains of this failed regime.

49
IRANIAN REGIME'S THREAT TO GLOBAL DEMOCRACY

In a revealing statement from the Office of the Director of National Intelligence (ODNI), the Federal Bureau of Investigation (FBI), and the Cybersecurity and Infrastructure Security Agency (CISA), the ongoing efforts of Iran to undermine the sanctity of the U.S. elections in November 2024 have been once again brought to light.

This proclamation underscores a harsh reality: Iran's regime is not merely a passive observer but an active participant in the democratic processes of the United States, aiming to pivot the outcome in its favor. It affirms that Iran's interference is a calculated, multifaceted campaign, extending beyond cyberspace into real-world subterfuge involving agents and misinformation peddlers who amplify Tehran's divisive agenda.

Iran's Persistent Threat:
The Intelligence Community's recent findings illuminate a disturbing trend of Iranian strategies poised to disrupt the U.S. political landscape. Iran's machinations are increasingly sophisticated, involving not only digital realms but also on-ground operations with local agents and so-called journalists who propagate Tehran's agenda under the guise of neutrality.

By infiltrating presidential campaigns through advanced cyber operations and social engineering tactics, Iran seeks to steal and leak sensitive information, hoping to sway public opinion and election outcomes. This modus operandi aims not just to skew public perception but to engender a broad spectrum of discord, manipulating election outcomes to favor Iran's geopolitical preferences.

Historical Context and Media Complicity:
Iran's approach to influencing global politics is not new but a refinement of tactics honed over decades. Tracing back to the 1979 Khomeinist revolt, the rise of the current regime was significantly aided by naïve U.S. foreign policy mistakes, under the CIA and Carter administration, and supported by transnational terrorist networks with covert backing from Moscow. During this period, Western media, particularly in the UK and USA, unwittingly became propagandists for the mullah's regime, lionizing Khomeini as a figure of religious and political renewal. This legacy of media engagement casts a long shadow, with these outlets today reluctant to revisit the praises they once heaped on Khomeini, likely due to a growing acknowledgment of the regime's true nature.

Echoes of Interference and Fear of Regime Change:
Recent statements by ODNI, FBI, and CISA highlight the Iranian regime's ultimate fear: regime change. It's crystal

clear that any move toward democratic values within Iran is seen as an existential threat by the criminal Shiite mullahs. Consequently, their foreign policy, particularly regarding the U.S., is focused on disrupting any support for such transformations, driven by a deep-seated paranoia about U.S. backing for regime change.

The notorious Iranian regime's pattern of interference in U.S. elections is part of a broader strategy observed in other nations, aimed at disrupting global democratic norms. Through strategic misinformation campaigns, Iran targets electoral processes and sways public policies and international perceptions.

Occasionally, Tehran and its intelligence institutions initiate a narrative, which is subsequently echoed by television and radio stations funded and operated with American taxpayers' money. Under the oversight of the CIA and FBI, these Persian TV stations in Washington and Los Angeles, along with a Persian radio channel in Prague, along with pseudo-experts who support the regime, parrot the propaganda of the Islamic Republic. This occurs without any apparent accountability, as if there is a complete lack of supervision in Washington.

Policy Implications and Enhancing Cybersecurity:
The U.S. faces a critical challenge in responding effectively to Iran's provocations without escalating tensions irreparably. A robust policy mix of diplomatic, informational, military, and economic strategies (DIME) is essential to curb further interference. This includes enhancing U.S. cybersecurity defenses, bolstering democratic institutions within Iran, and imposing targeted economic sanctions against entities involved in election interference.

Strengthening cybersecurity protocols is crucial to counteract these threats. Recommendations from the FBI and CISA—such as using strong passwords, enabling multi-factor authentication, and exercising caution with email attachments and links—need to be part of a broader public awareness campaign. This campaign should educate citizens on the signs of foreign interference and the importance of cybersecurity hygiene.

Global Democratic Solidarity Against Iran's Influence:

To effectively counter Iran's expansive influence operations, a global coalition of democracies is essential. This unified front should focus on sharing intelligence and best practices to preemptively address and neutralize Iran's tactics. Key activities include securing digital infrastructure, countering misinformation, and enhancing public awareness about foreign interference. Moreover, this coalition should advocate for aligned legal frameworks and policies that bolster defenses against such external threats. By collaborating closely, these nations can safeguard their elections and public discourse, presenting a strong barrier against the disruptive ambitions of authoritarian regimes. This approach not only protects individual nations but also strengthens global democratic integrity and resilience.

***

As the 2024 U.S. elections approach, the persistent threat of Iranian interference not only tests the resilience of American democratic institutions but also highlights the broader geopolitical stakes. The regime in Tehran is particularly alarmed at the prospect of Donald Trump's return to the White House, fearing a shift in U.S. policy that could aggressively counter their ambitions. Similarly, the potential election of Kamala Harris offers no guarantee of policy continuity from the Biden administration, adding to the regime's uncertainties. Even the promotion of figures like Pezeshkian does little to assuage their fears of facing a more confrontational U.S. policy post-November 2024.

This complex geopolitical landscape requires more than mere acknowledgment of the threats posed by Iran; it necessitates a robust, unified response from all levels of government and the public to uphold the democratic values we hold dear. The situation underscores the need for global democratic solidarity, not only to counteract Iran's strategies but to fortify the collective defense of democratic integrity worldwide. In this context, pushing for regime change in Iran through diplomatic and economic measures is more than a strategic necessity—it is a moral imperative to support a global order where democratic norms can thrive against authoritarian overreach.

The international community must engage actively, not just in denunciation but in taking concrete steps to ensure that democracies worldwide are safeguarded against the machinations of a regime driven by its fear of its citizens' demands for freedom and justice.

50
A FEARFUL AND PERILOUS FUTURE AWAITS IRAN'S NATION

The current regime in Iran is fundamentally unfit for the time and place it governs. It was founded on a flawed and historically distorted premise, and the political Islam established by Khomeini and the mullahs has caused significant harm to both Iran and the broader Middle East. The global community has observed how this ruling ideology, rooted in a particular interpretation of political Islam, has become an obstacle to the prosperity and well-being of the Iranian people. This regime is a hollow structure lacking substance, which has reduced Iran to ruins.

The ideological underpinnings of Tehran's oppressive and archaic regime stem from a fusion of Islamic and Communist principles. The actions and policies of its corrupt and duplicitous leaders demonstrate a level of rationality and comprehension that falls significantly short of Iran's middle class. This backward-looking, delusional, and crisis-ridden regime proves incapable of effectively governing Iran's complex society or meaningfully engaging with its young population

The regime's worldview is distorted by a sense of deprivation and delusion. From Khomeini's book on "Velayat-e Faqih" to Khamenei's recent speeches in November 2024, the Shiite clerical leadership perceives itself as the rightful successors to the Islamic Caliphates that emerged after Islami's Prophet Muhammad. This self-perception echoes the historical caliphates, which were often characterized by internal strife over the spoils of conquest. Both Khomeini and Khamenei view themselves as Muhammad's spiritual and political heirs, guided by a religious mindset that blends elements of superstition, misinformation, and populist rhetoric. Their actions suggest a relentless pursuit of unchecked authority, savagery and dominance, often at great cost to their own people and the region.

For 36 years, Iran has been ruled by a senile, despotic mullah who surpasses the likes of Hitler, Mao, Lenin, Stalin, Mussolini, Pol Pot, Kim Jong-un, Fidel Castro, Idi Amin, Franco, Gaddafi, Saddam Hussein, and Ceaușescu in terms of danger and brutality. Over the past half-century, Iran's two vicious dictators, Khomeini and Khamenei, have proven to be even worse than the Mongols, leaving an indelible stain on modern history and humanity. The Islamic caliphate system currently governing Iran—with its first caliph, Khomeini, and its second, Khamenei—bears no significant difference in essence from the murderous Safavid sultans or the inept Qajar dynasty.

For Iran's Khomeinist rulers, power is about domination,

devoid of accountability or willingness to engage in dialogue. The current leadership views society as an enemy, a competitor, or a herd to be shepherded. Concepts like human rights and civil society are illusory, and the notion of law holds no meaning in Iran. Civil society and adherence to laws are absent in today's Iran. Although the complexities of Iran's socio-political layers are challenging to articulate fully, the current regime is a continuation of the infamous terrorist group "Fada'iyan-e Islam."

In this regime, intellectualism, rationality, and logic are absent. Despite significant social transformations within Iran's relatively young population, the political system remains a harsh dictatorship ruled by eulogy, sycophancy, mafias, and religious gangs. This mirrors the Islamic caliphates of the past 1,400 years, where leaders neither dared to retire nor embraced change. Delusional rulers avoid reality, shut their eyes and ears to internal and external criticism, and consistently proclaim their divine right to rule through a propaganda machine. Every success is framed as a victory for their imaginary Islamic ideology, while every failure is attributed to Iran as a nation.

Since 1979, the mullahs and the current regime have devastated Iran's history, civilization, Ecosystem, and culture. Iran is ravaged, plundered, and off-track from the trajectory of its once-thriving civilization. The mullahs have had one mission: to spread poverty and destruction, enforce despotism, and propagate superstition and falsehoods. They have accomplished this mission. Not even the Mongols and Tatars inflicted such devastation on Iran. In the long winter of 1979, under the guise of divine will, Khomeini laid the foundation for the most bloodthirsty and corrupt theocracy on Earth. It is a grotesque and horrific system rooted in a regressive, brutal ideology masquerading as "pure Muhammadan Islam."

In the regime's discourse, they frequently reference an "Islamic Ummah." The Shiite leaders in Tehran, exhibiting blatant arrogance and narcissism, assert their legitimacy while simultaneously fostering terrorism, sedition, and chaos to maintain their grip on power. Their ideological foundation is rooted in charlatanism and radicalism—the core elements of Khomeinism. It is essential to clarify that Khomeinism is not merely a toxic ideology; rather, it represents a complex amalgamation of over 64 distinct schools of depravity and villainy, including anarchism, anti-Semitism, barbarism, Bolshevism, charlatanism, communism, demagoguery, despotism, dogmatism, expansionism, extremism, fascism, gangsterism, militarism, propaganda, ruffianism, savagery, Stalinism, terrorism, vandalism, vulgarity, and more.

The dangerous mafia-like rulers in Iran, outwardly Shiite Muslims but inwardly malevolent criminals, lack the intellectual capacity to navigate crises or renounce their antagonism toward peace and stability. Their dogmatic beliefs and deceitful façade have driven Iranian society into a tunnel of fear and darkness. As the late Shah, Mohammad Reza Pahlavi, of Iran once warned: "The Grand Horror." Meanwhile, Islamic leftist , or the pro-regime reformists, continue their charade of advocating for reforms in Iran, hoping to repaint the façade while selling illusions of hope and change. They refuse to address the chaos, insecurity, and destruction within Iran.

The regime's ideological foundation fundamentally opposes global friendship, order, and peace. Domestically, a hardline core governs through force and violence, while abroad, it actively fosters terror and fear. The regime's propaganda machine thrives on sensationalism, hollow slogans, and chaos, often spinning even its failures as "victories." Its displays of military and intelligence prowess are both absurd and farcical. However, when faced with serious challenges or threats, the regime retreats into defensive postures, hiding in proverbial shadows.

As history teaches us, such a regime cannot endure indefinitely. It will inevitably collapse, though not before plunging Iran and the region into turmoil for years to come.

Khomeini and Khamenei famously declared, "We will stand until the end!" Yet no one asked what the "end of the line" truly meant. Could it signify the complete destruction of Iran as a nation? Alarmingly, it appears so. Ultimately, one must conclude that this regime is not Iranian; these occupiers are enemies of Iran. The younger generation of Iranians is gradually arriving at this undeniable truth.

Meanwhile, some within the regime are already campaigning for Mojtaba Khamenei, the son of the current dictator, to inherit power. History reminds us that during the corrupt and criminal Umayyad Caliphate, Yazid succeeded his father, Mu'awiya I, through hereditary succession. Must Iranians once again endure the same tragic cycle of illegitimate "leaders"—embezzlers, plunderers, and murderers? — only to To what end?

The reality is that Shiite Imamate history is replete with hereditary power transfers, where authority is handed down like an inheritance. This regime, steeped in arrogance and corruption, dreams of creating a "Union of Islamic Theocratic Republics" (UITR). Yet such an idea is both absurd and doomed from the outset.

    Despite this, Iran will weather this storm and overcome this wave of destruction as it has countless others throughout its history. Though the regime betrays its people and creates immense challenges, the spirit of Iran remains unbroken. The nation will persevere and find its way forward.

51
BEHIND MULLAH'S IRON CURTAIN: PROPAGANDA AND REPRESSION

Iran finds itself on a dangerous downward spiral. Governance has led the country into complete deadlock. The situation in Iran has become a complex, inextricable knot, with governance accelerating destructively and absolutely, placing Iran's existence under the threat of complete destruction. The situation in Iran is extremely concerning.

Yet, the Iranian society and the world still do not fully comprehend the depth of this disaster. Since the springless winter of 1979, the regime has acted as an exploiter and occupier. The oppressive political system continually repeats its mistakes without any intention of correction. The dreams of the Iranian nation and its governance are not aligned. The Tehran government, with its unchecked power and immense wealth, fails to recognize the Iranian people, who deeply resent this governance. This tension and conflict will continue until the regime's fall.

The Iranian nation faces a governance that cannot understand language and with which dialogue is impossible. Dialogue between the oppressor and the oppressed does not occur with whips, bullets, and batons. However, the governance, acting like an unyielding horseman, has no intention of dismounting. From atop its horse, it lashes out with clubs and whips or shoots bullets at all the pedestrian citizens.

The military governance operates like a mafia, continuing its repression while the regime's propaganda machinery works overtime. All propaganda tools serve to bolster the regime's authority, which still seeks to consolidate its power across all platforms.

Relative to the potential of its people, Iran's governance is backward, incapable, and fraught with countless deficiencies. It holds no esteem among the Iranian people and is isolated on the international stage. The regime knows it has no national standing among the Iranian society, especially the younger generation, because it does not recognize the identity and name of the Iranian nation. The barrier between the governance and the nation is not just the outdated, bankrupt, and Khomeinist ideology.

Now, the oppressive and absolute evil regime, among an alienated and dissatisfied Iranian society, has no legitimacy or popularity. The government's discourse has also faced failure, consistently denying the interests of everyone but itself, which leaves no unity in society; everything is damaged and cracked.

With its irrelevant language and logic, the regime demands that society be submissive, viewing itself as the guardian overall, even grandiosely claiming to lead the Muslims of the Milky Way galaxy. How can one reason with a ruler who, after 35 years, only understands the language of force? None! The regime always points its finger of threat at everyone. Society cannot breathe freely.

A governance that recognizes the right to vote, civil rights, and freedom of speech and press only among its supporters and inner circle, selects and censors. This governance and system are not open to the future; they are very closed, dark, unwise, and irrational.

Intellectualism in Iran deals with terror, imprisonment, and absolute deprivation. The absolute evil governance in Iran has neither the desire nor the ability to understand anything beyond itself. A governance that is populist, repressive, and absolutist on one side, and a protesting, suppressed, and wholly lost society on the other are in conflict and opposition. There is no understanding or dialogue except through interrogations, revolutionary courts, and threatening calls from the Ministry of Intelligence and other security institutions. Indeed, no one in Iranian society is safe from arrest, suppression, and threats.

On the other hand, the current regime in Iran has utterly failed and is a symbol of absolute evil. Therefore, peaceful coexistence with this savage governance is impossible. The current regime does not recognize the people of Iran as a nation but sees them as the Islamic Ummah, and Iran for the regime is like war spoils, as if the country is occupied. But in fact, the Islamic Ummah is thousands of miles away from the Iranian nation, and it must be said that the Shiite regime and the Guardianship of the Islamic Jurist are not the Iranian nation. It must be said that the regime's narrow-minded politics and literature are completely contrary to the society and nation of Iran. In total, it is a failed system that contradicts freedom and law. It continuously suppresses but lacks authority.

The poor, suppressed, hopeless, and deprived society of Iran feels a deep dissatisfaction, public hatred, and both overt and covert anger towards the regime. The reason for the behavior of Iranian society is that after 1979, people lost their national pride and their national identity to the mullahs, leading the country into deadlock, downfall, and decay.

A governance in power that cannot understand language and has whips and bullets is a savage oppressor that is ready to commit any crime to preserve its irrational, non-modern, reality-averse, and deaf governance, and it is not ashamed of committing crimes. And the tragedy of the matter is that the mullah governance, with its sophistry and fallacy, claims religiosity and heavenly status, which is actually a display of superstitions and delusions and emptiness for political and religious fraud. Although Iranian society has moved beyond religion, a governance that calls the terrorist uproar of 1979 a revolution, but the bitter story of 1979, if it was a revolution, was a display of the savagery of Khomeini and his associates who returned Iran to 1400 years ago.

A few harsh and oppressive people are ready to sacrifice all of Iran for their invalid opinion and belief. The current religious despotism and religious governance in Iran expect the entire society to respect the terrorist uproar of Khomeini and also that the entire society should have the temperament of slavery and servitude and absolute obedience. And the structure of the Guardianship is the embodiment of despotism, delusion, ignorance, and superstition.

The path to institutionalizing democracy in Iran is also a long, rocky road full of ups and downs. A dangerous and threatening outlook awaits the Iranian nation. The regime is in decline. It is possible that soon, similar to economic and cultural collapse, environmental and industrial and agricultural collapses, a social and ethical collapse will also occur in Iran that can no longer be controlled.

Throughout history, the institution of the mullahs or the Shiite mullah system has been full of power-seeking, deception, law evasion, lies, propaganda, corruption, and terror and suppression. Change in this institution is impossible. Now, the Tehran regime has two tools: internal suppression and external aggression. The regime's terrorist institutions such as the Ministry of Intelligence, the IRGC, the police force, the Quds Force, and the army, as well as other proxy groups in the Shiite crescent to transnational criminal organizations, will continue their work as long as this regime is in power. The death of Raisi and others will not change or affect the system of this regime.

Predicting the situation in crisis-stricken Iran is challenging, especially with the elections commencing this Thursday as candidate registrations begin. However, I must state that:1. There will be no enthusiasm, participation, or competition in these elections. The atmosphere is severely restricted within a quasi-caliphate structure, and the government shows no interest in public involvement. 2. Amidst the media frenzy, the role of the Guardian Council, under Khamenei's supervision, is overlooked. 3. Candidate approvals will be limited to a few radical figures loyal to Khamenei. 4. The government aims to continue the current harsh conditions and seeks someone akin to Raisi.

52
COUNTERING THE IRGC: A GLOBAL CALL TO ACTION

The recent move by Canada to list Iranian regime's Islamic Revolutionary Guard Corps (IRGC) as a terrorist organization under its Criminal Code marks a significant moment in the international effort to curb Iran's malignant activities on the global stage. This decision comes after years of extensive lobbying and is a clear indicator of the growing concern among nations about the IRGC's role in fostering instability both regionally and internationally.

Iran's IRGC, established in the aftermath of the 1979 mullah's terrorist Revolt, is not merely a military organization; it is an influential political actor within Iran, wielding substantial economic power and executing the ideological and strategic intentions of the regime both domestically and internationally. More ominously, the IRGC's mandate transcends traditional military duties, involving itself deeply in Iran's political sphere, influencing its economic landscape, and most notably, orchestrating complex networks of proxy warfare across the Middle East and beyond and threaten global peace.

In the name of the IRGC, the word "Iran" doesn't appear. Essentially, this terrorist organization is active in protecting the Islamic Caliphate of the Khamenei and promoting the destructive ideology of Khomeinism under the guise of Islamic Resistance (but in reality, it signifies Islamic Terrorism). This terrorist institution is a criminal organization with a global reach, shining wherever the name of terrorism is mentioned. The radical thugs of IRGC are currently engaged in the domestic oppression and massacre of Iranians and is expanding its global terrorism network abroad.

Strategic Export of Revolution

The core of the IRGC's strategy has been to support non-state militant groups across the region, providing them with funding, weapons, and training to foment unrest and carry out attacks that align with Tehran's strategic interests. This has been vividly demonstrated in their support for Hezbollah in Lebanon, various militia groups in Iraq, the Houthis rebels in Yemen, and their ongoing military support to the Assad regime in Syria. Such actions are not merely regional security issues but are illustrative of the IRGC's broader strategy to reshape Middle Eastern politics, counter Western influence, and promote Iran as the preeminent regional power.

Global Terror Operations

Internationally, the IRGC's Quds Force, the branch responsible for extraterritorial operations, has been actively involved in planning and executing operations that clearly fall within the realm of international terrorism. These operations range from the orchestration of bombings and assassinations in Europe and South America to the provision of arms and tactical support to various militant groups. The infamous case of the 1994 AMIA bombing in Buenos Aires, which killed 85 people, is a stark reminder of the deadly reach of the IRGC's operations, directed and facilitated by its commanders.

Adapting to Modern Conflicts

In more recent years, the IRGC has adapted its methods and expanded its reach. It has increased its cyber capabilities, engaging in cyber espionage and attacks against foreign governments and industries, which constitutes a significant threat to global information security. The IRGC has also been implicated in military confrontations, such as the attacks on commercial shipping in the strategic waterways of the Middle East, which threaten global supply chains and international trade.

The international community must recognize the necessity of a robust, multi-faceted response to the IRGC's activities. While the designation of the IRGC as a terrorist organization by nations like Canada represents a crucial step forward, it is an inadequate measure if not part of a broader, cohesive strategy that includes enhanced sanctions, targeted legal actions against IRGC affiliates, and a comprehensive international legal and diplomatic framework aimed at curtailing its operations globally.

International Sanctions and Diplomatic Efforts

This behavior has significant implications for international security and necessitates a concerted global response. The designation of the IRGC as a terrorist organization by countries like Canada is an important step, but it is insufficient alone. Such actions must be part of a broader strategy that includes stronger international sanctions, targeted actions against individuals and entities connected to the IRGC, and a cohesive international legal and diplomatic framework to limit the Corps' operations.

Humanitarian and Ideological Counteractions

Moreover, nations must work together to address the humanitarian crises precipitated by the IRGC's actions or the IRGC-supported conflicts, particularly in war-torn regions like Syria and Yemen. The international community must prioritize diplomatic and humanitarian strategies to mitigate the suffering of civilians, who are often the most affected by the IRGC-supported conflicts. Additionally, the global community must counteract Iran's propaganda by supporting democratic values and human rights narratives within Iran and among its regional allies.

Strengthening Global Alliances

It is also essential for countries to cut off the financial streams that support the IRGC's extensive network. This includes stricter controls on international banking and finance channels to ensure that funds cannot be funneled to the IRGC or its proxies. Collaborative international efforts are required to dismantle the sophisticated networks that the IRGC uses to fund its operations, including those involving illicit trade and smuggling.

The global community's response to the IRGC must also be ideological. It involves countering Iran's extensive propaganda machinery, which justifies its actions and spreads its revolutionary ideology. Supporting counter-narratives within Iran and among its allies, emphasizing democratic values and human rights, is crucial.

In essence, the IRGC represents a profound challenge to international peace and stability, necessitating a concerted global response. A comprehensive approach that includes legal, financial, military, and ideological responses is vital. The international community must be unified and resolute in its actions against the IRGC to effectively curb its influence and operations. Failure to take decisive action risks not only further regional destabilization but also increased global insecurity. In confronting the IRGC, the international community must demonstrate both resolve and strategic foresight, ensuring that measures taken are comprehensive and sustained to dismantle the power structures that support the IRGC's global terrorist activities. This is not merely a regional necessity but a global imperative.

53

DONALD TRUMP'S CHALLENGES WITH THE IRANIAN REGIME

Donald Trump is preparing to re-enter the White House in a few weeks, having assembled his intelligence team. His administration faces significant challenges from the Islamic Republic of Iran. A major and ongoing threat to the U.S. remains the mullah's regime in Tehran. Naturally, this will pose problems for Trump; since 2023, Iran's terrorist sleeper cells in the western hemisphere have repeatedly attempted to assassinate him. In reality, the threat extends beyond the former president, targeting U.S. borders and institutions.

From the White House to the U.S. borders, these locations will remain targets of aggression by the Islamic Republic and its affiliates. Tom Homan, Trump's appointee for border management, brings extensive experience in combating terrorism and organized crime. Well-acquainted with the Islamic Republic and Islamic terrorism, border czar's vigilant monitoring of Special Interest Aliens and cartel activities at the US-Mexico border underscores the persistent threats from organized crime and potentially Iran-linked terrorism. His efforts demonstrate a profound understanding of the complexities at the border, focusing on protecting national security without any prejudice against Iranians or any other nationality.

Meanwhile, the deceptive lobbies of Iran's regime have long been established in the U.S., repeatedly attempting to influence American policymakers with distortions far removed from reality. For instance, the Islamic Republic's propaganda apparatus claims to U.S. officials that "the CIA and America orchestrated a coup in Iran in 1953, toppling a democratically elected prime minister"—a laughable and egregious falsehood. It remains unclear why such a narrative should be perpetuated, especially given the murky historical details surrounding the supposed election of that populist figure, Mosaddeq.

They also often assert that reformists differ from conservatives or hardliners. Yet, no one questions what changes they genuinely aim to implement within the dictatorial theocratic system. What distinguishes these factions in their promotion and expansion of Islamic terrorism? Absolutely nothing! None of these corrupt factions has opposed severe domestic repression. On another note, Persian media outlets under the influence of the U.S. Department of State, swayed by networks linked to these pro-regime factions, are ineffectual, unwatched, and widely disliked. Despite this, millions of American taxpayer dollars are wasted on broadcasting futile Persian-language programs and hosting repetitive guests. This represents a grim reality.

Moreover, the media, some American think tanks, and even universities have become echo chambers for Tehran regime's propaganda, shamelessly disseminating misleading narratives about Iranian history and politics.For example, major American media outlets travel to Tehran to interview regime officials, provide them designed platforms in New York, or publish the aggressive views of Tehran's intelligence officials in English. Similarly, an American think tank might host a dinner and offer a platform to Tehran's notorious figure, Ebrahim Raisi, while several American universities provide positions to individuals tied to NIAC or the Islamic Republic, including elements of its terrorist network.

On the other hand, hundreds of hours spent by previous Democratic administrations on diplomacy and negotiations with Iran's Khomeinist regime have been fruitless, leading to no substantive outcomes. The fundamental DNA of the Islamic Republic of Iran is entwined with terrorism, missiles, drones, and fostering crises and animosity towards America and Israel. Expecting reform and change within this framework is not only unwise but illogical, setting unrealistic expectations for any genuine reform or meaningful change. Conversely, the lives of hundreds, possibly thousands, of American servicemen in the Middle East are endangered by Iran's terrorist networks. Without a redefined intelligence policy, similar to the past four years, American forces may continue to suffer casualties without an adequate response from the White House.

Indeed, there have been instances where American officials preemptively informed Iranian officials about military maneuvers in the Persian Gulf, highlighting the need for a sharply defined security policy to effectively manage these risks and threats.

After the presidential elections following the demise of Raisi, the general anticipation pointed towards Trump's resurgence from Iran's regime. A prominent affiliate of Khamenei, fueled by deceitful propaganda and empty rhetoric, emerged from the electoral fray. Pezeshkian not only failed to uphold his promises but also exacerbated the prevailing conditions. Trump faces the daunting task of confronting the Islamic Republic and its terrorism-linked network alone, with minimal reliance on European allies. The Islamic Republic, leaning on support from China, Russia, and North Korea, persists in its antagonism towards the United States and Israel, actively maintaining its terrorist operations.

Trump and his intelligence team are fully cognizant of Iran's nuclear ambitions. U.S. intelligence agencies are well-informed about the Mullahs' pursuits to develop a nuclear weapon and atomic bomb, underscoring the critical need for vigilant and strategic responses to these ongoing threats.

They recognize that all Islamic terrorist networks within the Shia Crescent have ties to Tehran. The intelligence and military committees in both the US Senate and House are well aware of how the American intelligence community views Tehran's threats, based on detailed intel reports. The name of the Iranian regime is a constant in discussions across American counter-terrorism centers or CIA's CTC. Additionally, intelligence services from Persian Gulf states and Israel's Mossad keep Washington thoroughly briefed on threats emanating from Tehran.

Despite this extensive knowledge, the failures of the past four years, and similar previous periods, remain indefensible. Yet, even with Trump's entry into the White House, no specific and impactful policy has been articulated to confront the Tehran regime decisively. The path forward remains muddled; despite possessing in-depth intelligence about Iranian threats, a clear and potent strategy to effectively address the Tehran regime is still lacking.

Media outlets connected to the Islamic Republic continue discussing negotiations with Trump, but what exactly is being negotiated? Trump and his intelligence team still face challenges in dealing with the Iranian regime. Any agreement with terrorists would merely legitimize them, akin to the absurd idea that one could "teach chess to a gorilla." Trump shouldn't be deceived by these Khomeinist tricksters - as the Iranian saying goes: they dye cats & sell them as canaries (one could sell snow to Eskimos).

In private conversations with members of Trump's transition team, I've highlighted essential strategic and operational measures regarding Iran. These include comprehensive intelligence briefings, intensifying the "maximum pressure" campaign, avoiding diplomatic interactions with Tehran, implementing robust counterterrorism efforts, safeguarding domestic interests, preparing for immediate responses, supporting the democratic aspirations of the Iranian people, and reforming Persian-language outreach programs to effectively counter regime propaganda.

Given Trump's staunch support for Israel, a decisive and serious stance against the Islamic Republic of Iran is anticipated. However, nothing definitive has materialized yet, and the Middle East remains a simmering cauldron. Meanwhile, the widely despised 86-year-old dictator of Tehran continues to plot chaos and crises.

54
EARLY ELECTIONS IN IRAN: PUBLIC APATHY AND THE SPECTER OF CONTINUED OPPRESSION

As the curtain falls on Ebrahim Raisi's turbulent tenure, his administration, marked not only by its ineffectiveness but also by its unwavering brutality, prepares to exit within the next 3-4 weeks. Over these last three years, Raisi's government, alongside its entire cabinet, has showcased a profound capacity for oppression but little else, leaving behind a legacy tarnished by the violent suppression of numerous groups and every form of domestic dissent including retirees, workers, students, farmers, teachers, and those defrauded by various schemes. This oppression has also exacerbated national crises.

The past two years have particularly highlighted the regime's draconian response to nationwide protests against both religious tyranny and a myriad of economic issues, with actions from the government and its military and security institutions intensifying—resulting in an alarming escalation of summons, interrogations, arrests, and a spate of executions.

Moreover, the regime has not confined its atrocities to domestic matters but has extended its reach abroad, collaborating with Russian forces in Ukraine and inciting Islamic terrorist groups against Israel, further cementing its reputation for savagery on the international stage.

Yet, the prospect of change remains bleak. However, any hope for reform or deviation from this path of brutality under the upcoming 14th government of the Islamic regime seems futile. The regime continues to turn the pages of a playbook filled with oppression and disregard for civil liberties, operating under a theocratic framework where the president serves merely as a figurehead, a puppet to the overarching authority of regime's Supreme Leader Ali Khamenei. The electoral voice and opinion of the populace are systematically ignored, highlighting a stark disconnect between the government's actions and the will of its people.

The imminent departure of Raisi has stirred little more than speculative debates on his successor, with the real contenders likely being maneuvered behind the scenes by Khamenei through the influential Guardian Council. Early assessments suggest a continuation of the status quo, with no genuine competition or public engagement in the farcical electoral process. This orchestrated approach to governance has led to widespread public disillusionment, prompting a significant portion of society to lean towards boycotting what they dismiss as a mere electoral charade.

The electoral landscape is cluttered with candidates from various factions of the regime, yet none command genuine public credibility or respect. Traditional conservatives may rally behind figures like Saeed Jalili and Mohammad-Bagher Qalibaf, although their impact and appeal remain uncertain. The IRGC are poised to endorse their own candidates, such as Hossein Dehghan and Parviz Fattah, both known for their hardline stances and loyalty to military doctrines and close to intelligence circles.

Furthermore, controversial figures like Mahmoud Ahmadinejad and Mohsen Rezaei are also in the fray, each bearing the burden of a problematic past that significantly undermines their appeal. The former, once disgraced and ostracized from the political elite, seeks a return, while the latter, known for his repeated and unsuccessful bids, faces ridicule both from within the government and the public at large. It symbolizes the regime's cyclic redundancy.

Reformists, tangled in their own web of corruption and closely tied to the existing power structure, express a desire to perpetuate the regime's longevity while masquerading as agents of change. Yet, they receive little support from Khamenei, who shows a clear reluctance to involve them meaningfully in the electoral process. This faction remains marginalized, with scant hope of gaining traction or investing in a viable candidate.

As for the mullahs like Alireza Arafi and Mohseni Ejei, their potential candidacies are anticipated yet predictably aligned with the regime's conservative ideologies. The ultimate lineup for the elections will depend heavily on Khamenei's endorsements and the Guardian Council's strategic selections, underscoring the orchestrated nature of

Iranian elections.

As registration for candidates begins on May 30, the Guardian Council, under Khamenei's watchful eye, will dictate the final slate of candidates, reinforcing the predetermined nature of the elections. Campaigning is set to commence on June 12, leading up to the vote on June 28. Yet, the outcome is all but certain—another display of manipulated electoral integrity where the true sentiments of the Iranian populace are likely to be overshadowed by fabricated voter turnout and state-sanctioned candidates.

Three years ago, Raisi purportedly secured 18 million votes against a backdrop of 4 million spoiled ballots—a statistic that today, amidst heightened public disillusionment, seems implausible at best. The regime, fearful of the true strength of public dissent, continues to rely on propaganda, number fabrication, and outright deceit to maintain its grip on power.

In conclusion, as Iran stands on the precipice of another orchestrated electoral exercise, the contrast between the democratic processes observed in more open societies and the theatrical displays within Iran could not be starker. The global community, particularly the international media, must strive to penetrate beyond the regime's narrative, shedding light on the genuine struggles and aspirations of the Iranian people who yearn for authentic change and democratic governance. As the regime prepares to stage yet another show of electoral compliance, the people of Iran continue their gradual but resolute march towards awakening, challenging the foundations of a theocracy that has long overstayed its welcome.

It must be noted that elections are not actually held in Iran; rather, what transpires is a farcical spectacle full of sophistry. These are neither free nor competitive events. Khamenei and the IRGC perceive America as vulnerable, having attacked American forces 175 times without any significant response from the United States. The White House, particularly under Democratic leadership, seems primarily interested in maintaining the status quo.

The main candidates in the upcoming U.S. elections, occurring five months after Iran's early elections, understand that the policies of the Islamic Republic will not change with the mere alteration of the president's name. They are aware that over 70% of the participants in Iran's elections are high-ranking commanders of the IRGC. The future president of Iran will not be a true representative of the Iranian people but rather a figure trusted by Khamenei and the IRGC—a repressor, anti-American, and anti-Israeli. Undoubtedly, U.S. intelligence and security agencies are aware that the Iranian people do not trust Khamenei's appointees and desire a regime change in Tehran.

55
ECHOES OF DISSENT: THE SILENT BOYCOTT AGAINST IRAN'S AUTHORITARIAN RULE

In the Islamic Republic of Iran, a landscape once rich with cultural and political heritage now suffers under the yoke of an authoritarian regime that has hijacked the once-sacred act of voting. The disenfranchised Iranian populace finds itself ensnared in a system where elections serve as nothing more than a spectacle of faux democracy, orchestrated to sustain the illusion of legitimacy for a government that has systematically eroded civil liberties and human rights.

The recent overwhelming boycott of the presidential elections is not merely a passive act of defiance but a pronounced indictment of a regime that has failed its people spectacularly. This boycott transcends mere political disillusionment; it is a profound statement against the regime's propaganda machine that paints participation as a civic duty, while in truth, it is a coerced endorsement of a predetermined outcome.

Within this context, the roles of presidential candidates become clear. Figures such as Jalili and Pezeshkian, perceived by the public not as pioneers of change but as stalwarts of the status quo, are emblematic of a broader political malaise. They are seen not as legitimate contenders for leadership but as cogs in a machine engineered by Supreme Leader Ayatollah Khamenei. His regime, epitomized by a relentless grip on power, manipulates every facet of governance—from the judiciary to the military—to ensure that no true opposition can emerge.

Ali Khamenei himself stands as a paragon of dictatorial excess, embodying the antithesis of the democratic values he purports to uphold. His plans to establish a dynastic succession through his son, Mojtaba, reveal a blatant disregard for democratic processes and a preference for monarchical rule disguised as religious governance. This maneuver is not just a perpetuation of personal power; it is an affront to the collective will of the Iranian people, signaling that even the semblance of choice is a privilege granted by the ruling elite, not a fundamental right.

The boycott, therefore, is a critical expression of political maturity and historical consciousness by a society that, despite being shackled by fear and repression, recognizes the futility of participating in a predetermined play. Over the decades, Iranians have cultivated a sophisticated understanding of their political landscape, informed by repeated cycles of promised reforms followed by inevitable retrenchment. This has led to a collective awakening, where the electorate refuses to validate a corrupt system through participation in its rigged elections.

The implications of this silent boycott extend beyond the immediate context of electoral politics to touch upon the very legitimacy of the regime. The 'vilayat-e faqih' system, which centralizes religious and political authority in the hands of the Supreme Leader, is fundamentally incompatible with the principles of democratic governance. It perpetuates a model of leadership that is inherently despotic, reminiscent of historical caliphates where rulers wielded absolute power, unaccountable to their subjects.

This model of governance has not only stifled political dissent but has also led to economic stagnation and social decay. Iran's economy, heavily sanctioned by the international community and mismanaged by corrupt elites, teeters on the brink of collapse. The regime's failure to effectively address these issues, combined with its oppressive tactics to suppress any form of dissent, has only deepened the resolve of the Iranian people to seek change.

The reformist factions within Iran, including groups like the Islamic Left and participants of the 1979 revolution, once heralded as agents of change, now find themselves in a precarious position. Their calls for reform, constrained within the parameters set by the regime, have failed to bring about any substantive change. Instead, they serve to perpetuate a facade of progress, even as the fundamental structure of the regime remains unchallenged.

As the regime continues to clamp down on dissent and tighten its authoritarian grip, the response from the populace has been one of increasing resistance. The silent boycott is not just a refusal to vote; it is an active strategy of non-compliance that challenges the regime's authority and exposes its vulnerabilities. This growing undercurrent of civil resistance is a testament to the resilience of the Iranian people, who, despite enduring decades of repression, are increasingly determined to imagine and fight for a future that aligns with their aspirations for freedom and justice.

In conclusion, the silent boycott of the elections in Iran represents more than a momentary expression of discontent. It is a profound challenge to a regime that relies on suppression and deception to maintain control. For the international community and observers of Iranian politics, this act of boycott is a crucial indicator of a shifting political consciousness among Iranians, a sign that the authoritarian grip of the regime is faltering under the weight of its own contradictions. As this political drama unfolds, it becomes increasingly clear that the path to genuine reform in Iran must be paved with the active participation of its citizens, demanding and implementing a system of governance that truly represents their will and respects their rights.

56
FANNING THE FIRES: THE ISLAMIC REPUBLIC'S GLOBAL TERROR CAMPAIGN

The structure of the mullahs' regime in Tehran, notorious for its proliferation of terror, operates multiple terrorist groups across the Middle East. Regrettably, there is a palpable lack of genuine intent among both regional countries and Western powers, notably the United States, to dismantle this pernicious force. Ironically, these same nations engage in negotiations and even promote these malign actors in Western media, contributing to a disconcerting normalization of terror.

Western media outlets frequently refer to figures like Ali Khamenei with the undeserved title of "Ayatollah," which translates to "Sign of God." This irony begs the question: Which divine being would sanction terrorism that Khamenei represents? Engaging with terrorists—malevolent individuals who thrive on chaos and destruction—yields no benefits. Yet, we observe years of fruitless Western negotiations with the mullahs' regime in Tehran, adorned with photo ops that symbolize these diplomatic failings.

Despite losing hundreds of soldiers in the fight against terrorism sponsored by the Islamic Republic of Iran, and enduring terrorist attacks on their own soil, Europe and America seem to lack a lesson learned. The West fails to recognize how its actions embolden the regime, even as the Islamic Republic continues its international campaign of terror, kidnapping, embassy attacks and other provocations. It is unclear what further atrocities the Islamic Republic must commit to awaken the world from this oversight.

The Intelligence and military apparatus of the Islamic Republic cunningly crafts narratives or fabricate irrelevant and false rumors that find their way into Western media, furthering their agenda. Even American think tanks and universities grant platforms and positions to known terrorists, a troubling testament to a misguided understanding of freedom of expression. As if the more murderous and criminal you are, the more popular you become. Even the families of Islamic Republic officials freely roam in the West and America.

These oversights and naïveté have rendered the global landscape perilously insecure. The Islamic Republic's terror network, akin to a plague, spreads across the Middle East, Europe, Africa, and Latin America, yet the 21st century world seems paralyzed by indecision on how to address this threat. The persistence of radical Islam and Islamic terrorism poses one of the greatest threats to global peace, yet there remains a significant segment of the international community that turns a deaf ear to these realities.

World-renowned intelligence agencies like the CIA spend months on end prioritizing peace talks over decisive action against terrorist entities like Hamas. It appears future generations may look back on our era astonished at our appeasement of bloodthirsty terrorists. This century, however, seems bereft of answers.

The Islamic Republic maintains clandestine diplomatic channels with both the US and Israel while simultaneously orchestrating terror attacks globally. It seems the regime holds the world hostage, playing a dangerous game with global stability. Even as Tehran engages in public diplomacy, it fosters a network of terror that destabilizes regions far beyond its borders. However, the Islamic Republic lacks the defensive and military capability to confront the US and Israel. . China and Russia, along with their puppet North Korea, manipulate their servants in Tehran. However, Tehran continues its enmity towards America, the West, and Israel.

The White House, over recent years, has shown a lack of strategic initiative to counter the Tehran regime's destructive influence. Iranian lobbyists , apologists and stooges operate freely in Washington, further complicating the narrative and enabling the regime's propaganda machine, funded unwittingly by American taxpayers.

In actuality, The Islamic Republic's lobbies in Washington are actively operating, and even Persian-language media funded by American taxpayers, supposedly to promote democracy, are under the control and influence of the Islamic Republic. These agents broadcast their propaganda from televisions and radios—from Prague and Washington to Los Angeles.

The Islamic Republic has mobilized all its terrorist branches. Shiite terrorists affiliated with Iran in Iraq have initiated drone attacks on Israel, and Hezbollah has started launching rockets. Both actions are instigated by the IRGC and Quds Force under Khamenei. In recent days, the Islamic Republic awaited the end of Arbaeen and the ideological display it entails. As soon as that curtain falls, the next stage of warfare and missile and drone launches will commence. It seems that the officials of the Islamic Republic derive psychological satisfaction from threatening Israeli and American officials with death in front of the media. Essentially, the psyche of terrorists is restless and unhealthy.

A regime thirsty for bloodshed, lawlessness, explosions, destruction, and displays of savagery does not understand the language of diplomacy, and peaceful coexistence with it in today's world is impossible. It is unrelated to the culture, history, and civilization of the Iranian people. In fact, the mullahs, with the help of terrorists, have occupied Iran.

Today, as the Islamic Republic orchestrates a broad spectrum of terror, the world watches, waiting for the next act in this grim theater of war. The question remains: How long will the international community tolerate the existential threat posed by the regime in Tehran?

From today, global news agencies, like the showcasing of a new action movie in cinemas worldwide, vividly reflect news related to the warmongering of the Islamic Republic and its terrorist branches like Hezbollah, Hamas, Houthis, and Popular Mobilization Forces... They prepare for public mourning for the potential elimination of Hamas and the killing of its leaders in Tehran, accompanied by critiques filled with advice and vain hopes for peace.

Israel has no choice but to surgically remove this malignant growth for its survival, but the snake's head is in Tehran, and until its head is cut off, this futile spectacle continues. The world, amidst Islamic terrorists, is restless, and the situation does not bode well...

It is time for the global community to wake up and take decisive action. The stakes are too high, and the cost of inaction is too great. We must confront this menace head-on, with all the tenacity and resources at our disposal, before it further engulfs the world in its dark shadow.

57
HRH PAHLAVI AT IAC: "UNITED FOR FREEDOM, TIME TO ACT TOGETHER"

The Crown Prince Reza Pahlavi's speech at the IAC conference was highly anticipated and received overwhelming support from both Iranian and Israeli communities. Before his address, supporters waved massive Iranian and Israeli flags outside the venue, showcasing the deep solidarity between these nations in their shared struggle against the common threats posed by the Islamic Republic. This enthusiastic public display underscores Pahlavi's continued prominence as the most influential political figure among Iranians, particularly admired by the younger generation.

The Crown Prince Reza Pahlavi stands as a beacon of hope for millions, representing Iran's rich history and its potential for a brighter, more democratic future. Despite continuous opposition from the remnants of the 1979 revolution—

whose criticisms are often driven by bitterness rather than rational discourse—Pahlavi's reputation only strengthens. Marxists, separatists, and so-called reformists frequently align their rhetoric with the Islamic Republic's propaganda machine, flooding Persian-language social media with negative portrayals. Yet, despite these efforts, Pahlavi's name shines ever brighter, while his detractors remain irrelevant—mere champions of their own delusions, disconnected from the realities facing the Iranian people.

Against this backdrop of attacks and challenges, Reza Pahlavi's recent speech at the Israeli-American Council was more than a recounting of past atrocities. It was a clarion call for decisive global action against the Islamic Republic, focusing on its support for terrorism and systemic violence.

A Call for Coordinated Action
The HRH Prince Pahlavi made it abundantly clear that mere solidarity between the people of Iran, Israel, and the United States is no longer enough. He urged that the time has come for coordinated action to overthrow the Islamic Republic: "Now it is time to do more than stand side by side... it is time to act hand in hand" (Pahlavi, speech). This collaboration, he argues, is the only way to free the region from the regime's terror.

A Legacy of Terror
Pahlavi's speech meticulously detailed the atrocities committed by the Islamic Republic of criminal mullahs since the 1980s, both inside Iran and globally. He pointed out that "these crimes... were all orchestrated by the Islamic Republic and the man at its bloody helm, Ayatollah Ali Khamenei" (Pahlavi, speech). The regime's trail of destruction stretches

from Lebanon to Buenos Aires, from Iraq to Iran's own streets, underscoring its unwavering commitment to Islamic terrorism.

The Futility of Reform Efforts

One of the most compelling aspects of Pahlavi's message was his rejection of any hope for reform within the Islamic Republic. "Iranians tried to deal with this regime. They tried to reform it... but the result was only more violence" (Pahlavi, speech). Even under so-called reformist leadership, the regime continued its brutal repression. Pahlavi's warning to the West is clear: engaging in negotiations with the regime is futile, as it will never abandon its violent and oppressive nature.

A Red Line Drawn in Blood

The HRH Prince Pahlavi grew emotional when addressing the tragic anniversaries of violent events that claimed innocent lives. He lamented, "Sadly, that red line had to be drawn with the blood of innocent civilians—our Nika and your Shani, our Pouya and your Hersh" (Pahlavi, speech). His words underscore the high cost of inaction and the urgent need for global leaders to stop the regime's barbaric violence.

The Need for Maximum Pressure

Pahlavi calls for the reinstatement of maximum pressure policies on the Islamic Republic, both politically and economically. He emphasized that this pressure must be coupled with maximum support for the Iranian people, who continue to fight against their oppressors without external help: "We need to reinstate maximum pressure on the Islamic Republic... and provide maximum support to the people of Iran" (Pahlavi, speech). His focus was on encouraging defections from the regime and facilitating a peaceful transition to a secular democracy.

A Vision for the Future

Despite the gravity of the situation, Pahlavi concluded his speech on a hopeful note, envisioning a future where Iran is free from theocratic rule and its people can live in peace: "When the Lion and Sun rises again, the world will witness a new dawn of peace" (Pahlavi, speech). His vision extends beyond solidarity, advocating for a collaborative, coordinated campaign that could expand from the Abraham Accords to a new Cyrus Accords—a partnership aimed at securing prosperity and dignity for both nations.

The Time to Act is Now

The Crown Prince Reza Pahlavi's speech at the IAC serves as a stark reminder of what is at stake. The atrocities committed by the Islamic Republic are not isolated events; they are part of a long, calculated campaign of terror. Pahlavi's call for unity and coordinated action is not merely a plea for help; it is a roadmap for achieving lasting peace and security in the region. His message is clear: solidarity is no longer enough. The world must act together to end the Islamic Republic's reign of terror and pave the way for a brighter future.

In an era clouded by misinformation and propaganda, Pahlavi's name continues to shine as a beacon of hope for millions of Iranians. His popularity among the youth is a testament to his enduring relevance and the powerful legacy of his family, standing in stark contrast to the fading revolutionaries of 1979 who have lost touch with reality.

Pahlavi's speech highlighted the need for collaboration between Israel and Iran's opposition. He stressed that simply reacting to threats posed by Iran's proxies, such as Hamas and Hezbollah, leaves Israel vulnerable. His message was clear: "Now it is time to do more than stand side by side... it is time to act hand in hand" (Pahlavi, speech). The call for maximum pressure on the regime and support for the Iranian people underscores the urgency of forming a united front to bring peace and stability to the region. His vision for expanding from the Abraham Accords to a potential Cyrus Accords is a powerful testament to his forward-thinking strategy—a partnership that would secure prosperity and dignity for both Iran and Israel.

58
HANIYEH'S ELIMINATION A TURNING POINT IN MIDDLE EAST

Criminals always face the consequences of their actions. Ismail Haniyeh was a servant of Khamenei's Islamic terrorism network. He committed every crime to please Khamenei, but ultimately, he was eliminated near Khamenei himself, marking a significant success for Israel. This event demonstrates that Israel's enemies, no matter where they are, even in the heart of the world's terrorism hub, will still be hunted down.

The assassination of Ismail Haniyeh, the head of the Political Bureau of Hamas Terrorists, marks a significant development in the geopolitical landscape of the Middle East. Haniyeh, along with one of his guards, was reportedly killed at his Tehran residence, an incident confirmed by Hamas and the IRGC. This targeted killing, allegedly orchestrated by Israel, underscores the high-stakes nature of regional power struggles and the far-reaching influence of intelligence operations.

A Blow to Hamas and Its Allies

Ismail Haniyeh's death deals a substantial blow to Hamas, the Palestinian Terrorist Organization he led. Haniyeh was not only a symbolic figurehead but also a strategic leader who played a crucial role in Hamas' political and military activities. His leadership was pivotal in fostering ties with regional powers, particularly Iran's regime, which has long supported Hamas in its opposition to Israel. The elimination of Haniyeh disrupts the organizational hierarchy and could lead to a power vacuum within Hamas, potentially causing internal strife and weakening its operational capabilities.

The Successful Role of Israel's Intelligence Apparatus

The reported involvement of Israel in this high-profile assassination highlights the capabilities and reach of its intelligence agencies, particularly the Mossad. Israel has a history of targeting key figures in hostile terrorist organizations to disrupt their operations and send a deterrent message. The successful execution of such an operation within Tehran, a city heavily fortified by Iranian security forces, is a testament to the sophistication and daring of Israeli intelligence. This act not only underscores Israel's commitment to neutralizing threats and Islamic Terrorists but also serves as a warning to other adversaries.

Implications for Iran-Hamas Relations

Haniyeh's presence in Tehran at the time of his death underscores the close relationship between Hamas and mullah's regime in Iran. His visit for the inauguration of Iran's new president was symbolic of the alliance between the two entities, both of which view Israel as a common enemy.

The assassination could strain this relationship, forcing Iran to reassess its security protocols and the safety of its allies within its borders. Additionally, it raises questions about Iran's ability to protect its allies and maintain its influence in the region.

Regional Repercussions
The elimination of Haniyeh is likely to have significant regional repercussions. It may embolden other countries to take more aggressive stances against terrorist organizations and their leaders. Furthermore, it could escalate tensions between Israel and Iran, with potential retaliatory actions from both sides. The assassination also has the potential to incite unrest within Palestinian territories, as Hamas and its supporters respond to the loss of their leader.

The Path Forward
In the aftermath of Haniyeh's death, Hamas will need to quickly reorganize its leadership and strategize its next steps. The terrorist organization will likely attempt to rally its supporters and strengthen its resolve against perceived adversaries. Meanwhile, Israel and its allies must remain vigilant and prepared for possible retaliatory actions. The international community should closely monitor the situation, recognizing the delicate balance of power and the potential for further destabilization.

***

The assassination of Ismail Haniyeh in Tehran is a landmark event with wide-reaching implications for the Middle East. It highlights the lethal efficiency of Israeli intelligence operations and exposes vulnerabilities within Iran's security apparatus. As Hamas grapples with this significant loss, the dynamics of regional alliances and enmities will undoubtedly shift. The international community must remain attentive to these developments, understanding that the path to stability in the region is fraught with complexities and challenges.

The influence of Mossad in Iran, as evidenced by this operation, cannot be understated. It signifies a bold assertion of Israel's commitment to its security and its willingness to take decisive action against threats, regardless of the geographical and political complexities involved.

59

HARRIS, TRUMP: THE RELUCTANCE FOR REGIME CHANGE IN IRAN

The cauldron of the Middle East is simmering. The blaze was kindled in 1962, a period marked by the rise of an obscure and deluded Shiite cleric named Ruhollah Khomeini. Later, his brother—identified as Pesandideh—disclosed, "We are originally of Indian descent!" This precise declaration was indeed published on January 9, 1978, in the newspaper Ettela'at, sparking protests by Khomeini's adherents and thugs in Qom, which resulted in six fatalities.

At that time, Khomeini, acting akin to a foreign agent and a soldier under Gamal Abdel Nasser in Iran, vociferously opposed the Shah of Iran. Owing to the intercession of SAVAK's chief—General Hassan Pakravan—the Shah of Pahlavi was conferred the title "Ayatollah," signifying "Sign of God," bypassing the customary clerical progression. This abrupt elevation spared him from execution and led to his exile to Iraq.

In Iraq, Khomeini was provided a radio by Saddam Hussein, continuing his diatribes against the late Shah, and in 1969, authored the book 'Velayat-e Faqih' (Jurist) published in Beirut. Within this so-called book, Khomeini delineated his strategy for seizing power, proclaiming the Shiite mullah as God's earthly representative and the envoy of an imaginary and non-existent entity known as the Hidden Imam, stating "the jurist is his representative and retains power until his emergence, after which the power will be transferred to him or Imam Zaman." In this instance, the mullahs' charlatanism was derided across the Islamic states, yet it went unexposed, and even global intelligence organizations such as the CIA and Mossad had not perused a copy of his book. This reality, frequently, has been recounted and documented by senior officials within these institutions.

From the time the late patriotic Shah acknowledged Israel de facto in 1962 until the grim winter of 1979, spanning approximately 18 and a half years, the Shiite mullahs engaged in extensive networking, fostering terrorism, and cultivating ties with Palestine, Ghaddafi, Saddam, Castro, Mao, the Soviet Union, etc. When Saddam, due to rapprochement with the Shah and normalization of relations with Iran, expelled Khomeini from Iraq, he relocated to France.

Concurrently, the Democrats in the U.S., under the guise of religious populism epitomized by Jimmy Carter, and the UK, propelled Khomeini, the veteran Muslim Brotherhood combatant, into the limelight. The majority of the global leftist media broadcast a fabricated and deceitful interview with Khomeini (orchestrated by Banisadr, Yazdi, and Qotb-zadeh) and no inquiries were made regarding the proliferation of baseless and brazen lies about the Shah of

Iran. With nauseating hyperbole, they portrayed a sanctified and fraudulent image of a criminal like Khomeini, a reality that went unchallenged. The leftist global media (comprising Communists and Marxists) transformed into mouthpieces for Khomeini, and Iran found itself ensnared by his regime. In his rhetoric, when he declared Islam was imperiled, it implied that Khomeini and his regime were under threat. There was not any fact-checking!

The malicious ideology of Khomeinism ascended to power in Iran and established the inaugural government of Allah on Earth, under the supervision of the notorious terrorist Yasser Arafat and the representative of Ghaddafi. Proponents of the Mosaddeq era—those who embrace the contrived account of the August 19, 1953 coup while conceding their cooperation with Britain and the U.S. for a quarter-century until 1979, scheming against the late Shah—along with leftist Islamist reformists, orchestrated the seizures of the U.S. and Israeli embassies to ingratiate themselves with Moscow. These populist thugs have continually displayed hostility towards Israel and the U.S. while demonstrating allegiance to Russia and China, simultaneously advancing the agenda of Islamic terrorism throughout the Shiite Crescent.

Yet, the flames of the Middle East continue to flare. The Shiite mullahs, in their quest to perpetuate their outlaw and evil regime, refrain from no act of oppression or atrocity within their nation. Abroad, their propaganda apparatus is active, with global leftist media at their disposal. They even disseminate the fabrications of the mullahs' propaganda machine in English and other languages, or broadcast programs in Persian from BBC London, ensuring that the prevailing sentiment within Iranian society does not lean towards regime change. It appears that neither America nor Europe contemplates the necessity of regime change in Tehran.

This week, the pro-regime reformists, known as Islamic leftists, are poised to nominate Masoud Pezeshkian (a populist loyal to Khamenei) as President. It is evident that within the framework of the Islamic Republic's theocracy or Velayat-e Faqih, no distinction exists between reformists and conservatives; both occupy roles within security (such as the Ministry of Intelligence, MOIS) and military institutions (such as the IRGC and Quds Force), united in their objective to sustain the Islamic Republic's lifespan and equally culpable in committing atrocities against the Iranian populace.

This week in America, Benjamin Netanyahu, the Prime Minister of Israel, underscored the threat posed by the Islamic Republic to the global community, yet the American leftists (Democrats) showed no inclination to heed his realistic warnings. Their new electoral contender is Kamala Harris, who formerly served on the Senate Security Committee.

In summary, the track record of Democratic U.S. presidents regarding the Islamic Republic over the last 45 years is dismal. Under Jimmy Carter's administration, the Islamic Republic of the mullahs in Tehran was born; during Bill Clinton's tenure, the deceptive 'Dialogue of Civilizations'—a product of reformist duplicity—was marketed. Under Barrack Obama, despite the nationwide Iranian uprising and the ensuing youth massacre, correspondence with Khamenei continued, as if a butcher like Khamenei comprehended the essence of dialogue with the civilized Western world and democracy. A stubborn, war-criminal dictator focused solely on appeasing Moscow and China, with aspirations to annihilate Western civilization, even hastened to aid the Kremlin in the Ukraine conflict.

During Joe Biden's presidency, his Iran policy also floundered. Like Donnald Trump, he labeled the Islamic Republic as the representative of the Iranian people. His primary aim was to resuscitate the moribund JCPOA, and his policy of appeasement only emboldened, intensified, and exacerbated the belligerence of the Islamic Republic, while showing scant regard for the widespread Iranian movement against religious tyranny. Both Biden and Obama provided artificial resuscitation to the corpse of the Islamic Republic.

And today, whether Harris remains in the White House or Trump makes a return, this 62-year-old inferno will only grow more intense, yet there lacks any serious intent or determination to extinguish it. Until the scourge of radical Islam and Islamic terrorism, originating from the mullahs of Tehran, is eradicated from the Middle East, there will be no prospects for stability, comfort, peace, and security. Whether Harris or Trump assumes power, this harsh reality remains inescapable. And should the mullahs, infatuated with Islamic terrorism, acquire nuclear capabilities, the 21st-century humanity will face a grave threat that is not easily mitigated.

60
ISRAEL'S NEXT FRONT? IRAN, HEZBOLLAH, AND THE COMING WAR IN LEBANON

The recent surge in hostilities along the Israel-Lebanon border marks a significant escalation in the longstanding conflict between Israel and terrorist Hezbollah. Over the past six months, nearly 400 Lebanese, including around 70 civilians and 3 journalists, have been killed, and 90,000 Lebanese civilians have been displaced from approximately 100 towns and villages along the border.

The Israeli Defense Forces (IDF) have responded to Hezbollah's intensified rocket and drone attacks with significant military force, leading to widespread destruction in Lebanese villages and olive groves. Hezbollah's barrage of rockets and drones into northern Israel has aimed to support Hamas and demonstrate its military capabilities. The terrorist group's attacks have targeted Israeli military installations and civilian areas, causing significant damage and prompting a robust retaliatory campaign from Israel. The conflict has created a humanitarian crisis, with thousands forced to flee their homes and communities. Displaced Lebanese civilians face harsh living conditions, lacking basic necessities such as food, clean water, and medical care.

This renewed conflict underscores the volatile nature of the Israel-Hezbollah relationship and marks one of the most severe escalations since the 2006 war. The current turbulent situation highlights the persistent threat Hezbollah poses to Israel and the significant impact of Israeli military responses on Lebanon. As both sides continue aggressive military actions, the risk of a full-scale war looms large, with potentially devastating consequences for the entire region. International efforts to mediate and de-escalate the situation are crucial in preventing a broader conflict that could further destabilize the Middle East. Conversely, the activities of the Quds Force are inciting Hezbollah to escalate tensions.

Since the 2006 war, a period of relative calm and deterrence has prevailed between Israel and Hezbollah, punctuated by occasional skirmishes but no full-scale conflicts. However, the situation has become increasingly fragile, especially after the psychological impact of the October 7, 2024, attacks, which have heightened Israeli insecurity. This heightened state of alert has led to higher levels of PTSD, depression, and anxiety among the Israeli population, compelling the government to adopt a more aggressive stance against perceived threats.

Israel's risk tolerance has shifted dramatically in response to the perceived threat from Hezbollah, which is now better armed and trained than Hamas terrorists. Despite a preference for diplomatic solutions, Israeli officials are prepared to undertake unilateral military action if necessary. The IDF's recent deployment of 100,000 troops to the northern border underscores Israel's readiness to escalate the conflict to secure its borders and ensure the safety of its citizens. However, the primary culprit is not Israel, but the Islamic terrorist groups affiliated with the Quds Force of the Islamic Republic in Tehran, which are aggressively pressuring Israel and have set the entire Middle East ablaze. Amidst this conflagration, it is possible that the Iranian terrorist-loving mullahs may reveal their nuclear bomb.

The conflict has displaced over 150,000 people on both sides of the Israel-Lebanon border. Israeli leaders face intense domestic pressure to improve security and resettle displaced persons, leading to a more aggressive military posture against Hezbollah. This displacement, coupled with the ongoing threat from Hezbollah's enhanced military capabilities, has created a volatile security environment.

Hezbollah has significantly enhanced its military capabilities since 2006, amassing over 120,000 stand-off weapons and improving its force design, including light infantry, anti-tank capabilities, air defense, and an extensive UAS arsenal. Its involvement in the Syrian civil war has further honed its military skills and provided access to advanced weaponry, making it a formidable adversary for Israel.

Hezbollah's violations of United Nations Security Council Resolution 1701 have exacerbated the conflict. By stationing forces in restricted zones and launching attacks on Israeli positions, Hezbollah has escalated the situation, prompting a strong Israeli military response. The resolution, which calls for Hezbollah's disarmament and withdrawal from the border region, has been largely ignored, leading to increased tensions.

Hezbollah's strategic objectives include the destruction of Israel and the defense of Lebanon, while also seeking broader popularity within Lebanon Shiite community only. Its enhanced military capabilities and experience pose a significant threat to Israel, despite Israel's technological and firepower advantages. Hezbollah's tactical use of anti-tank missiles and UAVs has increased the intensity of the conflict, challenging Israel's security infrastructure.

Israel faces several strategic options: returning to deterrence, engaging in all-out war, conducting limited war, or pursuing coercive diplomacy. Each option carries significant risks and implications. Returning to deterrence may stabilize the situation temporarily but may not address the underlying threats. Engaging in all-out war could neutralize Hezbollah but at a high cost in terms of casualties and regional instability. Limited war could degrade Hezbollah's capabilities without a full-scale conflict, while coercive diplomacy, led by the United States, aims to manage the crisis through negotiations.

The United States plays a crucial role in preventing an all-out war through coercive diplomacy. By leveraging its influence and advocating for diplomatic solutions, the U.S. seeks to manage the crisis and prevent further escalation. However, the effectiveness of these efforts is contingent on the cooperation of all parties involved and the broader geopolitical dynamics in the region. Although Biden's paralyzing policy, reminiscent of the failed strategies of Jimmy Carter and Obama in appeasing the mullahs in Tehran, is ineffective and provides no tangible benefits for

Israel.

Hezbollah faces significant strategic dilemmas. While it remains a potent military force, its legitimacy within Lebanon is waning due to the country's ongoing political and economic crises. Iran, its primary backer, is urging Hezbollah to expand its operations against Israel and support militant groups in Iraq, Yemen, and other countries. However, Hezbollah must balance its commitment to Iran's foreign policy with its need to maintain domestic support and avoid actions that could lead to all-out war.

Hezbollah's close relationship with mullah's theocratic regime Iran is central to its operations. As Iran's most successful proxy, Hezbollah serves as a key component of Tehran's regional strategy, providing military support and training to other Iranian-backed groups. Despite differing religious backgrounds, Hezbollah and Hamas have found common ground under Iran's "Axis of Evil." Their cooperation has intensified, particularly in response to the ongoing conflict with Israel.

The current conflict between Israel and Hezbollah has significant regional implications. The potential for a broader conflict involving other Iranian proxies in Syria, Iraq, and Yemen remains a concern. Israel's continued military operations against Hezbollah and other Iranian-backed groups could lead to a wider regional war, destabilizing the Middle East further.

The escalating conflict between Israel and Hezbollah represents a critical juncture in the broader geopolitical dynamics of the Middle East. With heightened tensions, increased military capabilities, and complex political landscapes, both sides face significant challenges and risks.

The role of international actors, particularly the United States, in managing this conflict through diplomacy and coercive measures will be crucial in determining the future stability of the region.

As the situation evolves, the potential for a broader war remains a significant threat, underscoring the need for sustained diplomatic efforts and strategic foresight. The involvement of regional powers, including Iran, further complicates the conflict, with Tehran's support for Hezbollah adding to the volatility. The U.S. and its allies must navigate a delicate balance, applying pressure to deter further aggression while encouraging dialogue to de-escalate tensions. Moreover, Indeed, the risk of a military attack on the nuclear and missile facilities of the Islamic Republic is now felt more acutely than ever before.

Ultimately, the path to stability in the region lies in a multifaceted approach that combines diplomatic engagement, strategic deterrence, and humanitarian assistance. The international community must remain vigilant and proactive, working towards a resolution that prevents further escalation and promotes long-term peace and security in the Middle East.

61
FANNING THE FIRES: THE ISLAMIC REPUBLIC'S GLOBAL TERROR CAMPAIGN

The structure of the mullahs' regime in Tehran, notorious for its proliferation of terror, operates multiple terrorist groups across the Middle East. Regrettably, there is a palpable lack of genuine intent among both regional countries and Western powers, notably the United States, to dismantle this pernicious force. Ironically, these same nations engage in negotiations and even promote these malign actors in Western media, contributing to a disconcerting normalization of terror.

Western media outlets frequently refer to figures like Ali Khamenei with the undeserved title of "Ayatollah," which translates to "Sign of God." This irony begs the question: Which divine being would sanction terrorism that Khamenei represents? Engaging with terrorists—malevolent individuals who thrive on chaos and destruction—yields no benefits. Yet, we observe years of fruitless Western negotiations with the mullahs' regime in Tehran, adorned with photo ops that symbolize these diplomatic failings.

Despite losing hundreds of soldiers in the fight against terrorism sponsored by the Islamic Republic of Iran, and enduring terrorist attacks on their own soil, Europe and America seem to lack a lesson learned. The West fails to recognize how its actions embolden the regime, even as the Islamic Republic continues its international campaign of terror, kidnapping, embassy attacks and other provocations. It is unclear what further atrocities the Islamic Republic must commit to awaken the world from this oversight.

The Intelligence and military apparatus of the Islamic Republic cunningly crafts narratives or fabricate irrelevant and false rumors that find their way into Western media, furthering their agenda. Even American think tanks and universities grant platforms and positions to known terrorists, a troubling testament to a misguided understanding of freedom of expression. As if the more murderous and criminal you are, the more popular you become. Even the families of Islamic Republic officials freely roam in the West and America.

These oversights and naïveté have rendered the global landscape perilously insecure. The Islamic Republic's terror network, akin to a plague, spreads across the Middle East, Europe, Africa, and Latin America, yet the 21st century world seems paralyzed by indecision on how to address this threat. The persistence of radical Islam and Islamic terrorism poses one of the greatest threats to global peace, yet there remains a significant segment of the international community that turns a deaf ear to these realities.

World-renowned intelligence agencies like the CIA spend months on end prioritizing peace talks over decisive action against terrorist entities like Hamas. It appears future generations may look back on our era astonished at our appeasement of bloodthirsty terrorists. This century, however, seems bereft of answers.

The Islamic Republic maintains clandestine diplomatic channels with both the US and Israel while simultaneously orchestrating terror attacks globally. It seems the regime holds the world hostage, playing a dangerous game with global stability. Even as Tehran engages in public diplomacy, it fosters a network of terror that destabilizes regions far beyond its borders. However, the Islamic Republic lacks the defensive and military capability to confront the US and Israel. . China and Russia, along with their puppet North Korea, manipulate their servants in Tehran. However, Tehran continues its enmity towards America, the West, and Israel.

The White House, over recent years, has shown a lack of strategic initiative to counter the Tehran regime's destructive influence. Iranian lobbyists , apologists and stooges operate freely in Washington, further complicating the narrative and enabling the regime's propaganda machine, funded unwittingly by American taxpayers.

In actuality, The Islamic Republic's lobbies in Washington are actively operating, and even Persian-language media funded by American taxpayers, supposedly to promote democracy, are under the control and influence of the Islamic Republic. These agents broadcast their propaganda from televisions and radios—from Prague and Washington to Los Angeles.

The Islamic Republic has mobilized all its terrorist branches. Shiite terrorists affiliated with Iran in Iraq have initiated drone attacks on Israel, and Hezbollah has started launching rockets. Both actions are instigated by the IRGC and Quds Force under Khamenei. In recent days, the Islamic Republic awaited the end of Arbaeen and the ideological display it entails. As soon as that curtain falls, the next stage of warfare and missile and drone launches will commence. It seems that the officials of the Islamic Republic derive psychological satisfaction from threatening Israeli and American officials with death in front of the media. Essentially, the psyche of terrorists is restless and unhealthy.

A regime thirsty for bloodshed, lawlessness, explosions, destruction, and displays of savagery does not understand the language of diplomacy, and peaceful coexistence with it in today's world is impossible. It is unrelated to the culture, history, and civilization of the Iranian people. In fact, the mullahs, with the help of terrorists, have occupied Iran.

Today, as the Islamic Republic orchestrates a broad spectrum of terror, the world watches, waiting for the next act in this grim theater of war. The question remains: How long will the international community tolerate the existential threat posed by the regime in Tehran?

From today, global news agencies, like the showcasing of a new action movie in cinemas worldwide, vividly reflect news related to the warmongering of the Islamic Republic and its terrorist branches like Hezbollah, Hamas, Houthis, and Popular Mobilization Forces... They prepare for public mourning for the potential elimination of Hamas and the killing of its leaders in Tehran, accompanied by critiques filled with advice and vain hopes for peace.

Israel has no choice but to surgically remove this malignant growth for its survival, but the snake's head is in Tehran, and until its head is cut off, this futile spectacle continues. The world, amidst Islamic terrorists, is restless, and the situation does not bode well...

It is time for the global community to wake up and take decisive action. The stakes are too high, and the cost of inaction is too great. We must confront this menace head-on, with all the tenacity and resources at our disposal, before it further engulfs the world in its dark shadow.

62
SHAM ELECTIONS: IRAN IS UNDER THE RULE OF A JUNTA

Overview of the Current Situation

Iran is currently grappling with severe internal crises and external challenges, firmly under the stringent control of the mullahs often described as main supporters of terrorism. Recently, the regime has orchestrated staged intra-mafia disputes, likely to divert public attention from more pressing issues. Ali Khamenei, acting as the "Godfather" within this mafia-like structure, oversees candidates who vie for power and influence in a highly corrupt system. This oppressive rule has ensnared Iranian society, trapping it in malignant cycles of manipulation and control.

The regime of mullahs in Iran announced the approved six candidates—or more accurately, those favored by Khamenei and the IRGC. Campaigning for these candidates will commence and will continue for 15 days. The winner will replace Ebrahim Raisi, who was killed in a helicopter crash in May.

The Regime's Leadership Dynamics

Khamenei is focused on perpetuating the regime's survival, actively searching for a "revolutionary" figure— someone who does not shy away from suppression and bloodshed— and a "jihadist," implying readiness for plunder and to commit corruption. Despite acknowledging the dire national situation, the candidates shirk responsibility for it, attributing no blame to themselves despite their active involvement in both domestic and international operations. Regardless of their factional affiliations, all candidates are committed to preserving the regime's corrupt structure, with their disputes amounting to nothing more than superficial disagreements. This pervasive corruption has deeply permeated every level of the regime.

Public Disillusionment and Regime Propaganda

The Khamenei regime has failed to uplift public expectations and remains steadfast in its refusal to retreat or to moderate its authoritarian stance. The regime's repression apparatus commits atrocities with impunity. Overwhelmingly, the public perceives Khamenei not as wise or sacred, but as deeply flawed and criminal.

The candidates present no viable solutions, offering instead a legacy marred by murder, oppression, and deceit. Their titles and promises are broadly viewed as fraudulent, lacking appeal, character, dignity, or legitimate status. During election seasons, the public engages in political satire, crafting jokes or punctures the regime's inflated portrayal of its values and leadership, indicating widespread disdain for the hollow grandeur projected by Khamenei.

Election Farce and the Illusion of Democracy

The regime's electoral process in Iran is nothing more than a mere show, a facade reminiscent of the performative republicanism seen in dictatorships like those of Saddam Hussein or Qaddafi. There is no democracy or genuine public voting within this theocratic dictatorship; the elections are neither free nor competitive, but rather deeply deceitful processes tightly controlled by Khamenei. He ensures that only loyal, obedient candidates, often from the IRGC (such as Qalibaf, Jalili), the Basij (such as Zakani) or the Ministry of Intelligence, MOIS (Pourmohammadi), are poised to emerge victorious from the so-called ballot box. Noticeably, all these dishonorable candidates are prepared to suppress and massacre the Iranian society in the national uprising against the regime, and will stop at nothing to preserve the mullahs' regime. The display of these six candidates indicates the regime's will to suppress domestically and support terrorism internationally.

Speculation and predictions are rampant in Iranian society, where All candidates, more committed to irrational populistic slogans than substantial policies, await their turn to serve Khamenei. The kleptocratic and corrupt regime needs to display numbers and candidates to sustain the facade of sham elections.

Khamenei personally holds the key to the Guardian Council, whose review process for qualifying candidates is notoriously opaque and arbitrary. Yet, official regime narratives and propaganda carry little weight with the public, who, recognizing the futility, manipulation, and deceit of these orchestrated elections, often opt for boycott or derision.

In oppressive regimes, humor becomes a potent tool for

public dissent, piercing through the facade of authority. Iran's current climate mirrors past communist regimes where humor was a subtle form of rebellion against stifling regime. Despite severe repression, the Iranian people find solace in humor, using it as a tool to undermine the regime's legitimacy and expose its inherent faults and vulnerabilities.

Ironically, after enduring numerous crackdowns, Iranian society has largely decided to boycott all the regime's charades. It is estimated that only about 10 to 15% of the Iranian population will participate in the elections. Nonetheless, the regime's propaganda machinery will likely try to display a participation rate of around 45 to 55%, which are undoubtedly fabricated figures.

Military Dominance and the Direction of Governance

Iran's ruling military is increasingly visible on the global stage. Under Khamenei's directive and bolstered by military and security forces, the regime is transitioning towards a militaristic dictatorship, shrouded in religious despotism. Dominated by the IRGC, Basij, and Ministry of Intelligence Service (MOIS), these groups' members are being groomed as puppets, perpetuating the regime's tyranny and its oppressive policies. Thus, the foreseeable future shows no signs of deviation from this trajectory: the mullah's regime is poised to continue its autocratic rule, stifling any potential for democratic change or progressive reform.

The military's pervasive control over the country's key institutions—including the presidency, parliament, and various security councils—further solidifies this shift, marginalizing any attempts at reform and further alienating the Iranian populace. Iranians view their rulers as part of a corrupt power mafia that denies them any genuine governance choices. The entire sky over Iran acts as the ceiling of a vast prison, containing 90 million inmates.

International Perspective and Isolation

Amid escalating confrontations with Western powers over nuclear issues and a lack of transparency with the UN, Iran's international relations have become increasingly strained. The military junta's refusal to engage in constructive diplomacy, coupled with its persistent obstinance, has pushed Iran into isolation, with its economy teetering on the brink of collapse, and its populace poised on the verge of civil unrest.

The regime's actions have deepened its international isolation and economic downturn, further aggravated by a lack of diplomatic efforts. Despite this, the junta remains resolute, receiving substantial support from major global players like Russia and China, who provide the backing necessary to sustain its oppressive mullah's regime in Iran. Essentially, the military rulers are more focused on consolidating their power domestically than addressing international concerns.

Human Rights Violations and Civil Unrest

The regime's response to opposition is characterized by severe repression of any form of dissent, whether it manifests as civil disobedience or outright militancy. In essence, the regime increasingly tightens its grip, harshly suppressing any dissenting voices.

Security forces regularly quell protests with violence, leading to widespread human rights violations, including arbitrary detentions, torture, and extrajudicial killings. The media and intellectual communities endure relentless persecution and censorship. Many activists and intellectuals have been imprisoned or subjected to even harsher penalties, underscoring the regime's deep-seated fear and intolerance of any critique or challenge.

Global Implications and Conclusion

The global community's response to Iran's regime has been tepid, marked by ineffective sanctions and diplomatic pressures failing to alter the junta's trajectory. The regime's economic mismanagement and isolationist policies have precipitated a crisis that not only threatens the stability of Iran but also poses significant risks to regional peace and global security.

As Iran continues under Khamenei's iron-fisted rule, its path towards a militarized, theocratic dictatorship becomes alarmingly apparent. This junta regime and its trajectory presents a dire threat not only to the Iranian people but also to regional peace and international stability, necessitating a robust and concerted global response to mitigate further deterioration and promote positive change in Iran and beyond. In actuality, the mullahs' regime intends to display democracy and legitimacy fraudulently, but the will of the Iranian people is to boycott the mullahs' circus.

63

THE IRANIAN PEOPLE REJECT WAR, BUT THE REGIME SEEKS IT.

The Islamic Republic of Iran stands on the precipice of collapse. After 45 years of tyranny, terrorism, and corruption, the regime faces mounting internal pressure from a disillusioned and oppressed populace, while its external ambitions of regional dominance and ideological war with Israel have only isolated it further. The future of the region, particularly the delicate balance between war and peace, hinges on how the coming months play out. The Iranian people, already fed up with a regime that has brought them nothing but misery, may finally be nearing their breaking point. For Israel, this moment presents both a grave threat and a golden opportunity—to decisively weaken the regime and potentially help usher in a new chapter for Iran.

The Iranian People's Struggle
For decades, the Islamic Republic regime has ruled Iran

with an iron fist, relying on fear, suppression, and barbarism to maintain its grip on power. The regime's ideology, rooted in Khomeinism, has fostered an environment where dissent is crushed, freedoms are curtailed, and life resembles that of a nation held hostage. The Iranian people, subjected to this tyranny, have no interest in the wars their government wages in their name.

The people of Iran are victims of the regime's warmongering. They never asked for a war with Israel or the broader West, yet for 45 years, they have been forced to endure the consequences of a government more interested in exporting revolution and terrorism than in the welfare of its own citizens. The Iranian regime has dragged the country into a mire of international isolation, crippling sanctions, and economic despair. The vast majority of Iranians do not support this war, nor do they harbor any enmity toward Israel or its people.

A Regime Built on Terrorism and Repression

The Islamic Republic came to power through a combination of deceit, manipulation, and violence. Its leaders, including the Ali Khamenei, have consistently used terrorism as a tool to maintain control, both domestically and internationally. From Hezbollah in Lebanon to Hamas in Gaza, the regime has extended its reach through a network of proxy terrorist organizations, destabilizing the Middle East while maintaining a facade of resistance against the West and Israel.

Yet this very strategy is unraveling. The regime's reliance on violence has not only alienated the international community but has also isolated it from its own people. Iranians see through the regime's propaganda, and their anger is palpable. Protests against the regime are frequent, and the regime's brutal crackdowns only further ignite the flames of dissent.

Internally, the regime has systematically oppressed its citizens, curtailing freedoms, imprisoning political opponents, and fostering a climate of fear. Economically, the country is in ruins, with rampant poverty, inflation, and unemployment. The Iranian people are suffocating under the weight of a government that cares more about exporting terror than addressing the needs of its citizens. Externally, the regime's aggressive posturing has led to multiple conflicts and a deepening isolation on the world stage.

Israel's Struggle Against a Terrorist State

While the Iranian regime has continuously provoked conflict with Israel, it is important to remember that Israel's conflict is not with the Iranian people. Israel's struggle is with the leadership of the Islamic Republic, which has consistently sought to undermine its existence through terrorism and proxy wars. Since the establishment of the Islamic Republic, the mullahs have worked tirelessly to instill hatred for Israel and the West, framing themselves as defenders of the muslim states, even as they impoverish and brutalize their own citizens.

Israel, facing missile and drone attacks orchestrated by the Iranian regime, has been forced to defend itself repeatedly. These provocations are not isolated incidents—they are part of a broader ideological war that the mullahs are waging against modernity, democracy, and the West. The regime's ultimate goal is to undermine Western civilization and establish a Shiite caliphate, with Israel being a prime target of this delusional ambitions.

But Israel is not willing to accept this. Faced with an existential threat from a regime that openly calls for its destruction, Israel has no choice but to strike back. The continued provocations from Tehran, including the firing of missiles and the orchestration of terror attacks through its proxies, have left Israel no alternative but to defend itself by dismantling the Iranian regime's terrorist networks.

The Options for Israel

As the situation escalates, Israel is faced with a range of options to neutralize the threat posed by the Iranian regime. First, Israel could continue to strategically dismantle the regime's terrorist arms in the region, such as Hezbollah, Hamas, and the Houthis. However, this decisive approach, though effective in curbing the immediate threat, may not be enough to change the broader regional dynamic or significantly weaken the regime itself.

The second option, and arguably the more decisive one, would be to directly target key figures within the regime. Eliminating thugs like Khamenei and senior military commanders such as Salami, Hajizadeh, and Qa'ani would strike at the heart of the regime's power structure. Such actions would not only disrupt the regime's military and ideological leadership but could also spark a domestic uprising within Iran. The Iranians, who have long suffered under the regime's oppression, could see this as an opportunity to rise up and overthrow the mullahs once and for all.

The final option would involve targeting the regime's nuclear and military infrastructure directly. The regime's nuclear ambitions are a grave concern for Israel, and a decisive strike on these facilities could neutralize the threat once and for all. The elimination of Iran's nuclear capabilities would be a significant blow to the regime's prestige, both domestically and internationally. It would also send a clear message to the mullahs that their pursuit of regional domination through terror and intimidation will not be tolerated.

The Role of the Iranian People

While Israel's actions are crucial in neutralizing the external threat posed by the regime, the real hope for lasting change lies with the Iranian people. They are the ones who will ultimately decide the future of Iran. The Iranian people have endured decades of suffering under the Islamic Republic, but their resolve remains strong. They yearn for freedom, democracy, and a future where Iran is no longer defined by terrorism and repression.

The regime's collapse, while inevitable, will not come without a fight. The mullahs will cling to power for as long as they can, using every tool at their disposal to suppress dissent. However, the Iranian people are ready. They have already shown their willingness to rise up against the regime, and with the right external support—whether through sanctions, diplomatic pressure, or military action—they could finally topple the regime and reclaim their country.

A Shared Future of Peace

The regime's time is running out. Its war with Israel, and indeed with the entire civilized world, has only hastened its demise. The Iranian people are fed up with a regime that offers them nothing but repression and misery, and they are ready for change. For Israel, the coming months represent a critical moment in history—a chance to not only defend itself from the regime's terror but also to help create the conditions for a new, free, and democratic Iran.

The collapse of the Islamic Republic will not only bring peace and stability to the Middle East but also restore hope and dignity to the Iranian people. It is a golden opportunity that history has presented, one that must not be squandered. For the sake of both nations—and indeed, for the future of the region—the mullahs' regime must be dismantled. Only then can the people of Iran and Israel celebrate not as adversaries, but as partners in peace and progress.

64
IRAN'S SHAM ELECTIONS: A THREAT TO U.S. AND ISRAEL INTERESTS

The potential second presidency of Donald Trump is causing considerable anxiety within the Iranian regime, which is fervently preparing for this possibility by seeking to preserve its oppressive system and ensure a smooth succession from Khamenei to his son. Driven by Khamenei's delusional ambition of expanding the Shia Crescent and challenging the global order, Iran is aligning itself more closely with China and Russia, further exacerbating its international isolation.

For Ali Khamenei and his heir, orchestrating a seamless transition after Khamenei's demise to uphold the Islamic Republic's doctrinal governance remains their paramount objective. This singular goal underscores the despotic nature of Iran's religious leadership, which continues to lean heavily on China and Russia while maintaining its antagonism towards the West, the United States, and Israel.

The Facade of Democracy
In the annals of political theater, few spectacles rival the farcical charade that is Iran's presidential elections. As the nation gears up for yet another orchestrated display of "democracy," the ruling clerical establishment's sole objective remains the preservation of its iron-fisted grip on power and the perpetuation of its archaic system of religious despotism.

The carefully curated slate of candidates, handpicked by the Guardian Council, is a motley crew of swindlers, fools, and stooges, each one a loyal servant to the regime's interests. Dissenting voices are swiftly disqualified, ensuring that the outcome is predetermined, a mere formality in the grand scheme of things. Voter turnout, whether high or low, is inconsequential to the ruling elite. Official figures are routinely inflated through a well-oiled propaganda machine, projecting an illusion of legitimacy to the outside world. The reality, however, is far more sobering, with genuine participation estimated to be a paltry 10-15% of the electorate.

Internal Dynamics and the Presidential Selection
The candidates, meticulously vetted and selected by the Guardian Council, are predominantly from the Islamic Revolutionary Guard Corps (IRGC) or the Ministry of Intelligence. This selection underscores a continuity in Iran's policy of militaristic and clerical dominance, with each candidate demonstrating unwavering loyalty to Khamenei's overarching vision.

Michael Morell's alarming assertion in *Foreign Affairs* that "The U.S. is on the brink of facing a significant terrorist threat," resonates deeply in this context. This narrative parallels the ignored warnings prior to 9/11, painting a foreboding picture of the consequences of underestimating the signals emanating from Iran. The regime's persistent support for networks like the Islamic Resistance, amid preparations for a possible Trump presidency, highlights a steadfast commitment to its long-standing strategies of regional and global disruption.

The Reformist Mirage and the Public Discontent

Even the so-called "reformists," once hailed as harbingers of change, have been co-opted into the system, pledging allegiance to Khamenei in a desperate bid to remain within the regime's fold. Their promises of moderation ring hollow, as they too are mere pawns in the grand game of power, their aspirations for reform sacrificed at the altar of self-preservation.

The Regime's Descent into Authoritarianism

As the protests of the past seven to eight years have demonstrated, the chasm between the regime and the people of Iran has grown ever wider. International isolation, coupled with the regime's conflict with Israel and its support for terrorist groups across the Shiite Crescent, have further eroded its credibility and legitimacy.

Khamenei, the self-proclaimed "Supreme Leader," cuts a pathetic figure – a vindictive, narcissistic, performative, and delusional clown, clinging to the status quo with a desperation that borders on the absurd. His preferred choice for the presidency is likely to be a candidate from the ranks of the Islamic Revolutionary Guard Corps (IRGC) or the Ministry of Intelligence and Security (MOIS), further entrenching the regime's authoritarian grip.

The next president will undoubtedly be chosen from among the candidates from the IRGC or the Ministry of Intelligence, as the IRGC is adamant about not weakening its Islamic terrorism network (Islamic Resistance) in any way. The regime has drawn its swords; it has no intention of compromising.[2] The presidential debates in Iran are set to be broadcast on the regime's television shortly. It's important to note that the primary audience for the candidates is not the Iranian public, but rather Khamenei himself. The candidates are keen on winning his favor by any means necessary.

As Iran seemingly transitions towards a junta-like regime, the ten critical aspects defining this shift include military dominance, authoritarian mullah rule, heightened suppression of opposition, centralized power, drastic curtailment of freedoms, rigorous control of information and censorship, utilization of military force, mafia-style economic dominance, rampant human rights violations, and continued international isolation.

The Path Forward: Regime Change or Perpetual Oppression

It is vital to recognize that both the regime's hardliners and the so-called moderates are merely two sides of the same coin, endorsing suppression, terrorism, and propaganda. The prevailing discourse of regime change significantly outweighs the rhetoric of electoral participation in this authoritarian theatre. The Iranian populace, largely indifferent and disenchanted, seeks alternatives beyond the stagnant and unyielding dichotomy of reformists and hardliners. The regime's quest is self-preservation, but Iranian society has already moved beyond both factions, with genuine support for the regime likely not exceeding 15%.

As Iran teeters on the brink of becoming a full-fledged military junta, the writing is on the wall. The regime's stranglehold on power, its suppression of dissent, its control over information and censorship, its human rights violations, and its international isolation are all hallmarks of a system that has long since lost its legitimacy.

The discourse of "overthrowing and regime change" has become the rallying cry for a populace that has grown weary of the empty promises and hollow rhetoric of the ruling elite. The Iranian people have spoken, and their message is clear: they reject the circus of sham elections, the charade of reform, and the false dichotomy between hardliners and moderates.

It is time for the world to recognize that the path forward for Iran lies not in the perpetuation of this farcical charade, but in the embrace of genuine democratic change, one that respects the will of the people and restores their fundamental rights and freedoms. As the world watches, the imperative for recognizing and addressing the true challenges posed by Iran's strategic maneuvers becomes not just necessary but urgent.

65
IRAN'S CROSSROADS:
A REGIME PARALYZED BY ITS OWN FAILURES

In recent years, the Islamic Republic of Iran has faced a series of escalating confrontations with Israel that have left the regime humiliated and increasingly vulnerable. Despite the fiery rhetoric and threats emanating from Tehran, the regime's inability to respond effectively to Israel's provocations has exposed deep fissures within its military-security apparatus and highlighted its broader strategic failures. As the corridors of power within Iran's ruling system, the Velayat-e Faqih, scramble to determine a course of action, it is becoming increasingly clear that the regime is at a critical crossroads—one where any misstep could lead to its sudden and catastrophic collapse.

At the heart of the Islamic Republic's ideology lies the destructive doctrine of Khomeinism, built on hollow slogans, intimidation, terrorism, and an obsessive focus on anti-Israel and anti-American rhetoric. Over the past 35 years under the tyranny of Khamenei, and the preceding 10 years under Khomeini, the regime's core leadership has relentlessly worked to expand its network of transnational terrorism. They have pursued the creation of a Shiite empire at any cost, unleashing chaos across the Middle East. In every terrorist operation, countless Israeli and American soldiers, as well as Europeans, have lost their lives. Behind the scenes, despite the public displays of hostility, clandestine negotiations with the United States continue through specific lobbying channels.

This regime's ultimate aim is to propagate Shiism and construct a nuclear-armed Shiite empire. To preserve its grip on power, it is willing to commit any atrocity. The path to regime change in Iran will be fraught with challenges, but it is essential for the stability of the region and the world. For Israel, confronting Islamic terrorism and the terror networks tied to the Islamic Republic is a matter of survival. However, if the world fails to support regime change in Iran, the cost will be high. The unchecked spread of radical Islam and Islamic terrorism across the globe is but one of the many dangers. The religious octopus that fuels this terror has its head in Tehran—a wild, 85-year-old cleric who holds the fate of the region in his grasp.

The roots of the regime's current paralysis lie in a complex web of internal conflicts, strategic miscalculations, and a pervasive fear of the superior military power of Israel and its ally, the United States. The Iranian regime, long reliant on its network of Islamic terrorism and proxy groups to project power across the region, now finds itself with few viable options. The internal discord within the regime's military and security sectors has further weakened its ability to present a united front against external threats. This lack of cohesion is compounded by the regime's failure to coordinate effectively with regional powers and countries on which it depends for support, leaving it increasingly isolated on the international stage.

One of the most glaring issues facing the regime is its inability to accurately assess different scenarios and their potential consequences. The leadership in Tehran has repeatedly underestimated the costs and ramifications of its actions, leading to a series of strategic blunders. This is particularly evident in its dealings with Israel, where the regime's threats and displays of anger have done little more than expose its impotence. The regime's fear of engaging directly with a militarily superior Israel, coupled with the realization that any conflict could quickly spiral out of control, has left it in a state of strategic paralysis.

The regime's limited options for action are further constrained by the growing discontent within Iranian society. Decades of oppression, economic mismanagement, and corruption have eroded the regime's legitimacy, and the Iranian people, weary of the endless cycle of conflict and repression, are increasingly unwilling to rally behind the government's foreign policy adventures. This lack of popular support has left the regime isolated, not only internationally but also domestically, further limiting its ability to respond to external threats.

Since July 31, eight days have passed, and the regime's leadership remains paralyzed, unable to formulate a coherent response to Israel's latest provocations. The corridors of power within the Velayat-e Faqih system are filled with confusion and disorientation, as the leadership grapples with the realization that it is no longer in control of its own destiny. The regime's fear of entering into a direct conflict with Israel is palpable, as the leadership understands that such a move could lead to the sudden collapse of the entire government. The power structure in Iran now stands at a crossroads, uncertain which direction to turn and whether or not to take the gamble of war.

The current crisis is a stark reminder of the inherent instability of authoritarian regimes. For decades, the Islamic Republic has ruled through a combination of repression, ideological manipulation, and strategic alliances with regional powers. However, the regime's ability to maintain control is increasingly being called into question. The internal conflicts and strategic miscalculations that have plagued the regime in recent years are not merely isolated incidents but rather symptoms of a deeper, systemic failure.

As the regime's leadership contemplates its next move, it must grapple with the harsh reality that its options are rapidly dwindling. The era of impunity, where the regime could act without fear of significant repercussions, is coming to an end. The strategic environment in the Middle East is shifting, and the Islamic Republic is no longer the dominant player it once was. The regime's fear of Israel's military power, combined with its inability to galvanize domestic support for its foreign policy, has left it vulnerable and exposed.

In the end, the Islamic Republic's current predicament is a reflection of the broader challenges facing authoritarian regimes worldwide. Such regimes, by their very nature, are prone to strategic miscalculations and internal discord. Their reliance on repression and ideological control to maintain power often blinds them to the realities of their strategic environment, leading to catastrophic failures. For the Islamic

Republic, the crossroads at which it now stands represents a moment of truth—a moment where the regime must decide whether to continue down the path of confrontation or to seek a new, more pragmatic approach to its foreign policy.

The inevitability of history suggests that regimes that fail to adapt to changing circumstances are doomed to collapse. The Islamic Republic of Iran, with its rigid ideological framework and increasingly isolated position, may soon find itself on the wrong side of history. As the regime's leadership grapples with the decision of whether to engage in a potentially suicidal conflict with Israel, it must also confront the possibility that its time in power may be drawing to a close. The crossroads at which the regime now stands is not just a strategic dilemma but a moment of existential crisis— one that will determine the future of the Islamic Republic and its place in the world.

66

ISRAEL'S WAR WITH THE WORLD'S TERRORIST SUPREME LEADER

Israel has not had and does not have a war with the people of Iran. Generally, the Iranian historical nation also has no enmity or war with Israelis. The Islamic caliphate of the Shiite Jurist (Velayat-e Faqih) is seeking a civilizational war with Israel and wants to destroy the West, civilization, and modernity with savagery and Islamic terrorism.

Regrettably, the Iranian people are also victims of vicious and barbaric rulers who have tied the name of civilized Iran and monarchy to Islamic terrorism for 45 years, and perhaps for many years after the collapse of the mullahs' regime, this shame will remain for the name of Iran due to crimes, oppression, and savagery, and gradually the Iranian nation will restore the name of Iran to its historical credit and reputation.

In the public opinion of patriotic Iranians, no one is with the mullah's regime, and no one has been or is seeking war. But the warmongering mullah and criminal ayatollahs, from the very first day, based the destructive ideology of Khomeinism on this terrorism, terror, horror, and destruction. And Israel has no choice but to break the bones of the Iranian regime for its survival and existence, a warmongering ideological regime that has so far fired hundreds of missiles and drones towards Israel and incited thousands of Islamic terrorists against the innocent people of Israel under different names cunningly. And naturally, Israel does not accept this humiliation that from time to time, the Shiite mullah fires against it. The one responsible for this destruction and turmoil in the Middle East region is none other than a savage and arrogant mullah named Ali Khamenei, who is willing to sacrifice all of Iran and Iranians for his absurd ideology.

Khamenei is someone who has translated the book of the father of Islamic terrorism (Sayyid Qutb) into Persian, and the terrorist organization of the Muslim Brotherhood has been among his supporters. Khamenei is someone for whom homeland, nation, and country have no importance; he is an agent of the country's destruction. Otherwise, Israel has not had and does not have a war with the Iranian nation and the country of Iran, and for Khamenei, only the transnational network of Islamic terrorism and the Shiite crescent are important.

These days, in response to the terrorist and missile attacks of the Islamic Republic, there are several options before Mossad and Israel government:

1. Do not show an immediate and serious reaction. And over time, cut off the terrorist arms of the Islamic Republic.

Which, due to the credibility of the name of Israel, such a reaction is humiliating and degrading for the Jews.

2. Eliminate the officials of the Islamic Republic or target the hated and corrupt military and political villains and thugs within the Velayat-e Faqih who have taken a historical nation hostage. Perhaps a few days of propaganda excitement and political mourning will be provided, but no one will shed a tear for Islamic terrorists, and it will even cause the national uprising of the Iranian nation to rise against their own thugs and remove the shadow of war from their beloved land. Because this war is not the war of the Iranian nation and Israel, it is the war and savagery of the Islamic Republic regime. And the elimination of any of the terrorist officials of the Islamic Republic will certainly cause the joy of the Iranian nation and the humiliation of the religious dictatorship. Weakening power in the structure of the Islamic Republic has a sweet fruit, and that is the new regional order that will bring stability and security in its wake, and the dominant regional power without the Islamic Republic will lead to security and stability. The disintegration of the Islamic Republic is also one of the wishes for the states of the Persian Gulf region, which are Israel's new allies. Just as no one shed a tear for Haniyeh and Nasrallah, the elimination of Khamenei and the villains of the IRGC and MOIS or Quds Force will have no result other than a wave of pride.

3. Destroy nuclear and chemical facilities and electrical and military infrastructure and economic mafias of the Revolutionary Guards. The only playing card of the Islamic Republic is this Islamic terrorist network under the name of Islamic resistance, but certainly, the terrorist mullah, with having nuclear weapons, will be a great loss for Israel and the land of the Jews. Twice this savage and delusional and

warmongering regime in Iran has fired hundreds of missiles against Israel, if it had an atomic bomb, it would certainly have fired that too, and if it has it, it will certainly fire it too. Basically, the Shiite mullah has no shame from crime and savagery.

The Islamic Republic, by provoking its translational terrorist networks and increasing tension, has been openly seeking a full-scale war for years, but the world had closed its eyes and ears to seeing and hearing the realities, and today, little by little and without a doubt, America's foot will be opened to the fateful dispute. It has become clear to the military and intelligence institutions of America and Israel that the Islamic Republic has neither military nor intelligence capability. It does not have the courage and ability to face military confrontation, and certainly China and Russia will not throw themselves in for the sake of savage mullahs with America and the West and Israel.

Israel is forced to seriously terminate this threat and cancerous tumor. Both Democrats and Republicans in America will stand behind Israel, and American security and military institutions have also given hundreds of casualties and victims due to the warmongering of the terrorist loving mullahs since 1979, but the White House has never had the bravery to openly express desire for regime change in Iran. Saying this phrase has always been among the forbidden words or taboos in Washington, although American military and inetelligence commanders are also in daily contact with Israel and know that peaceful coexistence with the Shiite mullah is not possible.

But Israel has a better understanding of the essence of the mullahs' republic. It knows that it has only remained based on three principles of foreign propaganda, internal repression, and foreign servitude. Mossad also does not adjust its strategy for the arena of Democrats and Republicans elections, they know that this government in Tehran is anti-human, anti-peace, anti-stability, and anti-tranquility. To guarantee survival, Israel has no choice but to remove this threat, and the Islamic Republic is also a weak, mafia and corrupt, isolated, hated government without popular support.

The fall of the Islamic Republic is more possible than any other moment in history. The intensity of Israel's military attack will change the equations in the Middle East. And the more the display of humiliation and inability of the Islamic Republic, the more the flame of internal uprisings in Iran will be. Of course, no one asks Israel to determine the leadership of the movement. The Iranian nation will choose their desired government themselves, currently in the current situation, the primary goal of the Iranian nation and Israel is the destruction of the mullahs' regime. In these sensitive historical days, Israel is a partner of the distressed and anxious and waiting Iranian nation.

It is a golden opportunity that history has given to Israel to address concerns about the Islamic Republic's nuclear program. From Netanyahu's meeting with the Crown Prince Reza Pahlavi, and then the message to the Iranian nation last week, it showed that Israel has purposefully and with a plan and strategy entered this game with combined attacks in a reciprocal war with terrorist mullahs. And it will certainly destroy the Islamic Republic's nuclear program at the current historical juncture, and it may be the only and loneliest historical opportunity for Israel! Simultaneously with the destruction of military and nuclear facilities, and the elimination of Islamic Republic officials, the Islamic

Republic will disappear like snow in summer. A large part of the Iranian people will finish the work with a national uprising. After breaking the terrorist arms of the Islamic Republic in the region - such as Hamas and Hezbollah and the Houthis and Hashd al-Shaabi - this government with the illusion of a nuclear program will not get anywhere.

Surely, the Israeli intelligence agencies know that the situation of the Islamic Republic is not good, and the life glass of this regime breaks at any moment.

67
ISRAEL'S NEXT FRONT? IRAN, HEZBOLLAH, AND THE COMING WAR IN LEBANON

The recent surge in hostilities along the Israel-Lebanon border marks a significant escalation in the longstanding conflict between Israel and Hezbollah. Over the past six months, nearly 400 Lebanese, including around 70 civilians and three journalists, have been killed, and 90,000 Lebanese civilians have been displaced from approximately 100 towns and villages along the border. The Israeli Defense Forces (IDF) have responded to Hezbollah's intensified rocket and drone attacks with significant military force, leading to widespread destruction in Lebanese villages and olive groves.

Hezbollah's barrage of rockets and drones into northern Israel has aimed to support Hamas and demonstrate its military capabilities. The group's attacks have targeted Israeli military installations and civilian areas, causing significant damage and prompting a robust retaliatory campaign from

Israel. The conflict has created a humanitarian crisis, with thousands forced to flee their homes and communities. Displaced Lebanese civilians face harsh living conditions, lacking basic necessities such as food, clean water, and medical care.

This renewed conflict underscores the volatile nature of the Israel-Hezbollah relationship and marks one of the most severe escalations since the 2006 war. The current situation highlights the persistent threat Hezbollah poses to Israel and the significant impact of Israeli military responses on Lebanon. As both sides continue aggressive military actions, the risk of a full-scale war looms large, with potentially devastating consequences for the entire region. International efforts to mediate and de-escalate the situation are crucial in preventing a broader conflict that could further destabilize the Middle East.

Post-2006 Deterrence and Recent Tensions

Since the 2006 war, a period of relative calm and deterrence has prevailed between Israel and Hezbollah, punctuated by occasional skirmishes but no full-scale conflicts. However, the situation has become increasingly fragile, especially after the psychological impact of the October 7, 2024, attacks, which have heightened Israeli insecurity. This heightened state of alert has led to higher levels of PTSD, depression, and anxiety among the Israeli population, compelling the government to adopt a more aggressive stance against perceived threats.

Increased Israeli Risk Tolerance

Israel's risk tolerance has shifted dramatically in response to the perceived threat from Hezbollah, which is now better armed and trained than Hamas. Despite a preference for diplomatic solutions, Israeli officials are prepared to undertake unilateral military action if necessary. The IDF's recent deployment of 100,000 troops to the northern border underscores Israel's readiness to escalate the conflict to secure its borders and ensure the safety of its citizens.

Displacement and Security Concerns

The conflict has displaced over 150,000 people on both sides of the Israel-Lebanon border. Israeli leaders face intense domestic pressure to improve security and resettle displaced persons, leading to a more aggressive military posture against Hezbollah. This displacement, coupled with the ongoing threat from Hezbollah's enhanced military capabilities, has created a volatile security environment.

Hezbollah's Military Improvements

Hezbollah has significantly enhanced its military capabilities since 2006, amassing over 120,000 stand-off weapons and improving its force design, including light infantry, anti-tank capabilities, air defense, and an extensive UAS arsenal. Its involvement in the Syrian civil war has further honed its military skills and provided access to advanced weaponry, making it a formidable adversary for Israel.

Violations of UNSCR 1701

Hezbollah's violations of United Nations Security Council Resolution 1701 have exacerbated the conflict. By stationing forces in restricted zones and launching attacks on Israeli positions, Hezbollah has escalated the situation, prompting a strong Israeli military response. The resolution, which calls for Hezbollah's disarmament and withdrawal from the border region, has been largely ignored, leading to increased tensions.

Hezbollah's Objectives and Tactical Capabilities

Hezbollah's strategic objectives include the destruction of Israel and the defense of Lebanon, while also seeking broader popularity within Lebanon. Its enhanced military capabilities and experience pose a significant threat to Israel, despite Israel's technological and firepower advantages. Hezbollah's tactical use of anti-tank missiles and UAVs has increased the intensity of the conflict, challenging Israel's security infrastructure.

Israeli Objectives and Options

Israel faces several strategic options: returning to deterrence, engaging in all-out war, conducting limited war, or pursuing coercive diplomacy. Each option carries significant risks and implications. Returning to deterrence may stabilize the situation temporarily but may not address the underlying threats. Engaging in all-out war could neutralize Hezbollah but at a high cost in terms of casualties and regional instability. Limited war could degrade Hezbollah's capabilities without a full-scale conflict, while coercive diplomacy, led by the United States, aims to manage the crisis through negotiations.

U.S. Involvement and Coercive Diplomacy

The United States plays a crucial role in preventing an all-out war through coercive diplomacy. By leveraging its influence and advocating for diplomatic solutions, the U.S. seeks to manage the crisis and prevent further escalation. However, the effectiveness of these efforts is contingent on the cooperation of all parties involved and the broader geopolitical dynamics in the region.

Hezbollah's Strategic Dilemmas

Hezbollah faces significant strategic dilemmas. While it remains a potent military force, its legitimacy within Lebanon is waning due to the country's ongoing political and economic crises. Iran, its primary backer, is urging Hezbollah to expand its operations against Israel and support militant groups in Iraq, Yemen, and other countries. However, Hezbollah must balance its commitment to Iran's foreign policy with its need to maintain domestic support and avoid actions that could lead to all-out war.

Hezbollah's Relationship with Iran and Hamas

Hezbollah's close relationship with Iran is central to its operations. As Iran's most successful proxy, Hezbollah serves as a key component of Tehran's regional strategy, providing military support and training to other Iranian-backed groups. Despite differing religious backgrounds, Hezbollah and Hamas have found common ground under Iran's "Axis of Resistance." Their cooperation has intensified, particularly in response to the ongoing conflict with Israel.

Future Prospects and Regional Implications

The current conflict between Israel and Hezbollah has significant regional implications. The potential for a broader conflict involving other Iranian proxies in Syria, Iraq, and Yemen remains a concern. Israel's continued military operations against Hezbollah and other Iranian-backed groups could lead to a wider regional war, destabilizing the Middle East further.

***

The escalating conflict between Israel and Hezbollah represents a critical juncture in the broader geopolitical dynamics of the Middle East. With heightened tensions, increased military capabilities, and complex political landscapes, both sides face significant challenges and risks. The role of international actors, particularly the United States, in managing this conflict through diplomacy and coercive measures will be crucial in determining the future stability of the region.

As the situation evolves, the potential for a broader war remains a significant threat, underscoring the need for sustained diplomatic efforts and strategic foresight. The involvement of regional powers, including Iran, further complicates the conflict, with Tehran's support for Hezbollah adding to the volatility. The U.S. and its allies must navigate a delicate balance, applying pressure to deter further aggression while encouraging dialogue to de-escalate tensions.

Moreover, the humanitarian impact of the conflict cannot be overlooked. The displacement of tens of thousands of civilians and the destruction of infrastructure exacerbate the already dire conditions in Lebanon. Addressing these humanitarian concerns through international aid and support is essential to mitigate the suffering of the affected populations.

Ultimately, the path to stability in the region lies in a multifaceted approach that combines diplomatic engagement, strategic deterrence, and humanitarian assistance. The international community must remain vigilant and proactive, working towards a resolution that prevents further escalation and promotes long-term peace and security in the Middle East.

68
ISRAEL'S NEXT FRONT? IRAN, HEZBOLLAH, AND THE COMING WAR IN LEBANON

The recent surge in hostilities along the Israel-Lebanon border marks a significant escalation in the longstanding conflict between Israel and Hezbollah. Over the past six months, nearly 400 Lebanese, including around 70 civilians and three journalists, have been killed, and 90,000 Lebanese civilians have been displaced from approximately 100 towns and villages along the border. The Israeli Defense Forces (IDF) have responded to Hezbollah's intensified rocket and drone attacks with significant military force, leading to widespread destruction in Lebanese villages and olive groves.

Hezbollah's barrage of rockets and drones into northern Israel has aimed to support Hamas and demonstrate its military capabilities. The group's attacks have targeted Israeli military installations and civilian areas, causing significant damage and prompting a robust retaliatory campaign from

Israel. The conflict has created a humanitarian crisis, with thousands forced to flee their homes and communities. Displaced Lebanese civilians face harsh living conditions, lacking basic necessities such as food, clean water, and medical care.

This renewed conflict underscores the volatile nature of the Israel-Hezbollah relationship and marks one of the most severe escalations since the 2006 war. The current situation highlights the persistent threat Hezbollah poses to Israel and the significant impact of Israeli military responses on Lebanon. As both sides continue aggressive military actions, the risk of a full-scale war looms large, with potentially devastating consequences for the entire region. International efforts to mediate and de-escalate the situation are crucial in preventing a broader conflict that could further destabilize the Middle East. Meanwhile, the Quds Force is actively agitating and persuading these terrorist groups to escalate tensions.

Since the 2006 war, a period of relative calm and deterrence has prevailed between Israel and Hezbollah, punctuated by occasional skirmishes but no full-scale conflicts. However, the situation has become increasingly fragile, especially after the psychological impact of the October 7, 2024, attacks, which have heightened Israeli insecurity. This heightened state of alert has led to higher levels of PTSD, depression, and anxiety among the Israeli population, compelling the government to adopt a more aggressive stance against perceived threats.

Israel's risk tolerance has shifted dramatically in response to the perceived threat from Hezbollah, which is now better armed and trained than Hamas. Despite a preference for diplomatic solutions, Israeli officials are prepared to undertake unilateral military action if necessary. The IDF's recent deployment of 100,000 troops to the northern border underscores Israel's readiness to escalate the conflict to secure its borders and ensure the safety of its citizens.

The conflict has displaced over 150,000 people on both sides of the Israel-Lebanon border. Israeli leaders face intense domestic pressure to improve security and resettle displaced persons, leading to a more aggressive military posture against Hezbollah. This displacement, coupled with the ongoing threat from Hezbollah's enhanced military capabilities, has created a volatile security environment.

Hezbollah has significantly enhanced its military capabilities since 2006, amassing over 120,000 stand-off weapons and improving its force design, including light infantry, anti-tank capabilities, air defense, and an extensive UAS arsenal. Its involvement in the Syrian civil war has further honed its military skills and provided access to advanced weaponry, making it a formidable adversary for Israel.

Hezbollah's violations of United Nations Security Council Resolution 1701 have exacerbated the conflict. By stationing forces in restricted zones and launching attacks on Israeli positions, Hezbollah has escalated the situation, prompting a strong Israeli military response. The resolution, which calls for Hezbollah's disarmament and withdrawal from the border region, has been largely ignored, leading to increased tensions.

Hezbollah's strategic objectives include the destruction of Israel and the defense of Lebanon, while also seeking broader popularity within Lebanon. Its enhanced military capabilities and experience pose a significant threat to Israel, despite Israel's technological and firepower advantages. Hezbollah's tactical use of anti-tank missiles and UAVs has increased the intensity of the conflict, challenging Israel's security infrastructure.

Israel faces several strategic options: returning to deterrence, engaging in all-out war, conducting limited war, or pursuing coercive diplomacy. Each option carries significant risks and implications. Returning to deterrence may stabilize the situation temporarily but may not address the underlying threats. Engaging in all-out war could neutralize Hezbollah but at a high cost in terms of casualties and regional instability. Limited war could degrade Hezbollah's capabilities without a full-scale conflict, while coercive diplomacy, led by the United States, aims to manage the crisis through negotiations.

The United States plays a crucial role in preventing an all-out war through coercive diplomacy. By leveraging its influence and advocating for diplomatic solutions, the U.S. seeks to manage the crisis and prevent further escalation. However, the effectiveness of these efforts is contingent on the cooperation of all parties involved and the broader geopolitical dynamics in the region.

Hezbollah faces significant strategic dilemmas. While it remains a potent military force, its legitimacy within Lebanon is waning due to the country's ongoing political and economic crises. Iran, its primary backer, is urging Hezbollah to expand its operations against Israel and support militant groups in Iraq, Yemen, and other countries. However, Hezbollah must balance its commitment to Iran's foreign policy with its need to maintain domestic support and avoid actions that could lead to all-out war.

Hezbollah's close relationship with Iran is central to its operations. As Iran's most successful proxy, Hezbollah serves as a key component of Tehran's regional strategy, providing military support and training to other Iranian-backed groups. Despite differing religious backgrounds, Hezbollah and Hamas have found common ground under Iran's "Axis of Resistance." Their cooperation has intensified, particularly in response to the ongoing conflict with Israel.

The current conflict between Israel and Hezbollah has significant regional implications. The potential for a broader conflict involving other Iranian proxies in Syria, Iraq, and Yemen remains a concern. Israel's continued military operations against Hezbollah and other Iranian-backed groups could lead to a wider regional war, destabilizing the Middle East further.

***

The escalating conflict between Israel and Hezbollah represents a critical juncture in the broader geopolitical dynamics of the Middle East. With heightened tensions, increased military capabilities, and complex political landscapes, both sides face significant challenges and risks. The role of international actors, particularly the United States, in managing this conflict through diplomacy and coercive measures will be crucial in determining the future stability of the region. As the situation evolves, the potential for a broader war remains a significant threat, underscoring the need for sustained diplomatic efforts and strategic foresight. The involvement of regional powers, including

Iran, further complicates the conflict, with Tehran's support for Hezbollah adding to the volatility. The U.S. and its allies must navigate a delicate balance, applying pressure to deter further aggression while encouraging dialogue to de-escalate tensions.

Moreover, the humanitarian impact of the conflict cannot be overlooked. The displacement of tens of thousands of civilians and the destruction of infrastructure exacerbate the already dire conditions in Lebanon. Addressing these humanitarian concerns through international aid and support is essential to mitigate the suffering of the affected populations.

Ultimately, the path to stability in the region lies in a multifaceted approach that combines diplomatic engagement, strategic deterrence, and humanitarian assistance. The international community must remain vigilant and proactive, working towards a resolution that prevents further escalation and promotes long-term peace and security in the Middle East.

69
KHAMENEI'S CALL FOR TOTAL WAR AGAINST ISRAEL

Khamenei's theatrical speech on Friday, 10/4/2024, in Tehran, amid tight security measures—though the IRGC thugs who ordered the missile attack on Israel were notably absent—offered nothing new, just the same repetitive and meaningless rhetoric. His speech was more directed at the Arab countries and the regime's transnational terrorist network, perhaps in an attempt to boost their morale. His audience was not the Iranian people but rather the so-called "Islamic Ummah," which seems to exist nowhere in the real world.

Although his remarks were from a position of weakness, lacking any logic or rationality, he deluded himself into sounding powerful. He attempted to downplay Israel's strikes on Islamic terrorism while stubbornly defending the IRGC and Quds Force, ignoring the fact that Hamas and Hezbollah have been decimated, with the Houthis and the Popular Mobilization Forces following the same path.

Khamenei's speech made it clear that he has no intention of retreating from his path of domestic oppression and regional warmongering. He wants to meddle in Arab world affairs under the guise of Islam, seeking to intrude on the security of Arab and Islamic countries in the Middle East and North Africa. He dreams of reshaping the region with his "Shia Crescent," a vision that is utterly unattainable. Among the Arab countries, particularly in the Persian Gulf, he holds no credibility. Aside from Qatar, which sides with Tehran due to the Muslim Brotherhood, Hamas, and Islamic terrorism, no Arab country has any affection for this lunatic dictator.

One striking observation was that Khamenei did not address the Iranian people at all. This cruel and bloodthirsty dictator knows he has no legitimacy or popularity among the people of Iran. The people despise the so-called Islamic Ummah and Islamic Resistance (Islamic terrorism and Islamic Jihad). In the eyes of the Iranian nation, Khamenei is a lunatic and anti-Iranian dictator who has taken the entire country hostage, dragging Iran into the abyss of destruction until the day his religious tyranny collapses. The people in Iran ask, why is war necessary? What do Hezbollah, Hamas, the Popular Mobilization Forces, and the Houthis have to do with us Iranians? But for Khamenei, the lives and opinions of the Iranian people have never mattered. Even as missiles were being fired, planes continued to fly over Iran's skies.

In his speech, Khamenei spewed lies, but it became clear to the world that beyond his empty boasts, he defended Hamas's crimes. It is now evident that he was the instigator and mastermind behind the October 7th atrocity. Today, he officially declared that every blow against Israel is a service to humanity. Sadly, this nonsensical and meaningless rhetoric was even broadcast by BBC Persian and BBC English.

In the end, it must be said that the command of evil in the Middle East lies in Khamenei's hands. As the people of Iran hope, may Khamenei be Israel's next target. With his elimination, the world will one day celebrate a joyful occasion in contemporary history. He is a stooge, harmful to humanity—a deadly virus.

Moreover, what we are witnessing in the Middle East is perhaps the most significant counterterrorism campaign of the 21st century—a defining moment in history. In this effort, Israel has neutralized more terrorists from the U.S. most-wanted list than the U.S. has since 9/11, specifically targeting key Islamic terrorists. The world should recognize the unwavering resolve of Mossad, the IDF, and the determined leadership of Prime Minister Netanyahu. I hope Israel continues by dismantling the transnational terrorist network of the mullahs' regime in Iran.

70
KHAMENEI'S ASSASSINATION THREATS AGAINST TRUMP

Shiite clerics, or mullahs, primarily use one tool to impose their beliefs and outrageous opinions: the display of barbarism, savagery, and murder. Throughout the history of Islamic caliphates, critics and opponents have been systematically slaughtered, poisoned, assassinated through conspiracies, or eliminated in staged incidents. The entire 1400-year history is fraught with crime, betrayal, and murder, with all dishonorable Islamic caliphates perpetually ready to commit any crime and perform any brutal act to preserve their survival and maintain their wealth and power.

The Islamic Republic's regime in Tehran is no exception. This outlaw regime came to power through terrorism, murder, bombings, manslaughter, bank robberies, highway robberies, infanticide, etc., and has continued in power these past 45 years through murder and terrorism. During these 45 years, they have consistently killed every opponent and critic. They know no bounds in committing crimes.

Even if there are criticisms of Trump's patriotic presidency, insisting on killing him is a display of savagery. These days, Trump remains a target and prey for Islamic terrorists because he killed one of the most murderous, despised, and brutal terrorists of the Shiite Islamic caliphate in Tehran – Qasem Soleimani – leaving only a ring behind (January 3, 2020). He also killed Abu Bakr al-Baghdadi – the caliph of ISIS (October 27, 2019).

Khamenei is also a codger, senile, bankrupt, despicable, vengeful, and psychotic mullah. This geezer falsely considers himself Lord's representative on Earth. When Trump's first cabinet was critical of him and eliminated his top terrorist, Khamenei's hatred flared. He has repeatedly attempted to murder this famous figure from American presidential history. Then he would rub his hands and lips together, meekly and hypocritically calling it a divine promise. Khamenei always easily orders the slaughter of his opponents. However, the bitter point is that American media, in an unwise, fantastical, and nauseating manner, still call this pathetic, psychotic terrorist an Ayatollah, meaning a sign of God! ... And no one knows which God's representative a bloodthirsty terrorist is.

Now, in a startling revelation, the U.S. Department of Justice has unveiled a murder-for-hire plot allegedly orchestrated by the Islamic Revolutionary Guard Corps (IRGC) to assassinate high-profile targets in the United States, including President-elect Donald Trump. This plot not only highlights the IRGC's extreme commitment to retribution for the 2020 death of Qasem Soleimani but also signals a disturbing escalation of Iran's aggressive tactics on U.S. soil, further intensifying national security concerns.

The primary individual charged in this case, Farhad Shakeri, an IRGC asset, allegedly coordinated with two New York-based associates, Carlisle Rivera and Jonathon Loadholt, to surveil and potentially eliminate an Iranian-American dissident. In a shocking twist, Shakeri also reportedly received directives to plan the assassination of President-elect Trump, marking a brazen move by the IRGC to extend its reach and vengeance-driven agenda far beyond Iranian borders.

The IRGC's Expanding Reach

The Iranian regime's continued reliance on its paramilitary arm, the IRGC, to target dissidents and adversaries outside Iran is not a new tactic. However, the allegations that it sought to assassinate a former U.S. president reflect an audacious new level of aggression. The IRGC thugs, already designated by the U.S. as a foreign terrorist organization (FTO), appears to be acting with near impunity, driven by a long-standing goal to avenge Soleimani's death and intimidate voices that oppose the regime.

The Iranian regime has historically suppressed dissent internally, with an iron-fist approach that includes arrests, torture, and forced confessions. But as the diaspora grows, and as voices of dissent find platforms internationally, Tehran's strategy has evolved to include overseas surveillance, abductions, and now, murder plots. Shakeri's recruitment of criminal associates on U.S. soil to aid in these operations demonstrates the IRGC's resourcefulness and highlights the vulnerabilities that adversarial powers can exploit within American borders.

The U.S. Response and Future Security Challenges
Attorney General Merrick Garland and FBI Director Christopher Wray have emphasized that the U.S. will not tolerate Iran's attempts to endanger American citizens or threaten its leaders. Their strong statements reinforce the Biden administration's stance that any attempt to harm a U.S. official would be viewed as an act of war. While these assertions are crucial in asserting U.S. commitment to protecting its citizens, this latest incident raises troubling questions about what Iran's continued provocation means for U.S.-Iran relations and the stability of international diplomacy.

The DOJ's successful disruption of the plot underscores the effectiveness of U.S. intelligence and law enforcement agencies in countering international terrorism. However, as adversarial powers increasingly seek to bypass traditional warfare by employing shadow operatives within the U.S., the DOJ, FBI, and other agencies face a daunting challenge in preemptively identifying and neutralizing such threats.

Implications for U.S.-Iran Relations
The implications of this foiled plot for U.S.-Iran relations are profound. Amid Iran's increased financial investment in retaliation against perceived enemies, it is clear that diplomatic channels have done little to curb Tehran's provocations. President-elect Trump's previous administration took a hardline approach, withdrawing from the Iran nuclear deal and reimposing sanctions. Although the Biden administration pursued a more diplomatic path, Iran's unwavering hostility suggests a need for a recalibrated U.S. approach to contain Iran's influence and protect American lives.

The Global Threat of State-Sponsored Terrorism

Iranian regime's plans to assassinate an American president, silence dissidents, and target citizens underscore the reality that terrorism, when state-sponsored, can evade geographical limits. For Iran's regime, avenging Soleimani's death has become a rallying cry that seemingly justifies cross-border violence. For the international community, this is a clarion call to confront the dangers of state-sponsored terrorism and to prevent these tactics from becoming normalized.

As Iran's regime intensifies its operations abroad, democratic nations must address the threats posed by authoritarian states that extend their violence beyond borders. Only by standing firm against such provocations can the U.S. and its allies preserve security, defend human rights, and protect the freedom of their citizens to speak out against oppression. The case of Farhad Shakeri and his associates is a sobering reminder that vigilance is more crucial than ever in a world where adversarial regimes willing to go to extreme lengths to settle scores.

***

It should be considered that American Intelligence agencies have gradually realized that they must eliminate the network of lone wolves and dormant terrorist cells of the mullahs within the United States and Latin America - which are mostly directed from inside the Islamic Republic's embassies in the South American hemisphere. Otherwise, the order issued from Tehran will not be subject to a statute of limitations, and this vicious snake will eventually spill its venom.

I have said time and time again that the snake's head is

in Tehran, and with the elimination of Khamenei - like Bin Laden, Abu Bakr al-Baghdadi, Nasrallah, Qasem Soleimani, and Mughniyeh - nothing but peace will be achieved in the world, and inevitably, no one will cry for a terrorist. A lunatic dictator who for years has masked himself with a fake sacred face and kills innocent people easily. The snake's head must be separated from its poisonous body.

71
KHAMENEI: IRAN'S WARMONGER LEADING THE NATION TO RUIN

The clerical regime in Iran, led by Ali Khamenei, has driven the nation to the edge of an inferno. Under his rule, Iran has become a pariah in the international arena, known for terror, repression, and a relentless, misplaced obsession with Israel's destruction. As Khamenei stokes the flames of conflict, his unyielding fanaticism reveals not a leader of vision or strength, but a delusional fanatic whose policies hinge on blind hatred, a warped interpretation of faith, and a willingness to sacrifice his people and region to achieve a dangerous agenda.

The roots of this tumultuous trajectory were laid in 1979 when the Shia mullahs rose to power in Iran with the assistance of Marxist and Islamist terrorist groups—all tied to the KGB. Even the followers of the popular and unruly Prime Minister Mosaddegh, who could be compared to

Ahmadinejad in his populism, joined forces with Khomeini, transforming into foot soldiers for a brutal theocracy. Many of them trained in the terrorist camps of Yasser Arafat, where they mastered sabotage and extremism, hiding behind Mosaddegh's portrait while ardently praying for Khomeini's theocratic dreams to succeed.

In 1980, Khomeini ignited one of the region's most devastating conflicts, a brutal eight-year war with Iraq. Though Saddam Hussein, with Arab backing, was ready for peace after the first two years, Khomeini dragged the conflict on, indifferent to the catastrophic toll on Iranian and Iraqi lives. His intent was neither righteous nor self-sacrificial but rooted in his Islamic caliphate's ambition. Khomeini's priorities lay in consolidating his influence, a ruthless goal that led him to even broker covert arms deals with Israel and the United States—the infamous Iran-Contra affair of 1985-1986. He auctioned off Iran's wealth to prolong the fight, all while quelling internal opposition. His slogan, "Allahu Akbar," echoed even as his forces killed thousands, mirroring Saddam's mantra on the other side of the border. Khomeini believed himself a divine emissary, but in the end, he drank his own "cup of poison" and perished in 1989.

One would have hoped that with Khomeini's death, the bloodthirsty drive of Iran's leadership might fade. But his successor, Khamenei, took up the mantle, declaring himself God's representative and the supposed deputy of the twelfth Imam, a mythic figure rooted in Shia superstitious. Khamenei's illusions have led him to push the Middle East into an abyss of war, spreading devastation in Yemen, Iraq, Syria, and Lebanon. His regime has left a trail of ruins and massacres wherever it has intervened. At home, Khamenei's quest for power has come at the expense of Iran itself, driving the country into bankruptcy and ruin. This warmongering, deceitful, and brutal leader's support for the recent events of October 7 illustrates the regime's unyielding thirst for conflict. Just as Iran's Islamic IRGC supported al-Qaeda in 2001, Khamenei's Islamic Republic continues to nurture similar groups today. Khamenei's boasts and threats, however, serve only as a facade of strength.

Inside Iran, Khamenei's reign has relied on a "success through spreading fear" strategy, enabling the mullahs to enforce years of brutal repression. Yet, barbarism and terror cannot build a stable foreign policy. When the regime orchestrated missile attacks on Israel, the mullah was exposed as a paper tiger, stripped of its supposed ferocity. In reality, despite the mounting tensions and frequent skirmishes between Iran and Israel, Khamenei lacks the courage for a full-scale confrontation and instead resorts to missile launches and inciting terrorist proxies to do his bidding.

Historically, tyrants like Khamenei have favored flatterers and sycophants who eagerly sing his praises, even crafting poetic fantasies of his supposed "conquests." Such praise inflates the regime's fragile ego, depicting Khamenei as a heroic figure whose army would supposedly march into Jerusalem by dawn, should he give the order. But these fantasies fall apart upon close examination. Why, if he is truly the "conqueror of wars," has he never led or won any?

While Iran is led by Khamenei, a snake poised to strike at any moment, the Iranian people themselves are not complicit in this aggression. The vast majority of Iranians do not harbor the mullahs' zeal for war or terrorism. Khamenei and his clerical elite have long used Iraq as a staging ground for attacks, often timed to align with politically sensitive moments, like the upcoming U.S. elections. The Quds Force, Iran's infamous paramilitary wing, leverages Shia networks in Iraq to exert influence, with silence from Arab, Sunni, and Kurdish factions, which could pose a threat to the region's fragile stability. Khamenei's grave miscalculation in provoking a potential war with Israel has set the Islamic Republic on a path to collapse, as its defense infrastructure lies in shambles, and its missile facilities stand defenseless and vulnerable.

Khamenei's contempt is, paradoxically, often greater toward his internal enemies—the dissatisfied Iranian populace—than toward foreign adversaries like Israel or the United States. He has shown an unrestrained willingness to crush dissent, branding his people as enemies if they refuse to support his deadly ambitions. The Iranian nation does not stand behind Khamenei; this is not their war, nor is it one they wish to fight. For many Iranians, any external act that challenges Khamenei's grip on power, such as an attack on his headquarters, might spark a glimmer of hope. After nearly 45 years of oppression, the idea of popular protests looms as a nightmare for the regime, while Iran's current leadership clings to power in its final throes.

Iran's situation is grim. Corruption and criminality among the regime's officials have drained the nation, with the world watching as Iran sinks further into the abyss. For decades, global leaders have placated this rogue state, choosing diplomacy over decisive action and wasting precious time. But the world can no longer afford such leniency; change is inevitable, and Israel's efforts to disrupt Iran's network of terror reflect this shift. The Iranian regime, a balloon inflated with its own propaganda, has begun to deflate. For the mullahs, there is no longer any hiding behind rhetoric and religion; Israel has seen through the facade and will not hesitate to remove this threat, regardless of the international political climate.

While Iran faces its greatest turmoil in decades, Khamenei and his propaganda machine downplay Israel's counterstrikes, trying desperately to mitigate the damage. Yet, doubts gnaw at the minds of the Islamic Republic's officials, who find themselves caught between fearing an escalation they cannot control and dreading the implications of appearing weak. Failing to respond to Israel could inflame hardliner pressures within Iran, stirring unrest and leading to accusations of capitulation from the regime's most fervent supporters.

Under Khamenei's rule, the Iranians live in a reality shaped by deceit, cruelty, and a sinister alliance of criminals who rob the nation of both its wealth and its humanity. Iran has been stripped of culture, wisdom, and intellectualism, with the criminal ayatollahs steering society toward superstition, violence, and ignorance. For 36 years, Khamenei's authoritarian rule has cast a dark shadow over the nation, fostering a culture where prejudice, vindictiveness, and ignorance take precedence over freedom and justice. There is no meaningful distinction between Khamenei, Abu Bakr al-Baghdadi, Osama bin Laden, Hassan Nasrallah, Yahya Sinwar, Ismail Haniyeh, and Qasem Soleimani—they all share the same doctrine of terrorism and oppression, their actions fueled by fanaticism and a disregard for humanity.

Israel has seen through the regime's bluster, understanding it as nothing more than a fragile facade. By disrupting the Iranian mullahs' terror network, Israel seeks to sever the regime's influence and further destabilize its grip. This mock empire, once exposed, will crumble. Whether it is Trump or Harris in the White House, the time for action is now, and Israel will not relent until this threat is eliminated.

Iran is in turmoil, with its propaganda machine faltering in the face of Israel's calculated responses to its provocations. The officials of the Islamic Republic may try to mask their growing panic, but the cracks are evident. They dread the consequences of further escalation, both politically and economically, while also fearing the backlash from hardline elements who expect unwavering aggression. As this vicious cycle continues, Khamenei's regime approaches its breaking point, while the Iranian people, weary and disillusioned, await the dawn of a new era.

72
KHAMENEI'S DICTATORSHIP AND PEZESHKIAN'S SERVITUDE ROLE

In the theater of Iranian politics, democracy serves merely as a grotesque masquerade. The recent elections, a grand charade meticulously staged to perpetuate the regime's dominance, drew a scant 10% to 15% of the electorate. This spectacle, steeped in intimidation and marred by violence, signals the continuity of despotism unless a profound transformation unfolds.

Iran's electoral ruse was crafted with dual purposes: it sought to sculpt international narratives while muffling the burgeoning domestic demands for transformation. A fresh onslaught of propaganda, aimed particularly at an American audience, attempted to veil the regime's savagery—a tyranny masquerading as governance. We must not be beguiled by this facade; beneath the guise of leadership lies nothing more than a mullahs' cabal.

Pezeshkian's rise, a scheme woven by Khamenei, casts him not as a beacon of reform but as a pawn entrenched in autocracy. His ascent only tightens the regime's stranglehold, intensifying the mechanisms of repression and bolstering the bastions of Islamic extremism, while hostility towards the West festers unabated.

Under Pezeshkian's guise of leadership, the landscape remains bleak. The regime's grip strengthens, ensuring the perpetuation of Islamic terrorism and its hegemony in the Middle East. The animosity towards America and Israel endures without wane. An informed leader in the U.S. must confront these truths. The figures propped up by the regime do not embody the Iranian will but serve the machinations of tyranny.

The entire political apparatus in Iran stands starkly against any notion of progress or reform. Khamenei's rule, an epitome of authoritarian control, smothers any semblance of hope beneath its oppressive weight. The electoral farce, a mere shadow play of democracy, showcases candidates who are but merchants of deception. Pezeshkian's 16 million votes, a mere fraction in a nation of 90 million, highlight the persistent shadow of religious despotism.

The schism within Iran's power echelons—between reformists and conservatives—serves only to perpetuate their dominion through ruthlessness. Though seemingly disparate, these factions are merely different faces of the same corrupt entity, entwined in deception and superficial reforms that yield no genuine progress.

Decades since Khamenei's controversial rise in 1981, the patterns of authoritarianism continue unabated. With

Pezeshkian's elevation, the regime's draconian practices persist—dissenters languish in prisons, and the state's terror reaches beyond its borders.

The groundwork for the regime's collapse is undeniably set, yet the voice of the Iranian populace is stifled, drowned out by the din of reformist propaganda. True change is a mirage as long as the existing order prevails, unchallenged by justice or the people's outcry for freedom.

As spectators and participants on the global stage, we must discern the reality behind this façade: a regime desperate to cling to control, terrified of its citizenry's potential for revolt. The electoral boycott has empowered the Iranian public, instilling a respect for their suffrage and a refusal to sanction their continued subjugation. The international community must remain vigilant; the touted change is but an illusion, a narrative spun to maintain a despotic rule that serves only the rulers.

Ultimately, the political masquerade in Iran, under the pretense of electoral democracy, is nothing but a regression—a tragic step back for a nation yearning for true reform and liberation from tyranny. The situation is ripe for change, yet constrained by an authoritarian grip that fears the voice of its people—a voice that, despite efforts to suppress it, resonates with an ever-growing demand to end the reign of terror.

73

KHAMENEI'S PAPER BOAT ON TURBULENT WATERS

Children often fold paper boats and float them in water, where they remain afloat until disturbed by waves. Similarly, Khamenei has kept his regime afloat for years through bluffing, grandstanding, and a facade of sanctity. Yet, the reality reveals that the Islamic Republic's paper tiger is soaked and on the verge of collapse. Behind the propaganda machine of the regime and its Western-affiliated reformist lobby lies a truth contrary to its claims of strength and resilience.

The regime's current efforts are focused on military exercises and maneuvers, designed to project an image of invincibility in the media. Today also marks the fifth anniversary of the IRGC's heinous crime of shooting down the Ukrainian passenger plane (January 8, 2002), an act following the death of Qasem Soleimani, the notorious Islamic terrorist commander of the Quds Force (January

3, 2020). Iranians have come to realize that as long as the Shiite mullahs and their centers of power persist, the nation's problems will remain unsolvable. As Persian poetry teaches, heroes break idols; similarly, this grotesque idol of the regime, which has sucked the lifeblood of Iranian society like a leech, must also be shattered. The Shiite mullahs have been a scourge on Iran's fertile land, preventing peace, humanity, and the rule of law.

In the modern 21st century, perhaps no country understands the mullahs' regime as deeply and accurately as Israel. During my research as a counterterrorism analyst in the Middle East, I have engaged professionally and socially with many experts in American, British, and Israeli intelligence agencies. Few possess the keen insight into the propaganda of the mullahs and Khamenei's cunning as my colleagues in the counterterrorism centers of Israeli military and Mossad. They remind me of General Patton, who defeated Rommel because he read his book. Similarly, Israel has read the "book of the mullahs," and its intelligence agencies, particularly Mossad, understand how they think. Alas, the U.S. and Europe lack this understanding and fail to recognize the tricks and deceptions of the Islamic Republic's regime.

Some American officials even accept speaking fees to participate in promotional events for pro-Khomeinist groups like the MEK, oblivious to their fraudulent nature. These individuals, tied to the 1979's Islamic-Marxist revolt, have no constructive solutions or credibility within Iranian society. Western intelligence agencies often overlook that groups like the MEK, Kurdish separatists, and other participants in the 1979 uprising have consistently failed in their policies, strategies, and actions, earning them no legitimacy among Iranians.

For instance, since the visit of Prince Reza Pahlavi—an influential and capable opposition leader—to Israel (June 2023), many masks have fallen. Most 1979 revolutionaries received their terrorist training in Palestine. However, Israel's intelligence agencies understand that working with honest, patriotic, and peace-loving individuals offers hope for a future Iran. Such collaboration ensures that after the potential collapse of Khamenei's regime, Iran's national talents can be harnessed, not squandered on violent, leftist ideologues filled with resentment and animosity.

The destructive ideological fervor of Khamenei and the IRGC is evident in their recent military maneuvers, ostensibly to intimidate Israel. Yet, the Iranian people see through this charade, recognizing that the regime, like a snowball under the summer sun, is melting away. It holds neither credibility nor popularity within Iran or the region. Israel's devastating strikes have severely weakened the regime's defenses, while Netanyahu's direct messages to the Iranian people are met with admiration akin to that of a national hero.

The criminal ayatollahs' dictatorship in Iran is deteriorating, with its own media acknowledging the dire state of the regime. A member of the Assembly of Experts recently admitted, "The Islamic Republic's time is up," and declared that "Iran is ready to explode."

The return of Trump, combined with Israel's partnership and Europe awakening from 46 years of complacency, has created a nightmare scenario for the regime. Meanwhile, the regime's U.S.-based lobbyists have been writing op-eds in Democrat-aligned media, advising Trump to re-engage in diplomacy with the terrorist-loving mullahs—essentially asking the world to repeat its past mistakes without understanding the regime's playbook.

No one appears willing to ask if the Iranian people want regime change to escape decades of misery since 1979. Meanwhile, those who ordered assassinations of figures like Netanyahu and Trump now engage in futile and absurd strategies, revealing their disconnection from reality

Now, they absurdly try to teach chess to a gorilla or put lipstick on a pig—actions as futile as their grasp of reality. The mullahs' very essence is inseparable from terrorism, chaos, sabotage, and deceit. Any attempt at diplomacy or dialogue with such entities only serves to legitimize their terror-driven agenda.

Ultimately, Khamenei's paper boat faces rising waves, drenched and crumbled. The regime's bluffs about daily military drills and countdowns to destroy Israel are no longer taken seriously. The stark reality of the Islamic Republic has become clear: after the destruction of its Islamic terror networks and Israel's dismantling of its defense systems, the regime clings to its last two cards—inciting its remaining transnational terror proxies (like the Houthis, Hashd al-Shaabi, and PKK) or declaring its nuclear capability.

Yet, despite its desperate propaganda campaigns, Iranian public opinion remains firmly against the regime, paralyzing its efforts. The regime's missile attacks against Israel have exposed its military weakness as hollow bravado.

This is a regime willing to endure any humiliation to cling to power but unashamed of committing atrocities to maintain its grip. However, this time, its efforts are futile—wet powder cannot ignite. Perhaps the global community, awakened in the 21st century, will rise against Khomeinism and Islamic terrorism, just as it opposed apartheid and communism in the 20th century. The world could once again see a time when the U.S. and Israel have embassies in Tehran, rekindling connections with Iran's rich culture, history, and civilization, reminiscent of the era of the late Shah of Iran, Mohammad Reza Pahlavi.

Failing this, even the Arab nations of the Persian Gulf may finally realize the futility of placing hope in corrupt regime-affiliated reformists, as they too face the looming specter of instability should the Islamic Republic persist.

74
LEFTISTS FEARING THE REGIME'S COLLAPSE IN IRAN.

Events in Iran could unfold at any moment. However, the Marxist and Islamic leftists who took part in the 1979 revolt have now positioned themselves as peace advocates, actively promoting it. Nevertheless, their primary concern is the collapse of the mullahs' regime, as they recognize that the majority of Iranians have rejected the destructive ideology of Khomeinism and the actions of the 1979 communist and Islamic terrorists who committed numerous crimes against Iran and the late Shah, resulting in their humiliation and loss of credibility in Iran's future.

Iranians are not free, living under a religious dictatorship known as the Guardianship of the Jurist. For 45 years, this historical nation has endured extreme tyranny. Life in Iran resembles slavery, marked by severe repression and exploitation, with the regime diverting all national interests towards terrorism while brutally suppressing even the mildest protests. Thousands of Iranians languish as political prisoners, and countless families have been shattered by the psychological strain imposed by this oppressive system. Over the last four and a half decades, the mullahs' regime has acted like a serial killer, instilling fear and terror, fabricating charges, and lying, while utterly disregarding any ethical standards for the Iranians. The regime wants to fence around society so that people do not see the free world. But the nation's anger with the regime has made it easier to circumvent censorship.

It is a ludicrous joke for a Shiite mullah, who trains Islamic terrorists, to claim they represent freedom and democracy. In the lawless state of Iran, there is no security, and the nation teeters on the brink of disaster. Communication from the regime comes in the form of bullets, with no other dialogue extended to the people. Fundamentally, the mullahs' regime harbors hostility toward both society and the nation of Iran. They have no desire for a society that is free, happy, or prosperous. A cocktail of injustice, oppression, humiliation, and destruction, coupled with pervasive false propaganda and antagonism towards the global community, has pushed Iranian society to the edge of eruption.

Corrupt and criminal elements within the Islamic Republic's regime, despite their fear of a national uprising and dread of collapse, continuously see a cohort of false, regime-backed opposition abroad attempting to sway Iranian public opinion and redirect the focus of protests. However, these efforts are in vain as the country deteriorates internally. There is no national consensus, and any minor spark of conflict gravely threatens the regime's survival due to the widespread resentment and fury among the populace. No signs of loyalty or cooperation with the regime are evident among the silenced majority. Optimistically, only 10 to 15% of the 90 million people might support the inscrutable regime. A brief exploration of Iranian social networks clearly reveals the deep-seated hatred the populace holds towards the illegitimate and unpopular mullahs' regime.

Despotism, autocracy, repression, censorship, and widespread poverty have plunged the country into a deep crisis and decline. Yet, the government remains proud of its military prowess—boasting missiles, drones, and a network of terrorism—and is increasingly eager to announce a nuclear capability. This ambition drives its hostilities and antagonism towards the entire Middle East and the Western world, further intensifying global tensions with war rhetoric and threats. However, their perception of power is delusional. Over the past 45 years, this approach has not only caused significant problems and incurred substantial costs but has also led to pervasive destruction. Countries like Iran, Iraq, Yemen, Syria, and Lebanon bear witness to this devastation, serving as stark examples of the regime's destructive impact.

Cunningly, the regime's propaganda machine claims to be liberating the Islamic world and purports to be striving to free Palestine and Gaza. Yet, this is merely historical manipulation. The regime lacks the military and security capability to achieve such feats, and it is also devoid of the necessary intellectual depth, ethical standing, and practical means to do so.

Currently, Iranian leftists who support terrorism—both Marxist and Islamic (pro-Khomeinist regime reformists)—are concerned about the potential collapse of the regime. They fear that an Israeli attack on Iran's nuclear, military, and chemical facilities could weaken the mullahs' government, spark a domestic uprising, and consign this despised regime to the dustbin of history, where it rightfully belongs.

Undoubtedly, the future of this regime is bleak. It lacks innovative and suitable solutions. There is no sign of development or growth. Iran is imploding from within. The regime's approach has been one of hostility towards its own people and creating a security crisis globally. Consequently, the government in Iran is at an impasse. The majority of the nation is actively seeking to overthrow the regime and is yearning for democracy.

The internal atmosphere of the country is akin to a war zone, yet the regime has not established any safe havens to protect the Iranian people. Particularly the younger generation is in search of a vibrant life, but the regime continues to pursue death and terror. The reality is that the unchecked and widespread power of the mullahs has pushed society to a breaking point, seeking alternatives amidst political paralysis, military inadequacy, diplomatic failures, economic collapse, and environmental devastation. Should there be an Israeli attack, the regime in Iran will face humiliation, a situation likely to embolden the populace to confront and destabilize the government further.

The regime of the criminal ayatollahs in Iran is morally and psychologically corrupt, yet leftists, aligned with the regime, seek to lull the awakened Iranian society into silence and submission. However, a government without the support of its people is destined to collapse. Despite enduring despotism and fear, the Iranian nation remains resilient, with nothing left to lose, as its identity and national pride were stripped away in the 1979 revolt.

Khamenei adheres to Shiite superstitions, myths, and religious falsehoods, comforting himself with the belief that he is paving the way for the emergence of Imam Zaman, even at the cost of the country's devastation. However, Iranian society, enlightened by intellectuals like Ahmad Kasravi—who was murdered by Khomeini's supporters, the Fadaian Islam, on March 11, 1946—has recognized these beliefs as fictitious and deceptive. Khomeini himself published the book "Velayat-e Faqih" in Beirut in 1969, advocating for an Islamic government grounded in the Guardianship of the Islamic Jurist and centered around the fabricated persona of Imam Zaman. This fabrication has emboldened them to view themselves as the perpetual rulers of Iranian society, unwilling to relinquish power. Nonetheless, Iranian society has progressed beyond these fabricated narratives.

Today, the influence of the mullahs in Iranian society lacks credibility and respect, and their nonsensical pronouncements fall on deaf ears as mosques stand empty. Yet, the Marxist left and the fanatical Islamic mullahs mirror each other, both steeped in outdated ideologies. However, the new generation in Iran is no longer enticed by prejudices, superstitions, and religious falsehoods. Perhaps Netanyahu's message to Iran's youth has ignited a spark of hope, inspiring them to courageously and independently reject the decrepit and destructive regime. Indeed, victory seems to await the Iranian nation as it forges a new path forward.

Today, Iranians fully understand who accepted radio equipment from Saddam Hussein, who obeyed KGB directives to send terrorists to train with Yasser Arafat, who established connections with Castro, and who received financial support from Gaddafi to fuel terrorism—it was Khomeini. Currently, numerous communists and Islamist thugs are abruptly declaring themselves patriots. However, this time around, Iranians are equipped with knowledge. Who knows, perhaps soon in Tehran and Jerusalem, the people of Iran and Israel will once again celebrate their friendship.

75
A TICKING TIME BOMB FOR THE MIDDLE EAST

The Middle East stands on the brink of an all-out war, primarily due to the machinations of Iran's ruling clerics, who have a notorious affinity for sowing chaos and crisis. These leaders are fundamentally opposed to peace, stability, and tranquility in the region. They consider any act of aggression against Israel and the United States as justified, displaying a blatant disregard for mercy, compassion, and humanity. Regardless of the presidency changes in Iran, the regime's support for Islamic terrorism remains steadfast, with Khamenei orchestrating attacks against Israel from behind the scenes. Sometimes, the denial of this fact by certain global media outlets seems absurd and laughable.

In the complex geopolitical landscape of the Middle East, Iran's influence is a perennial point of contention. Recent events have illuminated a particularly disturbing trend that involves Iran's leadership fostering alliances with known terrorist organizations, which significantly escalates regional tensions and posits Iran as a pivotal player in potential conflicts.

The recent validation of the so-called "reformist" Pezeshkian by Khamenei was swiftly followed by meetings with leaders of recognized terrorist organizations like the Palestinian Islamic Jihad (PIJ) and Hezbollah.

These interactions are more than diplomatic gestures; they are explicit demonstrations of Iran's strategy to extend its influence through proxy forces. The regime's president unabashedly defends Islamic terrorism and the clerical regime's sponsorship of such terrorist activities.

The roles of Iran's Ministry of Intelligence (MOIS), the Revolutionary Guards Corps (IRGC), and its Quds Force, under Khamenei's direct supervision, are well-documented and particularly alarming. The Quds Force has actively supported and collaborated with various Shia terrorist militias across the region, including the Houthis, Hashd, PIJ, and others, positioning them as major adversaries of Israel and other perceived foes. This not only destabilizes the Middle East but also places Iran at the core of potential widespread conflict.

Although the Islamic Republic also enjoys tacit approval from China and Russia, who are keen on challenging regional order, countries like Turkey—under its authoritarian leader Erdogan—support Islamic terrorist organizations like Hamas. The relationships among the Muslim Brotherhood, Turkey, the Islamic Republic, and Qatar in supporting terrorism are overt and official. Iran, along with Syria and North Korea, maintains warm relations with the terrorist group Hezbollah.

The possibility of a full-scale war remains high as these alliances and the resulting actions perpetuate regional unrest. Directed by Khamenei and often seen as a puppet of Russian interests, the Tehran regime increasingly poses a threat to both its neighbors and the broader stability of the Middle East.

As global tensions simmer, the connections between Tehran and terrorist activities demand a robust response from international powers. Iran's alliances with these groups highlight a strategic approach to regional dominance, leveraging proxies under the guise of religious and political objectives. This scenario casts a dire shadow over the region, hinting at an impending all-out war with Tehran at its heart, orchestrating discord.

The international community must wake from its slumber and address this threat decisively. The stakes are extraordinarily high, and the cost of inaction could be devastating—not only for the Middle East but for global peace and security. The time to act is now, to dismantle these alliances and reintroduce stability to a region long haunted by the specters of war and terrorism.

But the international community is asleep. There is no inclination to support regime change in Tehran, and until the head of the snake is cut off in Tehran, this crisis and chaos will remain in the region. In Tehran, criminals rule, and like during the Safavid era, they are busy committing every imaginable atrocity. These regional wars will only end when the Islamic Republic is dismantled. Otherwise, this grim and erosive tale will continue to claim victims.

76
FEAR OF MOSSAD: SHAKING IRAN'S INTELLIGENCE COMMUNITY

Israel hasn't claimed responsibility for eliminating Haniyeh. Mossad's threat has shaken the Islamic Republic's intelligence community. They can't counter Mossad and Israel, but rumors persist. For the mullahs, only propaganda counts; they claim to defeat Mossad in their delusions, but reality differs.

Assuming we accept the delusions of the Iran' regime and view the situation from their perspective for a moment that Mossad has executed one of the most astounding counter-terrorism operations globally. In Iran, ruled by Shiite mullahs and a hub for a sponsoring Islamic terrorism, the leaders staged a spectacle for themselves.

From this perspective, Mossad eliminated a significant figure in the Islamic terrorism network in Tehran. This took place in a highly secured area, guarded by the IRGC and the Ministry of Intelligence (MOIS). Telecom technology is key in modern operation. The day before Pezeshkian's presidency, the so-called Mossad's precise strike achieved three goals: it removed a major Hamas strategist, caused chaos among Iranian officials, and humiliated Iranian intelligence again. Now, how do we tell these delusional Mullahs amidst this rumor mill that Mossad has not yet claimed responsibility?

Over the past 50 years, SAVAK (during the Shah's reign), Mossad, and the CIA carried out many joint operations, greatly disturbing the Soviet Union and KGB. History couldn't foresee that 45 years later, Tehran's Shiite Caliphate regime neglecting its own country, and oppress protesters savagely, all while dreaming daily of destroying Israel and the US.

In today's Middle East, an irrational mullah, reminiscent of the cruel leaders of historical Islamic caliphates throughout history—from the Rashidun, Abbasid, Umayyad, Fatimid, Ottoman, ISIS, and beyond—delusionally declares himself Amir al-Mu'minin (Commander of the Faithful) and the global ruler of the Muslims. His entire efforts are focused on promoting Shiism, creating the Shia Crescent, and establishing a dangerous transnational terrorist network across Iraq, Syria, Lebanon, and Yemen. Under his leadership, these non-state actors operate under an umbrella dubbed the Axis of Islamic Resistance.

This malicious coalition has devastated four Middle Eastern capitals, with the Quds Force and the MOIS perpetrating atrocities in these four capitals. They even maintain terrorism training camps inside Iran. These malevolent forces bring nothing but destruction, darkness, and poverty wherever they go, squandering Iran's resources in their quest to build a Shia empire and confront Saudi Arabia.

To the Tehran authorities, absolutely, not even the security and stability of the Persian Gulf matter. They continue, under the pretense of defending Shiites, to incite chaos, deception, infiltration, and coups from Bahrain to Morocco. It is no longer surprising that on July 31, 1987, pilgrims were armed with intentions to bomb the Kaaba and blow it up. It was an international scandal that embarrassed Khomeini.

For instance, the Islamic Republic collaborates with the Muslim Brotherhood, Qatar, and Turkey to continuously support Hamas terrorists against Israel. Concurrently, they back the terrorist organization PKK to ensure that Turkey does not overshadow Iran's role or influence in this complex geopolitical game, or to prevent Syria's collapse. As well, they engage the Barzani tribe to distract Turkey. Alongside the PKK and Hezbollah, they facilitate drug trafficking, and with the Barzanis, they conduct money laundering. Moreover, they maintain collaborations with various Kurdish parties and organizations, regardless of their political stance.

Their sinister influence reaches into Africa, where they recruit, create terrorist networks, and operate from Sudan to other areas. The Islamic Republic also arms terrorist groups in Somalia, with its ties to Al-Shabaab growing unmistakably.

Parts of the Quds Force and the MOIS also collaborate with transnational criminal organizations in Latin America, posing a threat to the security of the Northern Hemisphere. Moreover, they maintain terrorist and propaganda networks within America itself. Under the eyes of the CIA, DHS and

FBI, agents of the Islamic Republic poison and contaminate the media, lobby, hold faculty positions in various universities, shamelessly spread falsehoods and propagate lies, speak at think tanks with financial backing, organize marches inside American universities, and collaborate with assassins from covert terrorist networks and running sleeper cells.

It appears that the world has become indifferent to being held hostage by the destructive ideology of Khomeinism. If no action is taken, the consequences that become increasingly more perilous, and regretably the Democrats are complicit in this alignment with the regime. The world has not taken serious action against the transnational terrorism network of the mullahs in Iran; the CIA helped to eliminate Bin Laden (who, in fact, was trained in Sudan during the days of Rafsanjani and Omar al-Bashir with the help of the Quds Force and Hezbollah, and returned to Afghanistan via Iran to orchestrate the September 11th attacks), or to kill the second-in-command of Al-Qaeda in Tehran on 7th August 2020, or perhaps the most dangerous terrorist of the Quds Force (Qasem Soleimani, who killed hundreds of American soldiers and was a key figure in activating the Shia Crescent and the Islamic Republic's transnational terrorism network).

While the American intelligence community has made significant efforts, it's clear that Mossad has been effective in both eliminating terrorists and undermining the mullahs' regime. Mossad has targeted key IRGC figures when they posed threats. Over the past 45 years, Mossad has periodically been the main force challenging Khamenei and his outlaw regime.

For instance, while praying over the bodies of Haniyeh

and his bodyguard, Khamenei looked to the sky out of fear, as if he were anticipating a Mossad drone or an Israeli missile before it struck. Cowardly, the Middle Eastern inept and spineless dictator is distrustful and suspicious of everyone around him.

Khamenei occasionally becomes intoxicated seeing the crimes of the Revolutionary Guards, security organizations, and his own terrorism network, and issues orders for terrorist operations—or as they call it, Islamic Jihad!—and when he rashly ordered missile launches toward Israel, he fled to Mashhad at night to escape Mossad's reach in his delusions. In the real world, what value or credibility does a fatwa from such a criminal have?

In actuality, the fear of Israel and Mossad has driven the regime's propaganda machine to the point of delirium. The situation is so dire and absurd that even former ministers of intelligence are constructing sentences with the words CIA and Mossad. Mossad probably views its cat-and-mouse game with Khamenei as a form of entertainment, but as long as this dictator is alives in Iran, the saga of war, blood, bombs, and terror in the Middle East persists. It is hoped that with support for "regime change" in Iran, this story will come to an end.

Just as Mossad never forgot Ismail Haniyeh's blessing prayer in a hotel in Turkey during the broadcast of Hamas's brutality against Israel on October 7, 2023, it will never forget the command center of the IRGC thugs, figures like Salami, Baqeri, Hajizadeh, and others, who ordered the launch of supersonic cruise missiles and kamikaze drones at Israel. But Mossad's ability in operations have compelled the Islamic Republic to consider replacing its main pieces and reorganizing the intelligence community's chessboard with the naive notion that it might block Mossad's infiltration. However, Mossad has already read the play of the game.

77
NETANYAHU'S DIRECT APPEAL: A NEW CHAPTER IN MIDDLE EAST POLITICS

In a surprising move that has caught the attention of political analysts and citizens alike, Israeli Prime Minister Benjamin Netanyahu recently addressed the Iranian people directly, bypassing the Islamic Republic's brutal leadership. This unprecedented communication highlights the complex and evolving dynamics in the Middle East, particularly the relationship between Israel, Iran, and the broader region.

Netanyahu's message, while ostensibly aimed at fostering goodwill with the Iranian populace, serves multiple strategic purposes. It attempts to drive a wedge between the Iranian people and their government, asserting that the regime's priorities do not align with the interests of ordinary Iranians. By emphasizing the potential for peace and prosperity in a post-Islamic Republic era, Netanyahu is subtly encouraging internal dissent and presenting Israel as a potential ally to the Iranian people.

However, this message comes at a time of heightened tensions in the turbulent region. The recent elimination of key terrorists in Iran's "Transnational Terrorist Network," including Hezbollah's leader Hassan Nasrallah, has significantly altered the strategic landscape. These developments have not only weakened Iran's regional influence but have also exposed vulnerabilities in its network of proxy Islamic terrorist groups.

The timing of Netanyahu's address is crucial. It coincides with a period of internal strife in Iran, marked by economic hardships and growing public discontent with the regime's policies. By highlighting the regime's expenditure on foreign conflicts and nuclear ambitions at the expense of domestic well-being, Netanyahu aims to exacerbate these internal tensions.

From a security studies perspective, this approach can be seen as a form of psychological warfare. It's an attempt to influence Iranian public opinion and potentially create internal pressure on the Iranian government. The effectiveness of such a strategy, however, depends on various factors, including how widely the message is disseminated within Iran and how it's perceived by the Iranian public.

Netanyahu's assertion of Israel's military capabilities and reach serves a dual purpose. It's both a warning to the Iranian regime and an attempt to project strength to the Israeli public and the international community. By mentioning the elimination of figures like Mohammed Deif and Hassan

Nasrallah, Netanyahu is signaling Israel's willingness and ability to act against perceived threats, even beyond its immediate borders.

The message also touches on a vision of a post-Islamic Republic Iran, painting a picture of potential cooperation and peace between Israel and Iran. This forward-looking approach is designed to appeal to Iranians' aspirations for a better future and to position Israel as a potential partner rather than an eternal enemy.

However, it's crucial to approach Netanyahu's message with a critical eye. While it presents a compelling narrative, it also simplifies complex historical and geopolitical realities. The longstanding animosity between Iran and Israel is rooted in more than just the policies of the current Iranian outlaw regime. Cultural, religious, and historical factors play significant roles in shaping these relations.

Moreover, the message's effectiveness in reaching and influencing the Iranian public is questionable. Iran's tight control over media and internet access means that many Iranians may never hear Netanyahu's words. Those who do might view them skeptically, given the long history of hostility between the two nations.

From Iran's perspective, this message could be seen as an attempt to interfere in its internal affairs. The Iranian criminal mullah's regime has long accused foreign powers, particularly Israel and the United States, of trying to destabilize the country. Netanyahu's direct address to the Iranian people could be used by the regime to reinforce this narrative and potentially strengthen nationalist sentiments.

The broader implications of this message extend beyond Iran-Israel relations. It signals a shift in Israel's approach to regional politics, moving from a policy of containment to one of active engagement, albeit with the Iranian people rather than the government. This strategy aligns with broader efforts to reshape the Middle East's political landscape, including the normalization of relations between Israel and several Arab states.

For the international community, particularly the United States and European powers, Netanyahu's message presents both opportunities and challenges. While it aligns with Western interests in curbing Iran's nuclear ambitions and regional influence, it also risks escalating tensions in an already volatile region.

The elimination of key figures in Iran's proxy network, if confirmed, marks a significant shift in the balance of power in the Middle East. It potentially weakens Iran's ability to project power beyond its borders and could lead to a reassessment of its regional strategy. However, it also raises the risk of retaliation and further escalation of conflicts.

As we analyze these developments, it's important to consider the human cost of ongoing conflicts and tensions in the region. The people of Iran, Israel, and neighboring countries continue to bear the brunt of geopolitical maneuvering and proxy wars. Any path forward must prioritize the safety, security, and prosperity of all people in the region.

In conclusion, Netanyahu's message to the Iranian people represents a bold but risky diplomatic maneuver. It reflects the changing dynamics of Middle Eastern politics and the ongoing struggle for regional influence. As the situation continues to evolve, it will be crucial for all parties involved to navigate these choppy waters with caution, always keeping in mind the potential for both conflict escalation and opportunities for peace.

The coming months and years will likely see further shifts in the regional balance of power. How Iran's terrorist loving regime responds to its weakened position, how Israel navigates its newfound strategic advantage, and how other regional and global powers react will shape the future of the Middle East. In this complex geopolitical chess game, the moves made today will have far-reaching consequences for generations to come.

Finally, Netanyahu and Israel are held in high regard among the people of Iran. This is partly because he invited Iran's Prince Reza Pahlavi to Israel and also due to Israel's destruction of terrorists linked to the mullahs, which has brought joy and amusement to the Iranian people. As a result, social media in Persian is filled with unique praise for Netanyahu and Israel, with some even viewing Netanyahu as a significant ally in the success of regime change in Iran. This clearly reflects the deep divide between the terrorist regime and the honorable and noble people of Iran, a fact that has certainly not gone unnoticed by Netanyahu.

78
PEZESHKIAN, KHAMENEI'S NEW OPERATIVE AND THE MIRAGE OF REFORM

In the theater of Iranian politics, democracy serves merely as a grotesque masquerade. The recent elections, a grand charade meticulously staged to perpetuate the regime's dominance, drew a scant 10% to 15% of the electorate. This spectacle, steeped in intimidation and marred by violence, signals the continuity of despotism unless a profound transformation unfolds.

Iran's electoral ruse was crafted with dual purposes: it sought to sculpt international narratives while muffling the burgeoning domestic demands for transformation. A fresh onslaught of propaganda, aimed particularly at an American audience, attempted to veil the regime's savagery—a tyranny masquerading as governance. We must not be beguiled by this facade; beneath the guise of leadership lies nothing more than a mullahs' cabal.

Pezeshkian's rise, a scheme woven by Khamenei, casts him not as a beacon of reform but as a pawn entrenched in autocracy. His ascent only tightens the regime's stranglehold, intensifying the mechanisms of repression and bolstering the bastions of Islamic extremism, while hostility towards the West festers unabated.

Under Pezeshkian's guise of leadership, the landscape remains bleak. The regime's grip strengthens, ensuring the perpetuation of Islamic terrorism and its hegemony in the Middle East. The animosity towards America and Israel endures without wane. An informed leader in the U.S. must confront these truths. The figures propped up by the regime do not embody the Iranian will but serve the machinations of tyranny.

The entire political apparatus in Iran stands starkly against any notion of progress or reform. Khamenei's rule, an epitome of authoritarian control, smothers any semblance of hope beneath its oppressive weight. The electoral farce, a mere shadow play of democracy, showcases candidates who are but merchants of deception. Pezeshkian's 16 million votes, a mere fraction in a nation of 90 million, highlight the persistent shadow of religious despotism.

The schism within Iran's power echelons—between reformists and conservatives—serves only to perpetuate their dominion through ruthlessness. Though seemingly disparate, these factions are merely different faces of the same corrupt entity, entwined in deception and superficial reforms that yield no genuine progress.

Decades since Khamenei's controversial rise in 1981, the patterns of authoritarianism continue unabated. With Pezeshkian's elevation, the regime's draconian practices persist—dissenters languish in prisons, and the state's terror reaches beyond its borders.

The groundwork for the regime's collapse is undeniably set, yet the voice of the Iranian populace is stifled, drowned out by the din of reformist propaganda. True change is a mirage as long as the existing order prevails, unchallenged by justice or the people's outcry for freedom.

As spectators and participants on the global stage, we must discern the reality behind this façade: a regime desperate to cling to control, terrified of its citizenry's potential for revolt. The electoral boycott has empowered the Iranian public, instilling a respect for their suffrage and a refusal to sanction their continued subjugation. The international community must remain vigilant; the touted change is but an illusion, a narrative spun to maintain a despotic rule that serves only the rulers.

Ultimately, the political masquerade in Iran, under the pretense of electoral democracy, is nothing but a regression—a tragic step back for a nation yearning for true reform and liberation from tyranny. The situation is ripe for change, yet constrained by an authoritarian grip that fears the voice of its people—a voice that, despite efforts to suppress it, resonates with an ever-growing demand to end the reign of terror.

79

QAANI IN BAGHDAD: MOBILIZING IRAN'S TERROR AXIS AGAINST ISRAEL

Since the collapse of Bashar al-Assad's brutal regime in Syria, Iran's Dictator Ali Khamenei has delivered four inflammatory speeches targeting Syria, including two recent direct threats against uprisings in the country. This rhetoric mirrors the era when Khomeini, the founder of Iran's Islamic theocracy, provoked Saddam Hussein and Iraq's army after seizing power in 1979. Khamenei, at 86 years old, remains one of the longest-serving and bloodiest dictators in the modern world, masking his tyranny under a veneer of false sanctity. In his worldview, the entire world is misguided, and only he holds the truth.

This duplicitous despot plays a double game, criticizing Trump through hardliners while pursuing new diplomacy through reformists. But the reality is stark: Khamenei's spiderweb of Islamic terror networks is collapsing. The million dollars spent on Hamas and Hezbollah have been squandered in defeat. He knows that if Israel, under Netanyahu, and the U.S., under Trump, dismantle his remaining terrorist proxies, like the Houthis, PIJ and Hashd al-Shaabi, the focus will shift to Iran's nuclear program. More critically, Khamenei understands that if his nuclear ambitions and producing nuclear bomb are curtailed, the Iranian people will rise in a nationwide rebellion, consigning his regime to the ash heap of history.

While global diplomatic norms often temper such blunt assessments, most Middle Eastern leaders, particularly in the Persian Gulf, recognize the truth. The criminal ayatollahs in Iran came to power through the chaos of 1979's revolt, riding on a wave of Islamic and Marxist terrorism. They have maintained their grip on power through violence, barbarism and coercion, devoid of legitimacy or popularity at home or abroad. Western diplomatic overtures to Iran betray a fundamental misunderstanding of history and the destructive ideology of Khomeinism.

Today, Esmail Qaani's arrival in Baghdad has once again dominated headlines across the Middle East. Despite rumors about his fate, Qaani remains a delusional and destructive figure, isolated yet dangerous. Unlike his predecessor, he has yet to earn Khamenei's Medal of Conquest. His deputies, Iraj Masjedi and Mohammad Reza Fallahzadeh, share his commitment to expanding Islamic terrorism within the Shia crescent. These three men, notorious for their crimes against Israeli and American forces, remain fugitives from justice. But what is Qaani's true mission in the aftermath of Iran's repeated failures in the Middle East?

Qaani's Multi-Faceted Mission

From an intelligence perspective, Qaani's mission appears to have several dimensions, none of which have escaped the vigilance of Mossad, the CIA, or allied intelligence agencies in the region.

1. Reinforcing the Proxy Network in Iraq: Qaani seeks to revive and consolidate control over Iraq's Shia terrorist groups. These militias, whether Arab, Sunni, or Kurdish (including the Barzanis and PKK), maintain close ties with the IRGC. Qaani aims to exert more direct influence over groups like Hashd al-Shaabi, preventing the collapse of Iran's proxy network in Iraq. Figures like Ali Sistani, who shares Khamenei's vision of a Shia crescent, are unlikely to oppose these efforts.

2. Provoking Anti-Israel Forces: Qaani's strategy includes mobilizing Iran's proxies against Israel to redefine their roles in the regional equation. For Qaani, his deputies, and even Iran's ambassador to Iraq—a Quds Force operative using the pseudonym Al-Sadeq—every proxy must be weaponized as a tool against Israel. Groups like Hashd al-Shaabi, equipped with missiles, drones, and intelligence from Iran's Ministry of Intelligence and IRGC, are being primed to pressure Israel.

3. Restoring Influence in Syria: Qaani's ultimate goal is to reestablish Iran's waning influence in Syria. For Tehran, Syria has long served as a vital corridor connecting it to Hezbollah, Hamas, and Islamic Jihad, preserving its strategic position against Israel. However, relentless Israeli strikes on Iranian positions in Syria have turned this once-reliable card into a liability, creating a nightmare for Tehran's military and security apparatus.

Strategic Adjustments and Regional Risks

Qaani's mission also involves mitigating regional pressures. For instance, he may seek to use Hashd al-Shaabi to shield the Houthis terrorist rebels, who are under increasing pressure from U.S. and allied forces. Simultaneously, Iran is investing in local and ethnic groups like the Kurds and PKK, attempting to establish new axes of influence. Yet, such maneuvers are unacceptable to Israel and its allies.

From a strategic standpoint, Qaani's presence in Baghdad signals a potential effort to redeploy Shia forces or pivot strategies to maintain Tehran's regional influence. However, these actions underscore the regime's inherent instability and belligerence rather than any meaningful strategy.

The Bigger Picture

Accompanied by his deputies Masjedi and Fallahzadeh, Qaani's Baghdad mission revolves around preserving and rebuilding Iran's proxy terror network, escalating pressure on Israel, and coordinating regional operations in Syria. These objectives highlight Khamenei's determination to maintain his destabilizing role in the Middle East. Yet, given mounting internal and international pressures, these desperate attempts to salvage Iran's terror network are fraught with challenges.

The CIA's new leadership, John Ratcliffe, in collaboration with the Pentagon and Israel, will likely block Tehran's ambitions to rebuild its aggressive influence. The reality is that Iran's regime is weaker than ever, grappling with repeated defeats on regional and international fronts. Khamenei's fragile spiderweb is unraveling, and the forces arrayed against him are growing stronger.

Qaani's visit to Baghdad, far from signaling strength,

reveals the regime's desperation to cling to its crumbling empire. For Tehran, the clock is ticking, and the stakes have never been higher.

80
REZA PAHLAVI: GUIDING IRAN TOWARD DEMOCRATIC CHANGE

"The Middle East is in a precarious state, brimming with changes and transformations. The entire region is undergoing shifts, power plays, and is plagued by brutal terrorism with terrorist actors and warmongers fearing the loss of their administrative and governmental authority through wars or popular uprisings. Khamenei's reckless gamble, his dangerous game with a transnational network of terrorism, has brought the Middle East to this precarious situation and threshold of change, but not the change he desired or envisioned.

The Islamic Republic in Iran is one of those governments at the heart and depth of these changes. It is a weak, rogue, warmongering government without popular support and illegitimate. A rebellious, losing, and illegitimate government that arose from a mixture of terrorist, leftist, and Islamic thoughts, derailing the train of Iranian civilization from its main track. Today, some delusional and narrow-minded individuals are prescribing solutions for the same devastated Iran.

It is evident that the current regime in Iran plays a significant and concentrated role intertwined with mafia-like terrorist groups, dragging the lands of Iraq, Syria, Yemen, Lebanon, and the rest of the region under the umbrella of the Shia Crescent, dominating the Middle East through terrorism and religious superstitions. However, this is not the reality.

Today's world has realized that the dark and oppressed people of Iran do not desire war, chaos, and destruction. But the occupying regime in Tehran is engaged in such a foolish fantasy and has been squandering Iran's wealth, interests, and national resources for 45 years, ignoring the desires of the society. The world has realized that the mullahs have remained in power with the help of terrorism and suppression, holding Iranian society hostage. Yet, in this noisy world, we see uneducated and pretentious politicians asleep, equating the Islamic Republic with the people of Iran. But the truth is otherwise.

Today's world has understood that the 1953 legend and the U.S. involvement in changing the government is a tasteless and shameless lie that is repeatedly told. A populist disrupted the country for a few days to remain prime minister longer, sending the country into the arms of the Russians, and shut down both the press and the parliament, driving the country into bankruptcy. Since that day, indebted leftists have been lying that the U.S. and the CIA staged a coup, and that populist was a democratically elected prime minister, but no one remembers when and where the public election referendum was.

What has also influenced the internal developments of Iran and significantly altered the domestic and foreign policies of the Iranian government is not the advancement and expansion of economic sanctions against the regime. Rather, it is the gradual destruction of the Tehran regime's Islamic terrorism network, whose arms are being severed one by one by Israeli counter-terrorism, and even if the trigger mechanism against the indebted and incapable Tehran government is activated soon, this downward trajectory will accelerate.

The world has realized that Israel did not start the devastating war and did not employ terrorist groups around Iran. Israel did not set the Middle East on fire with the destructive ideology of Khomeinism. But the warmongering Shia mullah, guilty of all these anti-human and anti-civilization crimes, daily schemes in Yemen, Syria, Iraq, and Lebanon against Israel, led by a stubborn, merciless, vindictive, and opportunist demagogue mullah named Khamenei, assigned to destroy Iran and the Middle East.

However, these complex developments in the Middle East, and the direct confrontation between Khamenei and Netanyahu, have also significantly stirred the global powers. The persistence in warmongering and regional terrorism and the fear of the mullahs' defeat in Tehran on one hand, and Israel's serious determination to combat evil and Islamic terrorism linked to the Revolutionary Guards on the other, have driven the region toward profound changes.

Moreover, undoubtedly, none of the ruling governments in the Middle East want the destructive, aggressive, and devastating role of the Islamic Republic of Iran in the region to expand, having experienced the consequences of the cancerous scourge of the Shia Crescent over these 45 years. Although these countries, despite various harassments, interventions, and threats from the Islamic Republic of Iran, are seeking to find the truth and experience a tangible change in their foreign policies that will gradually free them from the calamity of the Islamic Republic after 45 years.

Here, the common ground between the people of Iran and the Middle East becomes apparent, and that is the effort to change the regime of the mullahs and restore peace, tranquility, stability, and peaceful coexistence to the cradle of civilization, one of the most historic regions in the world, which has likely had 124,000 claimants of prophecy from the creator of the world.

A remarkable and surprising point in today's world is that Iranian society is pleased with the humiliation and defeat of the despised and isolated mullahs' regime. Iranian society regards the mullahs and the Revolutionary Guards as worse than ISIS and al-Qaeda, with 45 years of vivid memories of the crimes of the mullahs and their savage regime, and for 45 years, with flesh, skin, and bone, they have understood the meaning of religious tyranny filled with curses and the darkness of the Islamic caliphate of the Guardianship of the Islamic Jurist.

Iranian society is happy to see the fear and terror of the mullahs' regime about an Israeli attack, but on the other hand, they are worried and anxious about the future. At the end of the tunnel of horror and this desert wasteland, they see a glimmer of hope, and that is the presence of Prince Reza Pahlavi to assist the wounded, afflicted, and suffering Iranian society on the rocky and difficult path to democracy, after the regime change in Iran.

In any case, the spider's web of uncivilized, cowardly, and evil mullahs is collapsing. Although the people of Iran want this regime to go peacefully and without bloodshed, the Shia mullah considers himself the representative of a fictional and imaginary character named the Imam of Time and sees himself as the representative of God, and these lies, deceptions, and superstitions signify their strong desire to create a bloodbath and civil war. But Khamenei, like the last moments of Yahya Sinwar's life when he threw his walking stick, uses his last terrorist, his last bomb, and his last missile for warmongering because the basis of his thought is enmity, stupidity, and barbarism.

Nevertheless, we are at a critical moment in the history of the Middle East. But ultimately, the symbol of peace and democracy among Iranians is the 65-year-old prince, and just as the 20th century witnessed the death of Nazism, communism, and apartheid, the 21st century will also witness the death of Khomeinism and Islamic terrorism.

81
SILENT VEILS: UNVEILING TEHRAN'S THEOCRACY

Iran is entrenched in a perilous decline, with its governance steering the nation toward utter stagnation. The complexity of the situation has evolved into an intricate dilemma, characterized by the government's accelerated and destructive policies, threatening the very survival of the state.

Despite the grave circumstances, both the Iranian populace and the global community have yet to fully grasp the magnitude of this crisis. Since the pivotal winter of 1979, the regime has positioned itself as both exploiter and occupier, perpetuating its flaws without any inclination towards reform.

The aspirations of the Iranian people diverge significantly from those of their rulers. Governed by an administration wielding unchecked power and vast wealth, there is a profound disconnect, as the government fails to acknowledge the legitimate identity and voices of its citizens, who harbor deep resentment. This ongoing tension promises to persist until the eventual collapse of the regime.

Iran is subjected to a regime that is fundamentally unable to engage in any meaningful dialogue, substituting repression for communication. Armed with whips, bullets, and batons, the regime acts with the brutality of an unyielding conqueror, unwilling to relent. From this position of power, it inflicts violence upon its citizens, treating them as mere obstacles in its path.Operating akin to a mafia, the military and governmental forces continue their relentless oppression, supported by an exhaustive propaganda machine designed to reinforce and expand the regime's dominion.

In comparison to its potential, Iran's governance system is markedly regressive and inefficient, riddled with deficiencies that have estranged it from its people and isolated it on the international stage. Particularly among the youth, there is a palpable disconnection, exacerbated by the regime's refusal to acknowledge the authentic identity and heritage of the Iranian nation, rooted in a history that predates the current ideological framework.

Today, the regime is perceived as an illegitimate force, devoid of any moral or popular support, operating under a facade of governance that has consistently failed to unite or even adequately address the needs of its people. Instead, it has inflicted widespread damage and fragmentation throughout the society.Employing language and logic that seem irrelevant and dictatorial, the regime demands subservience, fancying itself as a celestial overseer entitled to dictate over a disenfranchised populace. It is a ruler who, after decades in power, remains impervious to the language of reason and diplomacy.

The regime selectively grants voting rights, civil liberties, and freedom of expression solely to its proponents, maintaining a strict regime of censorship. This governance is not poised for future reform; it remains closed, obscure, and fundamentally misguided.

The intellectual environment in Iran is stifled by terror, imprisonment, and profound deprivation. Governed by forces that neither desire nor possess the capability to transcend their own narrow viewpoints, the administration remains staunchly populist, repressive, and absolutist, standing in stark opposition to a society that yearns for liberation and truth. There exists no platform for genuine dialogue, only forced compliance through coercive interrogations and judicial manipulations. The populace lives under constant threat, vulnerable to arbitrary arrest and repression.

Moreover, the current regime is emblematic of absolute failure, symbolizing the epitome of tyranny. It does not regard its citizens as constituents of a legitimate nation but rather as subjects of a theocratic conquest, treating Iran as a prize of war. The disparity between the regime's vision and the vibrant cultural and historical identity of the Iranian people is stark and irreconcilable. Consequently, Iran's governance structure opposes not only the principles of freedom and law but also fails to command genuine authority or respect.

The plight of the Iranian populace is one of profound disillusionment and pervasive resentment, fueled by decades of lost national pride and identity erosion since 1979. Governed by an administration that communicates only through coercion and is unashamed of its propensity for violence, Iran is led by rulers whose claims to religious and celestial authority only mask their underlying deceit and ideological bankruptcy.

As it stands, the path to institutionalizing democracy in Iran is fraught with immense challenges. The nation faces a precarious future, teetering on the brink of societal collapse akin to its economic and environmental breakdowns. The regime's stubborn reliance on suppression and external aggression serves only to perpetuate its rule, unaltered by internal changes or the loss of figureheads.

Anticipating the outcomes of the imminent elections is fraught with difficulty, especially given the restrictive environment crafted by the regime, which shows scant interest in genuine electoral participation or public engagement. The oversight of the Guardian Council, under strict supervision, ensures that only a select few loyalists are deemed eligible, continuing the cycle of autocracy under the guise of electoral process.

This analysis reveals a regime intractable in its ways and detached from the realities of its people, destined to maintain a course that could ultimately lead to its undoing. The Iranian nation stands at a crossroads, with the potential for significant transformation if only the shackles of theocratic despotism can be broken.

82
STATUS QUO REMAINS:
THE PERSISTENT STAGNATION OF REGIME

This week, Masoud Pezeshkian unveiled his cabinet, featuring corrupt and brutal figures from intelligence and military sectors, all committed to maintaining the status quo. Iran's regime increasingly militarizes, supported by reformists who inadvertently helped establish a military regime—a loss in their gamble. Pezeshkian's administration merely continues Ibrahim Raisi's policies.

Iran is fundamentally ruled by a corrupt military and intelligence mafia. The current cabinet, already deemed a failure, is unlikely to change. Resembling military barracks, it includes MOIS stakeholders and IRGC thugs, creating an ineffective coalition.

In Iran, elections are a farce. Javad Zarif, cunningly, using tactics reminiscent of Goebbels during the Hitler era, maintained his facade until the end, hiding the behind-the-scenes truth. This has confirmed to Iranian society that all promises by him and Pezeshkian were mere lies and deception.

Since Khomeini's death, Khamenei has been a detrimental presence in Iran. His regime, characterized by terror, warmongering and aggression, is a significant barrier to democracy. The people of Iran are held captive by an irrational Shiite mullah. A key ministry in cabinet is the Ministry of Intelligence [MOIS] of the Islamic Republic, which has played a crucial role in fostering terrorism and is subject to sanctions from Europe and America. The mullahs' regime, a harbinger of death and a merchant of religion, filled with self-righteous zealots armed with fanaticism and superstitions, has become a nightmare for the helpless and hopeless people of Iran and a source of fear for its neighbors. These religious fanatics, pretentious in faith and backward, have created their own intelligence and espionage apparatus.

To date, seven mullahs have led the intelligence throne of MOIS, committing numerous crimes, barbarities and atrocities. Esmaeil Khatib, the eighth mullah spy, rose to power under Raisi, traditionally appointed to issue death fatwas under their distorted religious laws.

Pezeshkian's reappointment of Khatib signaled a lost cause, confirming his cabinet as the executor of Iran's ruin. Khatib's inclusion dismisses Pezeshkian's empty promises, signaling to Iranians and the world that Tehran's oppressive intelligence policies persist, fueling domestic and international terror. With Khatib at MOIS, Iran remains mired in a security crisis.

Khatib, lacking educational and security expertise, was embroiled in internal regime terrorism networks during Ali Fallahian's terrifying tenure at the MOIS (1989-1997). He directed intelligence in Qom, clashing with a reformist terrorist loving faction.

Later, as head of the Judiciary's Intelligence Center (2012-2019), Khatib's tenure, marked by torture and repression, ended when Raisi dismissed him, only for Khamenei to appoint him as MOIS minister. His radical approach deepened under MOIS, where he aligned the judiciary's, IRGC's, and MOIS's security apparatuses closely with Khamenei.

Perhaps if Raisi were alive today, he might have dismissed Khatib for his incompetence and repeated intelligence failures. But today, not only has Khatib not been dismissed, but he also remains in a cabinet that claims to champion change and protect the people's rights. His intellectual and rational capabilities are far from ministerial standards. A sickly, weak, delusional, and arrogant minister, Khatib pursues delusions of "exporting the revolt of Khomeini," viewing the entire Middle East as under the clerics' command and considers the Islamic Republic a global superpower officially recognized by the world. He views the United States as the dominant enemy of Iran.

Influenced by Khamenei's rhetoric and intellectually submissive, Khatib shares similar catastrophic views, consistently demonizing opponents and glorifying the 1979 clerics' uprising as "the miracle of the Imam's sunlight"—mere hogwash!

When the terrorist group Hamas attacked Israel on

October 7, 2023, he compared it to the barbaric Arab invasion of the Achaemenid Empire in Iran, the Arab conquest of Persia (632-654). In Khatib's delusions, Khamenei is the leader of Muslims worldwide, and the entire world should be held hostage by him. However, he does not shy away from committing any atrocity to please Khamenei.

In his meaningless speeches, often devoid of logical structure, Kahatib always describes himself as a "soldier constantly on the path of Velayat (Islamic Jurist or Shiite mullah's rule) and martyrdom," always ready to sacrifice his life for victory. He believes in Islamic terrorism but according to the usual literature in the Islamic Republic, he calls it the path of ideals and jihad and martyrdom!

He holds Khomeini and the religiously extremist structure in Iran in high regard, viewing the 1979 Islamic caliphate system as sacred. From his biased perspective, the world deviates, engaging in psychological warfare and media campaigns against Khamenei's dictatorship.

This deceitful and unethical mullah, Khatib, has been a nightmare for Iran's political and cultural figures. A proponent of terrorism, repression, and censorship, he has actively pushed for internet filtering and tightly controls the production of books, films, and music in Raisi's cabinet.

Indifferent to Iran's national interests, Khatib and Khamenei focus on eliminating perceived threats and fostering regional chaos. Intelligence agencies worldwide anticipate a resurgence of terrorism under his watch. Deluded, Khatib sees himself as an intellectual, oblivious to Iran's borders and the real threats, and advocates for cultural aggression, showing a profound lack of awareness. From Khatib's perspective, terrorist organizations like the Quds Force and the IRGC are "sacred and the honor of the religion of Islam and the ornament" of the regime. He knows no path other than terrorism and, in his misbeliefs, seeks to ensure that the face of the clerical regime and the system's authority is not tarnished.

A staunch opponent of America and Israel, Khatib harbors deep anti-American and anti-Israeli sentiments and has orchestrated several cyber operations in America. A major concern for U.S. intelligence community is the MOIS-linked terrorist sleeper cells on U.S. soil, with Khatib implicated in assassination plots against Trump and his close associates. This week, he announce ""the MOIS's top priority is to fight against Israel."

He harbors illusions of completely dismantling the CIA and Mossad networks. Despite confirming with CIA and Mossad officials three times, all assert that his claims are entirely fabricated. Khatib perceives that global intelligence agencies do nothing but plot against the mullahs' outlaw regime, which he labels as seditious. He frequently invokes the CIA and Mossad to construct naïve sentences.

During the anti-regime nationwide protests in 2021, Khatib deceptively reported that all protests were foreign-instigated and imprisoned female journalists reporting the incident as spies, falsely suggesting that Mahsa Amini's death was a foreign-orchestrated plot. Khatib did not shy away from committing atrocities against unarmed protesters. He shares Khamenei's fear of popular uprisings, attributing all public dissent to the CIA and Mossad and threatening Europe with terrorist acts.

Neither the CIA, nor Mossad engaged in the killings, torture, blinding, or sexual assaults reported in Iran—these are the actions of a regime led by individuals like Khatib and Khamenei, who exhibit psychopathic and extremist tendencies. Khatib staunchly supports brutal oppression, mercilessly crushing movements involving laborers, teachers, students, women, and intellectuals. From his worldview, any dissent against Khomeini's and Khamenei's regime justifies brutal suppression.

Khatib, marked by a history of vindictive and accusatory behavior, sees all opposition as foreign aligned, portraying himself as a harsh and unethical figure. He remains a pivotal figure within the regime's harsh crackdowns, indifferent to human rights and oblivious to the actual needs and voices of the Iranians.

However, in the real world, the face of the religious octopus in Iran is cracked, and it could collapse at any moment. The intelligence community of the Islamic Republic is bankrupt, corrupt, inefficient, and penetrable.

83
THE BATTLE FOR IRAN'S PRESIDENCY AMIDST POWER STRUGGLES

Over the past 45 years, the Islamic Republic has committed numerous crimes. It might be wise to establish a museum similar to the Holocaust Museum, named the Museum of Mullahs' Crimes, in various locations worldwide after the regime's collapse. This would help future generations understand what has transpired in Iran and the Middle East. Ebrahim Raisi, a notorious criminal figure, met justice accidentally, much like Qasem Soleimani. Both were killed harshly, and their deaths may have been a response to their roles in massacring innocent people. Raisi's sudden death or removal from the power scene was unexpected and its full implications and dimensions remain unclear.

Raisi, known as the butcher of Tehran, was superficially respected by entities such as the European Union, the US government, the United Nations, Hamas, the Barzani tribe, the Muslim Brotherhood, and Sistani in Iraq. This was met with ridicule and serious criticism from the Iranian people, who saw it as a trivial display of artificial respect. Imposed by the Islamic Caliphate system of the Guardianship of the Islamic Jurist, Raisi was inappropriately labeled an Ayatollah and a doctor, and declared a martyr upon his death, despite never winning a free election. It was a dirty plan of the regime's propaganda machine. In truth, Raisi was devoid of personality, educational background, knowledge, or a distinct political stance. He was merely a compliant figure, trusted by Khamenei but mocked by the Iranian populace.

It's notable that Raisi, the vice president of the Assembly of Experts—whose sole purpose is to appoint leadership—was removed or eliminated 48 hours before a critical meeting, which might have elevated him to the presidency of the Assembly. Tragically, Raisi died and burned to ashes in the worst horrific manner on May 19, 2024. Khamenei has thus lost one of his chief executioners or the signatories of the killing machine and must now appoint a successor.

The upcoming days in Iran are fraught with tension as power-hungry factions jockey for proximity to the leadership. The next few weeks will reveal a true power struggle among the wolves, with the contenders openly attacking each other. However, in the Islamic Caliphate system, the competition for more power and the elimination of rivals are both commonplace and well-known matter.

In the next 48 days, the internal societal atmosphere will be bleak and lifeless as the significant gap between the populace and the rulers becomes more pronounced. Although the candidates will quickly try to engage the disenchanted and estranged society by publicly undermining and defaming each other, this ridiculous show is all too familiar to the Iranian people. The gap between the rulers and the nation is serious.

On one side, the economic cartels within the regime, such as Astan Quds Razavi, the Mostazafan Foundation of Islamic Revolution (MFJ), the Executive Headquarters of Khomeini's Order (EIKO), and the IRGC, are intent on preserving the status quo. Conversely, all terrorist groups involved in the 1978 riots are committed to the regime's survival. Moreover, it is crucial to reiterate that both pro-regime reformists (Islamic Left) and conservatives (Hardliners) represent two sides of the same coin.

Khamenei chooses the president based on three criteria: obedience in executing orders without question, loyalty to the system and the Islamic Caliphate or regime of mullahs, and readiness to defend the regime by any means, including crime and suppression. Unfortunately, the common traits of all candidates share common traits: they are uneducated, vile, compliant, criminal, thoughtless, incompetent, corrupt, and opportunistic.

Being president in the Islamic Caliphate system means being willing to suppress demonstrations and commit murder to maintain the regime's security. These three traits ensure the continuation of a presidency that values loyalty over competence, efficiency, education, expertise, and merit. With this setup, elections are rendered meaningless. The opinions of the people are disregarded by the Islamic Republic system at all. Only the extent of trust in loyalty to the mafia-like ruling establishment of the mullahs is important. So, the elections in Iran's regime are worthless.

For the mafia regime, public participation is irrelevant. The mullah's regime requires only the semblance of involvement for propaganda purposes. Notably, the response to the elections three years ago, where invalid votes frequently came in second, and in the last parliamentary elections, where they sometimes came in first, underscores this disconnection. Possibly, the upcoming elections may see a similar pattern. The Islamic Republic holds no genuine place in the hearts or minds of the Iranian people.

In the upcoming 48-day electoral period, figures such as Bagher Qalibaf, Saeed Jalili, and Mohseni Ejei are can be mentioned. Others, like Ali Larijani, are less favored. Meanwhile, Ali Shamkhani is known for his ties to Saudi Arabian intelligence service, and Mohsen Rezaei, who failed to secure a visa to speak at a Washington Institute think tank about war, is seen unfavorably, even as his son made it to America. However, later he appeared as a worthless clown, and America avoided getting close to him.

Ultimately, the specific electoral candidates are irrelevant to the Iranian populace, who see all as indistinguishable and unimportant, particularly when appearing in the regime's farcical electoral displays with invalid votes.

The ruling power structure always holds potential and foresight for significant shifts, but it is clear that under the new presidency, after Khamenei's possible death, these dynamics will undergo major changes. The role of Russia in the succession process is also crucial, as their acceptance of Mojtabi Khamenei shows no signs of concern. Russia's presence remains a significant barrier to the success of democracy advocacy and the national movement for regime change in Iran. The regime in Tehran is messy and ineffective, solely focused on continuing the Islamic Caliphate of the Guardianship of the Islamic Jurist and serving as a vassal state to Russia and China.

Interestingly, the timing of Iran's elections, occurring 4 to 5 months before those in America, may not significantly impact U.S. policy. However, currently, behind-the-scenes talks between the White House and the Islamic Republic are ongoing. Iran faces a severe security crisis, and any incident could disrupt the regime's plans, with no assurances of stability. no one knows if the Islamic Republic will remain in power for the next 4 years. The ongoing competition for leadership, filled with conspiracies and demonic plots akin to historical Islamic caliphates, shows the regime's fragility.

With Raisi gone from the scene, the Islamic Republic in Iran is likely to continue its current course, showing little inclination for change. The regime is becoming more militarized and closed-off, increasing the likelihood of further internal and external conflicts. The security and military sectors are set to expand, pushing the government towards greater militarization and authoritarianism. The power centers within Iran are complex and layered, but the country remains vulnerable to any disruptive events, highlighting the lack of stability.

84
THE CIA IN THE BIDEN ERA: SUCCESSES AND FAILURES

As President Joe Biden's administration reaches its midpoint, it is an ideal time to evaluate the performance of the Central Intelligence Agency (CIA), a critical pillar of U.S. national security. Under Biden's leadership, the CIA has faced significant challenges, including the chaotic withdrawal from Afghanistan and rising tensions with global powers like Russia and China. These events have tested the agency's ability to remain agile and effective in an increasingly volatile world.

According to Larry Pfeiffer, a former intelligence official who served under six CIA Directors, Biden values intelligence in decision-making and has worked to ensure it remains free from political interference. Pfeiffer also highlights the unique role of CIA Director William Burns, whose background in diplomacy has shaped the agency's approach under Biden's tenure.

While much remains behind closed doors, this analysis reflects a small portion of what can be publicly examined. This essay explores the CIA's successes and failures during the Biden era, assessing how it has navigated modern geopolitical challenges. From counterterrorism operations to a strategic pivot toward great power competition, the CIA's performance offers insight into the Biden administration's approach to national security.

1. Operational Successes and Strategic Shifts

One of the primary metrics for evaluating the CIA's effectiveness is the success of its operations. During Biden's tenure, the agency has continued its counterterrorism efforts, achieving significant victories, including the targeted killing of high-profile terrorists, such as the drone strike in Kabul in July 2022 that killed Al-Qaeda leader Ayman al-Zawahiri. This operation demonstrated the CIA's enduring capability to execute impactful counterterrorism missions.

However, the CIA has also faced notable setbacks. The withdrawal from Afghanistan in August 2021 was marred by intelligence failures regarding the rapid collapse of the Afghan government. Despite warnings, the agency misjudged the speed at which the Taliban would overrun the country, leading to a chaotic evacuation that damaged the credibility of U.S. intelligence globally.

Biden's presidency has also seen a strategic pivot with a renewed emphasis on countering China and Russia. Under Director William Burns, the CIA has shifted resources toward great power competition, moving away from the counterterrorism-heavy approach of the post-9/11 era. This includes intensified efforts to gather intelligence on the geopolitical moves of these major state actors. However, while the CIA's intelligence regarding Russia's invasion of Ukraine was accurate, the agency misjudged the timeline, predicting that Russia would win swiftly. This miscalculation underscored the complexities of assessing military capabilities in rapidly evolving conflicts.

One key aspect of this shift has been expanding operations in the Indo-Pacific, countering China's growing influence by monitoring military activities and economic espionage. Intelligence-sharing partnerships with Japan, Australia, and South Korea have been crucial in enhancing regional security.Similarly, the CIA has refocused on Russia, particularly during the ongoing Ukraine conflict. The agency provided intelligence on Russian military movements and cyberattacks, shaping U.S. and NATO responses, including sanctions and military aid. However, the conflict has tested the CIA's ability to provide real-time, actionable intelligence in a highly fluid situation.

While the pivot towards China and Russia has been necessary, balancing these new priorities with ongoing threats from non-state actors remains a challenge. The redistribution of resources has sparked concerns about gaps in intelligence coverage, especially in regions where terrorism and instability persist. Critics argue that the CIA may struggle to maintain effectiveness across multiple fronts.

Despite these concerns, the CIA has made strides in bolstering intelligence capabilities, particularly through expert recruitment and enhanced cyber and surveillance technologies. Collaboration with international partners remains a key factor in adapting to evolving threats, although the overall success of this strategic shift remains debated.

The CIA's focus on great power competition under Biden represents a necessary adaptation to global dynamics. However, the long-term success of this strategy will depend on the agency's ability to remain agile and responsive as the lines between state and non-state threats continue to blur.

2. Leadership and Organizational Changes

The appointment of William Burns as CIA Director during Biden's term marked a significant shift in the agency's leadership. Burns, a seasoned diplomat with extensive experience at the State Department, has focused on integrating intelligence with diplomacy and emphasizing cybersecurity and human intelligence (HUMINT) capabilities.

Under Burns' leadership, the CIA has undergone several internal adjustments to align with the evolving global threat landscape. One of the key shifts has been the restructuring of priorities to focus on great power competition, particularly with China and Russia. This has involved reallocating resources to critical regions and investing in advanced technologies to strengthen intelligence capabilities. Burns has also underscored the importance of maintaining the CIA's independence and integrity in intelligence analysis, ensuring that political factors do not compromise the agency's assessments. This commitment to objective, fact-based intelligence has been essential in navigating complex geopolitical issues.

In addition, the CIA has increased its focus on cybersecurity and counterintelligence under Burns' guidance. Specialized units dedicated to combating cyber threats have been established, reinforcing the agency's defenses against state and non-state actors in the digital domain.

Enhancing human intelligence capabilities in challenging environments like China and Russia has been another priority. The agency has invested in training operatives with regional expertise and leveraging new technologies to support covert operations.

Burns has also fostered a culture of accountability and transparency within the agency. By improving communication across divisions and ensuring adaptability to emerging threats, his leadership aims to modernize the CIA and position it as a forward-looking intelligence agency capable of addressing both current and future challenges.

Burns' leadership has brought significant structural and operational changes, with a strong focus on integrating intelligence and diplomacy, cybersecurity, and human intelligence. These adjustments reflect a broader effort to ensure the CIA remains agile and relevant in addressing the complex security challenges of the 21st century.

3. Intelligence Accuracy and Technological Adaptation
The accuracy and timeliness of intelligence provided to the Biden administration have played a crucial role in shaping U.S. foreign policy, particularly during major geopolitical events such as the Ukraine crisis and the Afghanistan withdrawal. The CIA's effectiveness in delivering reliable intelligence has been key to the administration's ability to respond to evolving global challenges.

During the Ukraine crisis, the CIA's intelligence was instrumental in predicting and responding to Russian military actions. In the months leading up to the invasion in February 2022, the CIA provided detailed assessments of Russia's troop movements, military preparations, and strategic intentions. This intelligence allowed the Biden administration to coordinate with allies, impose sanctions, and provide military support to Ukraine. The accuracy of these predictions enhanced U.S. intelligence credibility on the global stage and enabled a coordinated response that significantly influenced the course of the conflict.

In contrast, the intelligence provided during the Afghanistan withdrawal in August 2021 highlighted significant challenges. Although the CIA had issued warnings about the potential for rapid Taliban advances, the speed and scale of the Afghan government's collapse surprised many. The failure to fully anticipate the swift takeover of Kabul and the subsequent chaos during the evacuation raised questions about the agency's ability to assess the resilience of the Afghan military and government. This intelligence shortfall complicated evacuation efforts and drew widespread criticism of the administration's handling of the situation, undermining confidence in U.S. intelligence capabilities.

Despite these advancements, critics argue that the pace of technological adoption within the CIA remains slow, failing to keep up with the rapid developments in adversary technologies. This lag hinders the agency's ability to fully leverage cutting-edge tools to meet emerging security challenges. The agency has increasingly relied on AI to process vast amounts of data and generate actionable intelligence in real-time, particularly in cybersecurity, where AI algorithms can detect and respond to threats more quickly than traditional methods. AI has also enhanced the CIA's capabilities in satellite imagery analysis, social media monitoring, and identifying disinformation campaigns, enabling more precise responses to emerging threats.

The CIA has also bolstered its cyber operations to counter the growing threats from state actors like Russia, China, and Iran. It has developed advanced tools to disrupt adversarial networks, safeguard U.S. infrastructure, and protect sensitive information. These capabilities have proven crucial in defending against high-profile cyberattacks, such as those orchestrated by Russian and Chinese hackers, and in retaliating against cyber incursions. The CIA's cyber defenses have played a vital role in safeguarding U.S. elections and government systems from foreign interference, a priority for the Biden administration.

However, the rapidly changing technological landscape presents ongoing challenges. The CIA must continuously adapt to new technologies being developed and deployed by adversaries, requiring sustained commitment to innovation and investment in cutting-edge research. The rise of quantum computing, for example, threatens current encryption methods, necessitating advancements in cryptographic techniques. Additionally, the proliferation of deepfake technology and AI-generated content complicates intelligence gathering, making it harder to discern authentic information from fabricated data.

The CIA has also developed countermeasures against the use of technology by non-state actors, such as terrorist groups and transnational criminal organizations. These groups increasingly use encrypted communications, cryptocurrency, and other digital tools to evade detection. In response, the CIA has enhanced its technical capabilities to intercept these communications, trace illicit financial transactions, and dismantle online networks used for recruitment and propaganda.

Notably, the CIA's intelligence under Biden has been a mixed bag, with notable successes during the Ukraine crisis but significant challenges during the Afghanistan withdrawal. The accuracy and timeliness of intelligence have directly impacted U.S. foreign policy, influencing key decisions. As the geopolitical landscape evolves, the CIA's ability to provide accurate and timely intelligence will remain critical to the success of U.S. foreign policy.

4. Global Influence and Partnerships

The CIA's ability to maintain and expand intelligence partnerships with allied nations is crucial for addressing global security challenges. Under the Biden administration, the agency has strengthened these alliances, recognizing that international cooperation is key to countering transnational threats like terrorism, cyberattacks, and rogue state activities.

One major success has been the revitalization of intelligence-sharing partnerships with key allies such as the United Kingdom, Canada, Australia, and New Zealand (the Five Eyes). These alliances have been instrumental in sharing intelligence on Russian military movements, Chinese espionage, and counterterrorism efforts, bolstering joint operations that have significantly impacted global security.

Beyond traditional allies, the CIA has deepened relationships with emerging partners in strategic regions like Asia, the Middle East, and Africa. Collaborations with countries such as Japan and South Korea have helped counter North Korean threats, while partnerships in the Middle East have focused on Iranian influence and terrorism. These efforts have expanded the CIA's influence, providing stronger support for U.S. foreign policy objectives.

However, the expansion of intelligence partnerships presents challenges. The CIA must navigate diplomatic sensitivities in intelligence sharing, especially with nations that have differing political agendas or human rights concerns. Joint operations in regions like the Middle East have at times led to diplomatic tensions or backlash, complicating U.S. relations.

Furthermore, intelligence operations carry diplomatic risks. Successes can strengthen alliances, but failures can strain relationships and erode trust. For example, flawed intelligence assessments may lead allies to question the reliability of shared information, potentially undermining broader partnerships.

Despite these challenges, the CIA has largely succeeded in expanding its global intelligence partnerships during Biden's term. Close collaboration with allies and emerging partners has been critical in addressing complex global threats and advancing U.S. strategic interests. As global threats continue to evolve, fostering strong and resilient alliances will remain vital to the CIA's mission.

5. Challenges in the Middle East: The Iran File

The CIA's role in managing the threat posed by Iran during Biden's presidency has been contentious. Despite efforts, the agency's performance in countering Iran's influence and dismantling its terrorist networks has been less than effective. Iranian-backed terrorist groups like Hamas, Hezbollah, the Houthis rebels, and the Popular Mobilization Forces (Hashd al-Shaabi) inside Shiite crescent continue to wield significant influence across the Middle East.

The CIA has struggled to disrupt these Khomeinist groups, which have maintained operations despite U.S. sanctions and targeted actions. Hamas and Hezbollah, for instance, remain active in Gaza and Lebanon, while the Houthis rebels in Yemen continue their military campaigns. In Iraq, the Popular Mobilization Forces maintain power, deeply entrenched in the country's political and security landscape.

This challenge can be attributed to Iranian regime's adeptness at circumventing international pressure through covert operations, regional alliances, and asymmetric warfare. Iran's transnational terrorist networks, built over decades, are difficult to dismantle through conventional intelligence and counterterrorism measures. Additionally, the Biden administration's diplomatic approach, particularly efforts to revive the Joint Comprehensive Plan of Action (JCPOA), has likely constrained the CIA's ability to take more decisive action against Iranian proxies, as aggressive moves could disrupt delicate negotiations.

Overall, the CIA's efforts to curb Iran's influence have not significantly altered the regional power dynamics. Iran's complex alliances and strategic use of proxy forces have limited the impact of U.S. intelligence operations. Addressing this challenge will require a more integrated approach that combines intelligence, diplomacy, and military strategies to effectively counter Iran's regional ambitions.

***

The CIA's trajectory during the Biden era reveals both significant successes and notable challenges. The agency has shown resilience, from counterterrorism victories to adapting its focus toward great power competition and embracing technological advancements. However, it has faced setbacks, particularly in intelligence accuracy during the Afghanistan withdrawal and its efforts to counter Iran's influence.

Under William Burns, the CIA has made progress in depoliticizing intelligence and strengthening global partnerships, but ongoing challenges demand further evolution. Embracing new technologies and refining strategies to counter threats from both state and non-state actors will be critical. The agency must balance secrecy with accountability to maintain public trust while executing its vital missions.

Ultimately, the CIA's performance under Biden reflects both continuity and change, underscoring the complexities of safeguarding national security. As the agency moves forward, its ability to learn from past experiences and address its weaknesses will shape its future success in protecting U.S. interests on the global stage.

85
THE CIRCUS OF "FOOLS, FRAUDS, AND FIREBRANDS" IN IRAN

The unprecedented presidential election registration process in Iran has concluded, marked by theatrical and irrational political behavior. The conduct and speech of the candidates have been a source of disgrace and regret for the estranged and angry Iranian society. None of the registrants in this circus considered the concerns, worries, or desires of the Iranian people. Instead, their efforts were focused on reading absurd statements, populist slogans, incoherent remarks, or words meant to please the authorities. They demonstrated no concerns or solutions for the country's crises and no intentions to alleviate the people's suffering, merely pandering to the internal regime mafias.

These thugs are willing to go to any lengths, even engage in bloody attacks, to secure lucrative and profitable ministries. Most are content with becoming ministers or deputies in another's cabinet. None of these political dwarfs possessed the principles and specific characteristics of a presidential candidate. They merely staged a show in front of reporters, posing as the president for moments in front of the cameras. In reality, they had nothing else to say. They all simply stated that the current situation in the country is chaotic. It was a repulsive and clumsy display of populism and demagoguery.

Starting next week, the Iranian people will be invited to another segment of this absurd show—the vulgar political debates on the regime's TV, where the candidates will fight with each other. Probably, between six to eight candidates will emerge from the Guardian Council's box, approved by Khamenei and the IRGC. The path to regime change, institutionalizing democracy, and eradicating the infection of corrupt mullahs and political mafias in Iran is long and requires more than ever the will and desire of the nation.

One notable example is Saeed Jalili, a rigid, radical, and fanatical thug who enjoys the support of like-minded followers in the Islamic Parliament and Khamenei's residence. Jalili opposes any interaction with the civilized world and was the least successful person during the negotiation period, bringing numerous sanctions upon Iran. He is both a servant and a propagandist for the Islamic regime. He belongs to the Steadfastness Front of the Islamic Revolution, a conservative right-wing political group, partly comprised of former ministers from Ahmadinejad's cabinet. This fanatic group, once led spiritually by Mohammad-Taqi Mesbah-Yazdi, is willing to massacre all Iranians to preserve the mullah's regime. With his potential arrival, Iran will sink deeper than ever into a mire and a tunnel of horror.

Another candidate likely to be approved by the Guardian Council is Mohammad-Bagher Qalibaf, a senior commander of the IRGC involved in suppression. Supported by Khamenei and the IRGC, Qalibaf is willing to do anything to achieve his dream of becoming president, even committing crimes and massacring people. He is a bloodthirsty individual, loyal to Khamenei, opportunistic, and corrupt. A corrupt person, a thief, a friend of smugglers, a criminal, and an oppressor of students, Qalibaf becomes the head of the ineffective and submissive Islamic Revolutionary parliament. A thug from the IRGC, his only life's pride is commanding the suppression of students and committing murders for the regime's benefits.

Mostafa Pourmohammadi, another mass-murder icon, also smiled in front of the cameras, showing off without any plan, design, popularity, or influence. Like his colleague Raisi, Pourmohammadi is an illiterate, blustering criminal, a lawbreaker, and a bloodthirsty man. Khamenei needs someone who, in suppressing protesting people and in loyalty to the Islamic Caliphate of the Velayat-e faqih, refrains from committing no atrocity. The more murderous, corrupt, and oppressive you are, the more beloved you are by the Caliph of the Muslims. Pourmohammadi, a former colleague of Raisi in the execution committee, briefly registered for stand-up comedy to perhaps reach the election circus in Iran.

Iranian society is disoriented, disillusioned, dissatisfied, and defiant. A dormant anger has led to despair and a break with the ruling authority. Mahmoud Ahmadinejad's registration for the elections signifies nothing new, merely the ongoing strife among thugs, wolves, and the multi-layered mafia within the Islamic Caliphate. To warm up the cold electoral atmosphere and deceive public opinion, the regime's propaganda machine has resorted to clownery.

However, this show is futile. Freedom and human rights in Iran have been dead since 1979. Elections are not held; it's a pledge of allegiance to Khamenei.

Ali Larijani, during his tenure as the head of state IRIB, aired security programs that paved the way for the character assassination and physical elimination of intellectuals, writers, and translators. He has played a significant role in the security policies and military operations of this savage regime. His unpopularity in Iranian public opinion stems from his actions as a member of the IRGC, a devout believer in Islamic terrorism, and his distance from the national spirit of the Iranian society.

The current elections and the infighting among the regime's power factions, the IRGC, and Khamenei's inner circle resemble a ridiculous and absurd show. It is a power struggle among wolves. Khamenei's loyalists want to ensure that power remains in the hands of Mojtaba Khamenei. Various power factions are striving to ensure that the president aligns with and complies with Khamenei's policies. For the Iranian people, these elections are meaningless, and they continue to boycott them. They know that whether the candidates are Larijani or Haqqanian, they represent the voice of repression and brutality of the regime and are symbols of the Islamic Republic.

In summary, this circus of fools, frauds, and firebrands is nothing but a deceitful and meaningless farce by the mullahs, having nothing to do with the honorable and noble people of Iran. Under Khamenei's despotic rule, concepts like voting, the right to choose, and freedom of speech have no meaning.

86
"MULLAHS' REIGN IN IRAN: DECADES OF DECEPTION AND BRUTALITY

The regime in Tehran mirrors the brutal reign of Ismail I of the Safavid dynasty (22 December 1501 – 23 May 1524), who, 900 years after the Arab invasion, rose to power and established Shi'ism as the official religion in Iran. Ismail I's rule, devoid of any national pride, was founded on extreme violence and bloodshed. He concealed his cruelty under the guise of religion, executing, dismembering, and torturing those who opposed him. When no external enemies were available, he even directed his violence towards his own family. Anyone opposing Shi'ism was condemned to death by the sword. Ismail I spread terror throughout the land with relentless massacres. Historical records, including those housed in the British Museum, detail his ruthless killings, including the burial of the living and the exhumation of the dead. Declaring jihad, he reshaped Iranian history through the lens of Shi'ism. On the day of his coronation at the central mosque in Tabriz, he brazenly proclaimed, "I have been appointed by God, and the prophets are with me. If the people resist, I will draw my sword and leave not one of the 300,000 people of Tabriz alive." After 520 years, is there any discernible difference between him and Khamenei or Khomeini?

Historically, Ismail's soldiers in Tabriz committed atrocities, slaughtering pregnant women and massacring 20,000 people, sparing not even the dogs. Ahmad Kasravi, an author later assassinated by Khomeini's followers, unveiled the bloodthirsty and barbaric actions of Shah Ismail. In Mazandaran, Ismail executed his opponents by forcing their necks into iron cages and setting them on fire. He also orchestrated the massacre of 7,000 people in Tabas. Obsessed with quelling dissent, the ruthless Safavid ruler burned several opponents alive. His successor, Sultan Ismail II, driven by deep-seated rage, continued the brutal massacres, killing and blinding 12,000 people during his brief reign. Sultan Abbas's 40-year reign was similarly marked by relentless bloodshed and massacres. He exiled opponents to the fortress of Alamut, blinded two of his sons, and killed one. It was only during his reign that the mullahs gained respect, as Sultan Abbas, cruel and tyrannical, repeatedly ordered massacres.

Khamenei, much like the bloodthirsty Safavid rulers, has demonstrated extreme savagery and barbarism, comparable to the Mongols and the Safavid Chagins (cannibals), in his brutal suppression of the freedom-seeking people of Iran. He has also established terrorist groups responsible for the deaths of innocent Israeli and American soldiers and civilians. During the Safavid era, a group of cannibal executioners, known as the Chagins, would, at the king's command, tear people apart and consume them alive in his presence. This group was active in the court of Sultan Abbas. Today, the executioners of the Velayat-e Faqih have not only killed young Iranians but have also aided Hamas in killing Israelis.

Five hundred and twenty years later, Khamenei appears determined to revive the brutal tortures of the Chagins from the Safavid era, tearing apart the people of Iran. He remains unchanged—a ruler entrenched in a culture of savagery, relentlessly crushing a devastated and collapsing country under his robe and sandals.

Forty-six years ago, it was nearly impossible to openly and truthfully assert in any global media that these individuals were lying and were merely a group of criminals, as no one would have believed it. The fire at Rex Cinema in Abadan City was a deliberate and criminal act orchestrated by revolutionary terrorists opposed to the late King Pahlavi. This tragic incident occurred on the night of Saturday, August 19, 1978, when four supporters of Khomeini, with the help of the cinema's caretaker and under the cover of darkness, locked the doors, trapping 630 people inside who were then burned alive. The death toll later exceeded 677. Khomeini's supporters falsely attributed this tragedy to the Pahlavi dynasty, laying the foundation of the 1979 revolt in Iran on lies.

The events of September 8, 1978, known as "Black Friday" or the "September 8 Massacre," were orchestrated by two mullahs with the help of Palestinian and Libyan terrorists, resulting in the deaths of 87 demonstrators in Tehran, Jaleh Square. These mullahs were well-prepared and quickly launched propaganda efforts. Many military personnel of the Imperial Iranian Army were killed, yet Khomeini's followers repeatedly blamed the massacre on the Shah's government through relentless media broadcasts. Unfortunately, 46 years ago, fact-checking or verification in Western media was virtually non-existent. It became almost fashionable to support the overthrow of the Shah, allowing radical Islam and Islamic terrorism to take root in Iran. For some leftist figures, praising Khomeini became a mark of intellectualism. Moreover, on December 11, 1978, a sergeant and a conscript soldier in the army opened fire on 35 officers at the Lavizan garrison during lunch, later declaring their allegiance to Khomeini.

This regime came to power through a legacy of crime, bloodshed, and barbarism. Countries like Iraq, Lebanon, Afghanistan, Libya, Syria, and Cuba all supported Khomeini. Many of Iran's leftist and Islamic terrorists, including the People's Mujahedin (MKO) and the Fedayeen, received military training in Palestinian camps. The MEK emerged from Mosaddeq's supporters (the National Front), who also backed Khomeini's terrorism. However, Mosaddeq himself sought help from Islamists to eliminate General Ali Razmara (7 March 1951) and later pardoned the assassin, a member of Fada'iyan-e Islam. Yet, in the Western world, it is falsely claimed that Mosaddeq was a democrat and a democratically elected prime minister chosen by the people, and that a coup took place. No one knows by what vote or how many votes he was elected, nor why the CIA would have staged a coup against a demagogue who ruled under martial law with torture in his prisons. And this falsehood persists to this day.

Contrary to all the interpretations and reports in the Western media of 1978 and 1979, Khomeini's followers were never supporters of democracy. They aspired to model Iran after the Soviet Union, Cuba, Albania, and Libya. Khomeini even secured airtime on Baghdad Radio from Saddam Hussein for his propaganda. Once in power, Khomeini supported Islamic terrorist groups worldwide, hosting terrorists from around the globe in Tehran under the guise of Islamic conferences, where they received military and tactical training. The Islamic Republic was established with the involvement of Yasser Arafat and a representative sent by Gaddafi. But the world media deceived humanity about Khomeini and his dogmatic followers.

The very essence and foundation of the Islamic Republic are inseparably linked with terrorism. In 2023, Khamenei incited Shia and Sunni terrorist groups in the Shiite Crescent against Israel, openly proclaiming in his speeches that Israel's destruction was imminent. Digital countdown clocks were set up in Tehran and other cities, marking the days until Israel's supposed annihilation. The flags of Islamic terrorist groups were visibly displayed behind Republic officials during official interviews in Tehran. The terrorist networks of the Islamic Republic, supported by the Ministry of Intelligence Service (MOIS), the Ministry of Defense, the Quds Force, the Army, and the Revolutionary Guards (IRGC), launched attacks on Israel, culminating in the October 7 massacre that claimed 1,200 lives. Almost immediately, the Islamic Republic's notorious lobbies abroad, using the same media that had supported the 1979 Khomeiniist revolt, began to defend the regime, declaring it innocent of Hamas's atrocities, while acting as both prosecutor and judge.

87
THE FINAL SOLUTION IS REGIME CHANGE IN IRAN

The current state of Iran is a powder keg of societal dissatisfaction, relentless repression, and environmental and economic collapse. Theocratic dictatorship under Iran's dictator, Ali Khamenei has pushed the nation to the brink of disintegration. Khamenei, an obstinate and irrational autocrat, clings to power despite cascading undeniable failures, deluding himself into fantasies of triumph while the country suffers under his rule. His tirades are laden with vitriol against Israel, the United States, and the modern West, yet they reveal his growing fear of the Iranian people's imminent uprising against his dishonorable regime.

Islamic countries, too, bear significant responsibility for nurturing this cancerous tumor. When Khomeini released his book *Wilayat al-Faqih* in Lebanon in 1970, neither the Islamic nations nor the Persian Gulf states denounced its deceitful and hateful rhetoric, steeped in Soviet-style communism and hollow autocracy. Fueled by delusions and backed by allies who subscribed to Islamic terrorism or Marxist militancy, Ruhollah Khomeini pursued his vision of 'Islamic jihad' and the establishment of a terror-driven Islamic regime. From the outset, the Soviet Union and its proxies—including figures like Yasser Arafat and Fidel Castro—actively supported this ludicrous venture in the Middle East. Even Saddam Hussein provided Khomeini with a radio platform, while Muammar Gaddafi funneled financial aid, enabling the rise of this malignant destructive ideology."

The Shia Crescent, a disastrous manifestation of clerical tyranny driven by the ambitions of the Islamic Republic, has extended its tentacles across the Middle East like a malignant octopus. It has fueled terrorism, ignited sectarian conflicts, and perpetuated regional instability—all at the devastating cost of Iran's wealth and its people's well-being. Only the complete dismantling of this theocratic project can open the path to peace, democracy, and the region's liberation from this destructive clerical empire.

For over half a century, Israel has stood as a witness to the relentless and malignant expansion of Islamic terrorism. Yet, when Israel advocated for regime change in Iran following the catastrophic 1979 revolt, the global community leaned toward appeasement and diplomacy with the Islamic Republic's terrorists or the criminal ayatollahs in Tehran. When Israel exposed the transnational terrorist networks orchestrated by the Shiite mullahs, the world chose to counsel Israel rather than confront Iran's regime. Even as Khomeini openly declared his intent to export the 'Khomeinist Islamic Revolt,' it appeared that Western intelligence agencies had not even bothered to read his *Wilayat al-Faqih*. This neglect was the true tragedy in 20th century.

Ahmad Kasravi—a historian and a visionary advocate for the 'Iranian Secular Identity' movement—courageously exposed the fabrications and manipulations of Shiite clerics, particularly their invention of the 12th Imam. His unyielding criticism of these deceptions led to his assassination on March 11, 1946, in a Tehran courthouse, where he was brutally gunned down and stabbed by members of the extremist group *Fada'iyan-e Islam,* loyal to Navab Safavi. These terrorists, blind to truth and reason, embody the same oppressive forces that continue to dominate Iran today. Both Khomeini and Khamenei have openly revered Safavi, a murderous and corrupt cleric who symbolizes their shared values.

Khomeini, in his 1944 book *Kashf al-Asrar (Unveiling of Secrets),* explicitly called for Ahmad Kasravi's execution in front of his religious followers. Why? Because Khomeini perceived himself as the earthly representative of the mythical 12th Imam—a delusion that Khamenei perpetuates to this day. Factually, both men have propagated the belief that the Islamic Caliphate under *Wilayat al-Faqih* must persist until the Day of Judgment, awaiting a sword-wielding savior to emerge from a well and redeem humanity. These two figures—Khomeini and Khamenei—audaciously claim to be the earthly emissaries of this imagined redeemer, using this narrative to justify their reign of tyranny and terror.

Ali Khamenei's regime finds itself ensnared in an unwinnable paradox or trapped in a lose-lose game, where each oppressive measure only heightens its international isolation and hastens its inevitable collapse. Meanwhile, the unyielding courage of the Iranian people signals that the era of religious despotism and terror-fueled governance is approaching its long-overdue demise.

Khamenei continues to deliver rambling, disjointed diatribes, resembling the behavior of a deranged autocrat. His tirades, filled with venom against Israel, the United States, the broader Middle East, and his own people, are often punctuated with threats to his adversaries. Yet, his delusional proclamations have become so detached from reality that they are met with little more than indifference or ridicule, even among his shrinking circle of supporters.

Iran's public anger is palpable—a nation suffocated by decades of corruption, authoritarianism, and the blatant criminality of its ruling clerics. The people's deep-seated hatred for the regime is rooted in the grim realities of everyday life: an economy in freefall, pervasive poverty, environmental collapse, and the oppressive chokehold of religious dogma. On the international stage, the regime's failures are equally glaring. Its so-called 'resistance axis' has unraveled, and its grandiose dreams of regional dominance have crumbled into disarray. The once-robust terror networks it cultivated across the Middle East are now faltering, serving as a testament to the regime's broader decay and diminishing influence."

Khamenei embodies the rot at the heart of his regime—a vindictive, unyielding despot trapped in denial. In a single month, he has delivered multiple speeches proclaiming hollow victories over Israel and the West, further exposing his detachment from reality. His rhetoric, steeped in aggression and delusion, highlights his descent into irrelevance. Cloaked in a facade of religious sanctity, Khamenei's true legacy is the destruction of Iran and the Middle East, leaving behind a trail of ruin and despair.

This Iranian dictator, consumed by delusions and an insatiable thirst for blood, tirelessly pursues new victims to satisfy his lust for oppression. Every day, he seeks a neck to tighten the noose around, embodying the cruelty and tyranny that define his rule. It is no surprise that Iranians have likened him to 'Zahhāk'—the malevolent figure from Persian mythology, infamous as the Snake Shoulder, a symbol of relentless evil and bloodshed."

Beneath the surface, a simmering fire of resistance burns brightly among the Iranian people. Decades of relentless suppression have failed to extinguish their unyielding desire for freedom. A tipping point seems imminent. The potential for an Israeli strike on Iran's nuclear facilities or the removal of Khamenei or his successor, Mojtaba, could spark a nationwide uprising. Such a catalyst would dismantle the remnants of the disastrous 1979 revolt, clearing the path for a new era in Iran and across the region.

This moment in history offers a rare and fleeting opportunity. The collapse of the regime would not only liberate Iran but also deliver a decisive blow to the roots of Islamic terrorism that have plagued the Middle East for decades. The world stands on the cusp of witnessing the demise of an 86-year-old dictator and the fall of a 46-year-old despised theocratic regime. This pivotal moment holds the promise of reshaping the future of the Middle East, bringing hope to millions and ending one of history's darkest chapters. Let this be the time Iran finally breaks free from the chains of tyranny, allowing the world to exhale a collective sigh of relief.

The Final solution lies in breaking free from the suffocating grip of clerical rule and dismantling the ideological, financial, and cultural networks that sustain the oppressive Shiite clergy. This would pave the way for a progressive, rational, and inclusive society, replacing superstition and fanaticism with humanity, logic, and equality.

International actors play an indispensable role in this transformation. Regional and global powers must collaborate to ensure that Iran's transition is peaceful and protected from external exploitation. By working together, they can help Iran emerge as a stabilizing force in the Middle East, free from the shadows of terrorism and tyranny.

For a moment, one can close their eyes and imagine a Middle East freed from Velayat-e Faqih (the Shiite clerical octopus) and the mafia-like networks of Islamic terrorism. Picture Crown Prince Reza Pahlavi guiding Iran through a transitional government—a compelling vision that, with safeguards against internal discord and external manipulation, could solidify a stable and democratic future. Envision Israel and the United States reopening their embassies in Tehran. Imagine the destructive ideology of Khomeinism and the chaos of 1979 finally consigned to the graveyard of history. Then, we could truly celebrate the birth of a new Middle East.

88
THE IRANIAN DICTATOR CONTINUES TO ORDER ASSASSINATIONS

On December 11, 2024, Khamenei delivered his first speech following Assad's fall, broadcast as a pre-recorded message. Its significance rested solely on the propaganda spread by his supporters. During the 51-minute ramble, he offered no ideas, messages, or meaningful content. His speech was riddled with delusions—a chaotic and unsettling display.

Khamenei's arguments came across as childish, riddled with lies and contradictions, and his sentences were often incoherent and disjointed. He embodies the traits of a stubborn, fearful, and vengeful and irrational dictator.

After my article in The Jerusalem Post on December 8, I appeared on "Iran International TV" at the invitation of Mehdi Parpanchi, the perceptive director of news, to discuss Assad's downfall and the potential domino effect threatening the

Islamic Republic. In advance, my friend Dr. Michael Rubin from the American Enterprise Institute (AEI) had written about the possibility of Iran and other regional nations facing collapse after Syria.

Khamenei lashed out in his December 11 speech, stating: "That ignorant analyst knows nothing about resistance, thinking it will weaken. Iran remains strong and mighty." I shared excerpts from both analyses on my social media. On 2022, after Khamenei criticized my book Trapped by Events—a dialogue with H. E. Parviz Sabeti, a former SAVAK official—my lawyer (J.S.) advised me to inform the FBI and DHS, which I did.

Desperately, Khamenei revealed how the humiliating defeat of the regime's "Axis of Evil" in the Middle East, particularly against Israel, has left him disgraced, isolated, and despondent. He resorted to issuing threats. He tacitly acknowledged the misery and failure of the outlaw regime he leads, lamenting that the U.S. and Israel had thwarted his ambitions for domination and continued violence. His frustration was evident as he admitted to Israel's success in disrupting arms and bomb shipments. For years, he has labeled the entire world as "enemies," yet paradoxically expects these "enemies" to tolerate his provocations, and terrorism.

Khamenei's obstinate and misguided behavior. While his fantasies of silencing dissidents persist, his reign of fear and violence can no longer stifle the free flow of information. The regime scrambles to suppress dissent, with the Attorney General swiftly announcing legal action against critics and targeting analysts and commentators in a desperate bid to reactivate dormant terror cells, specifically on U.S. soil.

Khamenei's transnational Shiite Islamic terrorist network has crumbled and is no longer capable of spreading chaos across the Middle East. Decades of oppressing the Iranian people and squandering their wealth on ambitions of regional domination have unraveled. The collapse of this network marks not only a strategic defeat for Khamenei but also a turning point for those who have long suffered under his regime's tyranny.

Khamenei revealed his inability to accept defeat while expressing deep concern over the regional failures. The loss of Hamas and Hezbollah, leaving only the West Bank, PIJ, Houthis, and PMU, highlights the disintegration of his once-influential network.

The special operations units in Lebanon and Syria within the IRGC have been rendered inactive, as they no longer have any practical capabilities. Khamenei's attempts to justify the regime's actions hinge on superstitious Shiite narratives manufactured by the religious octopus. Despite his claims of fighting for Shiite shrines, even the IRGC's commanders have admitted to intervening in Syria to save Assad long before ISIS appeared. Khamenei claimed that Iran's involvement in Syria was to preserve security, but where in the world does an anti-security terrorist seek to protect security?

Khamenei repeatedly lied in his speech. For example, he claimed he wanted to help the people of Syria and Lebanon, but this was untrue; he had no intention of sending rice, flour, or oil—his aim was to send weapons. Another lie was his justification for intervention in Syria, where he stated that Syria helped Iran during the eight-year war. However, he failed to mention that even then, Khomeini prolonged the war to such an extent that in November 1987, Syria, along with other Arab countries, condemned Iran for delaying the acceptance of Resolution 598 and explicitly expressed "solidarity" with Saddam Hussein—the criminal leader of Iraq. Syria also signed a strongly worded statement from Arab countries in support of Saddam Hussein against Iran. In the *Kayhan* newspaper on Thursday, February 8, 1979, it was reported that how Syria had supported Khomeini and his terrorist gang before 1979. Notably, Assad's fall brought joy to the Iranian people. Another defeat for Khamenei came when the terrorist group Hamas congratulated the anti-Assad armed forces on their victory in Syria. This is reminiscent of the time when Khomeini formed his interim government in front of Yasser Arafat and Gaddafi's envoy—both of whom later supported Saddam Hussein.

One point was glaringly evident: Khamenei is buried under the rubble of defeat, yet he still plots new schemes to create chaos and incite war, despite no longer having the power or energy to carry them out. The stubborn old fool refuses to learn from developments and fails to understand that killing, threats, and suppression will lead him nowhere. This is a path that dictators around the world have trodden, reaching no destination, and he too will remain buried in this sewer.

The ruthless tyrant of Iran—demonstrated that he still lacks any understanding of reality. He fundamentally fails to comprehend international relations and remains immersed in his own delusions and fantasies. For his own consolation, he delivers long speeches that resemble incoherent rambling. His words lack scientific basis, are not grounded in reality, and have no foundation in reason or logic. All of Iran's wealth has been squandered on expanding Islamic terrorism, arms trafficking, and financing terrorism. Thanks to Israel, all of his deterrence power, defensive military capabilities, and his so-called axis of evil have been destroyed.

Khamenei and his incapable regime failed to launch a third military attack on Israel and know that Trump is on his way to the White House. The Islamic Republic has effectively become weaker, and its survival faces serious danger. In these circumstances, he is merely content with announcing the construction of an atomic bomb, but this will certainly lead to a military strike on nuclear facilities, coordinated by the CIA and Mossad. The powerless, exhausted, and humiliated loser of the Middle East is Khamenei and his regime. These are villains and thugs who lack the support of the Iranian people. Iranian society has no dialogue even with a weak dictator.

American and Israeli intelligence agencies also know that without regime change in Iran, there will be no peace, stability, or calm in the Middle East. Seeing the Islamic Republic fall into a downward spiral of weakness and defeat is a pleasing scene for them. They know that the weaker it becomes, the less ability it has to ignite fires and wage war, and it is forced to retreat, surviving only through its repression machine and propaganda. The regime in Tehran is severely lacking in any tools or resources. They know that in the eyes of the people, the Islamic Republic is dead and should be buried. The mafia and military junta regime is on the verge of collapse.

He continued his speech with empty promises and hollow slogans, his face crumpled and devastated. He offered no substance in his claims or military displays. His terrorist organizations have collapsed, his imaginary resistance front has been destroyed, and he lacks the ability to rebuild. Like a defeated army in war, he has no possibility of reconstruction. In his mind, the whole world is to blame, and he judges everyone.

The mullah's regime has been rhetorically disarmed and is at an impasse. The regime is rotten to the core and will be uprooted with a single shake—a regime without allies or friends, with a worn-out structure and internal crises. Crisis-ridden, impoverished, and politically paralyzed Iran, locked under a harsh political blockade, needs no further explanation. The continuation of this erosive game by the regime is no longer viable.

Khamenei—barefacedly—did not even dare to mention the names of Turkey or Russia in his speech. He neither criticized Bashar al-Assad nor uttered a single word against Putin or Erdogan. Instead, he threatened the Iranian people, critics, and analysts. He remains committed to continuing the path of rebellion, as his survival depends on it. He is fundamentally unwilling to coexist with the modern world.

Amidst lies and threats and failing to address consecutive defeats, he promises the appearance of something that doesn't exist, and crisis has engulfed all pillars of the corrupt regime. History assures us that the day will come when the Iranian people will no longer hear that trembling, discordant voice. Iranians, well-versed in Ferdowsi's Shahnameh, know the truth: Tyranny leads to destruction.

89
THE MOIS: A LEGACY OF SHAME FOR MULLAHS

Echoing the tradition of American Presidents who visit Langley to engage with the CIA, Masoud Pezeshkian attended a ceremony at the Ministry of Intelligence Service (MOIS) to mark its 40th anniversary. Known in Europe and America as a terrorist organization, MOIS is implicated in numerous international crimes and supports the destructive ideology of Khomeinism and Shiite clerical tyranny. Claiming to be the 'unseen soldiers of Imam Zaman,' a figure considered mythical and nonexistent outside of Shiite lore or superstitions, MOIS exposes Pezeshkian as a populist.

For history, the MOIS, later to become MOIS, was established in 1983, amalgamating revolutionary-era intelligence units. It evolved into a formidable force coordinating sixteen intelligence and counterintelligence bodies. Despite nominal control under the president, MOIS's ministers require approval from Khomeini or Khamenei, reflecting the regime's theocratic grip.

In the geopolitical arena, the United States' intelligence community has long recognized Iran's MOIS as a significant intelligence apparatus intertwined with the criminal mullahs who govern Iran. This establishment, MOIS, has been directly linked to the loss of many CIA officers over the years, a testament to its ruthless operations.

MOIS utilizes all means at its disposal to protect the Islamic Republic's interests, employing infiltration, monitoring, arrests, and cooperation with foreign intelligence agencies. The infamous "Chain Murders" of Iranian dissident intellectuals during the 1990s serve as a grim reminder of MOIS's brutal operations, with the agency later claiming responsibility. MOIS has been involved in various types of terrorist activities—sabotage, espionage, bombings, and the assassination of dissidents—all within and outside Iran. This transnational suppression has persisted since the inception of the Islamic Republic, intensifying even during periods marked as 'pragmatist' regimes.

In light of MOIS's ruthless and manipulative activities, the international community must remain vigilant, holding the agency accountable for its transgressions. The recent sanctions imposed by the US underscore the imperative to curb MOIS's malevolent reach and protect human rights and democracy from its insidious influence. The legacy of Iran's MOIS is one of terror and subversion, and acknowledging this reality is crucial for fostering a safer world.

In the contemporary era led by Esmail Khatib, the MOIS is actively operating and orchestrating a transnational terrorist network across the Middle East and Latin America. What is particularly alarming is MOIS' concerted effort to establish numerous "sleeper cells" within the United States. On the international stage, it has always been alongside the IRGC and the army in developing terrorism and providing financial and logistical support to the terrorism network in the Middle East and even Central Africa and Latin America, etc. Hundreds of cases of kidnapping, murder, human trafficking, drug transit with the help of Hezbollah and PKK, etc., have been recorded.

Throughout its existence, MOIS has been a primary instrument of violence, assassinations, and manipulation under various administrations, whether reformist or hardliner, with core policies of repression and coercion remaining unchanged. This has cemented the agency's malign role in supporting Islamic terrorism.

Within Iran, MOIS is first despised among the people, and later globally. Its only skills are hitting, killing, blinding, torturing, raping, confiscating, and harassing ordinary people, political and social activists, and interfering in all artistic, cultural, and intellectual works within Iran. It has done the least to help the peace, comfort, and security of the Iranian people. Forty years ago, Khomeini established the dark clerical dictatorship in Iran, five years after the 1979 uprising and the rise to power of the Shiite mullahs, this ministry has since been, alongside the police force and Basij, the arm of repression of the mullahs' regime. In the sinister and black record of this terrorist organization, hundreds of cases of murder of intellectuals, artists, activists, prisoners, etc., have been recorded.

From the day of its establishment until today, several mullahs have reached the presidency in this sinister and mafia ministry. Khomeini only had one Minister of Intelligence,

Reyshahri, who was present in this ministry for 5 years of Khomeini's crime-filled caliphate. Before 1979's revolt, he was arrested by SAVAK (the National Security Agency of Iran during the reign of the late, and patriotic Shah of Iran) due to terrorist activity in an Islamic group. After 1979, he was also one of the Islamic judges who issued death sentences for hundreds of people in Islamic kangaroo courts. He was one of the famous bloodthirsty figures of Khomeini's era. He was the Islamic judge of Khomeini's Islamic courts. Later in his life, he was supported by reformists to be present in the Assembly of Experts.

During the caliphate and dictatorship of Khamenei from 1989 until today, which has been 35 years, great terror has been institutionalized in Iran, and he has had 7 spy mullahs in the MOIS, although few have reached 8 years of tenure in this ministry. From Fallahian, Dori Najafabadi, Younesi, Mohseni Ejei, Moslehi, Alavi to Khatib, the machine of repression and terrorism by this ministry never ceased.

During Fallahian's time, Interpol was after his arrest due to the AMIA explosion in Argentina (18 July 1994), the Mykonos murder (17 September 1992), chain murders, murders outside the country, etc., but this did not happen. Factually, Europe did not cooperate with Israel and the United States. He was also one of the Islamic judges before becoming minister and killed hundreds in Abadan, Mashhad, Kermanshah, and Mashhad. One of the cold-blooded slaughterers who is a major violator of human rights in the Islamic Republic.

After him, Dori Najafabadi was also one of the notorious mullah prosecutors whose hands are stained with the blood of innocent massacres. During Khatami's presidency and his ministry, chain murders among Iranian intellectuals occurred, and he resigned. But in the prosecutor's office, he issued so many torture, prison, death, and murder orders that Europe eventually issued a statement against him.

Following his tenure, Ali Younesi reached the ministry, but he was also among the heads of military courts and directly participated in the massacre of military figures opposing the Islamic Republic. But because of populism, he sometimes points to points of interest in Iranian history.

Then it was Ejehi's turn. He was also previously an interrogator. He worked in the prosecutor's office and was always associated with important and sensitive cases in high-security ranks, and he still maintains this position. He is globally known for violence and repression. From mass executions to the brutal suppression of protesters. He also teaches training courses at the Baqer al-Olum Faculty of the MOIS and also in revolutionary courts. His name is tied to the suppression of protesters, shutting down the internet, and harassing prisoners.

Next in line, Moslehi came to power. From the first day of 1979, he was one of the thugs of the Islamic Revolution Committee and supporters of Khomeini and participated in the executing and harassment of citizens supporting the late Shah of Iran. He was later the representative of the Supreme Leader in the military forces (IRGC and Basij). He is one of the savage repressors, and even the European Union on October 10, 2011, banned Moslehi from entering EU countries due to severe and widespread human rights violations in Iran and the rights of Iranian citizens, and symbolically said that all his assets in Europe would also be seized. Then, according to common practice, the U.S. Treasury Department also sanctioned Heidar Moslehi in September 2022 due to cyber activities against the United States and its allies. His education was solely in Islamic jurisprudence and he was a student of Khamenei, having little connection with intelligence studies or political sciences.

This is the record of 7-8 Ministers of MOIS in Iran's outlaw regime, all involved in crime. They lack academic education and security expertise. They have all played an overt role in repression and terrorism. They are under international pursuit and sanctions.

One must ask Pezeshkian, with this disgraceful and shameful history, what is there to be proud of? A history filled with crimes and murder that has supported terrorist groups within the transnational terrorism network tied to the Islamic Republic in the Shia Crescent for years is not something to be proud of. Even if there isn't an international tribunal to condemn the mullahs' crimes, perhaps in the future, akin to the Holocaust Museum, there might emerge a museum dedicated to the crimes of the mullahs.

90
THE MIRAGE OF REFORM IN IRAN'S ETERNAL THEOCRACY

In the shadow of Iran's turbulent history, the election of Masoud Pezeshkian as president is heralded by some as a sign of potential change. However, this perception is misguided. Pezeshkian's presidency is not a harbinger of reform but a continuation of the Islamic Republic's enduring theocratic rule, skillfully orchestrated by Ali Khamenei to maintain his grip on a nation teetering on the brink of socio-political upheaval.

1. The Illusion of Election Integrity

The recent elections in Iran were anything but democratic; they were a tightly controlled spectacle with Khamenei ensuring only those loyal to the regime's foundational theocratic principles were in the running. The claim of a 70 percent voter turnout for Ebrahim Raisi in previous elections has been widely ridiculed as fictitious—a manufactured statistic designed to project a veneer of popular support. This manipulation of electoral integrity is a strategic ploy by the regime to legitimize its authoritarian grip while dismissing international and domestic calls for true democratic reforms.

2. A Puppet of the Regime

Far from being an agent of change, Pezeshkian is undeniably another of Khamenei's puppets, installed to placate international scrutiny while ensuring the continuation of the status quo. His presidency does not signify a shift in power but is rather a calculated move to refresh the regime's tarnished image in response to growing domestic discontent and international isolation. This strategic positioning helps the regime to mask its authoritarian practices under the guise of superficial change, misleading the international community about the nature of governance in Iran.

3. Economic Despair and Mismanagement

Under Pezeshkian, Iran's economy continues to languish under the weight of corruption, mismanagement, and stringent international sanctions. Despite his promises of economic reforms, these are likely to be nothing more than rhetoric, with little substantial policy change to address the deep-seated issues of graft and economic inefficiency. The regime's economic policies have historically prioritized its survival over the welfare of its citizens, leading to a cycle of poverty and despair that fuels widespread dissatisfaction.

4. Suppression of Dissent

The regime's response to civil unrest and public dissent has been characterized by brutal repression. The nationwide protests ignited by the tragic death of Mahsa Amini are a clear testament to the regime's fear of losing control. These protests, demanding basic human rights and freedoms, were not quelled through reform or dialogue but through violence and intimidation. This approach reveals the regime's true nature—an entity that will not tolerate opposition or relinquish control, regardless of the cost to its people.

5. The Farce of Social Reforms

Any minor concessions on social issues, such as the mandatory hijab, are merely superficial gestures that fail to address the systemic oppression embedded within the regime. These "reforms" are strategically deployed as a smokescreen to distract from the regime's authoritarian practices and to give a semblance of progress where there is none. The state continues to enforce rigid control over personal freedoms, demonstrating that the regime's primary concern is maintaining power, not the welfare of its citizens.

6. A Compromised Foreign Policy

Pezeshkian's potential overtures towards renewing diplomacy with the United States and alleviating sanctions are likely to be ineffective and superficial. Iran's foreign policy, deeply intertwined with Khamenei's vision, remains focused on expanding its nuclear capabilities and supporting regional militias, actions that are fundamentally at odds with the interests of the Iranian people and global peace. This policy stance ensures that Iran will continue to face international isolation and economic hardship, further exacerbating the challenges faced by its population.

***

Masoud Pezeshkian's presidency is not a dawn of reform but a continuation of a deceitful narrative crafted by a regime desperate to maintain power at any cost. The international community and the Iranian people must recognize the enduring authoritarianism that defines the Islamic Republic of Iran. The path to genuine reform in Iran is obstructed not by external pressures but by an entrenched leadership unwilling to relinquish its totalitarian control over the nation.

Pezeshkian's election, far from being a step toward liberalization, is a calculated maneuver to sustain the regime's theocratic autocracy under the guise of moderate reformism.

91
THE PAPER TIGER HAS COLLAPSED

In a few days, it will be the anniversary of October 7th, when terrorist groups within the Shia Crescent committed crimes against humanity in Israel, brutally slaughtering 1,200 people. Perhaps in the history of Iran, the Arab invasions (between 632 and 654 CE), the Mongol invasion (1219), or the rise of the Shia clerics (1979) are painful and well-remembered events. But for the people of Israel, after the Holocaust (between 1941 and 1945), witnessing such a horrific and agonizing scene was unimaginable.

From the very beginning, when the Shia cleric in Iran pursued power and wealth, we can refer to Khomeini's 1961 speech, where, like Nasser's soldier, he spoke out against the Shah and brought up the name of Israel. From the day the Shah of Iran recognized Israel de facto until the winter of 1979, roughly 18 and a half years, the Shia cleric engaged in terrorist network-building and training terrorists. Khomeini's book, *Velayat-e Faqih*, was published in Beirut in 1970. Khomeini's entire destructive ideology was built on enmity towards Israel and the U.S. After gaining power in Iran, the Shia clerics committed every atrocity against Israel and the U.S. Every year, hundreds of innocent and defenseless Israelis were killed by the Islamic Republic's terrorist network.

The U.S. lacked a clear and informed policy towards the Islamic Republic, often turning a blind eye to many realities. It mistakenly believed that the so-called reformists were different from the hardliners. However, these same reformists, in the summer of 2000 – one year before 9/11 – awarded an honorary doctorate to Nasrallah at Tarbiat Modares University in Tehran. Nasrallah was the very person who ridiculed Iran's ancient civilization, referring to these Islamic terrorist networks as the "Islamic civilization." Yet Iran, before the rise of Islam, was an empire. Nasrallah is the one who called Khomeini and Khamenei, the mad and bloodthirsty executioners, the descendants of the Prophet of Islam. Of course, all these words were said in exchange for money, and there was never any real difference between reformists and hardliners in the advancement of Islamic terrorism.

Khomeini later formed a transnational terrorist network, which, according to mafia-style propaganda, was named the "Resistance Front." Khamenei expanded it, and Hezbollah became the main center of its terrorist operations. Whenever any terrorist branch, like the Houthis, Hamas, or the Popular Mobilization Forces, needed help, Hezbollah was there to assist. Even during Rafsanjani's era (1993), in Sudan, Hezbollah, the Quds Force, and Al-Qaeda formed an unholy triangle, and Iran became a training ground and sanctuary for Islamic terrorists, eventually leading to the events of

September 11, 2001. Yet again, the U.S. failed to grasp the reality on the ground, clinging to the deceptive smiles of the reformists, a mere mirage.

Years passed, and Khamenei installed an electronic countdown clock for the destruction of Israel in Iranian cities. The air force commander of the IRGC posed in front of the flags of the terrorist network, but global media continued to claim that the Islamic Republic was not behind the events.

However, after one year, the fog of confusion has cleared, and it has become evident that the source of all these crimes and wickedness is the Velayat-e Faqih regime's treasury in Tehran. For this reason, the Israeli people have realized that the people of Iran are friends, supporters, and sympathizers of Israel, and that the Islamic Republic is an occupier of Iran and has nothing to do with Iran's history and civilization.

After one year of pain and suffering endured by the people of Israel, the Middle East has also realized that in all criminal acts, the Quds Force, the IRGC, and the Ministry of Intelligence of the Islamic Republic stood alongside these terrorist groups against Israel. As long as this regime remains, such heartbreaking scenes will repeat. Perhaps after destroying the Islamic Republic's terrorist arms, Israel will also confront the root cause to prevent Iran from acquiring nuclear weapons, or else it will pose a threat to all of humanity.

Yet Israel, with persistence, strong leadership, accurate intelligence, and patriotic motivation, has risen to destroy the Islamic Republic's transnational terrorist network. While both the U.S. and Europe did not stand by its side, it has now become clear after a year that their paper tiger has collapsed one by one as autumn begins, and within months, Hezbollah has been relegated to the dustbin of history.

Now, the world is awaiting the end of the story. Certainly, according to the judgment of history, this arduous journey will continue, and this soggy cardboard network will fall. Khamenei is gradually losing the ability to rebuild and activate Hamas and Hezbollah. Though Hezbollah, a criminal mafia organization involved in everything from drug trafficking to gambling and human and arms smuggling, has no more strength to rebuild. The Middle East has also realized that wherever the Islamic Republic set foot, nothing but destruction, devastation, explosions, and terror followed. Yemen, Lebanon, Syria, Iraq, Iran... all were consumed in the flames of the Shia cleric's savagery. But the Middle East is awaiting a rebirth, and Israel's name will shine as the greatest power in the region. The future of Iran, after the collapse of the clerical regime, is a rebirth.

The terrorist Republic of Khomeini in Tehran was formed in the presence of Yasser Arafat. Its members were trained in Palestinian terrorist camps. However, the future of the Middle East will shine brighter in the friendship between Iran and Israel.

Nowadays, Iran's regime finds itself in a precarious situation, uncertain of how to proceed. Even if Israel were to launch a ground attack in Lebanon and eliminate Nasrallah, Iran's regime, despite being under immense pressure, lacks the capability to engage Israel in warfare. Khamenei is terrified of engaging in a war with Israel. He knows that the Iranian people are not supporting him. The younger generation, in particular, has celebrated the deaths of Islamic terrorists like Haniyeh and Nasrallah. The Quds Force, the MOIS, and the IRGC are nothing but a group of brainwashed, unskilled thugs. If Khamenei engages in war with Israel, he will lose, and his outlaw regime will collapse. He prefers to remain dishonored and discredited, hiding in a corner, issuing empty threats, but avoiding a direct conflict with Israel. He is fully aware that Israel would destroy his missile and nuclear facilities. In the end, Khamenei is merely a delusional, wild and coward mullah.

Finally, the puppet of Khamenei or Nasrallah was eliminated on 27th of September , and surely Khamenei would die and Israel would remain proudly standing. Khamenei's destructive policies (the head of the octopus in Tehran) wouldn't go anywhere. The removal of Hamas and Hezbollah was a great victory for Israel. The paper tiger and spider's web of the Shiite Islamic caliphate collapsed. The world of 21st century will be a safer place after the abolition of Islamic terrorists.

92
THE REGIME OF LIES, TERROR, AND DECEPTION

This regime in Tehran echoes the brutal reign of Ismail I of the Safavid dynasty (22 December 1501 – 23 May 1524), who, 900 years after the Arab invasion, rose to power and established Shi'ism as the official religion in Iran. Lacking any sense of national pride, Ismail I's rule was built on a foundation of extreme violence and bloodshed. He masked his cruelty and hatred under the guise of religion, beheading, dismembering, and torturing those who opposed him. If no enemies were found, he would even turn his violence on his own family. Anyone opposing Shi'ism faced death by the sword. Ismail I spread terror across the land through relentless massacres. Historical accounts, including those in the British Museum, document his ruthless killing of Iranians, burying the living and exhuming the dead. He declared jihad and reshaped Iranian history through Shi'ism. On the day of his coronation at the central mosque in Tabriz, he brazenly declared, "I have been appointed by God, and the prophets are with me. If the people resist, I will draw my sword and leave not one of the 300,000 people of Tabriz alive." After 520 years, can we see any difference between him and Khamenei or Khomeini?

Factually, Ismail's soldiers in Tabriz even slaughtered pregnant women and massacred 20,000 people, not sparing even the dogs. Ahmad Kasravi, an author later assassinated by Khomeini's followers, exposed the bloodthirsty and barbaric deeds of Shah Ismail. In Mazandaran, Ismail killed his opponents by forcing their necks into iron cages and setting them on fire. He also massacred 7,000 people in Tabas. Obsessed with suppressing dissent, the ruthless Safavid ruler burned several opponents alive. After him, Sultan Ismail II, driven by deep-seated anger, continued the brutal massacres, killing and blinding 12,000 people during his brief reign. Sultan Abbas's 40-year reign was also marked by bloodshed and massacres. He exiled opponents to the fortress of Alamut, blinded two of his sons, and killed one. Only during his reign did the mullahs gain respect, as Sultan Abbas, cruel and tyrannical, repeatedly ordered massacres.

Khamenei, much like the bloodthirsty Safavid rulers, has shown extreme savagery and barbarism, akin to the Mongols and the Safavid Chagins (cannibals), in brutally suppressing the freedom-seeking people of Iran in the streets. He has also created terrorist groups that have killed innocent Israeli and American soldiers and civilians. During the Safavid era, there was a group of cannibal executioners who, at the king's command, would tear people apart and eat them alive before his eyes. This group, known as the Chagins, was active in the court of Sultan Abbas. Today, the executioners of the Velayat-e Faqih have not only killed young people in Iran but have also supported Hamas in killing Israelis.

Five hundred and twenty years later, Khamenei seems intent on reviving the brutal tortures of the Chagins from the Safavid era, tearing apart the people of Iran. He remains the same—a ruler steeped in a culture of savagery, who continues to crush a devastated and collapsing country under his robe and sandals.

Even though, forty-six years ago, it was nearly impossible to openly and truthfully assert in any global media that they were lying and merely a group of criminals because no one would have believed it. Primarily, the fire at Rex Cinema in Abadan City was a deliberate and criminal act orchestrated by revolutionary terrorists opposed to the late King Pahlavi. This tragic incident occurred on the night of Saturday, August 19, 1978, when four supporters of Khomeini, with the assistance of the cinema's caretaker and under the cover of darkness, locked the cinema's doors, trapping 630 people inside who were then burned alive. The death toll later exceeded 677. Khomeini's supporters attempted to falsely attribute this tragedy to the Pahlavi dynasty. The foundation of the 1979 revolt in Iran was built on lies.

Then, the events of September 8, 1978, known as "Black Friday" or the "September 8 Massacre," involved two mullahs who, with the help of Palestinian and Libyan terrorists, orchestrated the deaths of 87 demonstrators in Tehran. These mullahs were prepared in advance and immediately launched propaganda efforts. Many military personnel of the Imperial Iranian Army were slaughtered, but Khomeini's followers repeatedly blamed the massacre on the Shah's government through continuous media broadcasts. Unfortunately, 46 years ago, fact-checking or verification in Western media was non-existent. It seemed almost fashionable for the Shah to be overthrown, and for radical Islam and Islamic terrorism to take root in Iran. For some leftist figures, praising Khomeini was a mark of intellectualism. Furthermore, on December 11, 1978, a sergeant and a conscript soldier in the army opened fire on 35 officers at the Lavizan garrison while they were eating lunch in the mess hall. They later declared their allegiance to Khomeini.

This regime ascended to power through a history steeped in crime, bloodshed, and barbarism. Numerous countries like Iraq, Lebanon, Afghanistan, Libya, Syria, and Cuba supported Khomeini. Even many of Iran's leftist and Islamic terrorists, such as the People's Mujahedin (MKO) and the Fedayeen, received military training in Palestinian camps. The MEK was born out of the supporters of Mosaddeq (the National Front), who also supported Khomeini's terrorism. However, Mosaddeq himself sought help from Islamists to eliminate General Ali Razmara (7 March 1951) and later pardoned the assassin, who was member of Fada'iyan-e Islam. Yet, in the Western world, it is falsely claimed that he was a democrat, an democratically elected prime minister chosen by the people, and that a coup occurred. No one in history knows by what vote or how many votes he was elected, or why the CIA should have staged a coup against a demagogue who ran the country under martial law and had torture in his prisons. And this lie continues to this day.

Contrary to all interpretations and reports in the civilized Western media of 1978 and 1979, Khomeini's terrorists were not supporters of democracy. They sought to emulate the Soviet Union, Cuba, Albania, and Libya. Khomeini even secured airtime on Baghdad Radio from Saddam Hussein for his propaganda. Once in power, Khomeini began supporting Islamic terrorist groups worldwide, hosting all the world's terrorists in Tehran under the guise of Islamic conferences, where they received military and tactical training. The Islamic Republic was conceived with the presence of Yasser Arafat and a representative sent by Gaddafi. But the world media lied to humanity about Khomeini and his dogmatic followers.

The essence and genes of the Islamic Republic are inseparably intertwined with terrorism. In 2023, Khamenei incited Shia and Sunni terrorist groups in the Shiite Crescent against Israel. He even promised in his speeches that Israel would soon be destroyed. The Digital Countdown clocks were installed in Tehran and other cities, counting down the days to Israel's destruction. The flags of Islamic terrorist groups were present behind the officials of the Republic in official interviews in Tehran. The terrorist arms and groups of the Islamic Republic, supported by the Ministry of Intelligence Service (MOIS), the Ministry of Defense, the Quds Force, the Army, and the Revolutionary Guards (IRGC), attacked Israel and orchestrated the October 7 tragedy, killing 1,200 people. Immediately, the Islamic Republic's notorious lobbies abroad, in the same media that promoted the 1979 Khomeiniist revolt, sprang into action and declared the Islamic Republic innocent of Hamas's crimes, playing the role of prosecutor and judge.

To this day, ten months after this crime, the role of Ali Khamenei—without the ridiculous and meaningless title of "Ayatollah" (Sign of God)—in this matter becomes more apparent every day. There is no serious will to fight the terrorist-loving mullahs in Tehran. It seems the world does not want to recognize that this terrorist regime has occupied Iran. The only nightmare for this regime of divine representatives on earth is an Israeli attack on the nuclear facilities and then a nationwide uprising of the people inside Iran.

Alas, the world turns a blind eye and deaf ear to Islamic terrorism and the epicenter of Islamic terror propagation. But sooner or later, Israel will be forced to eliminate the nuclear facilities of the savage mullahs for its survival. The Shiite rulers of Iran have disturbed the peace, tranquility, and security of the Middle East with their missile facilities, drones, and terrorist networks. The gap between the sorrowful people and the incomprehensible government has widened. Nowadays, the children of the Islamic Republic's officials seek to protect their wealth, power, and status, and they are even willing to kill for it.

The mullah's regime survives only through repression and propaganda. The new president, loyal to Khamenei, is a demagogue who spouts lies and superstitions that do not address the pain of the Iranian people and, if strikes or uprisings break out, would easily order massacres. In essence, if the mullahs obtain nuclear weapons, there will be no safe place left on earth. They are the plague and the cancerous tumor of the 21st century.

93

THE RETURN OF TRUMP: THE MULLAHS' NIGHTMARE OF DEATH IN IRAN

As Donald Trump's supporters and Republicans prepare to celebrate his glorious return to the White House, beyond America's borders—especially in the Middle East—there is a starkly different atmosphere. For Khamenei's circle and the terrorist-loving ayatollahs in Iran, it is a time of mourning. Khamenei's fear, loathing, and rage are exacerbated by the prospect of a pro-Israel ally resuming residence in the White House.

Khamenei has not only repeatedly called for Trump's assassination but also maliciously proclaimed that Trump would be consigned to the "dustbin of history." Yet, Trump returns to power more formidable than ever, and the past three years of Democratic engagement, characterized by appeasement of the mullahs' regime and ineffectual diplomacy, have been decisively shelved.

Trump is the same triumphant leader who consigned Qasem Soleimani, the world's most dangerous terrorist, to the dustbin of history. Names like Brian Hook and Mike Pompeo are rumored to be returning to Trump's cabinet, much to the mullahs' dismay. These are experienced individuals who understand that the narrative surrounding the 1953 coup in Iran is a shameful fabrication without merit. They recognize that no elections have ever produced a populist prime minister in Iran, dismissing Mosaddeq as nothing more than a demagogue rife with grievances.

Trump champions the imposition of sanctions and maximum pressure on the Islamic Republic, aiming to sever its tendrils of influence throughout the Middle East. This strategy is poised to once again undermine the confidence of the Islamic Republic. Even prior to Trump's anticipated return, Bashar Assad, influenced by Israel's decisive actions against Hamas and Hezbollah thugs, has momentarily distanced himself from the Islamic Republic. Trump seeks to further Israel's relationships with Arab nations, and unlike before, the security and military advisors in his cabinet are not inclined to restrain Israel's efforts against Islamic terrorism. Israel finds itself confronting terrorism on eight different fronts, all instigated by the Islamic Republic of Iran. Over the past year, despite repeated calls for compromise directed at Netanyahu, orchestrated by Ali Khamenei's directives, terrorists have been gearing up for all-out war to annihilate Israel.

Trump returns to the White House, even as Khamenei, an aging isolated leader at 86, has expressed desires to see him eliminated and has persistently dispatched terrorist agents to American soil. Indeed, all Counter-Terrorism agencies within the DHS, FBI, and CIA are acutely aware that "sleeper cells" and "lone wolves" from the Ministry of Intelligence, MOIS, and the IRGC are present within the United States and could become active at any time. However, during Trump's presidency, a transition in leadership from Khamenei is anticipated in Iran. Trump and his security team are well aware that neither Khamenei nor any potential successor hold any sanctity, religious authority, or respectability; they are simply rulers or merely caliphs within a regime of religious despotism and profound dictatorship in Iran that perpetuates its existence through propaganda, terrorism, and oppression.

Trump is committed to maintaining maximum pressure on Iran's mullahs' regime, and his return is likely to reignite a global consensus against what is considered the most perilous terrorist power in the 21st-century world. Throughout the turbulent Middle East, there is a palpable sense of relief at Trump's comeback. The nations of the Persian Gulf are particularly aware of how Iran's hardliners, the Quds Force, and the MOIS have subjected them to tragic risks and dire threats. However, Trump's return symbolizes a "sword of peace," wielded by a patriotic leader who resolutely opposes terrorism and seeks to alleviate regional tensions. This marks a departure from predecessors who, despite publicly aligning with Arab and Jewish interests, covertly engaged with and even financed terrorists, remaining silent on the aggressive policies and regional disruptions orchestrated by the Quds Force and the global acts of terrorism perpetrated by Iran's MOIS.

Fundamentally, engaging in diplomacy with a mullah who supports Islamic terrorism is futile and degrades the very essence of political integrity. The Islamic Republic brings nothing to the negotiation table but terrorism, and in its military efforts, such as blindly firing missiles towards Israel, it has revealed profound weaknesses. Its indiscriminate missile attacks on Israel have not only exposed its military deficiencies but also demonstrated that its only assets are a propaganda machine and a penchant for hurling insults at America and Israel through the media.

The funds Iran received post-Trump have been squandered on fostering terrorism, escalating tensions, and enforcing suppression, with the oil revenues failing to alleviate the growing impoverishment of the Iranian populace. Although Trump has expressly stated he does not aim to change the regime, his presence has been a source of joy for the Iranian people, who oppose the current barbaric regime. The oppressive mullahs, having lost their national pride and identity since the downfall of the late Shah in 1979 due to Jimmy Carter's ill-advised policies, now face humiliation under Trump's gaze. The elimination of Khamenei's favored commander at Baghdad airport was met with rejoicing among Iranians, who prayed for Trump, viewing him not as a terrorist but as a liberator.

By withdrawing from the JCPOA, imposing stringent sanctions, and vocally supporting anti-regime nationwide protests in Iran, Trump has signaled that, despite the global complexities, he is not in favor of regime change in Tehran. However, he resolutely refuses to adopt the placating and indirectly supportive policies toward the mullahs' regime as seen in the administrations of Carter II (Obama) and Carter III (Biden).

Trump's electoral victory represents a decisive rebuke to the policies endorsed by three successive Obama-led administrations. It halts the continuation of strategies that seemed favorable to Middle Eastern dictators under a potential Harris administration, often dubbed Obama's fourth term. Obama's approach inadvertently taught dictators that survival through oppressive tactics would not only be tolerated but indirectly supported by the U.S., as seen in his inconsistent demands for regime change. While he demanded the ouster of leaders like Ben Ali and Mubarak, he notably refrained from calling for Khamenei's departure, despite Iran's escalating regional aggression and proxy wars.

His administration's focus on appeasing Iran and containing China, at the expense of traditional U.S. allies and regional stability, ultimately strengthened both the Islamic Republic and China, contradicting his own policy objectives. Trump's presidency interrupts these patterns, potentially redirecting U.S. foreign policy in the region for the next four years and diminishing the influence of Obama-era policies on global diplomacy.

Trump's return has emboldened the Iranian people to bravely confront their cruel, warmongering, opportunistic, and ruinous regime. His policies are set to immobilize the mullahs once again. Just as Americans have reinstated their leader in the White House, it is now time for Iranians to restore their monarch to the Niavaran Palace. HIH Prince Reza Pahlavi, a leading figure in the Iranian opposition, has publicly celebrated and congratulated Trump's comeback.

Trump's return heralds a decisive shift in Middle Eastern diplomacy, characterized by a robust stance against the mullahs' destructive policies and the broader fight against Islamic terrorism, alongside a commitment to fostering peace. By reinforcing security ties with Israel, he will significantly mitigate the military and security threats posed by the mullah regime. The "push back" policy will be reactivated and implemented, with the Iranian people poised to be the principal agents of change. Soon, influential Iranian-American lobbying groups will emerge to heighten global awareness of the regime's realities, effectively countering the unabashed tactics of Islamic lobbies in America. While it remains uncertain who will serve as the CIA director during Trump's term, it is evident that the counterterrorism center will intensify its focus on the Islamic Republic.

94
AN OPPORTUNITY FOR REGIME CHANGE: REJECTING THE ILLUSIONS OF DIPLOMACY

In the aftermath of the catastrophic failures of the Obama and Biden administrations—both of whom perpetuated the Carter-era approach toward the Islamic Republic of Shiite mullahs in Iran—it is evident that turning to diplomacy is a grave miscalculation, a futile strategy, and a naive fantasy.

Pro-Iran lobbyists and apologists, entrenched within the propaganda machine of the Islamic Republic across Europe and the United States, continue to echo this discordant message. However, former President Trump must avoid being drawn into this lose-lose game.

The era of "maximum pressure," coupled with mechanisms such as the reactivation of the "snapback" sanctions, revealed the regime's vulnerabilities like never before. The only viable path forward, if the goal is to establish a new Middle East and eradicate Islamic terrorism, is unwavering support for regime change in Tehran. Anything less will prolong this sinister game, sacrificing American and Israeli forces to the whims of a barbaric regime.

The Islamic Republic, under the guise of governance, has long operated as a state sponsor of terrorism. Its terrorist proxies, including Hezbollah, Hamas, and the Houthis, have perpetuated instability, leaving behind a trail of destruction. The regime's domestic repression is no less egregious, as Iranians endure a collapsing economy, relentless corruption, and rampant human rights abuses. However, beyond the potential threat of U.S. or Israeli strikes on its nuclear facilities, the Islamic Republic's greatest fear lies in the prospect of a nationwide uprising by the Iranian people. This fear is compounded by the regime's existential challenge of succession.

Ali Khamenei, known for his paranoia, vengefulness, and delusional tendencies, is deeply concerned about the fate of his son Mojtaba, who has been groomed as his successor. Khamenei is haunted by the memory of how Ahmad Khomeini was eliminated in a power struggle by Khamenei and Rafsanjani, and he dreads a similar fate for Mojtaba.

Khamenei's distrust has led to the creation of overlapping intelligence and security agencies, each operating parallel to the other. This complex web of control reflects the dictator's deep insecurity. Even in his final days, the disgraced tyrant of Iran continues to sow chaos and ignite conflict, demonstrating his insatiable thirst for bloodshed. He is determined to maintain his grip on the pinnacle of power, even from beyond the grave.

Diplomatic overtures at this critical juncture risk legitimizing and emboldening the regime. The cycle of negotiations, concessions, and betrayal is a well-worn tactic of Tehran's theocratic regime. It is a distraction meant to buy time for their nuclear ambitions while appeasing global powers with hollow promises. Returning to this flawed approach would not only empower the regime but also squander the momentum gained by maximum pressure policies.

Now, more than ever, the focus must shift to supporting the Iranian people's quest for freedom. Empowering dissidents and pro-democracy movements, combined with strategic international pressure, could pave the way for a future free of theocratic tyranny. Such a transformation is essential for a secure Middle East and the eradication of state-sponsored terrorism.

This is a once-in-a-generation opportunity to reshape the trajectory of the region. Failure to act decisively will result in a prolonged cycle of violence, instability, and missed potential. History will not forgive those who chose appeasement over justice and pragmatism. The time is now to stand resolutely against the Islamic Republic and champion the formation of a new Middle East—one defined by freedom, peace, and security.

Trump's intelligence team—and all intelligence agencies with new leadership—understand that the Iranian regime faces both internal and external challenges. The regime's crisis of legitimacy, public dissatisfaction, economic hardships, rampant inflation, widespread repression, and the growing divide between the people and the ruling establishment, coupled with mismanagement and governance failures, are clear signs of its fragility. On the external front, the looming threats of U.S. and Israeli military intervention, the possibility of the regime losing its nuclear ambitions, and the paralysis of its global terrorist network create a short-term outlook fraught with peril for Tehran.

These critical factors collectively strengthen the case for reviving the maximum pressure strategy and the snapback mechanism. It is neither logical nor politically prudent to give a hostile, isolated, and crisis-ridden country another lease on life under the guise of negotiations. The regime's "paper tiger" is laid bare before the eyes of U.S. and Israeli military and intelligence centers. Its theatrical displays and the bluffs of its propaganda machinery lack credibility.

This combination of internal crises within a dictatorial regime has created a golden opportunity. Any new nuclear deal would simply act as artificial life support for Iran's dictator. Why give a regime that champions terrorism another chance to survive? Why should Trump be swayed by the mirage of diplomacy and use a meaningless tool against a country that sought to assassinate him and destroy Israel? Offering diplomacy to a regime that is anti-peace, anti-humanity, and anti-regional stability is a futile, hollow, and failed endeavor.

The Tehran regime can only be restrained by one thing: the demonstration of strength and power. This would embolden the Iranian people to overcome their fears, solve the fundamental equation, and bring about regime change. The prevailing mindset in Iranian society is now firmly in favor of regime change, and the awareness of the Iranian people today cannot be compared to 1979, when a handful of Islamic and Marxist terrorists hijacked the country.

This golden opportunity must be seized to build a new Middle East, rather than pursuing the futile illusion of diplomacy that leads nowhere. Establishing a democratic Iran based on modern principles and human rights would align with the strategic interests of both the United States and Israel. Conversely, failing to achieve regime change in Iran would strengthen the Russia-China axis, pushing them toward forming new relationships with the emerging Israel-Arab alliance.

95
IRAN'S ENDLESS WINTER AND A NATION IN RUINS

Iran is engulfed in an unprecedented state of despair. The nation is paralyzed—choked by relentless air pollution, soaring inflation, authoritarian rule, unqualified leadership, a lack of strategic governance, and a pervasive disregard for the rule of law. These compounded crises have driven its citizens to the brink of psychological and physical collapse, with many succumbing to life-threatening conditions. The country teeters on the verge of internal upheaval, where an inevitable collapse could unleash long-suppressed fury and a wave of uncontrollable, bloody retribution.

How many grieving mothers have been left to mourn their innocent children, executed or gunned down by this regime? How many families have been shattered under the weight of prolonged imprisonments of political activists and intellectuals? How many vibrant young lives, full of passion and promise, have been extinguished—blinded, crippled, or paralyzed by the regime's relentless brutality? How many cemeteries have been expanded, standing as solemn testaments to the relentless grief and despair endured by the Iranian people? In this land, joy and the essence of life have become distant, forgotten relics.

From the very beginning, the criminal Ayatollahs resorted to Islamic terrorism as a means to impose their delusional and barbaric ideology. Cloaking their actions under the guise of Islamic movements, they established terror cells to further their agenda. When Reza Shah the Great departed Iran on September 16, 1941, his deepest concern was the resurgence of the Shiite clerical mafia.

During the reign of Mohammad Reza Shah Pahlavi—an adored ruler known for his patriotism, modern vision, adherence to the law, and humanitarian values—this dishonorable clerical mafia operated without shame, committing egregious crimes against humanity. Ultimately, through alliances with Islamic terrorist groups, Marxist factions, certain Arab nations, and even the KGB, they seized power and amassed wealth in Iran.

The Islamic terrorist factions sought to drive the late Shah out of power, threatening to destroy the country if their demands were not met. Meanwhile, supporters of Mosaddeq—the populist and lawless Prime Minister—joined forces with Khomeini, fabricating a sanctified yet entirely false image of him in the global media, one that bore no resemblance to reality. The so-called "people's prime minister" is a title falsely attributed to a man for whom no one can explain when, where, or in what election he was ever chosen by the people. What is often conveniently omitted is that, under constitutional law, it was the Shah of Iran who appointed him. When this very prime minister dissolved the parliament, leaving the nation in disarray, the Shah had no choice but to issue a decree for his dismissal. In retaliation, the prime minister plunged the country into three days of chaos, desperately clinging to power.

Even more egregiously, the followers of this prime minister were involved in conspiracies ranging from assassination attempts against the Shah to other destabilizing plots. They later aligned themselves with Khomeini in a movement that fundamentally betrayed the nation's future. The bitterness and resentment that lingered from August 19, 1953, to February 11, 1979, continue to this day, with the same baseless rhetoric, falsehoods, and fabrications being obsessively and relentlessly echoed in leftist media. This is a forbidden story, one that remains deliberately untold in English. To perpetuate the myth, they even fabricated the title of "Doctor" for this individual, presenting him as a national hero—a blatant falsehood. For the past 45 years, Iran's history has been ensnared in such fabrications, its narrative distorted by deceit and deliberate obfuscation.

Since 1979's Khomeinist revolt—the long winter of the Iranian nation without a spring—the regime has relentlessly spread hatred, violently crushed dissent, plundered national resources, sponsored terrorism, manipulated the narrative with propaganda, and fueled a cycle of destruction and malice.Both reformists and hardliners within the regime are united in one aim: preserving their financial and ideological interests at any cost. Beyond Iran's borders, a second "Islamic Republic" operates, infiltrating and corrupting Persian-language media like a pervasive cancer, entangling the truth in a web of deceit and making it nearly impossible to escape this multi-layered mafia.

When the late Shah of Iran, Mohammad Reza Pahlavi, left the country, he tearfully foretold that under the rule of these lawless and inhumane rebels, the brainwashed and euphoric masses would come to regret their actions within three months. Today, Iranian society—particularly the younger generation, who despise the upheaval of 1979 and the barbaric regime of the mullahs—has embraced a profound sense of nationalism and pride in their Iranian identity. In the figure of Crown Prince Reza Pahlavi, the only credible opposition leader, they find a poignant reminder of their national pride and the grandeur of Iran, eroded since the winter of 1979. Under the current occupiers, the country has been reduced to a lawless ruin, plundered by a gang of looters.

The growing wave of internal dissatisfaction has deeply unsettled the regime. In response, they have staged military maneuvers involving 110,000 Basij and IRGC forces, exercises so chaotic that casualties occurred even during the drills. To the Iranian people, these spectacles evoke haunting parallels to the parades of Saddam Hussein and Muammar Gaddafi—hollow displays of power that preceded the swift and total collapse of their oppressive regimes, bringing down the walls of tyranny with them.

Israel and America serve merely as scapegoats, while the regime's true enemy is the Iranian people, poised to rise at any moment. A nation suffocated by oppression and tyranny, desperate for change, anxiously awaits the inevitable collapse of the regime. Reformists and the state's propaganda machine cannot mask the grotesque reality of this monstrous system with superficial embellishments.

Even many of those who participated in Khomeini's 1979

chaos—figures with tarnished records and zero credibility—have lost all popularity among the people. Most are little more than media figures, lacking real influence or a genuine base within Iran. Trapped in their delusions, they continue to wage imaginary battles against the late Shah, ignoring Khamenei and his theocratic dictatorship.

This regime is rotting from within, like a tree hollowed out by worms, its scorched roots incapable of sustaining its structure. Long-term rule cannot be upheld by bayonets, clubs, or bullets. The nation is paralyzed, grappling with crippling energy shortages, while the remnants of the national treasury are squandered—either to fund terrorism and wage futile wars against Israel or to sustain the machinery of propaganda and repression.

The future of Iran appears destined for collapse, an inevitability that the Middle East, too, seems to anticipate. Such a collapse will almost certainly usher in a period of unrest and chaos. Yet, given the shallow roots of the destructive ideology born in 1979, there is reason to hope that the regime's hysterical reactions and relentless propaganda will fail to gain traction or establish any semblance of legitimacy.

We would do well to reflect on the parting words of the late Shah of Iran, who, upon leaving Niavaran Palace, urged: *"Let us all think of Iran in these critical times!"* But in the harsh reality of today, little of Iran as he envisioned it remains. Decades of mismanagement by incompetent and unqualified rulers have driven this once-beautiful nation into the abyss of destruction. And still, in this devastated land, the winter persists...

96
KRISTI NOEM: A TERRORIST'S WORST NIGHTMARE - A NEW ERA OF AMERICAN HOMELAND SECURITY

The recent appointment of Kristi Noem as the Secretary of Homeland Security represents a transformative moment for the Trump administration, signaling a robust commitment to strengthening the nation's security infrastructure against a complex array of threats. This strategic decision comes amidst pronounced opposition from Democratic legislators, highlighting a contentious yet pivotal shift in the United States' approach to national security. Known for her dynamic leadership and strategic acumen, Noem is now at the helm of critical security domains—ranging from enhancing border security measures, intensifying counter-terrorism efforts, fortifying cybersecurity initiatives, coordinating responses to domestic attacks, and ensuring the security of the nation's transportation systems. These areas are integral to safeguarding the United States' internal stability and its resilience against external threats, underpinning Noem's comprehensive security mandate.

During her confirmation hearings, Kristi Noem articulated a clear and forceful understanding of the national and international challenges that lie ahead. She conveyed a staunch determination that no adversary, nor any so-called ally, would be able to breach American borders or successfully facilitate terrorist infiltrations. This resolve is particularly vital amid escalating global tensions and the persistent threats posed by rogue states like the Islamic Republic of Iran, which actively supports various terrorist factions. Her assertive posture reassures allies and serves as a warning to adversaries, emphasizing America's renewed vigilance under her watch.

Under Noem's vigilant leadership, a strategic overhaul in counter-terrorism is anticipated. The focus will sharply pivot towards aggressively countering threats both from external and internal sources, specifically targeting and dismantling sleeper cells that have connections to foreign regimes such as Iran. These cells represent ongoing severe threats, capable of orchestrating attacks from within the fabric of American society. By addressing these covert dangers, Noem aims to fortify the nation's defenses against the multifaceted nature of modern terrorism, ensuring a security landscape that is both resilient and adaptive to the dynamics of global terror networks. This proactive approach seeks not only to neutralize immediate threats but also to dismantle the infrastructural and logistical networks that facilitate terrorist activities on U.S. soil, reflecting a comprehensive strategy to safeguard national security.

Kristi Noem is also preparing to confront the intricate networks of influential lobbies and individuals connected to Tehran, which operate under the façade of civic and religious organizations. These entities seek to penetrate and destabilize American security infrastructure, employing tactics that surpass conventional acts of terrorism. They extend their operations into sophisticated cyber-attacks aimed at critical American and Israeli systems. In response, Noem's administration is prioritizing the safeguarding of these essential infrastructures, mandating the implementation of advanced cybersecurity defenses and the strengthening of international collaborations, notably with Israel. These measures are crucial for defending against cyber threats that are increasingly becoming tools of modern warfare.

Furthermore, under Noem's leadership, the integration of the Department of Homeland Security (DHS) with other key U.S. intelligence and security agencies is set to intensify. This enhanced collaboration aims to create a more cohesive and unified front against security threats, improving information sharing and strategic operational alignment. Despite these efforts, the persistent menace of Islamic terrorism on American soil remains a significant concern. This reality compels Noem's strategy to focus on devising and implementing effective counter-terrorism measures that not only track and neutralize threats but also prevent the radicalization and mobilization of terrorist elements within the U.S. These strategies are essential for maintaining public safety and ensuring the protection of American citizens and their allies, illustrating Noem's commitment to a proactive and preemptive security posture to combat the evolving landscape of global terrorism.

Under Secretary Kristi Noem's leadership, the Department of Homeland Security (**DHS**) is set to significantly enhance its scrutiny of radical ideologies within academic environments. This initiative stems from the recognition that organizations such as Hezbollah and Hamas have established influential platforms within American universities. These groups, often collaborating with Marxist professors, engage in activities that promote anti-Western sentiments and glorify figures like **Khamenei, Sinwar, and Nasrallah**. Such activities not only raise alarms about foreign influence but also about the potential indoctrination of students with extremist ideologies. To counteract these influences, Noem plans to implement a robust strategy designed to disrupt extremist activities on campuses, ensuring that universities continue to serve as centers for learning and not become breeding grounds for extremist indoctrination. This approach will involve enhanced cooperation between Homeland Security and educational institutions, including monitoring and, if necessary, intervening in university affairs where support for terrorism under the pretense of academic freedom is detected.

The primary goal of this strategy is to preserve the integrity of educational environments, safeguarding them from exploitation by extremist groups and maintaining a focus on educational and scholarly pursuits free from ideological manipulation. This concerted effort reflects DHS's commitment to a proactive defense of educational spaces from infiltration by entities with links to terrorism.

Under the stewardship of Kristi Noem, the Department of Homeland Security is gearing up to confront and navigate through a spectrum of complex security challenges with a revitalized and strategic approach. Noem's leadership is poised to steer homeland security policies toward a more rational and meticulously focused direction. Her leadership philosophy appreciates the multifaceted nature of national security, recognizing that the scope of threats extends beyond physical dangers to include significant ideological confrontations. This nuanced understanding is crucial for devising strategies that effectively address both traditional security challenges and the subtler, yet equally perilous, ideological conflicts that have profound implications for national stability.

This strategic realignment under Noem is designed to bolster the internal security mechanisms of the United States, shielding the nation from external manipulations that seek to undermine its sovereignty. The anticipated policies are expected to create a more robust internal security landscape, capable of withstanding the pressures and influences from foreign entities. By enhancing the security framework, Noem aims to ensure comprehensive protection that covers all aspects of national security, from border control and anti-terrorism measures to cyber defenses and the safeguarding of the nation's ideological integrity.

In conclusion, Kristi Noem's leadership at the Department of Homeland Security signifies a revitalized commitment to strengthening America's security infrastructure. Her tenure is set to equip the nation adequately to confront and prevail over the modern, multifaceted threats that characterize today's global security environment. As this new chapter in American security policy unfolds, Noem is dedicated to maintaining a delicate balance between liberty and security. This focus is crucial in fostering a resilient and secure nation, prepared not only to face current security challenges but also to anticipate and neutralize emerging threats. In this era of global uncertainty, Noem's proactive and comprehensive approach to homeland security promises to reinforce America's standing as a secure, free, and stable nation, ready to navigate and triumph over the complexities of an increasingly intricate global landscape.

In this new era of homeland security under strong female leadership, Islamic terrorists will no longer attack synagogues, Jewish tourists, students, and activists, allowing their religion and culture to develop and thrive in utmost security. Wishing Kristi Noem success in advancing these worthy goals.

97
SHIFTING SANDS: THE MULLAHS' NIGHTMARE IN THE U.S. DEFENSE DEPARTMENT

The appointment of the new US Secretary of Defense is poised to profoundly influence regional policies in the volatile Middle East, an area where the United States holds significant strategic and military interests. The Secretary of Defense is pivotal in sculpting America's military and defense strategies. His decisions on troop deployments, defense budgets, and military priorities in regions such as the Middle East have the potential to reshape the conflict dynamics within the region.

Pete Hegseth, Trump's latest appointee as Secretary of Defense, is instrumental in fostering military collaborations with allies like Israel and Saudi Arabia, and managing tense military engagements with adversaries such as Iran's Shia Mullah regime. His policy directives are set to distinctly affect the regional power balance. Hegseth's leadership on military missions and his approach to engaging with terrorist and criminal non-state actors, as well as counterterrorism efforts, are critical to the ongoing security and stability of the Middle East. Moreover, Hegseth is expected to significantly influence the security framework of the Middle East and play a pivotal role in the Russian Ukrainian conflict.

In the Middle East, formulating strategies to combat terrorism linked to the mafia and the transnational terrorist network supported by the Islamic Republic demands time, keen insight, and a sophisticated, layered approach. With his dynamic approach to military diplomacy, the new Secretary of Defense is expected to play a crucial role in security negotiations with nations and in interactions with international bodies.With Hegseth's arrival at the Pentagon, his role sends potent signals to regional and international stakeholders, catalyzing shifts in U.S. policies in the Middle East. Hegseth, a proponent of assertive power projection, shows no inclination towards appeasing Islamic terrorist and criminal elements in the region. His leadership marks a decisive stance against forces undermining peace and stability in the Middle East.

With the recent shifts in U.S. government leadership, including the appointment of a new Secretary of Defense, the Defense Intelligence Agency (DIA) is poised for transformative operational enhancements. The DIA plays a crucial role in gathering and analyzing military data crucial for shaping American defense strategies and foreign policy. Under Pete Hegseth's leadership, significant reforms in the DIA's methodologies and operational tactics are anticipated. These include refocusing intelligence priorities on major global threats from China, Russia, and Iran, enhancing interagency collaboration for greater operational efficacy, and bolstering resources and capabilities to improve intelligence analysis and threat identification. These strategic changes within the DIA are likely to influence U.S. defense and security policies profoundly. Notably, these modifications in the Department of Defense's leadership will directly affect the nature and extent of U.S. support to Israel in its efforts to counter the Iranian regime and combat Islamic terrorism in the Middle East.

I hope that for Hegseth, the situation the DIA faced in 1978-1979 will not recur. Despite their presence in Iran at that time, they were unaware of how the Soviet-affiliated Islamic and communist mafias orchestrated the 1979 uprising. Frankly, the DIA lacked a clear understanding of the unfolding crisis.

From his first day in office, Hegseth has delved into security reports, emphasizing the importance of solidifying military and intelligence collaboration between the U.S. and Israel. This focus is particularly on enhancing missile defense systems, intelligence sharing, and joint training initiatives. Such cooperation is vital for Israel's readiness to tackle the Iranian threat and its associated terrorist networks.

During Hegseth's tenure, increased military and technological support to Israel is anticipated, including the provision of advanced weaponry and defense systems to fortify its defense capabilities. Moreover, these measures are expected to bolster deterrence without any obstacles impeding support for Israel within the Pentagon. However, in the Middle East defense sector, there remains a risk from individuals possibly linked to the Iranian regime or known Iranian notorious lobbies in the U.S., such as Quincy and

NIAC. These apologists and affiliated stooges, driven by the destructive ideology of Khomeinism and anti-Israel sentiments, could potentially act as covert operatives of the Islamic Republic, complicating U.S. defense operations against Iranian activities. A significant concern for Hegseth is the potential infiltration of these pro-regime's elements within the Pentagon's security apparatus, which have historically managed to embed themselves in various administrations.

Pete Hegseth's approach as the new Secretary of Defense could significantly reshape U.S. strategies concerning Iran and its affiliated groups. His support for sanctions against the Iranian regime and his proactive stance on countering groups influenced by Iran, such as Hezbollah, Hamas, the Houthis, Hashd al-Shaabi, and the PKK, underscore a commitment to curbing Iran's influence and mitigating regional threats. This includes bolstering military and intelligence operations and supporting sanction measures against these entities.

Hegseth's advocacy for peace agreements and the normalization of relations between Israel and Arab nations also plays a crucial role in reducing tensions and limiting Iran's regional dominance. His policies could contribute to a more secure Middle East by fostering stability and reducing the likelihood of conflict. However, for the Tehran regime, Hegseth's policies might indeed be seen as a significant threat, especially given his support for aggressive measures like targeting the Revolutionary Guards' nuclear facilities. Hegseth recognizes the strategic placement of these facilities across Iran, which complicates direct military actions without significant risks. His distinction between the Iranian people and the regime indicates a nuanced approach, emphasizing support for the citizens while opposing the governmental structure.

Moreover, his known anti-terrorism stance, particularly against Islamic terrorism, aligns with previous U.S. administrations' efforts but may introduce more direct actions against perceived threats. His support for the targeted killing of Qasem Soleimani by the Trump administration highlights his belief in assertive military actions against key figures within the Iranian regime.

In summary, Hegseth's role as Secretary of Defense is likely to involve strong measures against Iran and its proxies, emphasizing security enhancements for allies like Israel and promoting stability in the Middle East. This approach, while potentially escalating tensions with Tehran, aims to reduce the capability and influence of hostile entities in the region.

98
THE FIRST SOLUTION IS REGIME CHANGE IN IRAN

The current state of Iran is a powder keg of societal dissatisfaction, relentless repression, and environmental and economic collapse. Theocratic dictatorship under Iran's dictator, Ali Khamenei has pushed the nation to the brink of disintegration. Khamenei, an obstinate and irrational autocrat, clings to power despite cascading undeniable failures, deluding himself into fantasies of triumph while the country suffers under his rule. His tirades are laden with vitriol against Israel, the United States, and the modern West, yet they reveal his growing fear of the Iranian people's imminent uprising against his dishonorable regime.

Islamic countries, too, bear significant responsibility for nurturing this cancerous tumor. When Khomeini released his book *Wilayat al-Faqih* in Lebanon in 1970, neither the Islamic nations nor the Persian Gulf states denounced its deceitful and hateful rhetoric, steeped in Soviet-style communism and hollow autocracy. Fueled by delusions and backed by allies who subscribed to Islamic terrorism or Marxist militancy, Ruhollah Khomeini pursued his vision of 'Islamic jihad' and the establishment of a terror-driven Islamic regime. From the outset, the Soviet Union and its proxies—including figures like Yasser Arafat and Fidel Castro—actively supported this ludicrous venture in the Middle East. Even Saddam Hussein provided Khomeini with a radio platform, while Muammar Gaddafi funneled financial aid, enabling the rise of this malignant destructive ideology."

The Shia Crescent, a disastrous manifestation of clerical tyranny driven by the ambitions of the Islamic Republic, has extended its tentacles across the Middle East like a malignant octopus. It has fueled terrorism, ignited sectarian conflicts, and perpetuated regional instability—all at the devastating cost of Iran's wealth and its people's well-being. Only the complete dismantling of this theocratic project can open the path to peace, democracy, and the region's liberation from this destructive clerical empire.

For over half a century, Israel has stood as a witness to the relentless and malignant expansion of Islamic terrorism. Yet, when Israel advocated for regime change in Iran following the catastrophic 1979 revolt, the global community leaned toward appeasement and diplomacy with the Islamic Republic's terrorists or the criminal ayatollahs in Tehran. When Israel exposed the transnational terrorist networks orchestrated by the Shiite mullahs, the world chose to counsel Israel rather than confront Iran's regime. Even as Khomeini openly declared his intent to export the 'Khomeinist Islamic Revolt,' it appeared that Western intelligence agencies had not even bothered to read his *Wilayat al-Faqih*. This neglect was the true tragedy in 20th century.

Ahmad Kasravi—a historian and a visionary advocate for the 'Iranian Secular Identity' movement—courageously exposed the fabrications and manipulations of Shiite clerics, particularly their invention of the 12th Imam. His unyielding criticism of these deceptions led to his assassination on March 11, 1946, in a Tehran courthouse, where he was brutally gunned down and stabbed by members of the extremist group *Fada'iyan-e Islam,* loyal to Navab Safavi. These terrorists, blind to truth and reason, embody the same oppressive forces that continue to dominate Iran today. Both Khomeini and Khamenei have openly revered Safavi, a murderous and corrupt cleric who symbolizes their shared values.

Khomeini, in his 1944 book *Kashf al-Asrar* (*Unveiling of Secrets*), explicitly called for Ahmad Kasravi's execution in front of his religious followers. Why? Because Khomeini perceived himself as the earthly representative of the mythical 12th Imam—a delusion that Khamenei perpetuates to this day. Factually, both men have propagated the belief that the Islamic Caliphate under *Wilayat al-Faqih* must persist until the Day of Judgment, awaiting a sword-wielding savior to emerge from a well and redeem humanity. These two figures—Khomeini and Khamenei—audaciously claim to be the earthly emissaries of this imagined redeemer, using this narrative to justify their reign of tyranny and terror.

Ali Khamenei's regime finds itself ensnared in an unwinnable paradox or trapped in a lose-lose game, where each oppressive measure only heightens its international isolation and hastens its inevitable collapse. Meanwhile, the unyielding courage of the Iranian people signals that the era of religious despotism and terror-fueled governance is approaching its long-overdue demise.

Khamenei continues to deliver rambling, disjointed diatribes, resembling the behavior of a deranged autocrat. His tirades, filled with venom against Israel, the United States, the broader Middle East, and his own people, are often punctuated with threats to his adversaries. Yet, his delusional proclamations have become so detached from reality that they are met with little more than indifference or ridicule, even among his shrinking circle of supporters.

Iran's public anger is palpable—a nation suffocated by decades of corruption, authoritarianism, and the blatant criminality of its ruling clerics. The people's deep-seated hatred for the regime is rooted in the grim realities of everyday life: an economy in freefall, pervasive poverty, environmental collapse, and the oppressive chokehold of religious dogma. On the international stage, the regime's failures are equally glaring. Its so-called 'resistance axis' has unraveled, and its grandiose dreams of regional dominance have crumbled into disarray. The once-robust terror networks it cultivated across the Middle East are now faltering, serving as a testament to the regime's broader decay and diminishing influence."

Khamenei embodies the rot at the heart of his regime—a vindictive, unyielding despot trapped in denial. In a single month, he has delivered multiple speeches proclaiming hollow victories over Israel and the West, further exposing his detachment from reality. His rhetoric, steeped in aggression and delusion, highlights his descent into irrelevance. Cloaked in a facade of religious sanctity, Khamenei's true legacy is the destruction of Iran and the Middle East, leaving behind a trail of ruin and despair.

This Iranian dictator, consumed by delusions and an insatiable thirst for blood, tirelessly pursues new victims to satisfy his lust for oppression. Every day, he seeks a neck to tighten the noose around, embodying the cruelty and tyranny that define his rule. It is no surprise that Iranians have likened him to 'Zahhāk'—the malevolent figure from Persian mythology, infamous as the Snake Shoulder, a symbol of relentless evil and bloodshed."

Beneath the surface, a simmering fire of resistance burns brightly among the Iranian people. Decades of relentless suppression have failed to extinguish their unyielding desire for freedom. A tipping point seems imminent. The potential for an Israeli strike on Iran's nuclear facilities or the removal of Khamenei or his successor, Mojtaba, could spark a nationwide uprising. Such a catalyst would dismantle the remnants of the disastrous 1979 revolt, clearing the path for a new era in Iran and across the region.

This moment in history offers a rare and fleeting opportunity. The collapse of the regime would not only liberate Iran but also deliver a decisive blow to the roots of Islamic terrorism that have plagued the Middle East for decades. The world stands on the cusp of witnessing the demise of an 86 year-old dictator and the fall of a 46-year-old despised theocratic regime. This pivotal moment holds the promise of reshaping the future of the Middle East, bringing hope to millions and ending one of history's darkest chapters. Let this be the time Iran finally breaks free from the chains of tyranny, allowing the world to exhale a collective sigh of relief.

The Final solution lies in breaking free from the suffocating grip of clerical rule and dismantling the ideological, financial, and cultural networks that sustain the oppressive Shiite clergy. This would pave the way for a progressive, rational, and inclusive society, replacing superstition and fanaticism with humanity, logic, and equality. International actors play an indispensable role in this transformation. Regional and global powers must collaborate to ensure that Iran's transition is peaceful and protected from external exploitation. By working together, they can help Iran emerge as a stabilizing force in the Middle East, free from the shadows of terrorism and tyranny.

For a moment, one can close their eyes and imagine a Middle East freed from Velayat-e Faqih (the Shiite clerical octopus) and the mafia-like networks of Islamic terrorism. Picture Crown Prince Reza Pahlavi guiding Iran through a transitional government—a compelling vision that, with safeguards against internal discord and external manipulation, could solidify a stable and democratic future. Envision Israel and the United States reopening their embassies in Tehran. Imagine the destructive ideology of Khomeinism and the chaos of 1979 finally consigned to the graveyard of history. Then, we could truly celebrate the birth of a new Middle East.

99
THE NEW CIA DIRECTOR AND THE TEHRAN REGIME HEADACHE

Approximately 1-2 hours following Donald Trump's inauguration as the 47th President of the United States, the Senate Intelligence Committee appointed John Ratcliffe as the CIA Director. He is tasked with leading the world's foremost intelligence and espionage organizations during this particularly critical period.

Unlike some former CIA directors who for mere thousands of dollars would disgrace themselves by attending fanatical Islamic terrorism events such as those hosted by the MEK, exchanging integrity for money, Ratcliffe would never fabricate baseless lies and empty rhetoric against Prince Reza Pahlavi, the most esteemed and influential figure of the Iranian opposition. He refuses to recognize that the Islamic Republic and the MEK are two sides of the same coin, with this terrorist group originating from the Freedom Movement

— supporters of Khomeini and Mosaddeq — and this notorious and shameful group having blood on their hands from Americans such as Colonel Paul Shaffer, Jack Turner, and Oveis Hawkins.

Ratcliffe is committed to ethics, principles, and the pillars of free thought. He understands that if Tehran's regime were to collapse, the transitional period would require a strong, reputable, and credible leader to guide society temporarily until it can choose its own path via democratic means—whether toward a modern democratic republic or a return to its monarchical roots, reflecting the true course of Iranian civilization and history. However, due to the absence of a monarchy and its cultural implications in the U.S., Americans might find it hard to envision that a monarchy could foster democracy, rule of law, peace, and stability, especially considering their relatively short history compared to Iran's 7000-year civilization, which has experienced such governance for millennia.

With Donald Trump's reelection and the commencement of his second term, the CIA faces shifting challenges and priorities in an increasingly unstable global landscape. In addition to addressing major challenges and structural changes—particularly the rotation of CIA station chiefs in the Middle East—the agency's current primary focus is on external threats. However, while China and Russia represent significant national security concerns, the hostile and destructive behavior of the Islamic Republic's mullahs in Iran continues to pose a daily challenge for the CIA.

As an advocate and supporter of the CIA, I wish to clarify that, unlike Islamic terrorists, mullahs, and followers of Mosaddeq and Khomeini, I do not intend to perpetuate the myth of the CIA's supposed meddling in Iran, such as the alleged role in the 1953 coup. Considering the CIA was only two years old at that time, it certainly lacked the capability to orchestrate such events, and the agency undoubtedly finds the repetition of this baseless claim amusing. However, it is evident that enhancing espionage networks and human resources among Iranians is crucial. Improving capabilities in handling confidential information and modernizing data collection and analysis systems are essential steps to effectively counter the contemporary threats posed by the Islamic Republic.

I have previously discussed the CIA's challenges during the Biden administration, but now, with enhanced engagement with Middle East and Iran specialists—whether they are CIA staff or allies—the review and evaluation of covert operations must rely on accurate and effective information. Successfully preserving American national security is contingent on addressing the threats posed by the Islamic Republic.

Currently, with Trump inaugurating his second term, prioritizing the CIA's challenges regarding Iran is crucial. Over the next four years, the agency will confront numerous issues related to the Islamic Republic of Iran. Among the most critical challenges, in conjunction with Israel, are thwarting the Iranian regime's nuclear ambitions and preventing the regime's leaders from acquiring nuclear capabilities.

The CIA, particularly its station chiefs in the Middle East and the Gulf countries, engage in daily cooperation and relationships with Mossad and Arab nations that are allies and partners of the United States, managing regional tensions which is a formidable challenge for all involved. Information sharing with intelligence services of allied countries about the Shiite Islamic Republic and coordinating strategies to counter threats from Iran are essential, yet they are just part of the task of monitoring the Islamic Republic's destructive activities in Iraq, Yemen, and covertly in Bahrain, Saudi Arabia, and Syria. These represent a complex and multi-layered threat landscape. The Quds Force and the Iranian Ministry of Intelligence continue to overtly support proxy groups like Hezbollah, Hamas, the Houthis, and Popular Mobilization Forces, among others, driven by Ali Khamenei's calculated risks on Iran's political strategies.

Moreover, alongside the routine efforts of the CIA's Counter-Terrorism Center and the Counter-Enrichment Center, combating the intelligence and espionage efforts of the Iranian regime is a staple of daily operations. Identifying and neutralizing Iran's espionage activities, whether conducted by the Ministry of Intelligence, MOIS, under Esmaeil Khatib, the Intelligence Organization of the IRGC supervised by Mohammad Kazemi, or safeguarding CIA intelligence sources and methods against infiltration by groups linked to the Quds Force under the leadership of individuals like Qaani, Falahzadeh, and Mesjedi, increases the workload but is crucial. A thorough understanding of both the internal and external dynamics of the Islamic Republic is vital in these efforts.

If the CIA intensifies its efforts to counter the influence of the Islamic Republic of Iran and its intelligence institutions across the unstable and volatile Middle East—such as identifying and neutralizing Iranian influence networks in regional countries and assessing the impact of Iran's policies on regional stability— focusing potentially on regime change in Iran, it could achieve greater success over the next four years.

I hope that my candid advice does not suffer the same fate as that of SAVAK to the then-CIA director during the years 1977 to 1979. Under President Carter, Stansfield Turner led the CIA but was reluctant to accept the negative role of the KGB in directing Islamic and Marxist terrorist groups, had not read Khomeini's writings, and was unaware of Khomeini's malevolent intentions. These oversights prevented him from fully understanding the catastrophe of 1978 in Iran. As a result, the country drifted into Russian influence, making Moscow a significant barrier to any regime change in Iran.

It is essential to have a logical and precise analysis of the political developments within Iran, closely assessing the regime's stability and the likelihood of political changes. Identifying the rifts and differences within Iranian governance is crucial, as the regime is on the verge of collapse, and a turbulent and destabilizing transition period is likely to follow without proper and logical analysis of usable talents and reliable resources. Merely enhancing the technical capabilities for collecting signals and imagery intelligence will bolster your archives, not your pragmatism.

The CIA should emulate Mossad's policy, which traditionally maintains a more accurate analysis of the decision-making within the Iranian regime and, by extension, a deeper understanding of the decision-making processes at the highest levels of the Iranian government. Correcting this issue within the CIA would simplify the prediction of Iran's potential reactions to regional and international developments.

Drawing on my professional expertise and 12 years of experience analyzing the Middle East and counter-terrorism, I am confident that under Ratcliffe's significant leadership, the CIA will carefully and delicately tackle these challenges to prevent the escalation of tensions while protecting American interests. However, it is crucial to be prepared to respond swiftly to unforeseen developments in Iran-U.S. relations because a volatile figure like Khamenei still exerts influence, and the survival of Israel and the stability of the entire Middle East hang in the balance.

100
TRUMP'S NSA AND THE FRAILTY OF KHAMENEI'S CHAOS

One of Trump's close associates, Michael Waltz, carries significant responsibilities. As the National Security Advisor (NSA) under President Donald Trump, he is also a friend and supporter of Israel, poised to play a pivotal role in global political history over the next four years.

Donald Trump's initial policies towards Ali Khamenei and the Islamic Republic of Iran can be analyzed through the lens of security studies, employing theoretical frameworks such as realism, liberalism, constructivism, and critical security theory.

From a realist perspective, which prioritizes power and national interests, Trump's primary objective was to diminish the Islamic Republic of Iran as a threat to the interests of the United States and its regional allies, particularly Israel and Saudi Arabia. Given the ineffectiveness of diplomacy, Trump appropriately implemented a maximum pressure policy by withdrawing from the JCPOA and imposing stringent economic sanctions on the Islamic Republic. These measures aimed to cripple Iran's economic and military capacities, thereby curtailing its regional influence across critical areas such as Iraq, Syria, Lebanon, and Yemen.

In terms of security, Waltz's role assumes greater significance. Trump and his team astutely distinguish between the Iranian populace and the Mullahs' regime, labeling the latter as a "rogue state" that necessitates control through stringent economic sanctions, diplomatic isolation, and military deterrence. Providentially diverging from liberalist principles, Trump's administration views the focus on institutions and multilateral international cooperation as ineffective in addressing the belligerence of the Iranian regime.

The reduction of international cooperation and the withdrawal from the JCPOA, deemed a defunct and irrelevant agreement, reflect a rebuke of the unsuccessful policies from the Obama administration and the delusive nuclear deal predicated on international cooperation—a strategy ineffectually perpetuated by Biden, leading nowhere as the Iranian regime merely mocked the international community with no real intention of cooperating.

The overarching aim of the Shiite mullahs is to develop nuclear weapons and atomic bombs, intended for use against American and Israeli forces. Had they possessed such capabilities, they would have without doubt deployed them against Israel and America repeatedly over the years. The Mullahs are neither useful stooges nor trustworthy; to defeat them, one must first understand their strategies, as outlined in their doctrines—a nuance the Democrats overlooked. Their failure to grasp this led to their disgrace, resulting from futile diplomatic engagements with the criminal Ayatollahs.

A critical outcome of Trump's policy was the isolation of the Mullahs. However, despite this isolation, some allies persisted in supporting the Mullahs, and Biden's actions inadvertently aided in the regime's survival. From a constructivist perspective, which emphasizes the significance of ideas, identities, and discourses in shaping policies, it is evident that the ruling regime of Shiite Mullahs in Iran shows minimal regard for identity and discourse in the contemporary sense. The foremost advocate for countering the discourse of the Islamic Republic—especially during the intense censorship of Obama's era—was General Michael Flynn, former NSA of Trump. Meanwhile, both previously and more recently, Trump has effectively utilized the "threat of Iran's regime" narrative, consistently portraying the Islamic Republic as a principal destabilizer in the Middle East. Waltz supports this narrative, and together with Trump, they strive to depict the Khomeinist regime not only as a destructive force but also as an ideological threat against Western values and the modern, 21st-century world order.

The goal is also to weaken the illegitimate legitimacy of the Islamic Republic and highlight the identity conflict between the United States (as a representative of democracy and modernity) and the Mullahs' regime in Iran (as a representative of religious despotism and Islamic terrorism), a regime leaning on Russia and hanging by Putin's decaying rope.

From the perspective of critical security theory, which focuses on human security, social justice, and broader security concepts, Waltz's role is illuminated further. He understands that Trump's policies, particularly the economic sanctions, have profoundly affected the everyday lives of ordinary Iranians. Waltz recognizes the potential for a popular uprising against the oppressive and inept Shiite Mullah regime, which has failed to manage shortages of essential goods, severe inflation, and widespread economic difficulties, leading to increasing detestation among the Iranian people. The weakening of the Iranian regime under Trump has highlighted to the Iranian populace that human security, social stability, and quality of life are unattainable under the current governance. Waltz is aware that the regime sustains itself through three primary mechanisms: internal suppression, a robust propaganda apparatus, and engagement in terrorism.

Trump's strategies against Ali Khamenei and the Islamic Republic of Iran meld realist approaches (aimed at diminishing Iran's power), constructivist tactics (fostering a discourse against the Islamic Republic), and flawed liberal decisions (eschewing multilateral cooperation). However, alongside Trump, Waltz should not anticipate illusory changes in the behavior of the Islamic Republic, such as a diminution of sovereignty, alleviation of pressure on the severely oppressed populace, or a decrease in internal suppression. Instead, they should adopt a more rigorous stance in addressing the challenges posed by the oppressive, undemocratic, and terrorism-supporting regime of the Islamic Republic of Iran.

Waltz, working with Trump, has the opportunity to support the real opposition that bolsters civil society and backs the democracy-seeking movements against Iran's despotic regime. Additionally, they should consider dismantling the ineffective network of Persian-language media funded by the U.S. government, which often acts more as a platform for Iranian government reformists rather than as a beacon for Iranian civil resistance.

Channels like VOA and RFERL have failed to provide the Iranian people with access to uncensored information, which could enhance public awareness and undermine the regime's domestic legitimacy. Instead, these outlets often serve merely to circulate narratives of Islamic terrorism, separatism, and government reformism. As an American taxpayer, one must question why funds are allocated to such ineffective media initiatives.

In the context of supporting genuine opposition and the quest for democracy, HRH Prince Reza Pahlavi stands out as a prominent figure who champions democracy, human rights, and freedom. He earnestly seeks to transition beyond the Islamic Republic, advocating for change both within Iran and internationally. Based on constitutional law, he is often regarded as a legitimate representative of the Iranian people to this day.

The efforts initiated by General Flynn could indeed be advanced by someone like Waltz, focusing on the political and diplomatic isolation of the Mullahs' regime. With Waltz's involvement, there is potential not only to prohibit representatives of the Islamic Republic from international institutions but also to target and dismantle the detested lobbies of the Tehran regime on American soil. These lobbies often include financial institutions affiliated with the IRGC and companies that support terrorism, furthering the isolation of this illegitimate and terrorism-supporting regime.

Supporting internal protests, bolstering internet access and free communications, and removing censorship are crucial steps in aiding the Iranian people to organize and sustain their protests effectively. By empowering Iranian elites, academics, and activists, we can weaken the regime's grip and lay the groundwork for future democratic reconstruction. It's essential to ensure these individuals do not become disillusioned or feel abandoned by America, as their role will be pivotal in shaping a democratic Iran. Waltz, with his expertise in military and intelligence operations, understands that neutralizing the military capabilities of the aggressive and terrorist-supporting regime is crucial. Collaborating with Israel, targeted strikes on military, missile, and nuclear facilities are vital steps in mitigating this global threat. Waltz is well aware of the significance of dismantling the Iranian regime's terrorist networks and its proxy groups that destabilize the Middle East, recognizing the necessity of these strategic measures to curb the regime's influence and threat.

The mafia regime in Tehran resembles an occupying, notorious, criminal, illegitimate, and unlawful entity that has enforced its political Islamist and terrorist ideology upon the population, effectively holding 90 million Iranians hostage to its oppressive rule.

Waltz and Trump understand that addressing the challenges posed by the Islamic regime in Tehran requires a multifaceted strategy, especially given that this regime does not truly represent the Iranian nation. For this reason, Trump has garnered popularity among democracy-seeking Iranians. His actions, such as the elimination of the Islamic terrorist figure Qasem Soleimani, his supportive tweets during Iranian protests, and his outspoken stance against the regime, have given hope to Iranian society. These actions signal the potential downfall of Khamenei's crumbling regime, which has shown fear in the face of Trump's policies.

101

THE US INTELLIGENCE COMMUNITY AND ITS HIDDEN ENEMIES

Tulsi Gabbard, nominated by President Trump for the role of Director of National Intelligence (DNI), is scheduled to undergo her confirmation hearing before the Senate Intelligence Committee in 48 hours, on Thursday, January 30th. If confirmed, she will be the second woman to lead and coordinate the sprawling American intelligence community, which encompasses 18 different agencies with a combined budget of approximately $70 billion. In her role, she would act as one of Trump's key advisors, responsible for the prompt dissemination of processed intelligence throughout the community to both the President and other national policymakers, while also managing interactions with foreign intelligence and security services and international bodies.

With her military background in the U.S. Army National Guard and her tenure on various House committees, Gabbard, if confirmed to this pivotal intelligence role, would need to exemplify a balanced and effective model of U.S. national security. She would tackle significant challenges within the intelligence community, transitioning for the first time from a military to an intelligence agency setting.

President Trump regards her as a loyal candidate, potentially prioritizing her ideological alignment over her specific security expertise. Conversely, critics argue that her lack of direct intelligence community experience could lead her to approach issues predominantly from a military perspective. As a Lieutenant Colonel in the Army National Guard, Gabbard, aligned with Trump's vision, aims to reform the intelligence community and its agencies. These agencies have faced numerous challenges in the ongoing war against terrorism, and enhancing counter-terrorism efforts has been pivotal to their success. Additionally, one of the significant and emerging threats to these major and complex intelligence and security agencies in the U.S. is their serious and effective confrontation with transnational organized crime, which threatens to erode the credibility and trust in the U.S. intelligence services.

The significance of Gabbard's potential appointment extends to its impact on national security, foreign policy, and the organizational structure of American intelligence. Despite her extensive military experience, she encounters numerous challenges in combating America's adversaries from an intelligence and security standpoint. The authoritative American intelligence community is dynamic, continuously evolving, and demands precision. Her appointment could trigger both domestic responses and substantial international repercussions. On a broader scale, U.S. national security concerns necessitate precise intelligence assessments of its principal adversaries, consistently identifying three nations: **China, Russia, and the Islamic Republic of Iran.** Each maintains a robust "separate and toxic propaganda machine," "corrupt and infamous lobbying groups," and "operational sleeper cells" within the soil of the U.S. Even the Islamic Republic, notorious for its "terrorist sleeper cells and anti-Israel propaganda machine," intensifies the security challenges faced by the American intelligence community. These states and bad actors also deploy "agents for infiltration" within the U.S. intelligence community, similar to how infamous lobbies from the Islamic Republic have penetrated the Defense Ministry of the USA.

Critics have previously questioned Gabbard's controversial views on Syria and Russia, though these may now be less pertinent. The greater her recognition of Tehran's malign activities as a destabilizing force in the Middle East and an adversary to America's regional allies, the better positioned she will be. By intensifying efforts to combat Tehran-backed Islamic terrorism, she can alleviate concerns regarding her potential impact on America's diplomatic relationships with its allies.

Although she switched her allegiance to the Republicans in October 2024, branding Democrats as warmongers, Gabbard's profound political transformation and shift in her political stance may not sufficiently equip her to tackle security challenges such as the war in Ukraine with Russia, or Tehran-backed Islamic terrorism, nor to conservatively influence international relations. In the strategic landscape of American politics, Gabbard must endeavor to bolster the credibility of U.S. intelligence, which significantly affects

America's relationships with allies like Saudi Arabia and Israel in the face of the malign influence of the criminal ayatollah's regime aligned with Russia in Iran. Recognizing Vladimir Putin as a war criminal and Ali Khamenei as a brutal dictator could accelerate her proactive measures. Despite potential widespread negative reactions from the international media during her tenure as the Director of National Intelligence under Trump's second term, these may not pose serious impediments.

Gabbard has participated in military operations in Iraq and Kuwait and, despite her commitment to the "America First" doctrine, the Iraq she served in witnessed the deaths of thousands of Americans who endeavored to establish democracy and freedom post-Saddam Hussein. Instead, Iraq fell under the influence of the Shiite crescent of the Islamic Republic, leading to significant limitations on American efforts in the region. Currently, the militia and criminal organization Hashd al-Shaabi, which takes directives from the Quds Force, presents a significant threat to Saudi Arabia and Israel.

Through her experiences and interactions in a rigorously trained environment, Gabbard will acquire insights and knowledge seldom taught with such detail and scope in academic settings. The challenge today is not merely in educating Gabbard; it is in the future political actions required to decisively confront America's adversaries. Among these threats is the potential development of a nuclear weapon by the terrorist-loving Khomeinist regime in Tehran, a prospect that endangers the 21st century and puts the existence of Israel and Europe at risk. Dependence on a quickly reversible fatwa from an uneducated mullah is futile. A profound understanding of both internal and external security threats, coupled with the ability to make decisions in complex and sensitive scenarios, is crucial for effective security management.

Although Gabbard harbors reservations about U.S. military interventions abroad—a stance that aligns with Trump's policies—the Middle East cannot achieve peace, stability, and comfort without addressing the leadership in Tehran, and without a regime change in Iran, the emergence of a new Middle East remains unlikely. In this context, cautious action and opposition to regime change prove ineffectual. Peaceful coexistence with a malignancy is impossible; it necessitates removal. No one desires American military intervention, yet no one favors a U.S. policy under Trump's potential second term that would engage diplomatically with the criminal mullahs who support Islamic terrorism, turning America into a global laughingstock like what critics argue happened under Obama and Biden. Engaging with such outlaw regimes is akin to putting lipstick on a pig. From my understanding of her character, I remain optimistic about Gabbard's intellectual independence and adaptability.

This seasoned veteran, who brings a distinctive political background and a record of military service, has demonstrated her patriotism through her commitment to the American flag. However, there should be no hesitation in addressing the threats to America's identity, sovereignty, and the safety of its allies. Decisive action is required.

If I were to encounter Ms. Gabbard in person on Thursday, I would warmly shake her hand and sincerely wish her success on her confirmation day. I would say, *"Madam Director, please prioritize regime change in Iran to facilitate the emergence of a new Middle East, and steadfastly support our Middle Eastern allies, including Saudi Arabia and Israel."*

102
DICTATOR'S NIGHTMARE: KHAMENEI'S FEAR OF THE TRUMP-NETANYAHU ALLIANCE

From the tunnel of time, let's go back 46 years, to when a man arrived at a cemetery in Tehran in a French plane and an American car. It seemed he had been tasked 1400 years ago to destroy Iran and the Middle East and was catapulted into the Middle East. In terms of personality and intellect, Khomeini was the essence of villainy and malevolence.

A month before Khomeini's arrival in Iran, Robert Ernest Huyser- on a special mission on January 4, 1979 - came to Tehran to assist the U.S. government in making subsequent decisions and keeping informed about the situation in Iran. He wanted to prevent Iranian army and SAVAK officials from staging a coup with the departure of the late Shah from Iran.

This four-star general left Tehran on February 3, 1979,

after a month of destructive mission. Of course, with his departure, Khomeini executed those senior army and SAVAK's patriotic commanders. Later, this general confessed in a hospital in Washington to Robert Armao that he felt guilty, but what good was it now, Iran had been thrown into the graveyard of history. It seems that the behind-the-scenes decision was that a backward and criminal mullah like Ruhollah Khomeini should merely witness the transfer of power and take control in Iran. Tehran regime's propaganda machine has called this turmoil of 1979 an Islamic revolution ever since and has deafened the world's ears, but the fruit of this turmoil was the destruction of the country and a bloodbath.

Israel and the U.S. lost their biggest friend and ally in the Middle East – the late Shah of Iran, Mohammad Reza Pahlavi – and from that day, the nightmare of American and Israeli forces in the Middle East began, and the word terrorism was associated with Iran, with Marxist and Islamic terrorist groups celebrating the rise of political Islam in Iran. But the same Islamic Republic grew like a cancerous tumor, and today the world faces a serious threat from Islamic terrorism, and after Iran's first dictator, Khamenei 36 years on, has added to Khomeinism's "Great Terror" in Iran and the Middle East. A criminal dictator who for years has committed atrocities against Israel and America on the one hand, and repressed the Iranian people on the other, sparing no crime.

Today, Netanyahu and Trump's meeting takes place in Washington. In the same Washington, a few days ago, the well-regarded and democratic son of that great emperor, by accepting the responsibility of leadership for the transition period after the collapse of the Islamic Republic of Iran at the Press Club, caused terror in the Islamic Republic and the terrorists linked to 1979's revolt. Secessionists, pro-regime's reformists, Islamic and Marxist terrorist groups, and the core power always have a common enemy, and that is Iran's Crown Prince Reza Pahlavi. Because they know he believes in democracy and human rights, and many of the apparent Iranian opposition do not want the collapse of the Islamic Republic, as the Pahlavi name becomes more prominent.

However, the meeting between Trump and Netanyahu adds to Khamenei's terror. Because a semi-closed and bankrupt country inside and defeated outside the country, is terrified of the union and cooperation of these two modern leaders. Trump and Netanyahu will discuss issues related to the Islamic Republic, hostages, and developing relations with Saudi Arabia. But their meeting has special significance that will have various effects on the Islamic Republic of Iran.

From those 46 years ago, Israel opposed diplomatic relations between the U.S. and the Islamic Republic and in the devastating war of two Islamic dictators – Saddam and Khomeini – both the U.S. and Israel tried to arm them so that they would destroy each other, and the Middle East would be rid of both.

From a security and intelligence perspective, such meetings in Washington DC are usually seen as opportunities for coordinating international policies and strengthening common positions against regional challenges. And the new CIA director – John Ratcliffe – and the new managers of the American intelligence community will gradually focus on their work in coordination with Mossad and the Israeli army.

From a security and intelligence perspective, meetings like the Netanyahu-Trump summit to discuss Iran not only indicate the coordination of international policies but also provide opportunities to strengthen common strategic positions against challenges mostly created by the Islamic Republic. These important meetings allow the new U.S. and Israeli governments to have better and deeper insights into each other's movements and intentions through the exchange of information and intelligence data. In this way, they can jointly plan more precise responses and quicker reactions to potential threats from the Tehran regime. But notably, the presence of Israel-supporting ministers in Trump's new cabinet will align with Israel's movements. For example, regarding the Islamic Republic of Iran, intelligence coordination could include exchanging information about military capabilities, nuclear activities for building an atomic bomb, and the Iranian regime's support for proxy terrorist groups in the region like the Houthis, Popular Mobilization Forces, Islamic Jihad, etc. This information could help create a unified and integrated perspective that ultimately leads to stronger and more effective preventive or responsive measures. But certainly, Trump's National Security Advisor (The Honorable Mike Waltz), the new Defense Secretary (The Honorable Pete Hegseth), etc., know that Israel must, by any means possible, remove the nuclear card from the mullahs' hands in Tehran.

In addition to the Trump-Netanyahu meeting, joint meetings between high-ranking Israeli and American intelligence and military officials act as opportunities for joint assessment and analysis of regional security threats and upcoming challenges. These assessments include long-term consequences of military actions, sanctions, and not empty diplomacy, all of which help strengthen intelligence and defense strategies and further isolate the collapsing regime of the Shiite mullahs in Tehran.

In summary, these meetings play an important role in strengthening bilateral security and intelligence cooperation between Israel and the U.S., and these collaborations are considered an essential part of the defense and national security strategy in dealing with complex global challenges. Perhaps agreement on military action against Iran's nuclear facilities, providing advanced military equipment like bunker buster bombs, or agreeing on the cessation of fruitless diplomatic relations with the terrorist loving ayatollahs in Tehran, can all impact the aggressive approach of the Islamic Republic of Iran and change the grounds for maximum pressure.

And the world's collective memory is not so weak as not to know that the Tehran dictator has repeatedly issued and even praised the assassination orders against Trump and Netanyahu, but he now witnesses the meeting of these two strong leaders at the White House, and the same terror in Khamenei brings joy to the Iranian people who are counting the moments for regime change.

103
THE FEARFUL MESSAGE OF IRGC TO TRUMP AND NETANYAHU

In just a few hours, Trump and Netanyahu will meet at the White House. While the details of their closed-door discussions with intelligence and military officials from Israel and the United States remain undisclosed, the terrorist organization known as the Islamic Revolutionary Guard Corps (IRGC)—the military arm of Iran's ruling mullahs—has already begun sending aggressive signals to Washington.

Over the past 48 hours, Iranian news agencies affiliated with the IRGC have suddenly ramped up their propaganda, boasting about unveiling underground missile cities in southern Iran and other locations. They have even claimed to have introduced a new type of missile while simultaneously celebrating the supposed victories of Hamas and Hezbollah terrorists.

This pattern of behavior is a familiar response to the increasingly erratic speeches of Iran's dictator, Ali Khamenei, who stubbornly refuses to acknowledge the failure of his policies. His loyal IRGC commanders, eager to please their leader, resort to grandiose displays of power. Some funnel cash to Syria and Lebanon in hopes of inciting terrorist groups, while others dominate Iranian state media with bombastic rhetoric, attempting to create the illusion that Trump and Netanyahu should fear Iran's military capabilities.

In the last 48 hours, the unveiling of new underground missile cities in Iran has been repeatedly mentioned in media outlets affiliated with the Tehran government. These facilities, inaugurated by the IRGC, are part of the mullahs' regime's broader strategy to showcase its military capabilities against potential threats. The underground missile cities, housing cruise and ballistic missiles, claim to be able to fire from underground to anywhere and assert that they are protected deep underground and can resist potential attacks from Israel and the United States. But all of this is part of an empty show.

Strategically, these incomplete and inadequate facilities do not realistically enhance the Iranian regime's ability to evade detection or improve crisis response capabilities. While these missile cities may bolster the mullahs' ego, they represent a serious threat to the entire Middle East region. With Trump's return to office and coordination with Netanyahu, Persian Gulf states will naturally seek the removal of this threat.

Beyond these military theatrics, Iranian regime's officials have also claimed to unveil new missiles with supposedly enhanced targeting capabilities. However, these efforts are not a genuine display of military prowess or deterrence, but rather a new bluff in the face of international pressure. The full extent of the mullahs' missile capabilities was revealed in two recent attacks on Israel. When Trump's return to the White House became certain, the Tehran regime, fearing retaliation, abandoned plans for a third attack and is now desperately attempting to rebrand its failed diplomacy with the U.S. and absurdly, even begging for an agreement with Trump.

At the same time, Iranian officials continue to fabricate narratives about the so-called victories of terrorists like Hamas and Hezbollah. This propaganda is meant to strengthen the Islamic Republic's image as a dominant force in the Middle East, but its effectiveness is fading. As Khamenei's bubble of delusions bursts and his regional network of Islamic terrorism crumbling, the Iranian regime stands weakened and bankrupt. These attempts to rally support from its proxy terrorist groups merely underscore its desperation, as the regime itself faces mounting internal and external challenges. The Islamic Republic is a weak and bankrupt country.

From an intelligence perspective, Iran's recent unveiling of underground missile cities and new missile technology is nothing more than a performative display, aimed at garnering attention rather than presenting a real military threat.

The upcoming meeting between Trump and Netanyahu will likely center on strategies to eliminate the Iranian regime's threat. Both leaders understand the necessity of a potential Israeli strike on Iran's nuclear facilities, factoring in the complex geopolitical and security implications. Unlike the Biden and Obama administrations, Trump will not be deceived by Iran's diplomatic charades, nor will he disregard Israel's concerns or Netanyahu's strategic assessments. This time, Trump and Netanyahu are not interested in appeasing Tehran. Trump has no patience for symbolic, weak agreements with the mullahs and certainly does not take their exaggerated military posturing seriously.

Trump's alignment with Netanyahu in confronting Iran's nuclear ambitions stems from the fact that if the Islamic Republic acquires a nuclear bomb, it will upend the balance of power in the Middle East and trigger an uncontrollable nuclear arms race in the region.

The mullahs' ultimate objective and the entire goal of the Islamic Republic has always been nuclear weapons, and their acquisition would pose an existential threat to Israel. Both Trump and Netanyahu, along with their respective military and intelligence teams, recognize that true victory lies in deterring Iran's aggression and curbing its regional ambitions.

Khamenei knows that any real concession—whether on terrorism, missile development, or nuclear ambitions—would mark the downfall of the Islamic Republic itself. Essentially, the Shiite mullah's regime in Iran thrives on projecting power, and it will only submit under extreme pressure—when survival becomes its only priority. If the nuclear issue is removed from Tehran's arsenal, just as its Islamic terrorism network has been weakened, Iran's internal instability could spark a national uprising against the regime's oppressive rule.

In Washington, the fundamental agreement between Trump and Netanyahu is clear: diplomacy with the mullahs is a futile endeavor. The Obama-Biden approach of prolonged negotiations and superficial diplomatic overtures is not a mark of rationality but of weakness. What is required is decisive action to permanently halt Iran's nuclear progress.

One of Trump's most critical achievements was the elimination of the notorious terrorist of Quds Force, Qasem Soleimani, along with his decision to withdraw from the flawed Iran nuclear deal (JCPOA). These actions humiliated the Tehran regime, demonstrating that a position of strength is the only language the mullahs understand. Later, Netanyahu has long adhered to a similar strategy, making both leaders widely respected among Iranians who openly hope for U.S. and Israeli intervention to topple the Tehran regime. This sentiment is no longer a secret—it is a growing reality.

The Trump-Netanyahu meeting is not just a symbolic gesture; it is a historic opportunity. Both leaders are well aware that tackling the Iranian threat requires decisive and coordinated action. While they seek to avoid a broader conflict in the Middle East and disruptions to global oil markets, they also understand that any retaliatory moves from Iran's weakened, and bankrupt regime will be feeble at best.

This moment presents a rare, perhaps once-in-a-century, opportunity for Netanyahu and Trump to reshape the future of the Middle East. In actuality, the actions of the Islamic Republic have pushed the country to the brink of war, with Iran's dictator, Khamenei, being solely responsible for this crisis. The Islamic Republic constantly relies on artificial authoritarianism and a facade of power, but it is all hollow. In reality, it is an illegitimate and unpopular regime among the Iranian people.

ACKNOWLEDGEMENT

This book is the result of more than 15 years of research and travels throughout the Middle East. I owe a profound debt to many people. Every so often, «Thanks « or «Thank you», does not quite seem to be adequate. I could not have written this book without warmhearted, and generous support from many individuals I have the privilege to know.

This is my third book in the USA since the end of my nightmare on July 28, 2020. It all started on March 6, 2017, as I, as an innocent victim of groundless illusions at one of the US Departments among the US intelligence community. I will never forget the brutality and inhumanity I was subjected to when they, on January 28 January, 2019, decided to assassinate me! I will never forget nor forgive them for this scandal.

I am sincerely grateful to all friends during the abovementioned frightening situation, especially The Honorable **Parviz Sabeti, Michael Payma, Dr. Nader Entessar, James Irani,** and **Ahmad Farassati.**

I was highly delighted to have the support of the greatly

skilled and former veterans of the Central Intelligence Agency (**CIA**) such as **General Mike Hayden**, **Larry Pfeiffer** and **Dr. Mark J. Rozell** who always supported me by twitting and sharing my articles in the well-known and prestigious Hayden Center (a center for Intelligence, Policy, and International Security in Schar School of Policy and Government - George Mason University) as well. I could not be more grateful to two well known and respectable figures of the CIA, the distinguished **Michael Morell** and **General David Petraeus** who kindly persuaded me to complete my book in their emails.

I also want to express appreciation to my wonderful friends such as **Dr. Michael Rubin** (AEI), **Douglas London** , former CIA analyst and station chief in Georgetown University and my friends in Israel National News , Jerusalem post and for their invaluable encouragement, inspiration and supportive kindness.

My greatest debt of all in this book has been to Ms. Judith Levy (Editor at the Begin-Sadat Center for Strategic Studies, Bar-Ilan University) who generously and patiently edited all my work and contributed with countless of ideas and improvements. She had a pivotal role in helping me write this book.

Also, I highly appreciate the endorsement of **Dr. Roxaneh Khosravi, Nader Dromani, Col. Houshang Vazin, Capitan Arya Bagheri** and **Mehryar Kaviani** for their supports.

Finally, I would also like to acknowledge long-standing debts to my lawyer, **Jonathan R. Struman** for his advice and guidance.

Erfan Fard
Beverly Hills, CA

INDEX

A

Abbasside; 18,21
Abdel Nasser, Gamal; 163,296
Abdolhossein; 18
Adib-Moghaddam, Arshin; 19
Afghanistan; 23,26,53,179,185,200,233,387,423,424,427,428,430,433,441,473
Africa; 18,23,24,52,85,98,141,189,206,218,283,308,353,386,430,457
Ahern, Tom; 41
Ahmadinejad; 114,275,362,435,436
Ahmadinejad, Mahmoud; 275,436
Aires, Buenos; 265,289
Akbari, Alireza; 186
Al-Assad, Bashar; 398,454
Al-Baghdadi, Abu Bakr; 356,360,365
Al Jazeera; 96
al-Mahdi; 19,20
Al-Mu'minin, Amir; 18,385
Al-Olum, Baqer; 459
Al-Qaeda; 31,96,387,424,466
Amanat, Abbas; 19
America; 23,24,25,27,28,29,46,82,83,109,141,148,179,189,199,206,221,236,237,
   238,265,269,270,277,283,284,299,308,309,337,359,368,386,396,413,416,
   421,422,455,456,457,476,479,481,490,493,496,497,498,516,520,523,524,
   525,526,528
Ames, Robert; 44
Amini, Ali; 47
Amini, Mahsa; 136,191,192,193,226,416,462
Andalus; 18
Arab; 15,17,50,78,88,98,105,113,114,115,132,134,135,144,162,163,164,185,208,
   221,223,352,353,362,364,374,393,400,415,438,452,465,470,477,478,486,
   488,501,511
Arafat, Yasser; 133,233,298,362,379,442,444,452,468,474,504
Arafi, Alireza; 275
Architecture; 19
Armao, Robert; 109,528
Armenia; 147
Arnold; 17
Arynana, Bahram; 47
Asia; 24,38,430
Astan Quds Razavi; 420
Azerbaijan; 147

B

Baghdad; 18,133,398,399,401,442,473,479
Baghdadi; 25,356,360,365
Bagheri, Arya; 539
Bahrain; 15,139,386,512
Banisadr, Abolhassan;; 47,114,297
Barnea, David; 148,160,176
Barzani; 386,419
Bayne Fisher, William; 19
Bazargan, Mehdi; 118,128
BBC; 118,172,238,298,354
Ben Ali; 480
Bennett, Naftali; 53
Biden, Joe; 13,23,32,59,60,61,62,78,80,84,116,138,139,148,151,159,176,188,190, 205,207,214,216,217,218,221,222,239,250,300,304,358,423,424,426,427,4 28,429,430,431,432,433,479,482,511,516,517,526,534,535
bin Laden, Osama; 57,365
Bolton, John; 80,116
Brzezinski; 44,45,237
Burns, William; 148,423,424,426,433
Bush, George; 236
Bush H.W., George; 110

C

Cairo; 18
Cambridge; 19
Canada; 55,100,151,175,263,265,266,430
Carter, Jimmy; 42,109,110,116,190,207,217,297,299,304,479
Central Intelligence Agency; 33,423,539
China; 39,60,119,188,205,271,284,298,300,309,316,324,337,382,422,423,424,425 ,426,427,429,480,486,499,510,524
Choueiri; 19
CIA; 24,30,33,34,35,36,37,38,39,40,41,42,43,44,45,46,47,48,49,50,51,63,64,67,89 ,90,109,110,121,148,152,153,164,176,185,188,189,197,205,206,232,237,2 38,247,248,269,271,284,297,309,385,386,387,388,400,401,404,416,417,42 3,424,425,426,427,428,429,430,431,432,433,441,453,455,456,473,478,481 ,509,510,511,512,513,514,529,539
Cinema, Rex; 440,472
CISA; 246,247,249
Clinton, Bill; 299
CNN; 54,58,218,226
Cotrell, William; 39
Cyrus; 101,159,165,167,168,170,290,291

D

David Kay, Eliyahu; 52
Dehghan, Hossein; 275
Deif, Mohammed; 391
DHS; 30,81,85,386,450,478,494,495
Dollinger; 17
Dromani, Nader; 539

E

Egypt; 22,39,47,105,108,163
Ejehi; 459
Ejei, Mohseni; 31,275,421,458
Erdogan; 56,382,454
Europe; 24,29,38,85,88,89,119,130,134,141,180,200,217,265,283,299,308,371,372,413,416,455,458,459,467,482,525

F

Fada'iyan-e Islam; 120,128,253,441,445,473,505
Fallahian, Ali; 414,458
Fallahzadeh, Mohammad Reza; 399
Fattah, Parviz; 275
FBI; 33,81,188,205,246,247,248,249,358,387,450,478
Ferdowsi; 454
Fidel Castro; 133,252,444,504
Frye; 18

G

Gaddafi; 104,109,252,379,442,444,452,474,490,504
Gamliel, Gila; 159
Ganji, Manouchehr; 47
Garland, Merrick; 358
Gaza; 56,209,210,211,319,377,432
General Flynn; 519
Georgia; 147
Germany; 63,66
Ghaddafi; 133,297,298
Ghaddafi, Muammar; 133
Ghorbanifar, Manucher; 49
Global Terrorism; 22,25,28
Grimme, Hubert; 17
Guardian; 186,261,274,275,276,314,325,411,435,436

H

Haines, Avril; 187,204
Haj 34; 17
Hajarian; 118

Hajizadeh; 150,151,152,153,321,388
Haley, Nikki; 219,220,221,222
Hamas; 27,52,53,54,55,56,58,66,75,76,96,97,113,139,143,161,284,285,291,292,29
3,294,301,302,305,309,310,319,321,339,340,341,344,346,347,350,352,353
,382,385,386,388,399,400,414,419,431,432,440,442,451,452,466,468,469,
471,474,477,483,495,501,512,532,534
HAMAS; 26
Haniyeh, Ismail; 56,292,293,294,365,388
Harris; 250,296,299,300,366,480
Harris, Kamala; 250,299
Hashd al-Shaabi; 339,373,399,400,401,431,501,525
Hashemi, Faezeh; 172
Hashemi Rafsanjani, Ali Akbar; 162
Haspel, Gina; 80
Hawkins, Oveis; 510
Hayden, Mike; 539
Hayom; 12
Hebdo, Charlie; 126,129
Helms, Richard; 34,46
Hezbollah; 14,27,28,49,66,75,76,82,83,113,118,119,139,161,175,210,264,285,291
,301,302,303,304,305,306,310,319,321,339,340,341,342,343,344,345,346,
347,348,349,350,351,352,353,382,386,387,391,399,400,431,432,451,457,4
66,467,468,469,477,483,495,501,512,532,534
Hijaz; 15
Hisham, Ibn; 16
Hitler; 217,241,252,412
Holocaust; 159,161,165,418,460,465
Homan, Tom; 268
Hook, Brian; 80,477
Hosseini Beheshti, Mohammad; 46
Houthis; 75,139,152,264,285,310,321,339,353,373,382,399,401,431,432,451,466,
483,501,512,530
Hussein, Saddam; 93,104,114,118,127,133,160,165,196,252,297,314,362,379,39
8,442,444,452,473,490,504,525

I

Imam Zaman; 19,20,297,379,455
Iraq; 14,23,25,26,46,48,53,93,139,179,196,197,200,264,285,289,296,297,305,310
,344,349,350,362,363,364,377,385,398,400,404,405,419,432,441,452,468,
473,512,516,525
IRGC; 14,22,23,24,25,26,27,28,30,48,51,56,63,74,76,77,80,82,83,84,96,97,106,11
2,113,117,119,120,121,124,126,127,129,130,131,134,136,138,139,140,141
,142,143,146,149,150,151,152,153,155,161,164,173,175,179,183,184,185,
186,188,190,199,205,207,210,211,223,230,261,263,264,265,266,267,275,2
77,285,292,299,310,312,314,315,325,326,327,336,352,356,357,363,370,37

2,382,385,387,388,400,412,414,416,420,435,436,437,442,451,457,459,467,468,474,478,490,512,519,532,533,552
IRGCQF; 23,24,25,27
IRIB; 229,437
Isaac Herzog; 160
ISIS; 53,75,82,96,97,113,119,155,356,385,406,451
Israel; 5,12,22,23,27,32,49,52,53,55,57,60,62,66,74,76,77,78,88,89,90,94,97,104,109,115,116,136,138,139,142,143,145,148,149,150,151,152,153,158,159,160,161,162,163,164,165,166,168,169,170,174,175,176,179,181,185,186,189,199,201,206,208,209,210,211,218,220,221,222,223,224,225,270,271,272,274,284,285,286,288,291,292,293,294,295,297,298,299,301,302,303,304,305,309,310,311,318,319,320,321,322,323,324,325,326,329,330,331,332,333,334,335,336,337,338,340,341,342,343,344,346,347,348,349,350,352,354,361,362,363,364,365,366,368,371,372,373,374,380,381,382,384,385,386,388,390,391,392,393,394,396,398,399,400,401,405,414,416,442,443,444,446,448,450,453,458,465,466,467,468,469,474,475,476,477,479,480,485,486,490,491,494,498,500,501,502,503,504,506,508,511,514,515,516,520,524,525,526,528,529,530,531,532,533,534,535,539

J

Jaleh Square; 440
Jalili, Saeed; 275,279,314,421,435
JCPOA; 87,116,120,140,143,188,205,217,220,222,300,432,479,516,536
Jen Schiff Kay; 52
Jerusalem; 12
Jerusalem Post; 12,449
Jesus; 19
Jihad; 17,57,139,143,161,208,209,210,211,353,382,388,400,530
Jihadism; 28
Jordan; 22,50

K

Kabul; 424,428
Kahrizak; 134
Kalp, Malcolm; 41
Kashf al-Asrar; 445,505
Kasravi, Ahmad; 379,439,445,471,505
Kaviani, Mehryar; 539
Kay, Eli; 52
Kazemi, Mohammad; 120,512
Kessler, Ronald; 239
KGB; 35,38,39,40,46,361,379,385,488,513
Khalgh, Mujahedin; 66
Khamenei; 20,21,23,57,58,87,89,93,96,99,106,110,111,118,119,124,125,126,127,129,132,135,137,143,167,169,180,184,200,210,213,223,224,234,235,241,243,252,255,261,262,264,271,274,275,276,277,279,282,285,288,292,299,30

7,310,312,313,314,315,317,319,321,324,325,326,327,330,335,336,352,353,354,355,356,360,361,362,363,364,365,366,367,368,370,371,372,373,379, 381,382,383,387,388,395,396,397,398,399,400,401,403,405,407,413,414,415,416,417,419,420,421,435,436,437,439,440,442,443,445,446,447,449,450,451,452,453,454,455,458,460,461,462,463,466,467,468,469,471,472,474,475,476,477,478,479,480,483,491,495,503,505,506,507,512,514,515,518, 521,525,527,528,529,531,533,534,535,536

Khamenei, Ali; 58,124,135,274,279,282,288,307,312,319,324,335,361,398,443,445,461,474,477,483,503,505,512,515,518,525,533

Khatami; 92,114,170,184,185,458

Khatib, Esmaeil; 120,413,414,415,416,417,456,458,512

Khomeini; 20,33,37,38,41,44,45,46,47,48,57,84,87,92,93,100,104,108,109,110,114,116,118,128,132,133,134,147,156,162,163,172,178,181,184,193,198,201,209,210,224,233,234,235,237,238,241,243,247,251,252,253,255,260,296, 297,298,330,362,379,386,398,413,414,415,417,420,439,440,441,442,443,444,445,451,452,455,457,458,459,465,466,468,471,472,473,474,483,488,489,490,503,504,505,510,513,527,528,529

Khomeini, Ahmad; 483

Khomeini, Ruhollah; 296,444,504,528

Khomeinism; 14,41,59,94,105,119,130,134,136,142,151,155,156,164,171,175,182,202,209,210,211,212,227,254,264,298,319,329,335,374,375,387,399,405,407,448,455,501,508,528

Khosravi, Roxaneh; 539

Khuzestan; 184,186

Kissinger, Henry; 42

Kremlin; 147,180,200,234,300

Krongard, Robert; 39

KSA; 186

Kurdistan; 63,94,134,191,192,193,194

L

Laden, Bin; 57,58,360,387

Larijani, Ali; 421,437

Latin America; 23,24,27,28,82,83,141,179,189,199,206,283,308,359,386,456,457

Lebanon; 26,45,139,163,264,289,301,302,303,304,305,319,340,341,342,343,344, 345,346,347,348,349,351,362,377,385,404,405,432,441,443,451,468,473, 503,516,533

Ledeen, Michael; 237

Lewis, Bernard; 16

Libya; 25,39,233,441,473

Loadholt, Jonathon; 357

London; 77,94,118,185,195,196,197,298,539,552

London, Douglas; 539

M

Madani, Ahmad; 47

Mahabad; 147
Makarem Shirazi, Naser; 118
Mandela, Nelson; 182,202
Marxist; 13,20,34,36,38,39,92,100,115,132,163,164,172,181,201,224,361,371,375
,377,379,399,444,485,488,495,504,513,528,529
Masjedi, Iraj; 399
Mediterranean; 26,149
Mehdi Karami, Mohammad; 125
MEK; 38,39,40,66,115,116,118,120,128,129,160,163,170,181,182,201,202,371,4
41,473,509
Mesbah-Yazdi, Mohammad-Taqi; 435
Meshaal, Khaled; 56
Mexico; 175,269
Middle East; 1,3,4,12,13,14,19,20,22,23,24,25,27,29,34,35,44,49,56,65,66,74,76,7
7,81,84,92,94,98,106,108,113,129,130,131,137,138,139,143,146,148,152,1
63,174,176,179,182,187,188,189,199,202,204,205,206,208,210,215,236,25
1,264,265,270,272,282,283,292,294,296,298,300,302,303,305,306,307,308
,319,323,330,332,335,338,341,344,345,347,350,351,353,354,362,368,371,
377,381,382,383,385,388,390,393,394,396,399,401,403,404,405,406,407,4
14,418,430,431,444,446,447,448,450,451,453,456,457,467,468,475,476,47
7,478,483,484,486,491,498,499,500,501,502,504,506,507,508,510,511,512
,513,514,517,520,524,526,527,528,529,533,534,535,536,538,552
MKO; 39,441,473
Mobilization; 26,285,310,353,431,432,466,512,530
Moghadam, Nasser; 40,118
Mohajerani; 117,185
Mohajerani, Ata'ollah; 117
MOIS; 28,30,49,50,51,83,84,92,93,95,96,97,106,111,112,113,115,120,121,123,12
4,131,136,155,164,173,186,188,190,205,207,210,232,299,314,315,326,33
6,382,385,386,412,413,414,416,442,455,456,457,458,459,460,468,474,47
8,512,552
Mojahedin-e-Khalq; 129
Molaverdi, Shahindokht; 172
Montazeri; 44,134,170
Morell, Michael; 51,325,539
Mosaddeq, Mohammed; 50,128,162,163,172,269,298,441,473,477,488,510
Moslehi, Alavi; 458
Moslehi, Heidar; 460
Mossad; 33,63,67,74,78,148,152,153,160,164,174,176,177,271,293,295,297,335,3
38,354,371,384,385,387,388,389,400,416,417,453,511,513,529
Mostazafan; 420
Movahedin; 118
Muhammad; 15,16,17,19,128,147,252
Muir, William; 17
Mykonos; 458

N

Nafisi; 18
Nahl 36; 17
Najaar, Mostafa; 186
Najafabadi, Dori; 458
Nasrallah; 336,360,365,391,392,466,468,469,495
Nasrallah, Hassan; 365,391
Netanyahu; 74,78,148,159,160,166,180,201,224,299,338,354,372,373,379,390,391,392,393,394,399,405,477,527,528,529,530,531,532,533,534,535,536
Netanyahu, Benjamin; 180,201,299,390
NIAC; 94,111,227,228,270,501
Nixon, Richard; 110,236
Noem, Kristi; 492,493,494,495,496,497

O

Obama, Barack; 13,83,84,220,239,299,300,304,479,480,482,516,517,526,534,535
ODNI; 246,247
OIPFG; 39,40,164
Oman; 15
Omar; 17,142,143,144,387
Ottoman Caliphate; 18
Oveissi, Gholam-Ali; 47

P

Pahlavi; 20,33,46,48,61,70,71,72,104,105,108,110,111,112,114,115,116,120,133,158,159,160,161,162,165,166,168,169,170,172,178,180,181,182,196,197,198,200,201,202,210,254,287,288,289,290,291,296,338,372,374,394,403,406,440,448,472,480,488,490,508,509,519,528,529
Pahlavi, Farah; 111
Pahlavi, Mohammad Reza; 104,160,162,254,374,490,528
Pahlavi, Mohammad Reza Shah; 33,488
Pahlavi, Reza; 48,61,71,72,104,108,110,111,112,115,116,120,158,160,161,162,165,166,168,169,170,172,178,180,181,182,196,197,198,200,201,202,210,254,287,288,290,338,372,374,394,403,406,448,480,490,508,509,519,528,529
Pahlavi, Reza Shah; 20,33,105,168,488
Palestinian; 53,54,55,56,135,144,162,163,164,165,208,209,211,223,224,225,293,294,382,440,441,468,472,473
Paul Shaffer; 510
Persian Gulf; 41,49,78,85,96,97,98,113,138,164,175,176,179,189,199,206,270,271,336,353,374,386,399,443,478,503,533
Petraeus, David; 539
Pezeshkian; 250,271,279,299,367,368,369,382,385,395,396,397,412,413,455,460,461,462,463,464
Pezeshkian, Masoud; 299,412,455,461,463
Pfeiffer, Larry; 423,539

Phillips Hart, Howard; 41
PIJ; 56,208,209,210,211,382,399,451
P.K.Hitti; 16
PKK; 373,386,400,401,457,501
Pompeo, Mike; 51,80,116,150,477
Pourmohammadi, Mostafa; 436
Powell, Jody; 239
Putin; 153,180,200,454,517,525

Q

Qaani; 150,224,398,399,400,401,512
Qaani, Esmail; 224,399
Qaddafi; 39,127,314
Qajar; 19,20,133,252
Qajar Dynasty; 19
Qalibaf, Mohammad-Bagher; 184,275,314,421,436
Qashqai, Khosrow; 47
Qatar; 26,56,95,96,97,98,101,353,382,386
Qotb-zadeh; 297
Quds Force; 23,30,113,131,146,149,153,164,174,175,190,207,210,223,224,261,26
4,285,299,302,303,310,336,347,352,364,370,382,385,386,387,400,416,442
,466,467,468,474,478,512,525,536

R

Radan, Ahmadreza; 133,134,135
Rafsanjani; 48,92,119,162,170,172,184,387,466,483
Raisi; 21,31,89,114,120,133,153,191,192,193,194,222,261,262,270,271,273,274,2
76,313,412,413,414,415,418,419,422,436,461
Raisi, Ebrahim; 21,31,222,270,273,313,418,461
Raisi, Ibrahim; 412
Ranfsanjani; 49
Rashid, Gholam Ali; 186
Rashidun; 16,17
Ratcliffe, John; 401,509,529
Razmara, Ali; 441,473
Reagan, Ronald; 109,110
Remarkably; 17,93,118,194,213
Reyshahri; 458
Rezaei, Mohsen; 184,185,275,421
Rivera, Carlisle; 357
Romanian; 99
Rossi, Melissa; 19
Rouhani; 172,185
Rouhani, Hassan; 172
Rozell, Mark; 539
Rubin, Michael; 450,539

Rushdie, Salman; 126
Russia; 38,39,40,44,45,46,60,119,146,147,148,179,180,188,199,200,205,220,271, 284,298,309,316,324,337,382,421,422,423,424,425,426,427,429,454,486,4 99,510,517,524,525

S

Sabeti, Parviz; 35,36,37,38,39,42,43,51,450,538
Saddam; 24,93,104,109,114,118,127,133,160,165,196,234,252,297,314,362,379,3 98,442,444,452,473,490,504,525,529
Safavid; 19
Safavids; 19,20
Salami, Hussein; 23,63,64,76,126
Salavati, Abolghasem; 123
Sanandaj; 64,193
Sassanid; 17,18
Saudi Arabia; 22,23,74,75,76,77,78,89,92,112,115,152,174,176,185,386,498,512, 515,525,526,529
SAVAK; 33,34,35,36,37,38,40,42,108,118,163,164,184,296,385,450,458,513,527 ,528
Sayyid Qutb; 210,335
Shaffer, Paul; 510
Shah; 20,33,34,35,36,37,40,41,42,43,44,45,46,47,48,50,104,105,108,109,110,111, 115,116,128,133,156,160,162,163,164,168,169,174,197,233,235,236,237,2 38,254,296,297,298,374,375,385,439,441,458,459,465,471,472,479,488,4 89,490,491,527,528
Shahnameh; 454
Shah, Reza; 20,33,105,111,156,168,235,488
Shakeri, Farhad; 357,359
Shamkhani; 120,183,184,185,186,421
Shamkhani, Ali; 120,183,186,421
Sham'sol'vaezin; 118
Shapour Bakhtiar; 47
Shkhaydam, Fadi Abu; 53
Sinwar, Yahya; 365,407
Sistani, Ali; 400
Smith, Donald; 39
SNSC; 183,184
Soleimani; 25,118,119,123,151,152,189,206,357,359,360,365,370,418,477,520,5 36
Soleimani, Qasem; 118,139,143,185,189,206,356,360,365,370,387,418,477,502, 520,536
South America; 29,82,83,265
Struman, Jonathan; 539
Sullivan; 236,237,238
Sunni; 19,133,209,364,400,442,474

Syria; 14,23,25,26,66,76,134,139,152,233,264,266,305,344,350,362,377,382,385,3
86,398,400,401,404,405,441,450,451,452,468,473,512,516,524,533

T

Tabari; 15,18
Tabriz; 147,439,470,471
Taheri, Amir; 111
Taliban; 26,96,113,119,143,424,428
Tehran; 12,13,20,25,34,35,38,39,40,41,43,44,45,48,53,55,56,77,78,83,84,98,106,1
11,123,142,146,147,148,151,159,169,175,176,179,183,185,187,195,199,20
4,208,210,212,213,216,231,246,247,248,249,251,254,257,261,264,268,270
,271,272,277,282,283,284,285,286,292,293,294,299,300,303,304,305,306,
307,308,309,310,311,321,329,330,331,338,344,345,350,351,352,353,355,3
56,357,358,359,360,374,380,383,384,385,386,387,400,401,402,404,405,40
8,413,418,421,438,440,442,444,445,448,453,466,467,468,469,470,472,473
,474,479,483,484,485,494,501,502,504,505,508,509,510,519,520,524,525,
526,527,528,530,531,533,534,535,536
Terrorism; 17,20,22,25,28,31,43,52,54,55,56,57,119,127,129,133,146,185,190,20
7,210,223,264,319,359,477,512,552
Toynbee, Arnold; 16
Tritton; 18
Trump; 24,51,80,139,150,151,220,222,249,268,271,272,296,300,324,326,355,356,
357,358,366,372,373,398,399,416,453,476,477,478,479,480,481,482,484,4
85,492,498,502,509,510,511,515,516,517,518,520,521,522,523,525,526,52
7,528,529,530,531,532,533,534,535,536
Trump, Donald; 51,150,222,249,268,324,356,476,509,510,515
Turkey; 47,56,163,382,386,388,454
Turkic; 19
Turkmenchay; 147
Turner, Jack; 510

U

Ukraine; 60,105,147,153,179,180,199,200,220,274,300,425,427,428,430,524
Umar; 17
Umayyad; 18,255,385
US; 22,23,24,25,26,27,28,29,30,31,34,35,36,37,38,40,42,45,46,48,55,60,61,62,76,
77,78,80,87,88,89,90,92,93,94,97,101,102,111,120,123,134,135,136,138,
139,140,142,143,147,148,150,151,152,153,159,160,185,187,188,189,190,
204,205,206,207,211,216,217,218,219,221,222,232,269,271,284,309,385,4
18,456,498,522,538
USA; 4,23,25,27,61,104,106,109,110,116,136,217,247,524,538
USSR; 34,39,40,146,164,179,200
Uthman; 17

V

Vahidi, Ahmad; 120,186

Vazin, Houshang; 539
Velayat-e Faqih; 133,252,297,299,329,331,334,336,379,440,448,466,467,471,508

W
Waltz'; 516
Waltz, Michael; 515
Ward, Phil; 41
West Africa; 23
Wilayat al-Faqih; 443,444,445,503,504,505
Wray, Christopher; 358

Y
Yazdi, Ebrahim; 46
Yemen; 14,15,25,40,139,152,264,266,305,344,349,350,362,377,385,404,405,432, 468,512,516
Younesi; 458,459
Younesi, Ali; 459
Youssef M; 19

Z
Zahedan; 64
Zahhāk; 447,507
Zarif, Javad; 412
Zarinkoob; 18

ABOUT THE AUTHOR

Erfan Fard is a Counter-Terrorism analyst and Middle East Studies researcher based in Washington DC.

He is in Middle Eastern regional security affairs with a particular focus on Iran, Counter terrorism, IRGC, MOIS and Ethnic conflicts in MENA.

He graduated in International Security Studies (London M. University, UK), and in International Relations (CSU-LA), and is fluent in Persian, Kurdish, Arabic and English.

Follow him on this twitter account @EQFARD / **www.erfanfard.com**